nagement
education

THE FUTURE OF MANAGEMENT EDUCATION

The Future of Management Education

Edited by
PROFESSOR ANDREW KAKABADSE
Cranfield School of Management
and
DR. SURESH MUKHI
New South Wales Institute of Technology,
Australia

NICHOLS

First published in the United States
of America in 1984 by
Nichols Publishing Company
Post Office Box 96
New York N.Y.10024

Library of Congress Cataloging in Publication Data

Main entry under title:
Future of management education.
    1. Management — Study and teaching — Addresses, essays,
lectures. I. Kakabadse, Andrew.
    HD30.4.F872   1984   658'.007   83–23788
    ISBN 0–89397–184–7

Printed in Great Britain

Contents

Contributors

John Bank
Present position: Lecturer in Industrial Relations,
Cranfield School of Management, UK.

Alan Barratt
Present position: Manager, Field Training Services of the
Middle East Department, Mobil Oil Inc, USA.

David Barron
Present position: Group Personnel Manager, Extel Group plc,
UK.

Roger Bennett
Present position: Reader in Management, Thames Valley
Regional Management Centre, UK.

Allan Bordow
Present position: Senior Lecturer in Organisation Behaviour,
The University of New South Wales, Australia.

James Boulgarides
Present position: Professor of Interdisciplinary Studies,
California State University - Los Angeles, USA.

John Burgoyne
Present position: Research Director, University of
Lancaster, UK.

Cary Cooper
Present position: Professor of Organisational Psychology and
Chairman of Department of Management Sciences, The
University of Manchester Institute of Science and
Technology (UMIST), UK.

Peter Forrester
Present position: Emirutus Professor of Cranfield Institute
of Technology. Former Pro Vice Chancellor of Cranfield
Institute of Technology, Director of Cranfield School of
Management and Professor of Industrial Management.

Ken Hall
Present position: Dean, Division of Business and
Administration, Western Australian Institute of Technology,
Australia.

Phil Harris
Present position: President, Harris International, USA.

Maurice Hayes
Present position: Consultant in Human Resources. Former Vice
President Personnel, Nicholas International Ltd, Australia.

Frank Heller
Present position: Director, Centre for Decision Making
Studies, Tavistock Institute of Human Relations, UK.

John Hunt
Present position: Plowden Professor of Human Relations,
London Business School, UK.

David Jamieson
Present position: Partner, Management Research Groups (MRG)
Associates, UK.

Andrew Kakabadse
Present position: Professor of Management Development,
Cranfield School of Management, UK.

Ivor Kenny
Present position: Senior Research Fellow, University College
Dublin, Eire.

Ronald Lippitt
Present position: Emirutus Professor of University of
Michigan. Also Vice President for Organisation Development,
Organisational Renewal Inc, USA.

Tom Lupton
Present position: Professor of Organisation Behaviour,
Manchester Business School. Former Director of Manchester
Business School, UK.

Charles Margerison
Present position: Director and Professor of Management,
University of Queensland Business School, Australia.

Suresh Mukhi
Present position: Associate Head, School of Business and
Public Administration and Head of Organisation and Management
Unit, The New South Wales Institute of Technology, Australia.

Len Nadler
Present position: Professor of Human Resources, George
Washington University, USA.

Denis Pym
Present position: Professor of Organisational Behaviour,
London Business School, UK.

John Roberts
Present position: Senior Personnel Officer, Cable and
Wireless plc, UK.

Tony Stevenson
Present position: Business Consultant and part time Lecturer
in International Management, The New South Wales Institute
of Technology, Australia.

Malcolm Warner
Professor and Research Co-ordinator, The Joint Graduate
Programme, The Management College, Henley and Brunel
University, UK.

Acknowledgements

I am deeply indebted to Sue Brown and Sarah Bishton for their diligence, perseverance and high quality work in preparing this document for publication. Thanks also to June Wardill, Heidi Crawford and Mairi Bryce.

Introduction

At a recent seminar on leadership, held at London Business
School, attended by key industrialists, directors of
business schools and influential academics and managers, it
became noticeable to all that the issues that dominated the
discussion concerned the development and education of
managers, now and in the future. The topic of leadership
fell more and more into the background. As one manager
stated:

> "The real problem is finding the right sort of training
> and development for the vast majority of managers.
> Potential top leaders make themselves visible in any
> case."

Similar opinions have been expressed by a number of senior
managers. What sort of training and development should be
considered for the future? What will be the needs of
organisations in the future, that managers should now be
considering? To whom can the line manager turn for help and
assistance to help develop his people in the organisation?

In an attempt to try and answer some of these questions,
Suresh Mukhi and I asked academics and managers to each write
a chapter on what they considered to be the important issues
for management education, now and in the future.

Although the contributions finally selected for this book
are varied, three distinct categories emerged; the manager and
the various changes he has to face; attempts at developing
management education/development in organisations and
exploring the future for management education? Hence, Mukhi
and I decided that these three broad categories should form
the three core sections of this book.

PLAN OF THE BOOK

To start, Kenny (Chapter 1) provides an insightful analysis
into the relationship between business, politics and society
with government acting as the central link to the three
factions. The consequences of government initiatives are
examined by identifying the stakeholders who are, or could
be, potentially affected by such actions. Men of government

1

are criticised for taking actions which result in far too many unintended and negative consequences. Equally, men of business do not emerge favourably from this scrutinising analysis, as they are identified as individuals unwilling or incapable of understanding the complex forces surrounding working life. The remedy? Break the old ways and styles of management; develop greater understanding of both present practise and future managerial needs. Only greater understanding provides the stimulus for more effective future performance.

It is Kenny's conclusion that provides our start.

Part I

In Part I, entitled "The Manager In A Changing World", five contributions are offered.

Bordow and Stevenson (Chapter 2) report a study examining the role of the chief executive and argue that the role is rapidly changing. No longer can chief executives look after the strategy of the business and do a PR job in the external world. With so many changes in society, chief executives must accept the responsibility of acting as change agents/catalysts to their own organisation. The skills of control and public relations have to be superceded by the skills of analysis, perception, sensitivity and understanding.

In contrast, Pym (Chapter 3) and Hunt (Chapter 4) bemoan the fact that the role of the middle manager has been undermined and his contribution not appreciated. Until the individual and the work group are given greater attention in terms of meeting work needs, mediocre performance from the majority of managers will continue to be the order of the day.

Heller and Warner (Chapter 5) explore the topic of shop floor participation in management decision making and policy development. They argue that the evidence from British research clearly indicates that management must pay far greater attention to the quality of work life of shop floor operatives.

Mukhi (Chapter 6) brings Part I to a close by examining the educational needs of managers in Australia. In conclusion, Mukhi provides a helpful list of criteria for identifying effective management development programmes.

Part II

The extent to which Mukhi's criteria are considered relevant is explored in Part II, entitled "Application In Organisations". Here case studies of attempts to introduce a systematic approach to human resource training and development in organisations are described.

Barrett (Chapter 7) examines some of the practical key issues to generating effective management development systems.

I, in Chapter 8, report of one case involving an intervention by external consultants, into a large police organisation. The behaviour of the consultants is discussed in detail. I conclude that in order to introduce major changes into organisations, strategies for appropriate third party behaviour need to be identified.

Hayes (Chapter 9) discusses both the problems and achievements of one company's, Nicholas International, experience in developing an effective performance appraisal system.

Boulgarides and Jamieson (Chapter 10) explore their involvement on a longterm organisation development (OD) programme designed to improve the managerial performance of the city managers of Culver city, a large urban area in California. The authors conclude by identifying sixteen questions concerning change and development in organisations, which should be addressed by both line managers and consultants if they wish to introduce substantial change to their organisation.

To close Part II, Baron and Roberts (Chapter 11) discuss how research studies can be a useful mechanism for introducing new approaches to training and development in an organisation. In particular, the long standing training partnership between Cable and Wireless, the world renowned telecommunications company, and Cranfield School of Management, is used as the case example.

Part III

In Part III, the issues and prospects for management education, now and in the future, are identified.

Hall (Chapter 12) explores what management development entails; reports on the results of a management development survey conducted in twenty organisations in Australia and finishes by identifying the key skills required by management educators and trainers in the near future.

Forrester (Chapter 13) adds to Hall's argument by offering a checklist of the pros and cons for the various types of management training programmes offered at business schools. Forrester then concludes by identifying the criteria for assessing the development of managers for the future.

Lupton (Chapter 14) continues the discussion of the role of business schools and in particular the effectiveness of management training in terms of value to client organisations. He considers that most university based management schools are ill-equiped to react quickly and effectively to the needs of clients in the private and public sectors. Recommendations are made concerning the reform of the university management school

In the two proceeding chapters, Bennett (Chapter 15) and

Margerison (Chapter 16) debate the likely future practises and objectives for management education. Although their analyses are divergent, their conclusions are similar. Improved managerial performance in the work place is the mission statement that emerges. Both writers indicate that training to increase work performance effectiveness can be best achieved by participative/action centred/sharing/group based learning approaches. The implication is that the lecture method and case study approach should be relegated to the bottom of the desired list of teaching practises.

Bank (Chapter 17) agrees and argues for participative/group based learning through the Outward Bound scheme; the approach that adds one more dimension to the learning experience - physical exertion. Based on a case study of one group undergoing a week's Outward Bound training, Bank examines both the value and problems of conducting Outward Bound training. The prognosis for participative learning coupled with physical exercise, seems good.

From an examination of training institutions and teaching approaches to learning processes, Cooper and Burgoyne (Chapter 18) offer a learning theory based on the concept of multiple values. The future of management education lies in helping people improve their understanding of themselves in relation to their work situation. To assist such understanding, Cooper and Burgoyne indicate that no single set of values are operant in any one organisation. All organisations are made up of multiple value systems. There exist as many differences of view and belief as there are people in the organisation. Hence, organisational politics, strife, difference and disagreement have to be taken as much into consideration in planned management development as the more traditional topics of leadership, sharing and open communication.

In keeping with the previous authors, I (Chapter 19) offer the view that the most effective training takes place in the work situation. The question is how to harness work experiences for further training, development and change. The answer is data feedback; the process of gathering, collating and feeding back relevant work oriented information to interested parties for them to discuss and debate. The purpose is to help people objectively examine their work situation and consider steps to change, if required.

Harris (Chapter 20) offers a futuristic view, postulating that we are experiencing a profound transition from an advanced industrial to a post industrial society. He clearly indicates that the management development needs of the year 2000 have to be considered and identified now.

Nadler (Chapter 21) also takes a futuristic view and offers the hypothesis that the world of work and organisation will be far more dependent on cooperation and interdependency between people as opposed to insularity, competition and selfgain. Hence, Nadler identifies the issues to consider,

4

and the means to achieve, great interdependence within and between organisations.

Lippitt (Chapter 22) equally takes a futuristic view. He identifies six key areas of change in society and organisations for which managers should be prepared. In order that managers be prepared for such changes, Lippitt identifies seven areas of needed competency development in order to enhance effective managerial performance.

The last three authors go some way to providing a management development blue print for the future and provide a guide for future management education practice.

FOR WHOM

For whom is this book intended? The answer is for two distinctly different, but interdependent, groups of management practitioners. For those directly involved in the business of management education/development, such as management academics, management trainers and personnel managers, this book provides an indepth examination of present issues and future concerns. Hopefully, this text will help in the planning of management education practice for the future.

For those indirectly involved in management education practice, such as line managers and senior executives, the book could be a valuable guide to identifying the key factors involved in the development of managers. In this way, the planning and development of managers can be neatly incorporated into the planning and development of the total organisation.

Andrew Kakabadse
August 1983

1 Business, politics and society

IVOR KENNY

In setting the scene I should like to make 2½ points. The
first is that that social entity known as the business
enterprise is under threat for which we have little precedent. The second is that, if the enterprise is to survive,
it will need new skills, new capabilities, a somewhat awe-
some prospect for the future of management education.

NOSTALGIA

The half point is that nostalgia will get us nowhere. Let
me deal with it first. In a New Yorker cartoon the chairman
of the board is saying, "And though last year, as in
previous years, your company had to deal with spiralling
labour costs, exhorbitant interest rates, and unconscionable
government interference, management was able once more,
through a combination of deceptive marketing practices,
false advertising, and price fixing, to show a profit which,
in all modesty, can only be called excessive".

I should be surprised if some entrepreneurial heart did
not beat a little faster at those words and if some one did
not murmur, "God be with the days". In twenty-two years
working with managers, I am impressed with the extent to
which we are prone to a recherche du temps perdu. But you
can't navigate with a rearview mirror, unless you are going
backwards. Even then what you see is distorted.

There is a more subtle form of nostalgia - or of self-
deception. Managers would claim that they are the ones who
know how things work. They know that you can't for long
spend more than you earn. They believe in their own rationality. Equally they believe in the irrationality of everyone else. Here is where the Blue Lagoon Syndrome appears:
the belief that some day governments will do the right thing
when they have exhausted all the wrong ones; the belief that
people, individually and in groups, will at last see sense,
will at last see the world the way managers do, will at last
see "reason".

And that, of course, is nostalgia at its best.

7

STAKHOLDERS

But if looking backwards is hardly the best posture to move forward into the future, looking forward brings its own problems.

A recent attempt to look forward was the Societal Strategy Project of the European Foundation for Management Development and of the European Institute for Advanced Studies in Management (1981).* It was a unique exercise in that it brought together for the first time in Europe over a sustained period a group of academics and managers. Its purpose was to meet the critical need to balance socio-political response and economic realities. When, in the course of the Project, we looked, through the eyes of managers, at a confused and threatening world, this is what we saw:

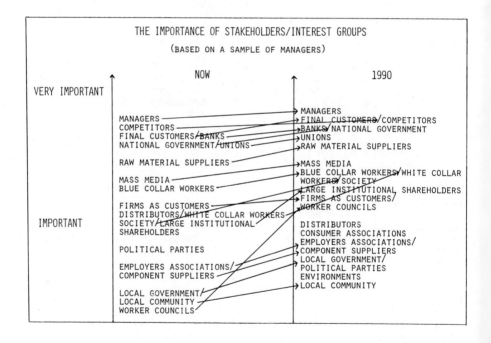

THE IMPORTANCE OF STAKEHOLDERS/INTEREST GROUPS

(BASED ON A SAMPLE OF MANAGERS)

---

* The report, <u>Facing Realities</u>, is available from the European Foundation for Management Development, 20, Place Stephanie, B-1050 Brussels, Belgium.

A group of six stakeholders is rated very highly over the
next decade:

    managers themselves,
    competitors,
    final customers,
    banks,
    national government, and
    unions.

The highest increase in relative importance centred
around other, emerging stakeholders:

    white collar workers,
    worker councils,
    consumer associations,
    raw material suppliers,
    local government,
    environmentalists, and
    society at large.

All the arrows point upwards. In other words, managers
saw the pressures from groups of stakeholders as growing
ever more intense.

I believe they are right.

PRESSURE GROUPS

One of the painful facts of modern life is the ability of
small, powerful groups to bring it to a halt. They can turn
off our lights, stop the trains, switch off the flow of
petrol. The public's frustration with them, its feeling of
powerlessness, is vented in denunciations through the news
media. These denunciations have two seemingly contradictory
but, in fact, parallel effects. One is to reinforce the
power group in its action. It becomes embattled,
determined, us against the world. The other is one of
righteous indignation, of having reached the end of our
tether, above all, of laying the blame. These groups are
increasingly ingenious in using legal, interventionist and
attention getting tools. They get large audiences. They
lead new and motivated constituencies. They are skilled in
whataboutery: the art of avoiding the issue.

For example, the 'them and us' argument is a uniquely
enduring one. It is even more full of nostalgia than the
managers I accused at the outset. It is, of course, mainly
a smokescreen, a convenient diversion from the real issue
which is that it is seldom 'them', in the shape of the
enterprise, that are being held to ransom. Costs can be
passed forward to consumers and backwards to suppliers of
labour, goods or capital. There is nowhere else they can
go. No entity called the firm can be made to bear the
ultimate costs. Recent Irish governments, with their

9

unerring eye for the soft option, have put a penal,
discriminatory tax on banks. There is no such thing as a
disembodied entity called a 'bank' to bear costs. Only
people bear costs: 47,639 shareholders in the two major
Irish banks alone. If the costs cannot be shifted, they
rest ultimately on the shareholders. But only the most
hardened capitalist baiter can take comfort from that.
Most of the shareholders will have bought their shares (or
the shares will have been bought by the institutions
through which they are providing for their pensions) for
prices that did not discount these new costs. And for an
essential good or service it is the community as a whole
that ultimately foots the bill.

PRESSURE GROUPS AND DEMOCRACY

Intervention by pressure groups is now a critical element
in democratic government. It was written recently of
American governance that it had become "uniquely
susceptible to special interest pressures. The cumulative
effect of this pressure has been the relentless rise of
government spending as well as the frustration of efforts
to enact effective national policies on most major issues".
Nearer home, in a paper to an Irish conference, I bemoaned
the fact that the government share of the Irish cake had
increased from thirty-seven to fifty-five per cent in ten
years. Now five years later it could touch sixty-six per
cent. It is now a reasonable assumption that Irish public
expenditure is out of control. Politicians' rhetoric
about the need to mend our ways is matched only by their
proclivity to throw a dollar at any pressure group that
says, "Booh".

THE UNPREDICTABILITY OF GOVERNMENT

Ask any top manager what he wants from government and he
will tell you stability and predictability.

   There are trends that persuade me that we are in
transition to a vastly more different set of arrangements
brought on by new forces, values and externalities. To put
it at its essence, the old roles of ordered government are
gone for good. They are replaced by dynamics that are
likely to bring about turbulence as the normal condition.
This would write full stop to the age of stability in the
relationships of government with those parts of society in
whose name it is supposed to act. It could make unstable
not only government for the people but government of the
people.

   Contributing to the uncertainty is a paradox. Despite a
healthy cynicism about the purposes and performance of
government, the public goes on demanding that it do more -
and more, always provided, of course, that they are not

asked to pay for it. And yet, in this country over the
past year or so, perhaps the beginning of a change can be
detected: the beginnings of a realisation that it is not
'the nation' that is 'living beyond its means', as political
fingerwagging would have had it, but that it is the
government that is living beyond our means, and that we are
getting damn bad value for the heavy taxes we have to pay.
(On a recent morning in the Dublin suburb in which I live
the telephones were out, the water supply had been cut off,
there was no garbage collection, and the traffic lights had
gone, adding, if that were possible, to Dublin's anarchic
traffic conditions. For these services, I part, quite
involuntarily, with a considerable portion of my earned
income). In a refreshingly frank recent talk, the Deputy
Secretary of the Irish Department of the Public Service
said, "Most government managers are not highly motivated to
define output, monitor productivity, set higher goals or
standards of performance or experiment with organisational
changes. Indeed there are positive disincentives to
productivity".

In his 1971 State of the Union address, President Nixon
declared that, "People everywhere are simply fed up with
government at all levels". That remark sums up the dilemma.
Many people are at or near the limits of patience with
government's disabilities. They cannot fathom its
objectives, accept its word, depend on its effectiveness, or
see where it is taking them.

In his inaugural address President Reagan said, "In this
present crisis, government is not the solution, it is the
problem".

The plain fact is that government has taken on more than
it can handle. One wonders, indeed, if a cabinet meeting
ever gets half way down the agenda. So long as government
is dense and crowded, nothing is going to alter its
proclivity to accumulate a stock of errors, nurse them to
the point of infection, and waste time, money and energy
defending itself against deserved criticism.

GOVERNMENT AND UNINTENDED DESTINATIONS

Adding to the uncertainty and unpredictability surrounding
government is the fact that, when it sets out to achieve
something, it can end up at an unintended destination.

Take, for example, its 'interventions' in the business
firm.

A firm may be defined loosely as a social organism that
has to make a profit to survive, innovate and grow or, in
the case of a State company, is limited in the amount of
loss it is permitted to make. (In Ireland, incidentally,
we have a unique obfuscation. We call State companies

semistate companies. There is, of course, no such thing).

What the firm can do is to identify and meet a market
need. It can, if it is a monopoly or oligopoly, manipulate
a market. It can innovate. It can create employment. It
can reduce employment. It can manage longterm investments.
It can deal with competitors under equal conditions.

What the firm cannot do is to operate without a market.
It cannot force customers to buy, as the government can
force citizens to pay taxes. It cannot create a need. It
cannot operate without clear rules of the game. It cannot
operate where the government subsidises competitors. In
sum, it cannot do things it was not designed to do.

When government asks it to do what it was not designed to
do, unexpected things happen.

For example.

The expected result of making dismissal impossible is to
secure employment and employee rights. The actual result
is some increase in security for those already in jobs and
a greater awareness by both employer and employee of
employee rights. So far, so good. But the inintended
result is no growth in employment, or even contraction, as
employees are gradually replaced by less troublesome
machines.

The expected result of government support for lame duck
industries is to maintain employment or a 'vital' industry.
the actual result is shortterm employment maintenance. The
unintended result is that government money runs out because
the original sore has been poulticed, not cured. There is
a brake on innovation and new employment creation.

The expected result of what is loosely (and inaccurately)
called industrial democracy is increased involvement of
employees. The actual result is that there is indeed some
increase in involvement, some learning. The unintended
result was described in Sweden in the course of the
Societal Strategy Project as "a stiff, decision stopping
bureaucracy".

The expected result of price control is to control
inflation, to protect the consumer or to limit monopoly
power. The actual result is that some inflation may be
modified or delayed. There is some shortterm consumer
protection. The unintended result is a decrease in
profitability, investment and innovation. Symptoms have
been tinkered with. Causes have not been attacked.

If government is to do anything well, against the clamour
of rising demands, it will have to offload peripheral, as
well as contentious, functions which are making a shambles
of public management and satisfying not even the benefitting

constituencies.

THINGS ARE GETTING WORSE

The troubling thought is that, at least in this country, the government shows no signs whatever of doing so. Worse, the figures for public expenditure show that it is continuing to go in the opposite, in the wrong, direction. Government shelves in Ireland are groaning under the weight of recommendations for reform from councils, commissions, working groups and task forces, all of them set up by government, all of them ignored by government.

Governments are riddled with restraints. The resultant conflicts do not give them the power and energy to do difficult and unpopular things. The concentration of constitutional power in the government does not produce political power. Pressure groups come up the back stairs and take command. This does not lead to venal government. Irish government is rarely venal. It is usually well meaning. But it is not far sighted. It is normally at least two steps behind events.

THE NEED FOR UNDERSTANDING

What I have been doing up to now is trying to illustrate just some of the forces at work on the enterprise. I have had to be selective. I would hope that, even within that selectivity, what I have said bears some relationship to the complexity of the forces with which managers have to contend.

I shall reach for my machine gun if some one suggests that what is needed to deal with complexity is flexibility. Of course we need flexibility, provided it is of the rapier, not the banana skin, kind. But we need a lot more besides.

First we need understanding. When we set out to analyse the stakeholders in the firm, this has been the traditional approach:

13

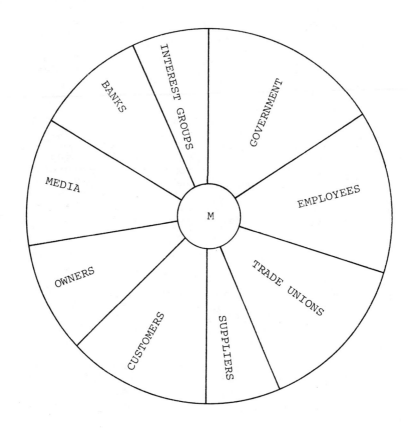

   Its main flaw, as we quickly saw in the Societal
Strategy Project, was that it was egocentric. It looked at
stakeholders through the eyes of the manager, from the
point of view of the firm.

   This next diagram is, perhaps, a little nearer the truth.
In it we see the firm as just one social organism among
several:

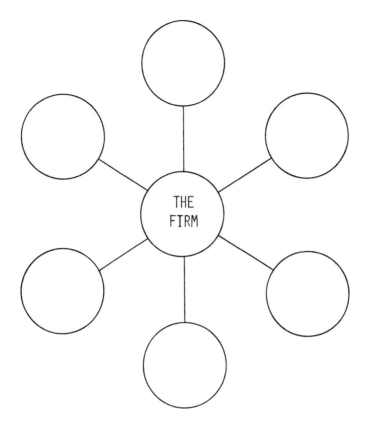

But then all those social organisms would have _their_
view of the world, _their_ stakeholders.

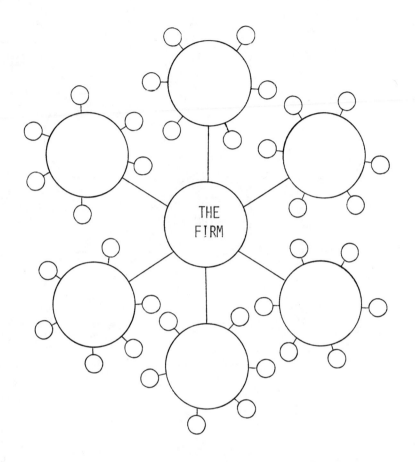

16

And the stakeholders would have stakeholders:

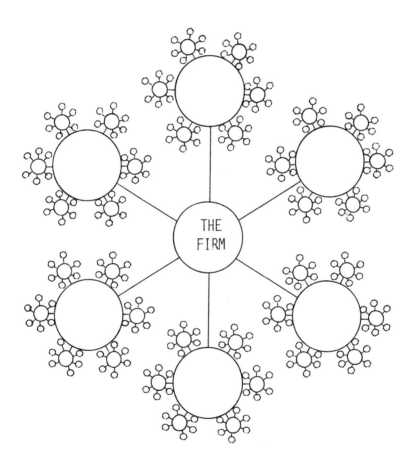

So, simple it is not. Unless the firm has within it the capability of understanding and dealing with that complexity, it will face a future full of surprises, most of them unpleasant.

A PSYCHOLOGICAL BLOCK

Here in the project, I for one detected a disappointing psychological block. While, among some senior managers, there was an intellectual, or theoretical, acceptance of the complex forces at work, there was a curious unwillingness so to rearrange the firm to deal with them.

This is a puzzling phenomenon. I can only hazard some guesses at the causes. They may lie in the narrow, specialised training of managers. They may lie in atavistic hangups that 'the business of business is business'. They may lie in the fact that senior businessmen, heavy with experience and past successes, attribute that success to their unique personal qualities. (I was told as a young consultant that, before I pointed out to Mr So-and-so how ineffective a manager he was, I should remember the symbol of his ineffectiveness parked outside; a shining Rolls Royce). They may lie in the very demands the job of managing, of minding the shop, make on the manager, causing tunnel vision. They may lie in the Anglo-American culture of Macho Management where the lonely, heroic figure is supported by folklore like "It's tough at the top" or "Management is not a popularity contest".

Or they may lie in the inertia, the comfort objectives, that stifle any organisation with the passage of time. As the 1549 preface to the book of Common Prayer puts it "There was never any thing by the wit of man so well devised, or so sure established, which, in continuance of time, hath not been corrupted".

BREAK THE OLD MOULDS

If the Societal Strategy Project means anything, it means that we have to break the old moulds of management, to break out of the crippling comfort zones of our precious little collections of traditional skills, to sally forth into a world that is threatening only because we do not understand it, to take on at their own game the pressure groups whose quest for power is dressed up in rosy hues of social concern, to become as politically active as those groups who would destroy that uniquely creative entity called the business firm.

And, in doing so, we must make crystal clear what our values are. We face ideologies that are well articulated and that command wide appeal. It is no use managers saying they can't stomach idealogy when, in spite of the way they like to contrast being practical with being ideological, they are walking exhibitions of ideology in action. The expression of an ideology can be largely unintended. Managers' actions project distinctive beliefs about feedom, authority, incentives, responsibility, happiness, distributive justice, and the role of government.

Throughout the project the ecumenical approach was encouraged. Ecumenism does not mean borrowing a bit of this religion and a bit of that. It means being consistent and being clear, so that, if other constituencies do not agree, they know where they stand with us. But it also means a willingness to listen, to move out into other constituencies, to make the difficult intellectual leap of trying to see the firm as others see it.

And we cannot do that within our present individual or organisational capabilities. We need to develop new skills. We need new organisational capabilities in the shape of time, thought, energy and resources. This is the real test. Are we prepared to make that transition - or simply pay lip service to it, and then business as usual?

It seems to me that 'usual' will not be a familiar word in a manager's future vocabulary.

I am not suggesting that it will be easy. Change is very hard indeed. But I am reminded of the words of de Gaulle. When asked if he was looking forward to old age, he said, "Yes, when I consider the alternative".

Part I
The manager in a changing world

2 Top management roles in a changing environment

ALLAN BORDOW AND TONY STEVENSON

The authors wish to thank Coopers and Lybrand, Sydney, chartered accountants, who sponsored this study; and The Public Relations Institute of Australia and Enterprise Australia, both of whom commissioned the work.

INTRODUCTION

In 1979 the huge United States automobile industry staggered under an aggregate loss of US$4,200 million. Business Week ('Why Detriot ...', 1981) reported this as the worst one year performance in the history of any US industry. The article said that this industry was now desperately fighting for survival.

The US automobile industry, long admired as one of the business success stores of modern industrialisation, has been plagued by problems both internally and externally. Those from without can be traced as far back as the mid 1960s when a General Motors product was attacked by Ralph Nader, self proclaimed advocate of the public interest. Since then the industry has been publicly scrutinised and criticised on the grounds of inadequate safety, emission of pollutants, planned obsolescence, and more recently failure to recognise the consumer demands for smaller, safer, and more energy efficient vehicles. It now faces possible permanent damage from imports, mainly Japanese products. In short, the industry may have had a near sighted view of society at large; unable to see public demands for safety and quality of the environment whilst being preoccupied with doing what it knew its engineers could do best - design and mass produce automobiles (Pfeffer and Salancik, 1978). More than a decade and a half ago, Cordtz (1966) saw the industry heading for trouble when he described officials at General Motors as products of the system which discouraged attention to matters outside the scope of their jobs. Now industry, reeling under external pressures, has been saddled with what Cordtz (1966) said (and General Motors abhorred) 'government instructions on how to build motor cars.'

The current plight of the US automobile industry begs this question: has this industry (or other industries for that matter) concentrated on annual and other short term goals at

23

the neglect of viability over the longer term? Profitability may be necessary, but is it simply sufficient? An organisation must also be viable in order to make future profits. For viability, an organisation must be alert to changing circumstances. To understand these changes and how they have come to affect top management, we need to look to the external environments of our organisation.

Examples of the effects of external pressures on business and other economic organisations appear to have increased since the acceleration of social and technological change following World War II, and more particularly since the 1960s. Demands for equal rights for women and ethnic minorities, demands for safety protection and honesty in advertising and packaging from consumers, demands for environmental protection and rehabilitation from conservationists, and demands for disarmament and the disengagement of industry from the military complex from pacifists have all left their mark, often financially, on companies throughout the modern, industralised world.

The study of management has now recognised these changes too. But, until the mid 1960s, the external environment of an organisation received little attention from theorists and other management thinkers of the day. At that time other factors, including employee motivation, internal social structure and culture, formal organisation arrangements, leadership and technology were the prime subjects of study (Kotter, 1979). In contrast to that period, Perrow (1978) believes that in the present mode of thought, the taking of an environment perspective is the new wave gathering force in modern organisation theory. For example, traditional management thinking attributes change within organisations to the direct intervention of its managers as based upon theories of individual effort. However, Lieberson and O'Connor (1972) and Salancik and Pfeffer (1977) found that such administrative actions actually accounted for only ten per cent of the variance in organisational performance. Other variables, one of which is the effect of the organisation's context or environment, accounted for the bulk of organisational change (Pfeffer and Salancik, 1978).

The first apparent attention that the management literature gave to an organisation's external environment was in Selznick's (1949) detailed description of how groups hostile to the Tennessee Valley Authority (USA) were eventually mobilised to support its development project. Thompson and McEwen (1958) emphasised "....the interdependence of complex organisations within the larger society...." and the consequences of this for organisational goal setting. In 1967, Thompson wrote the first systematic text that expanded on that idea (Thompson, 1967). Emery and Trist (1965) became well quoted for their notion that environments differ, and that these environments directly affect the structure and decision process of organisations embedded within that environment. The 'turbulent' contexts in which many organisations exist, they said, are comprised of interdependent elements and are themselves changing as well as the organisation itself. More recently, Trist (1977) said that skills would be needed in future to identify the internal and external stakeholders who ought to be brought 'in the room' when (multi) organisational problems were being discussed. Heenan and Perlmutter (1979) provide one example of the concept of a stakeholder as a group or institution with a <u>stake</u> in an organisation's success. Stakeholders may directly or indirectly give or withhold support by way of resources or influence. They could include employees, investors, customers, suppliers, government regulators, neighbours, and community interest groups.

This new emphasis on externalities is likely to change the role of top management at the very least. Lerbinger and Sperber (1975), believe that senior company officers can no longer cloister themselves in the hushed 'isolation of the executive suite and dispassionately view the world'. Bennis (1981) would apparently agree: 'This much can be said about leadership for the 1980s: those responsible for governing the enterprise will be spending more and more of their time managing external relations.' Bennis also said there was a 'virtually unanimous' response from a study of ninety chief executive officers that the impact of government regulations or the raised voice of a variety of increasingly eloquent stakeholders had wrought the most significant change in the role of the chief executive. Lerbinger and Sperber (1975) believe the growing number of constituents who are affected by corporate decisions see the chief executive as the dominant target - the person at the top of the executive structure and, along with government, at the summit of national power. The chief executive has been flushed from behind protective office walls and is now the chief actor in a 'theatre in the round' - totally exposed.

A spokesman for a leading US management consulting firm, McKinsey and Co., as quoted by Lerbinger and Sperber (1975) said that where the chief executive of a big company a few years ago spent ten per cent of his time on external matters, the figure today is generally forty per cent. Lerbinger and Sperber (1975) claim studies have shown that even before the age of external confrontation, chief executives had spent between two-thirds and nine-tenths of their time in contact with others, either inside or outside the firm. About thirty-five per cent of that time had been spent specifically on representation, including preparing for meetings, travel, business luncheons and contact with government officials, suppliers, trade union officials and others.

With the recognition that top management needs to relate to its external environment comes the identification by others of the chief executive's external role for his firm. Rock (1977) lists external relations as one of the fourteen accountable functions of the chief executive officer. He defines that function as monitoring the social, economic and political climates, fashioning a favourable image as spokesman, and maintaining liaison with major external

influencers to develop and keep effective working
relationships. Mintzberg (1973), has identified ten roles
for the manager. All implicitly involve contact with the
external environment, seven explicity; figurehead, liaison,
monitor, disseminator, spokesman, entrepreneur, and
negotiator.

After a career in British boardrooms, Sir Walter Puckley
(1973) saw the links with a company to its neighbours and
consumers, the government and other companies as becoming an
important point of concentration for the board of directors.
Reginal H. Jones, a former chairman of the General Electric
Company, lays the responsibility squarely on the shoulders of
the chief executive officer. In Business Week ('The corporate
image....', 1979), Jones said he then spent about half his
working hours managing externalities, speaking out on such
issues as tax reform, capital formation and inflation. All
chief executives would need to have '...extremely long
antennae and be extremely sensitive to public opinion. They
will have to become activists rather than adaptive.'

But, says Heller (1976), the chief executive - the very
person whose concentration, at least some of the time, should
be on the distant horizon - is often the least able to focus
on anything much further away than his immediate concerns.
Chief executives can delegate the responsibility for
contacting the environment. This role often goes to public
relations specialists such as Mobil Oil's vice president for
public affairs, Herbert Schmertz, whom Business Week ('The
corporate image....', 1979) describes as a national PR
celebrity. The magazine claims he has won his colleagues'
admiration for his confrontation of the critics of his
company and the industry and the way he sells his ideas to
top management

The chief executive has traditionally delegated the major
responsibility for managing an organisation's relationships,
particularly external, to the public relations practitioner.
Public relations, based in corporate journalism (Cutlip and
Center, 1978), is usually charged with improving the flow of
information between the organisation and its publics -
stakeholders. This is done through concise, clear and
interesting writing and illustration in publications and
audiovisual productions, sometimes getting feedback through
opinion research. But much more than information is involved
in such relationships. There is an exchange of other
resources which include money, people, goods and services.
The recent management literature looks at these relationships
in a wider sense than does the literature pertaining to
public relations.

Fortunately, the practice of public relations today has
taken cognisance of what is happening within the environment
surrounding big business. Public relations practitioners
have advocated that senior management must pay more
attention to the management of external relationships as
compared to the time they spend on day to day internal

matters. Because of this, the Public Relations Institute of Australia, with Enterprise Australia, decided to conduct a survey of Australian chief executives to determine what proportion of their time was being spent on public affairs outside their organisations and to what extent they expected this proportion to change. The development and results of that study are reported here. Its findings were also made available for discussion at the 8th National Public Relations Convention in Sydney, July, 1981.

A STUDY OF EXTERNAL RELATIONS ACTIVITIES OF CHIEF EXECUTIVES OF AUSTRALIAN FIRMS

Study development. It was decided that a mail out questionnaire would be used to survey the public affairs activities of a sample of chief executive officers of companies located in Australia. In order to define a working list of external public affairs activities of senior management, and to properly distinguish these from continuing internal activities, discussions were arranged with small groups of chief executives similar to those who would be included in the survey to follow. Then, from a list supplied by Enterprise Australia, personal invitations were sent to sixty chief executives of Australian companies in Sydney requesting their participation in the pilot study.

Five chief executives came to the first session and nine to the second session. The first session formed into one group and the second into two groups, one of four and one of five participants. An outline of the proposed study was explained to the three groups. This was followed by a statement to set a mental framework for this discussion: 'Irving Shapiro, chairman and chief executive officer of DuPont Company, has pointed out that he - and the top people in most large companies - now spend as much time on public affairs and public relations as on running the business itself.' (Drucker 1980).

Each group member was asked to list privately the public affairs activities in which he was currently involved as chief executive. Each participant's list was announced to the group and recorded on a flip chart. A composite list of approximately twenty activities was finally put to each group and the participants asked to evaluate them in order of priority for their current and anticipated role as chief executive. The activities mentioned by the most number of participants in all groups were those ultimately used in the survey questionnaire. The three groups also discussed the kind of information chief executives felt would be useful in their job and the method most appropriate for sampling their colleagues by mail. These opinions were taken into account in designing the format of the questionnaire and sampling methods.

Survey method. As no single, published directory is available to cover all Australian business enterprises, it was not possible to have a readily accessible means of defining the total and specific population of Australian for profit firms, trading in this country. The Jobson's (1980) directories were the sources finally chosen to define the population to be surveyed. Jobson's includes all companies listed with offical Australian stock exchanges, including minerals and oil explorers, non listed public companies, and at least the major foreign owned companies. These directories encompass the more conspicuous companies doing business in Australia.

In order to test the survey questionnaire's format and coverage, a pilot questionnaire was printed and mailed to a randomly chosen sample of sixty Sydney companies taken from Jobson's. This was done to test whether the questionnaire would be understood by its intended audience and to determine the expected rate of return. It was also considered as a trial run for a telephone contact method of following up responses which had not been mailed in voluntarily about a week after mailing.

Fourteen completed questionnaires (fifteen per cent of the pilot sample) were returned after the pilot survey had been in the mail one week. Then a person with experience in interviewing executives by phone, arranged to interview every second remaining pilot sampled executive over the phone. The telephone interviewer in this way found that the pilot mailing had occurred during the school holidays and also at the end of the financial year work load. This and the absence overseas by many executives seemed to account for the rate of return of the pilot questionnaire. It appeared that some promises of completion could be expected if a telephone follow-up was used during the actual survey.

As a result of the pilot study, it was concluded that all companies listed in Jobson's would be included in the survey population. Each company listed in Jobson's was subsequently identified and a letter and questionnaire sent to the chief executive inviting his participation. Those in the pilot survey and those with headquarters in New Zealand and Papua New Guinea were excluded. The chief executive of all the selected companies were each mailed a questionnaire, which was modified only slightly from that used in the pilot. The covering letter, personally addressed, explained the nature of the study with an offer to send a summary report to each person completing a questionnaire. Anonymity was promised for respondents in any published material, with their names being used only for mailing a summary report of the survey. A total of 1,016 questionnaires and covering letters were mailed. A team of telephone interviewers also endeavoured to phone and secure replies from those not responding by mail after the first week of the mail out. A sample of 148 completed questionnaires (fifteen per cent of the population surveyed) was eventually accumulated and used for analysis of the survey.

Survey Results. Returns came in from across the nation except

The Northern and The Australian Capital Territories. Of the
148 replies, 128 of the respondents' firms (or eighty-six per
cent) were in capital cities whereas seventeen (twelve per
cent) were located elsewhere. No location could be discerned
for three (two per cent) of the respondents. The medium size
of a company was 430 employees, with the most frequently
reported size being 200 employees, the actual size having
ranged from 3 to 6,000 employees. As for the executives, the
medium tenure in their present office was just over five
years. There was a wide range in their years of service,
from two months to forty years.

The industries represented by respondents and their
relative percentages in the sample were:

Manufacturing	29%	Mining, electricity and gas	28%
Wholesale and retail	16%	Finance	8%
Communication and entertainment	6%	Construction	5%
Community services	2%	Transport	2%

A further four per cent could not be classified; and no
other demographic statistics were collected. The findings
are examined by taking each questionnaire item in turn.

Question 1a. Which of the following functions, relating
to public affairs outside your organisation, do you now
perform in your role as chief executive?

Each respondent could tick as many of the twenty listed
activities as he wished; and the resultant ordering of most
to least number ticked for the entire sample is given in
Table 2.1. These results indicate that the ten most
frequently endorsed items, when summarised, are more
indicative of the figurehead role of management than the
bottom ten items. A figurehead role is a relatively passive,
ambassadorial function where the chief executive represents
his organisation to the larger world mainly in matters of
formality. By contrast, the less frequently chosen items
summarise a chief executive's active negotiation for his
company within a broad, diversified external environment. At
present it appears that in the role of external relations,
top management still favours complying with the more narrowly
prescribed protocols of their office over that of deliberately
carrying the interests of their organisation into the wider
social environment.

Question 1b. What percentage of your time, in your role as
chief executive, do you spend on the activities you ticked
in Question 1a?

As can be seen from Table 2.2, the average time given to
external relations by a chief executive in this sample was

Table 2.1

Percentage of sample endorsing items from Question Q1a as part of their current public affairs activities

ITEM	PERCENTAGE
Thinking	91
Keeping informed	84
Attending social functions	84
Meeting with clients	78
Hosting interstate and overseas visitors	75
Being involved with industry and/or professional associations	74
Meeting with shareholders	71
Attending seminars	70
Attending board meetings of associated companies	68
Meeting with politicians	66
Meeting with government administrators	56
Meeting with consultants	48
Involved with government regulators	45
Making speeches	41
Involvement with education	39
Meeting with unions	32
Advising government consultative committees and statutory bodies	32
Meeting with community groups	30
Attending board meetings of outside companies	28
Meeting with mass media	27

32.3 per cent of his working time, with a standard deviation of twenty per cent. That is, the typical chief executive now spends only about one-third of his time with public affairs activities that relate his company to its external environment, and that for the bulk of these chief executives somewhere between ten per cent but no more than fifty per cent of their time is being given to external affairs management.

Table 2.2

Amount of time currently spent on public affairs activities
by chief executives as a percentage of their total working
time for the total sample

% of time spent	Absolute Freq	Relative Freq (PCT)	Adjusted Freq (PCT)	Cum Freq (PCT)
5.	5	3.4	3.4	3.4
10.	17	11.5	11.5	14.9
15.	15	10.1	10.1	25.0
20.	22	14.9	14.9	39.9
25.	6	4.1	4.1	43.9
28.	1	.7	.7	44.6
30.	24	16.2	16.2	60.8
35.	6	4.1	4.1	64.9
40.	17	11.5	11.5	76.4
45.	2	1.4	1.4	77.7
50.	17	11.5	11.5	89.2
60.	4	2.7	2.7	91.9
65.	2	1.4	1.4	93.2
70.	3	2.0	2.0	95.3
75.	1	.7	.7	95.9
80.	2	1.4	1.4	97.3
90.	2	1.4	1.4	98.6
100.	2	1.4	1.4	100.0
Total	148	100.0	100.0	

Mean - 32.318   Median - 29.667   Std Dev - 20.006

Question 1c. How do you expect the percentage of your time
(or that of your successor), on external public affairs
activities to change within the next five years?

Although the overall results found for this question did not
correlate significantly (rho = -.06, p = .45) with the overall
results for question 1a, the negative coefficient suggests
that those spending a high percentage of their present time on
external matters might reduce their future activities in this

31

Table 2.3

Direction of expected changes in the amount of public affairs
activites likely to result during the next five years

Category Label	Absolute Freq	Relative Freq (PCT)	Adjusted Freq (PCT)	Cum Freq (PCT)
Considerably less	3	2.0	2.1	2.1
Slightly less	16	10.8	11.0	13.0
No change	26	17.6	17.8	30.8
Slightly more	70	47.3	47.9	78.8
Considerably more	31	20.9	21.2	100.0
No reply	2	1.4		
Total	148	100.0	100.0	

area over the next five years whereas those now spending
little time might in future increase their efforts
accordingly.

Table 2.3 specifies the number of respondents who chose one
of five categories of change that might be expected in regards
to their future involvement in external relations. For the
category 'no change', only eighteen per cent of all
respondents indicated that they expected no change to occur
over the next five years from their present level of
involvement in external affairs. Interestingly, and for
these twenty-six executives, none had stated that he now
spends more than fifty per cent of his time in public affairs
activities outside his respective organisation. In fact,
this 'no change' group on average now spends only about a
quarter of its time on public affairs activities (as compared
to the total sample average of thirty-two per cent). For the
categories reflecting a future change, sixty-nine per cent of
the sample (101 respondents) predicted that they would be
more involved with public affairs than they currently are -
forty-eight per cent qualifying this to be slightly more time
whereas twenty-one per cent said considerably more time than
at present. On average, this 'increased change' group now
spends slightly more than a third of its time on such
activities. Finally, some thirteen per cent indicated that
they would be lowering their present level of public affairs
activities into the future, eleven per cent of those giving
the category of slightly less time and two per cent

considerably less time than at present. This 'reduced change' group was found on average to be now more active in public affairs than the other two comparison groups, spending already about thirty-seven per cent of its time managing the company's external relations.

Question 2. Relating to public affairs activities outside your organisation, what activities that you are not doing now should you (or your successor) be doing?

The responses written in by each manager who replied to this question were categorised into similar content areas. The replies given to this question were often found to overlap between respondents, and were usually broad in scope and intention. Therefore, in summary, a verbatim list of representative statements is given as follows: 'training leaders of the future', 'encouraging public interest in companies', 'better informed concerning industry trends', 'improved dissemination of information to consumer groups', 'explaining company's philosophy and objectives to all groups in the community', 'sponsoring disabled trainees', and 'writing letters to the editor'.

Question 3. To which statement in Question 2 above should you (or your successor) give top priority?

The replies to this question were also content analysed; and can be summarised into three groups as follows:-

1. First priority was to representations with political groups, unions and community bodies.

2. Second priority was representations with clients, schools and business.

3. Third priority was representations with media and consumers.

Question 4. Which of the following strategies for managing your organisation's social environment would you consider desirable for your organisation within the next five years?

First, it was observed that those who are presently both very active and varied in public affairs outside the organisation also continue advocating an equally numerous set of desirable activities for the next five years. As for Table 2.1 in question 1a, the actual number (and percentage) of chief executives endorsing each item of question 4 is listed in Table 2.4, where the items have been placed in order of most to least preferred over the entire sample. The results tend to corroborate the notion put forward by individual respondents in question 2 that chief executives in future see themselves as being more actively involved in the wider social environment that directly or potentially may bear on the conduct and responsibility of that firm. It is further to be expected that such activity will be to

Table 2.4

Percentage of sample endorsing items from Question 4 as part
of their expected involvement with public affairs over the
next five years

ITEM	PERCENTAGE
Speaking out on behalf of the business system	65
Informing the public about business enterprise	64
Increasing dialogue with unions	62
Counselling young people	51
Getting the attention of government	48
Assessing community needs and expectations	46
Exploring alternative points of view	43
Monitoring the social environment	36
Corporate advertising and publicity	35
Reporting on the organisation's social performance	32
Sponsoring scientific activity	31
Donating to charity and/or the arts	27
Talking to non related industry	25
Exchanging executives for short term engagements in other organisations	16
Communicating with constituents	14

unequivocally enhance the mission of business rather than
simple to maintain visibility in the eyes of the community.

Discussion of Results. The results show that the
questionnaire appeared reliable. For instance, the overall
number of items ticked for any one chief executive on Question
1a, was an average of 11.5, with a standard deviation of four.
Similarly, for Question 4, his average was six items ticked,
with a standard deviation of three. This data shows a
significant correlation ($r = .50$, $p < .01$) between the number
of items ticked in Question 1a and those ticked in Question
4. Furthermore, the total number of activities ticked in
Question 1a corresponded significantly (Rho = .17, $p < .05$)
with actual time spent in public affairs activities outside
the organisation, as described in Question 1b. These two
findings suggest that respondents were consistent in reporting
the nature and frequencies of their external activities over
the six different questions asked in the survey.

Table 2.5

Average percentage of their working time spent on public
affairs activities by chief executives within specified
industries

	MEAN	STD. DEV.	N
ENTIRE POPULATION	32.318	20.006	148
Mining	27.286	14.670	35
Manufacturing	26.163	14.994	43
Electricity - Gas	43.333	26.013	6
Construction	40.625	16.133	8
Trade	38.250	24.156	24
Transport	45.000	7.071	2
Communication	61.250	45.162	4
Finance	32.500	20.170	12
Services	40.000	10.000	3
Entertainment	31.000	18.841	5
Other	33.333	23.166	6

In addition to the findings for each particular question,
there are results that bear upon combinations of questions
and/or types of respondents. As might be expected, the
replies related to the respondents' industry classification
to some extent, details of which are given in Tables 2.5 and
2.6. Those in mining or manufacturing enterprises were
below average (twenty-six per cent) as compared to the
entire sample (thirty-two per cent) in total time given over
to their public affairs activities. However, three-quarters
of those industry executives see an increase in such
activities within the next five years. Those in wholesale
or retail trade industries are somewhat above average
(thirty-eight per cent) in their present activity level with
sixty-two per cent of these executives seeing more change
over the next five years whereas twenty-five per cent view
less change during that time (thirteen per cent indicated no
change to present activity levels). Members of the finance
industry were right on average for the sample but were split
in their perceptions of future direction. Only fifty per
cent of those in finance saw themselves as slightly more
active within five years whereas thirty per cent saw no
change occurring and the remaining twenty per cent viewed
that period as one for slightly less change. The results
for other industry classifications cannot be reported in

Table 2.6

Expected extent of changes in the amount of time spent on
public affairs activities likely to result in the next five
years for chief executives specified by industries

	MINING	MANUFACT- URING	ELECTRIC- ITY - GAS	CONSTRUC- ION	TRADE	ROW TOTAL
Considerably Less	2.9	2.3	O	O	O	2.1
Slightly Less	8.6	2.3	O	O	25.0	11.0
No Change	14.3	20.9	33.3	25.0	12.5	17.8
Slightly More	48.6	44.2	50.0	50.0	50.0	47.9
Considerably More	25.7	30.2	16.7	25.0	12.5	21.2
TOTAL	24.0	29.5	4.1	5.5	16.4	100.0

	TRANSPORT	COMMUNI- CATION	FINANCE	SERVICES	ENTER- TAINMENT	ROW TOTAL
Considerably Less	O	O	O	O	20.0	2.1
Slightly Less	O	O	20.0	66.7	20.0	11.0
No Change	50.0	O	30.0	O	O	17.8
Slightly More	50.0	75.0	50.0	33.3	40.0	47.9
Considerably More	O	25.0	O	O	20.0	21.2
TOTAL	1.4	2.7	6.8	2.1	3.4	100.0

	OTHER	ROW TOTAL
Considerably Less	O	2.1
Slightly Less	16.7	11.0
No Change	16.7	17.8
Slightly More	50.0	47.9
Considerably More	16.7	21.2
TOTAL	4.1	100.0

36

this manner as there were too few respondents in each of the other industry groups to give reliable indications of their respective trends.

The location of respondents' firms, whether in one of the six capitals or in another city or town, also had bearing upon their respective executive's public affairs activities. The data in Table 2.7 shows that non capital city top management not only on average spent about thirty-seven per cent of their time on external affairs today as compared to about thirty-one per cent for capital city managers; but even more strikingly, non capital city respondents are today engaging in more numerous and different activities than are their capital city counterparts. For instance, non capital city executives are now meeting with community groups and with unions and are involved with education whereas capital city managers are not yet doing so. For these three types of external affairs activities (as taken from items in Question 1), there is a definite separation in present management trends between capital and non capital city executive groups.

When considering the future, similar differences are also forecast in the type and frequency of public affairs activities depending upon the executive's location (Table 2.8). For capital city executives, sixty-seven per cent see an increased use of their time in such engagements and a further nineteen per cent see no change. A final twelve per cent actually see a reduction in such activity. Whereas for the non capital city executives, eighty-three per cent see an increased use of their time on such activities, twelve per cent see no change, and only six per cent see any reduction at all. With regards to the frequency and variety of those activities in future, again non capital city top management expect to be more varied in their approach than those in capital cities. In particular, the data from Question 4 showed that the former will be significantly more conscious of the social role of their firms (e.g., reporting on the organisation's social performance, monitoring the social environment) than can be expected from those in capital cities.

Other significant trends appeared. When the results of endorsed present (Question 1a) and future (Question 4) public affairs activities are broken down by certain other categories, the size of a chief executive's firm, in terms of number of employees, did have a bearing on several specific types of external affairs activities but not overall with amount or variety of such activity as presently engaged in or as anticipated to be the case within five years. Executives from the smaller companies report now spending more time meeting with clients than those representing larger firms whereas the latter are more likely to meet with politicans and the mass media than are executives from smaller companies. For the sample as a whole, chief executives who are spending ten per cent or less of their present time in public affairs activities are opting not to do the following when compared to those who are presently spending fifty per cent or more of their time in the external environment: meeting with

Table 2.7

Percentage of present time spent on public affairs activities
by location of the chief exective's company

	MEAN	STD. DEV.	N
Capital City	31.430	18.490	128
Non Capital City	36.471	27.994	17
MISSING CASES	2.0%		

Table 2.8

Expected amount of time to be spent on public affairs
activities over the next five years by location of chief
executive's firm

	CAPITAL CITY	NON CAPITAL CITY	ROW TOTAL
Considerably Less	1.6	0	1.4
Slightly Less	11.1	5.9	10.5
No Change	19.0	11.8	18.2
Slightly More	46.8	58.8	48.3
Considerably More	21.4	23.5	21.7
TOTAL	88.1	11.9	100.0

politicians, thinking, keeping informed, and attending board
meetings of outside companies. In the reverse situation,
those who are active are meeting with mass media as a stated
preference as compared to the more inactive in today's public
affairs work, the latter stating no such preference.
Finally, the more senior the executive in terms of length of
service with his company, and who also tends to be found in
non capital city locations as well, the more he has a marked
preference not to attend social functions such as business
luncheons and cocktail parties. In future, the newer chief
executive in opposition to his more seniored counterpart
anticipates spending his public affairs time in the
broadening of his business experiences by exchanging
executives for short term engagements in other organisations,

and by talking to non related industry.

To conclude, on average, chief executives in Australian
business enterprises spend one-third of their time on public
affairs activities outside their companies, and most of them
expect this to increase. Today's chief executives spend
their time largely in a figurehead role, acting as
ambassadors rather than actively advancing their company's
relationships to its environment. However, and most
importantly, they expect this to be reversed in future at
which time they see themselves speaking out about business
to specific segments in the community and at the same time
scanning the environment for feedback and future targets for
their next appeals. How this switch in roles will come
about was not answered in the present research investigation.
However, management education must be a vital step in that
process. The issues immediately involved in the education of
chief executives for the job of managing their external
environments is therefore worthy of discussion at this point.

IMPLICATIONS FOR MANAGEMENT EDUCATION

For the Practitioner. The results of this study clearly
portray the chief executive as being in a transition state -
schooled and practising as the traditional and rather passive
emblem of his company, yet seeing the need to embrace a more
assertive and confrontive style especially towards the firm's
external environment. It is unlikely that today's chief
executive will be able to make this transition successfully
given their often long, seat of the pants climb to the top,
which was nurtured in times when change was slower and their
authority to manage was seldom challenged. For instance,
witness the change in appointing vice chancellors to
Australian universities. No longer does academic excellence,
research prowess, or types of degrees held count as the major
criteria for selection to these posts. Today's candidates
must be able administrators with proven track records, tough
fighters both to student activists and professorial staff,
and aggressive money seekers from governments and the public
alike. Most ivory towered academics would be hopelessly
incapable of executing those latter tasks. Thus it is the
younger, middle manager who is likely to breakthrough to the
newer roles of chief executive when he gets his chance at the
top. While waiting for that generation to take its place,
what can be done in the short term?

Fortunately this evoluntionary time can be speeded up
within today's management teams. There are changes now going
on in the way a chief executive manages his other managers -
namely, by delegation of authority and responsibilities to his
middle management. It is not uncommon these days to see the
chief executive of a firm in the company of several immediate
subordinates during visits around the plant, office or
factory. It should be just as common for them to accompany
the boss to the nation's capital or to the company's
headquarters overseas, not because of the subordinate's

financial genius or strategic marketing capabilites, but to
enable them to see first hand (and even try out occasionally)
how to bargain over a new contract for their firm or
negotiate an employee dispute with the union. On the job
experience as the company's spokesman and not simply as
another advisor to the chief will be crucial training for
tomorrow's job in top management.

   Middle management must be given visiting rights to their
company's board meetings in order to see top decision making
in action. They will also need expanded access to
information vital to long term policy and planning formation
as well as facts and figures of what is going on in their
environments in addition to the external data bases now
being developed for management. This information should not
be seen merely as aids to better decision making within the
company, but as an expanded knowledge base that will be a
critical prerequisite for the chief executive in the art of
public confrontation and direct negotiations in the external
worlds of his firm.

   Regardless of the attention to such activities, there is an
urgent need for top management to just get out into the
environment and see for themselves what is happening in their
surroundings. For example, a trip to the seat of government
for the day could be an eye opener to many an executive, who
never thought of such a journey as being part of his
strategy as chief executive. This mere exposure to the
workings of government would be a good start towards
developing a better perspective on the external worlds of
modern business for today's chief executive.

For Continuing Education. As the current management
literature does not provide the immediate answers for
continuing education of chief executives in relation to
their environments, the first step would be a search through
cross disciplinary boundaries. Sections of political science,
international relations, public and company law, economic
history and perhaps even modern literature would seem to be a
logical starting point for an educational foundation to top
management. Since chief executives themselves have their
experiences partly cataloged on record but mostly in their
heads, a second step would be to get them together for pure
information giving and discussion of mutual experiences. Such
information could be then used as case studies for the
continuing education of current and prospective chief
executives and as a beginning to further research and
investigation. As a third step, selected chief executives
must be brought in as guest lecturers to the current crop of
business and management students in an effort to exchange
views and develop theories and applications for the emerging
field of managing the external environment. Simulation and
other management games when coached by the guest lecturer
would help to provide realism and continuity in the classroom
as well.

   The base for continuing education of top management, it

must be concluded, is now clearly experiential. It is nevertheless insular due to the small pool of actual chief executive officers, who usually have a one company history as their background as well. A further way to expand such limited horizons is for the exchange of top management between companies, setting and functions. For instance, a high ranking manager of a company doing frequent business as a contractor with governments could spend a 'sabbatical' with a neutral part of that government's bureaucracy in order to experience first hand how government works. Upon returning to his company, that manager could teach his colleagues what he has learned; and from the collective pool of such experiences by other members of that management team, a more valid approach to dealing with governments could be established by that company. The chief executive would then have more collected advise from which to act when negotiating with that government. The next chief executive would of course have had access to that pool of advise as well, making his transition to the new job all that easier.

For the Curriculum. In view of the new concern to manage an organisation's social relationships, tertiary institutions may find themselves paying increasing attention in their curricula to the social structure in which an organisation is embedded. This structure is the complex network of people and other organisations which make up the society of any organisation.

New subjects. Several institutions already offer subjects to undergraduate and post graduate students with titles such as Business and Society and Changing Society. The content covered by such subjects, and new ones to be developed, does or should include:-

- The structure of society and social change.

- The process of government, at three levels - local, state and national - and in the administrative, executive and judicial branches.

- Futures studies, particularly the art of looking ahead for new social issues.

- Monitoring and evaluating social trends and issues (sometimes called Issues Management).

- The art of negotiation and conflict resolution.

- Interpersonal communication.

A brief overview of each of these subjects now follows.

Social Structure. The study of social structure is no longer the concern mainly of academics and student social workers, but of all who must understand the place and interrelationships of people and organisations in the wider social fabric. Managers of business, political and other

41

social and economic organisations are among those with this
need. An organisation exchanges money, goods, services,
information and people across its boundaries. It needs and
is needed by the rest of society. Such exchanges take place
in a complex set of relationships among its various
constituents who have the ability to supply or withhold the
things being exchanged, including social and political
consent.

The mesh of an organisation with the rest of society both
affects and is affected by social change. Managers can no
longer ignore trends in public opinion and emerging social
issues as their own organisation itself affects these trends
and issues as well. By implication, they are already
involved.

Government Relations. The last two decades have seen a rise
in government involvement in business, especially in
traditional industralised societies such as Great Britain,
the United States and Australia. Government involvement can
be unilateral by way of legislation and regulation; for
example, environmental protection, product packaging and
advertising restrictions represent relatively recent examples
of government involvement. But involvement is increasingly
multilateral, with the parties becoming involved in
discussion and trade-offs before legislation is drafted.
There has been an increase in the employment of public affairs
officers within companies to manage their firm's involvement
in public policy. Management needs to understand the
processes of government which develops and administers public
policy before it can hope to influence such policies.

Monitoring. Management regularly monitors financial progress
with regular feedback on monthly sales according to budget,
rates of return on investment, price earnings ratios on
shares, profits and other indicators. In future, management
subjects must cater for the need for management to learn how
to monitor its social performance with regular feedback on
social indicators, such as level of acceptance by investors,
clients, and government legislators. Some studies are
already made in this area with opinion research to test how
well a corporation is regarded by its stakeholders, and
corporate identity studies to measure the image that
stakeholders have of a given organisation. The social audit
(Abt, 1977) is a relatively new tool for measuring an
organisation's social performance against subjective and
objective criteria. The principle of a social audit is to
quantify the extent of an organisation's contributions to
society with variables such as employment opportunities
offered to the local community, corporate donations, worker
training and plant development schemes. An attempt is
made to compare this with the other side of the ledger,
putting quantities on variables such as level of pollution,
disruption to traffic and employee retrenchments. In certain
social audits, attempts are being made to account for such
things in dollar values and incorporate the extent of social
goods and bads in the annual reports which quantify

financial performance (see Baumol, Likert, Wallach and McGowan, 1970). Issues Management is another function which has been recently developed (Brown, 1978) to help corporate management identify the social issues and trends likely to impact in the immediate and mid term on an organisation's profitability and viability. Issues, such as the ageing of the population and trends to do-it-yourself products like handyman kits, are identified and their likely impact evaluated in terms of threats and opportunities. Similarly emerging issues - those which have not yet surfaced but may be in the making - are forecast and evaluated. By giving the issues and their impact priority ratings, in terms of their urgency and implications for an organisation, and by identifying the key players, or stakeholders, involved with each issue, management may be better informed on what actions to take to stave off or minimise threats and exploit opportunities from changing circumstances. Futures studies, is a way of searching the future, rather than researching the past and is involved intimately in issues management and social and technical forecasting - now more likely to be called strategic planning (Ackoff, 1981) or strategic management (Mitroff and Mason, 1980).

Communication. Interpersonal communication is already offered widely as a separate subject in mangement studies curricula. It covers the processes of writing, self presentation and sometimes audio visual and other graphic and audio communications. Some subjects go beyond this into the art of negotiating and conflict resolution. Interpersonal communication at the one to one level is not new to management studies. But the process of interorganisational communication is largely ignored in curricula. Public relations subjects sometimes attempt to impart the skills and understanding involved with communication, but the emphasis is largely on publicity, sales promotion, publications, audio visual presentation and public speaking. The management of stakeholder relations surely demands more than this, especially an understanding of power differences, political influence and the supply and demand of resources.

EPILOG

It is clear that the role of top management is destined for change owing to the impact that our environment is making upon people, organisations, and societies embedded within it. In the shortrun, new strategies to confront and negotiate more effectively with relevant sectors in the business environment are likely to be used by these executives. Over a longer time scale, changes in management education will aid future top executives in understanding why the need for change and perhaps even in predicting the nature of that change before it actually arrives. Eventually, these changes are likely to bring about change at another level which will in turn alter drastically the very essence - the value systems - upon which management is based. That would involve a change in perception.

We all perceive reality somewhat differently. It appears that our perspectives may at least partly be a function of our conditioning. Some people reared in the economic security of an upper middle class family may value individual freedom higher than social cohesion, and money making more than leisure especially if such values are associated with good outcomes. On the other hand, others brought up in a similar background, and who have suffered under such values, may rebel against their own family values. It still happens that today's management class is drawn from yesterday's managerial class and are persons happy in those values systems. But such traditions are gradually disappearing as increased opportunities for management education are being made available to a wider cross section of society, not only to those from working class backgrounds, but to those whose first language is not English.

New value systems are beginning to form a basis for altering managements' perception of things. These new values include a recognition of social interdependence, as opposed to the independence-dependence perspective of employer-employee (master servant) relations. Using alternative scenarios as perspectives on what is going on outside the organisation gives the corporate manager more information about the nature of these interdependencies. Understanding the values of others - their points of view and their rationale from <u>where</u> they stand - opens the way for top management to work on building relationships of understanding and mutual respect for those it deals with in its external boundaries and even beyond.

Just how to get bring about this change is unclear at this time; nevertheless, there is an urgency to proceed while a choice is still available. That process ought to begin by changing the notion that organisations can be run independently of their environments, which is the way Detriot largely acted until its recent crisis in 1979. Rather, organisations should be both seen to be interdependent with their environments and be run as if they are contributing to and utilising resources in concert with others. If they don't, the environment will surely remind them of their neglect.

BIBLIOGRAPHY

Abt, C, (1977), 'The Social Audit of Management', New York: Amacom.

Ackoff, R C, (1981), 'Creating the Corporate Future', New York: Wiley.

Baumol, W J, Likert, R, Wallich, H C, and McGowan, J J, (1970), 'A New Rationale for Corporate Social Policy', Supplementary paper No. 1, New York: Committee for Economic Development.

Bennis, W, (1981), 'Warren Bennis on Leadership and Development', Training and Development Journal, October, pp. 7-9.

Brown, J K, (1979), 'The Business of Issues: Coping with Company's Environment', New York: Conference Board.

Cordtz, D, (1966), 'The face in the mirror at General Motors', Fortune, No. 74, pp. 117-118.

Cutlip, S M, and Center, A H, (1977), 'Effective Public Relations', 5th Edition, Englewood Cliffs, N.J. Prentice-Hall.

Drucker, P, (1980), 'Rethinking the role of top management', Undated newspaper clipping.

Emery, F, and Trist, E L, (1965), 'The causal texture of organizational environments', Human Relations, 18(1), pp. 21-32.

Heenan, D A, and Perlmutter, H V, (1979), 'Multinational Organization Development', Reading, Mass: Addison-Wesley.

Heller, R, et al, (1976), 'The Once and Future Manager', London: Associated Business Programmes.

Jobson's Mining Year Book, (1980), 23rd Edition, Melborne: Dun & Bradstreet.

Jobson's Year Book of Public Companies in Australia and New Zealand, (1980), 52nd Edition, Melbourne: Dun & Bradstreet.

Kotter, J P, (1979), 'Managing external dependence', Academy of Management Review, 4(1), pp. 87-92.

Lerbinger, O, and Sperber, N H, (1975), 'Key to the Executive Lead', Reading, Mass: Addison-Wesley.

Lieberson, S, and O'Connor, J F, (1972), 'Leadership and organizational performance: A study of large corporations', American Sociological Review, Vol. 37, pp. 117-130.

Mintzberg, H, (1973), 'The Nature of Managerial Work', New York: Harper & Row.

Mitroff, I I, and Mason, R D, (1980), 'A logic for strategic management', Human Systems Management, Vol. 1(2), pp. 115-126.

Pfeffer, J, and Salancik, G R, (1978), 'The External Control of Organizations: A Resource Dependency Perspective,' New York: Harper & Row.

Perrow, C, (1979), 'Complex Organizations: A Critical Essay', 2nd Edition, Glenview, Ill: Scott-Foresman.

Puckley, W, (1973), 'The board's relationship with the community', in Taylor, B, and MacMillan, K, (Eds.), 'Top Management', London: Longman, pp. 14-38.

Rock, R H, (1977), 'The Chief Executive Officer,' Lexington, Mass: Lexington Books.

Salancik, G R, and Pfeffer, J, (1977), 'Constraints on administrator discretion: The limited influence on mayors on city budget', Urban Affairs Quarterly, 12(4), pp. 475-490.

Selznick, P, (1949), 'IVA and the Grass Roots: A Study in the Sociology of Formal Organizations', Berkeley, Calif: University of California Press.

'The corporate image: PR to the rescue', (1979), Business Week', January 22nd, pp. 47-61.

Thompson, J D, (1967), 'Organizations in Action', New York: McGraw-Hill.

Thompson, J D, and McEwen, W J, (1958), 'Organizational goals and environment: Goal-setting as an interaction process', American Sociological Review, Vol. 23, pp. 23-31.

Trist, E L, (1977), 'The concept of organizational ecology', Mimeograph paper, Philadephia: Wharton School of Finance, University of Pennsylvania.

'Why Detroit still can't get going', (1981), 'Business Week', November 9th, pp. 72-76.

3 The manager in a less powerful industrial order

DENIS PYM

As the dominant organisations within advanced industrial societies have grown larger and outwardly more complex, so their ownership has become abstracted, diffuse and isolated from their administration. These are the circumstances in which ownership has passed to the State, to foreign interests and to private and institutional stockholders. Such are the circumstances also in which the central position of authority, whether apparent or real, passes to the manager. The health and effectiveness of both manager and industrial order are inextricably linked. The first observation we might make on manager and enterprise is that neither is in good shape. Indeed, by their own criteria of success, it could be argued that the direction of their condition is one of further deterioration.

My concern is to advance a more optimistic view of the manager's role based on the prospect of a less dominant industrial system which we are already acknowledging through the abandonment of the myth of universal employment. To remind the reader, in this myth the institutions of employment monopolise the creation of wealth and wellbeing and our economic efforts are optimised through 'full employment'.

In essence, it is my argument that we should replace our structural view of organisation and its attendant problems with a cultural perspective. More specifically, less emphasis should be given by managers to the rational basis of enterprise and to problem solving in terms of high technology, and altering divisions of labour, rules and procedures and more to cultivating a way of life based on the commitment of employees to their primary task and to shared beliefs about human conduct. Within this cultural perspective, the managers' 'integrative' function as exemplar, fixer and master of ceremonies would be given more credibility. His immediate task is to build up that system of beliefs and weed out and abandon the bad ritual associated with thinking about organisation wholly as rational entities, a perspective within which authority is seemingly located beyond the people who make up the organisation.

47

THE PROBLEM SUMMARIZED

I shall begin this analysis of the problem and how we might
handle it with a summary of observations and opinion
reported elsewhere (see Pym 1976, 1981 and 1982). Suffice
it to say that these are based on field studies conducted in
the petrochemical, tobacco, airline and electronics
industries and in several government agencies in the UK over
the past two decades.

The circumstances which bring the authority of the manager
to the attention of social observers do not necessarily
alter his essential relationship with ownership. With few
exceptions, he remains an employee. His authority is as a
servant of the enterprise, a fact which must not be
discounted even if it is ignored by managers and their
allies. For, it is the implicit need of the manager in
collusion with the growing cohorts of professional employees
and advisers to conceal the real limitations of his power
which now plays a key role in impoverishing the employment
experiences of management in large enterprise.

The quest for economies of scale and extended hierarchies
in organisation that marked the postwar years of expansion,
though justified in terms of efficiency and the requirements
of new technology, was more closely linked to managerial
aspirations and to the belief in full employment as the
foundation of wealth creation and social wellbeing.

These developments had two detrimental outcomes. Firstly,
the large number of employees now occupying posts with the
title of manager. Secondly, the growth in physical distance
between these 'managers' and the essential operations of
product development, production and sales. In the service
sector too the problem of distance has emerged. Here,
contacts between advisers and clients for all 'the
improvement in relations' have become more formal and less
real through organisational excess. Much of this excess is
the consequence of imposing literary forms of communication
on these relationships. The phenomenon is popularly called
bureaucratisation, a label which seems to absolve too many
of us from our own complicity in organisational excess.

The question of physical distance and its link with social
distance has been examined at some length, particularly by
social psychologists, and shown to be a critical factor in
many of the worst villanies that man has bestowed on his
fellows. (See, for example, Milgram 1965). More recently,
Guirdham (1982) has explored the links between distance and
the beliefs people hold about transactions between parties
in different organisations. Those directly involved in such
exchanges were found to stress the importance of task or
product and the convivial relations between the parties when
they talked about interorganisational relations. By
contrast people removed, through hierarchy or division of
labour, from direct involvement emphasise their instrumental
and political basis and depended on more abstract language

48

to explain them. It is but a short step from the way we perceive such everyday exchanges to our beliefs about the basis of social order.

The personal experience of distance and isolation and their adverse effects on social order are reinforced by the authority vested in communicating through written words and numbers in all advanced industrial societies. Bureaucratised organisation, the education system, the scientific estate and the mass media reflect and uphold that authority and the dominating influence of employment in our lives.

To return to the managerial role. Researches into management activity by Jasinski (1956), Stewart (1967), Pym (1967) and Mintzberg (1973) point to the manager's substantial engagement in communications of a lateral kind and with people with whom he is not directly associated in a physical sense. If the complaints of subordinates about the unavailability of bosses are heeded, then the emphasis in managerial folklore has shifted over the past two decades from ' managing people' to 'managing situations'. This is certainly a characteristic of those organisations in which I have conducted my researches.

Much of the manager's associations today are with the growing cohorts of advisers and professional and technical employees, the scale of whose numbers (>one fifth of all employees) the manager is in no small measure responsible. These are also the parties who vest enormous importance in information and communication based on written words and numbers as their support for the invasion of the world of employment by computers, duplicators, photo reproduction systems, visual display units, word processors and a vast collection of electronic gadgetry illustrates. The implications are more serious than we recognise for the content of such media are abstract symbols whose authority is constructed on the assumption that man's many senses can be reduced to one.

Experience, the concrete, our very notion of reality itself is now seemingly reducible to abstract symbols. Value is not in people and their acts but in their abstract artefacts. All organisations are judged in terms of their economic viability. Even our national priority is expressed as an abstraction - single figure inflation. Balance sheets are reckoned to reflect the health of enterprise. Unemployment is not an experience but a number. The sick and destitute are cases and clients on file. In this world view those who make, do and look after are not just the low paid and of lowly status but are a kind of enemy whose activities ought to be the prospective fodder of some new microprocessor revolution. In some pre-literate societies the insane are ordained with godlike qualities, we accord this honour to economists, bankers, accountants, computer programmers and Mrs Thatcher's ministerial mechanics to whom we continue to look for salvation. It is precisely because we are all more or less literate and because literacy provides the foundation for our institutional dinosaurs that we remain insensitive to the threat to personal wellbeing and social order this new totalitarianism represents.

There is surely something perverse about the place of this abstract totalitarianism in a society which claims materialism as its raison d'etre? But the contradiction is more apparent than real. In our culture, words and numbers gain concrete and permanent qualities through the process of being written down. When we can express a phenomenon as a number or in terms of an abstract concept, it becomes a fact and therefore something worthy of our most serious attention. In the 1950's Senator Joe McCarthy discovered the advantage to be won by prefixing an opinion with a precise number. So fifteen cardcarrying communists in the State department became something more than an opinion or even a mere fact, a dangerous truth beyond question.

As Guirdham (1982) has observed, the parties who trade and transact most comfortably in the language of abstractions are the professionals, academics and managers who have been dispossessed of direct contact with making, doing and helping others. Abstraction is their political weapon and a shield behind which to conceal their impotence. Contrary to the observations and predictions of many social enquirers (e.g. Shepard (1957), Burns and Stalker (1961)) of conflict between the authority of hierarchy (management) and expertise (advisers, professionals, technologists etc) such differences have emerged over only superficial matters. The dominant relationship between these parties today is a collusive one, a collusion designed to promote their mutual protection and conceal their shared plight as employees. With its technical, social and legal enforcements, literacy provides the foundation for the implicit maintenance of false worth, the manager's <u>consequence</u> and the professional's relevance.

The declining influence of the manager is also concealed behind a growing array of status symbols - a new car, smart secretary and office, all the latest gadgets - each of which is justified in terms of his importance to the enterprise. But these in their turn further reduce his potency by detracting from his major responsibilities and separating him from task and workforce.

The examples of this implicit collusion are many. The social scientist's objective (and therefore legitimate) interest in the manager as a leader (man of consequence) and his total disregard of the manager's status as employee (servant) is part of this deception.

The Information Technology Year (IT 1982) was promoted on the same basis. Gloomy predictions for British industry and our way of life are promised if this latest technological bandwagon is not embraced. Such is the weight given to the purveyors of machines which process visual literary symbols that no voice is raised in objection to such absurdities. Experts in the new technology have only to press their demands in the language of industrial mythology (efficiency, cost reduction, faster and better decisions, improved performance) and bureaucracy (more visual/literary information) and victory is theirs. In actuality many of these innovations undermine industrial mythology while those applications designed to liberate man come nowhere.

Towards a solution: the cultural perspective

In terms of my argument thus far the real issues to pursue are those of managerial powerlessness and professional irrelevance and strategies for handling the problems they create.

I have argued that the role of manager and professional in relation to the primary task is an appropriate starting point. However, we must also recognise that the manager's most fundamental contributions may be of a different kind to those normally claimed for him, not as leader, innovator or decision taker, which imply a mastery of task, but as organisation man, master of ceremonies and guardian of the enterprises and its primary task.

Are these not what planning, forecasting, surveying, budgeting and record keeping, with respect to people, materials, and money, couched for legitimation, in the language of the industrial ethos are all about? Are these not also the essential concern of all those formal meetings in employment which absorb so much time and energy?

If the answers are in the alternative then maybe we ought to embark on a very different tack to that advocated by just about every observer of management.

Is it not possible that instead of denying the importance of task as a consequence of his separation from it, the manager instead recognises, accepts and develops his role in sustaining a social system which uses task as the basis of its integration and direction*. In this perspective the concept of organisation as divisions of labour, hierarchies, rules and procedures could give way to one based on shared beliefs and commitments. Culture might take priority over structure and myths, folklore, exemplars and rituals cease to be aspects of social life which we trivialise, joke about and reject, and instead become essential to the maintenance of order.

---

*The end of universal employment will also enable the act of work to regain its authority as a major determinant of organisation.

If much of the manager's energy is already absorbed in upholding the industrial ethic through ritualised activity, where is the problem? All social organisation is characterised by repetitive activities in which the link between means and ends is unclear. However, industrial man, whether as manager or professional, rejects folklore and ritual. Yet we need our myths, our heroes and rites to articulate meaning, reduce collective anxieties, provide social cohesion and generally integrate our lives. So organisations in bad shape are those whose guardians act in bad faith by not sustaining their values and norms and whose rites lack authenticity for their members.

The institutions of advanced industrial society have become the purveyors of bad faith and inauthentic ritual through the very acts we believe to be solving our problems. Governments increasingly reduce their wider responsibilities to legislation - a process by which authority is transferred from people to their artefacts. Of course, we need some rules and regulations but we forget the origins of our rules and the place man plays both in formulating them and living them out. Legislation begins as a way of solving the problems of disorder and soon becomes a primary cause of that disorder. We become confused by the multiplicity of rules, divisions and procedures and individually and collectively divert ourselves of responsibility for our actions. These we load on the law, our institutions, the police and even technology.

Because he gives much weight to the rational basis for what he does, the manager has also overplayed this ritualised way of solving the problem of organisation. In the context of total confusion some divisions of labour and written procedures may help us to sort ourselves out. Further applications of the principle of divide and rule to fragmented, overformalised organisation just adds to confusion and disaffection.

The over use of and overreliance on structural solutions to the problems of organisation brings us back to the authority of literary communications and the collusion of managers and professionals. Rites based on literacy, whether as format or content, are not inherently lacking in authenticity but there are aspects of these media which do not live comfortably with the function and meaning of rites. Written words and numbers help us to elaborate, clarify and differentiate experience rather than integrate that experience. Indeed the more we discriminate the less easy it is for us to connect. A letter, memo, report, or computer printout has ritualised form but the recipient's level of arousal or anxiety is increased even if the senders is reduced by the act. In this transaction, literary media act as instruments for exporting anxiety and arousal rather than as reducers of collective anxiety. Furthermore, the nuances contained in a document, like this article, may be meaningful to their architect but will be

52

less so to their readers. Again good ritual involves all
our senses, literary forms concentrate on one - the visual
sense. When formal meetings, whose format and contents are
based on literary media, are felt by participants to be
timewasting and confusing, then they have degenerated into
bad ritual. The further our rites get away from the primary
task the less likely they are to possess authenticity for
the participants. In many respects the proliferation of
bad ritual, which reduces commitments and increases
employee disaffection, has occurred because we have ignored
organisation as it is exhibited in a way of life and
over emphasised the rational basis of organisations. A
cultural view of enterprise both highlights the excesses
and failures of belief in the rational basis of
organisation and offers a route to greater employee
involvement in and commitment to its activities.

The cultural perspective explored a little further.

Perhaps I ought to begin this quest for strategies to
retrieve the manager's position in industrial organisation
by reiterating the argument so far.

    The existence of many divisions of labour and long
hierarchies of control separate the manager from the primary
task of organisation. These also encourage him to take
refuge, along with the cohorts of professional employees,
in an abstract perspective which compounds his isolation.
The totalitarian threat from the abstraction of experience
is concealed behind a vast edifice of implicit collusive
transactions between managers and between managers and
professionals which also camouflages the extent of their
respective powerlessness and irrelevance. The vehicle of
the abstract perspective and of the collusive games
sustaining them is literacy. It is our unquestioning
dependence on media of a literary kind in the rising tide
of bad faith and unauthentic rites in modern employment
that now threatens social order.

    The familiar structural perspective, which I am also
disputing, recommends as solution to this situation fewer
managers, fewer levels of management, less dependence on
written words and numbers in communication and more
emphasis on task in transactions. Though these may help a
little they would not of themselves challenge the rational
view of organisation which in its excesses contrives the
problem. We must instead shift the emphasis from
organisations to organisation as the basis for raising the
levels of human energy and commitment and improving the
coordination of human effort. In short we need to exchange
the structural view of organisation with a cultural
perspective.

    This is an approach to human activity more feudal than
industrial and undoubtedly more familiar in Japanese than
in British business circles. However, it is in keeping

with the prediction of several social observers, including my colleague John Hunt, of the revival of a more feudal view of the industrial corporation. In this perspective the basis of organisation derives from shared beliefs about the primary task and the implicit roles of human transaction. So the task of the manager would include the identification and communication of 'good' example; the evolution of appropriate mythology and the instigation and operation of rites to communicate and sustain those shared beliefs.

Beliefs, as rational man is so very aware, are dangerous. The more so if they are not based on his own commitment to rationality. The cultural perspective may not hold man as the measure of all things, more likely those with the power will be seen as the embodiment of organisation. When people with strongly held beliefs are drawn together they tend to exclude nonbelievers. In the context of universal employment this raises all manner of antidemocratic overtones. Indeed, it must be admitted that among enterprises which adopt a more cultural view of organisation, autocratic and paternalistic style of management predominate. However, the end of universal employment also marks some decline in the authority of industrial enterprise and the beginnings of a revival of community life. Both offer better prospects for organisation based on more democratic beliefs.

Here too it is timely to question the widely held belief within industrial societies that industrialisation and democracy complement each other. Much has been made, for example, of Theory Y management styles but seldom has the pursuit of this ethos been associated with changes in the basis of ownership. The pursuit of democracy within conventional employment, a subject and subordinate state, is mere window dressing. That is why, in my experience, those enterprises which show a measure of genuine concern about human relations and the welfare of employees also make no attempt to disguise the real basis of power and authority. Furthermore, within the rational perspective of organisation, notions like predictability and equality don't seem to go together. Indeed when and where man is equated with machine, equality is a misnomer for interchangeability, a concept more in keeping with predictability. By fudging the ownership issue and failing to recognise the implications of their total commitment to the rational perspective, managers and professionals have done much to denigrate the democratic ideal.

Exemplars and Myths

A cultural perspective of organisation would emphasise example as one basis of control. The highest form of example is the heroic figure. In our antipersonal, antihero way of life good example is difficult to find. The true heroes have gone underground. Heroes and exemplars do

54

exist as some concerted probing into our private dreams and thoughts will show, but these no longer provide the basis for example in our more public actions. Meantime public figures, (the politicians, film stars, TV personalities, jet setters and financial fiddlers) and those the media would have as heroes offer no example and little integrity. These are evidence of an order devoid of ideals.

However, not every aspect of contemporary life is as impoverished as the mainstream. Many of the readers will be familiar with the game of cricket, a sport which itself has been constipated by rules, tactics, technology and the belittlement of its players over recent decades. However, it now shows signs of recovering from the doldrums thanks to the example of a few individuals like Botham, Lillee, Imran Khan and Kepil Dev. Let us take just one example, probably the best, from English cricket, to explore the components of the heroic figure.

Perhaps the most important observation to make about Ian Botham as a cricketer is his total dedication to the task of cricket - winning games, making runs and taking wickets and his religation of method to a secondary place. His style of batting ranges from the exhilarating to the clumsy. His bowling has been described by one commentator as of the licorice-all-sorts variety. His success, in terms of methods is impossible to explain. He is dedicated to the task of cricket but apparently cannot manage others in that pursuit. Yet in his own performance he has the capacity to astonish and amaze us. His game has magical dimensions. Heroes are never saints or paragons of virtue. They have roguish elements to their character. Botham is not known to be averse to an occasional punchup over a good cause. In being totally human and yet an outstanding cricketer he reinstates the authority of man over his artefacts and gives the game a much needed boost.

Sometimes the heroic figure is both player and manager

Robert Townsend's (1970) very personal views of how to go about running a business and his achievements at the Avis Rent a Car Corporation illustrates the manager in the role of hero. Like Botham, Townsend's beliefs and actions hold closely to the purpose of his game, business, as he sees it which is money making and having fun. His convictions and his capacity to live by them helped him as a manager to discriminate between activities which prosper enterprise and those which constrain it.

Many of the readers will be familiar with the giant retailer Marks and Spencer and its unique place in British business. Some may also know the story of how that company first came to wage war against the excesses of paper work. Folklore has it that a late chairman, Sir Simon Marks, chanced to observe two sales girls in one of the company stores lost in the completion of stock inventory replacement cards while a queue of customers waited for service. These employees had relegated selling merchandise and serving customers to a minor place in their priorities. A companywide purge on all paper work followed. Clock cards were banished, sales girls were given access to store rooms, stock controls, order records, wage and staff records and head office procedures were either simplified or abandoned. Within three years it was estimated that twenty-six million pieces of paper weighing 120 tons had been eliminated annually. To put it crudely, but also in terms of a widely shared belief within the company, Marks and Spencers found it cheaper to trust employees, cheaper in fact to allow pilfering and dishonesty than to apply stringent controls on employee conduct and work procedures.

This piece of mythology and others like it have powerful implications for organisation. Through it, the sacredness of the primary task of selling merchandise is reinstated and the necessary view of human conduct to go with that task is acclaimed. Furthermore, it involves the rejection, by a key person in company, of rational processes which get in the way of the primary task and the statement of a belief in 'good staff relations'. Such stories do not just illustrate the paternalisation, caring, service oriented management ethos of Marks and Spencers, they provide example and precedent for its managers. In this way myth and folklore becomes basic to good organisation.

Rites

If organisation is to be maintained, essentially on the energy of shared beliefs, then the myths, examples and achievements embellishing those beliefs need to be celebrated regularly. Industrial man's commitment to rationality necessitates the rejection of other kinds of religious activity and, since ritual is fundamental to all social organisation, many of the rites of the industrial system lack authenticity. Consequently it is not easy to find industrial organisation with a good portfolio of rites. Professionals and managers, with the aid of high technology, have swept them away. To remind the reader, to be authentic, rituals must articulate meaning, enhance social cohesion and help people to interpret experience.

The writer first became aware of the positive role that rites play in social organisation in the early 1960s. A colleague, David Piper, was conducting some studies of bell making at the Whitechapel Bell Foundry, one of the oldest manufacturing concerns in Britain. He included the writer in the venture. It is easy to become mesmerised by the wonders of the bell making crafts and the mass of quaint activities in which the whole workforce engage to sustain their belief in the brotherhood of bell founding. Here, everything else, including technology and working conditions, was subordinate to the primary task and the craftsman's relationship to it. For example, use was made

56

of a sophisticated piece of electronic equipment to obtain
the fine tuning of the bell as the metal was turned on a
lathe but in the final act the craftsman dispensed with his
equipment and tuned with his ear. Piper had been invited
to contribute to making the centuries old production
operation 'more efficient' and he quickly recognised that
his ideas of efficiency might lead to a serious assault on
the customs and habits of the workplace. Being a person of
broad taste and concern he refused to engage in such an act
of wanton destruction.

As the above examples suggest, and in my experience, the
best rites are nearly always linked with task. In fine
papermaking, for example, these include handling, smelling
the mash before it is rolled into sheets, and meetings to
examine the finished sheet and the sheet of competitors.
In production much final inspection, though justified in
terms of quality control, is designed to protect the
mysteries of the product and the process which produced it.
The same goes for the content of managerial discussions.
If our concern is with authentic rites then matters to do
with the task should not be converted to abstractions - the
games of professionals.

To return to the Marks and Spencer illustration outlined
earlier. In the saga of Sir Simon Mark's attacks on
excessive control we find the possibility of setting up a
ritualised activity designed to reaffirm the primary task;
confirm the company's trust in its employees to advance
that task and, at the same time, encourage a continuing
campaign against the rites (paper work) of bad faith.

Some rites are largely social like, for example, people
from the same office meeting at the pub on Thursday nights.
Though the meeting may exclude shoptalk, the value of such
get togethers is closely allied to those of all ritualised
activity. Unfortunately many good rituals which begin this
way lose their meaning and significance as external
organisation in the form of agendas, specific times
devoted to company business etc is imposed upon them.

The point to remember here is that every organisation
needs ritualised activities and the manager has a key part
to play in the design, establishment and maintenance of
rites appropriate to the organisation and its primary task.

In summary, when we perceive organisations as systems of
belief we get much closer to the dynamics of organised life
than we can hope to do when we perceive them as rational
entities. We also keep people and their activities in the
forefront of our consideration. We put people before
machines, money, technology and abstractions. Within the
cultural perspective, the manager will find the scope to
affirm his central position in employing organisations.

BIBLIOGRAPHY

Burns, T and Stalker, G M, (1961), The Management of
Innovation, Tavistock, London.

Guirdham, M, (1982), Individual's Beliefs and
Interorganisational Relations, unpublished Doctoral
Thesis, University of London.

Jasinski, F, (1956), 'Foreman relationships outside the
work group', Personnel, vol.33, pp.130-136.

Milgram, S, (1965), 'Some conditions of obedience and
disobedience to authority', Human Relations, vol.18,
pp.57-76.

Mintzberg, H, (1973), The Nature of Managerial Work, Harper
and Row, New York.

Pym, D, (1967), unpublished report No.5, Training
Evaluation Study, at Esso, Fawley, Department of
Occupational Psychology, Birbeck College, London.

Pym, D, (1976) 'The demise of management and the ritual of
employment', Human Relations, vol.28, pp.675-698.

Pym, D, (1981), 'Professional mismanagement, Futures,
pp.142-150, April.

Pym, D, (1982), 'Emancipation and Organisation' in
Nicholson and Wall, (eds.), The Theory-Practice of
Organisational Psychology, Academic Press, London.

Stewart, R, (1967), Managers and Their Jobs, Macmillan,
London.

Shepard, H A, (1957), Superiors and Subordinates of Research
Establishments, paper 12, Symposium on Direction of
Research Establishments, National Physical Laboratory,
HMSO, London.

4 Where have all the general managers gone?

JOHN HUNT

DEVELOPING MANAGERS FOR THE TOP

Management Development Programmes are based on the
necessity of upward mobility for organisational survival.
There will always be a need for those few at the top who
try to run organisations. Yet, despite the most
elaborate development plans, top management talent is
always in short supply, even though the pool from which it
comes is extremely large. This outcome seems endemic to
work organisations ... insufficient talent, which was
painfully and patiently recruited years earlier, survives
to inherit the top. What interests us here is, where do
the good people go? Why do they die off? Where are the
general managers that developers promise to deliver?

Several immediate responses occur. First, as people move
into senior positions their earlier experiences and talents
may no longer be relevant to the task. Second, the middle
manager with his concentration on profit or productivity or
getting the product on the market may not be the
conceptualising, analysing type needed for senior
corporate management. Third, it may be that top people are
simply exceptional and the population of exceptional people
is exceptionally small ... most of us have to learn to live
with our mediocrity. Forth, the shortage may reflect our
tendency (as Freud noted) to look for godlike leaders who
embody all that is good and virtuous in man. Such a model
exists in our minds (and in our religions) and the reality
and fantasy are impossible to reconcile ... general
managers are inevitably disappointing - simply because they
are human and do not embody our visions of the ideal.

Many of these explanations have merit. We do need
different people at the top. We do lose many good people
because their rate of learning outstrips the pace of
organisational growth or the rapidity of the career plan.
We do produce organisational death or at least
psychological withdrawal as a result of the unsatisfactory
compromise between individual and collective. We do simply
get older and one third of managers suffer from midcareer
setbacks (Hunt and Collins, 1982) from which some never
recover.

59

We also know some have more energy, will fight and lose and come back to fight again. Others lose and fight no more; careers are about luck, politics, projecting oneself and not all are willing to play these games. We also know some commit a form of professional suicide (Cole, 1981) because the situation overwhelms them.

Markets change, objectives change, the superstar we look for must fit the current situation and what was current is no longer. In this way, being right for 'the top' cannot be controlled because what is needed is only partially within our control.

My purpose in this paper is to suggest that the shortage of talent arises from more subtle processes. The way we manage and develop people in organisations leads inevitably to a shortage of the very people it was intended to produce. So much of what, in good faith, is designed as advancing and developing managers is self defeating, leading to learned helplessness. My second objective here is to suggest an alternative process - one that enhances rather than limits managers' potential and one that may produce more not fewer general managers.

THE CURRENT PROCESS

A man or woman joins an organisation after school or university. The job is usually highly differentiated and segmented. There is a built in assumption that the individual, even the highly educated one, can only cope with a relatively simple process. Specialisation is the name of the game and 'development' is restricted to skill training both on and off the job. Not surprisingly, job dissatisfaction will reach its zenith in these early years.

However, if the individual performs well he or she will be promoted from segmented job to supervisor to manager within a relatively short period of his or her life. Upward mobility as a reward is promised and in the 20s and early 30s it is readily available. Not surprisingly by the 30s job dissatisfaction has dropped, our man or woman is on 'the way'.

The supervisor or manager of a team is usually chosen for his or her technical competence (he was a good engineer, or works study man, or personnel trainee, or investment banker, she was a good secretary, or programmer or biologist). Yet management is primarily an interpersonal process so the shift from technical expertise to a 'wishy-washy' world of managing people is not easy. First, there are no rewards attached to managing people - technical skills still matter more than managerial skills. Output is still the recognised measure of performance. Second, most managers have had little or no formal training for managing others on a day-to-day basis.

To amend this second problem, managers are put in the hands of the 'management developers'. A few lucky ones are sent off on an interpersonal skills programme to correct whatever personal shortcomings they may have in the new game of managing. One week is normal. Why the one week is offsite and without his or her subordinates is not explained, but the reasoning is simple ... the company cannot afford to take the manager and his team away together for one whole week. Such is the indispensability of the team. So training uses surrogate subordinates and role playing to avoid a total closure of one section for one week. The offsite location is preferred because it, ironically, minimises the very situational effects the manager has to manage.

Our manager and twenty others (most of whom have never met before) are isolated for a week in a management training centre some of which compete with the Hilton for luxury and magnificence. At last the help he or she needs is at hand. Or is it?

Management development programmes rarely consider the sort of idiosyncratic problems managers have. Certainly, a manager is taught the skills of managing people but the people, the tasks, the problems he or she has in the office or plant are not on the training programme. For the first of several such experiences the manager has to accept that those he manages and the situation he has to manage are excluded from his development process. The logistics of taking the entire team on a training programme are apparently beyond us, even though providing surrogate experience is not. It is analogous to training members of families to understand each other by training one parent.

Yet, despite the shortcomings of this developmental exercise, the relief is there. The manager usually learns more from the other participants than he does from the instructors. The more audacious members begin to reveal their own problems, their own early disillusionments with the organisation. Jokes about 'Head Office', the 'system', the chairman, the MD, 'the boss', abound providing light relief through nervous confessions of similar perceptions. Yet most of these confessions occur outside formal sessions as though managing is about something else and Head Office, the 'system', the people are accidently involved.

Following this initial training, other training or management development programmes ranging from interpreting the balance sheet to negotiating with unions are offered to our developing manager. Most of these programmes have little or no relevance to his immediate problems. They rely heavily on reducing those attending to the lowest common denominator and successfully avoid the immediate pressing problems of being a manager. Already, some managers begin to wilt.

PROFESSIONAL SUICIDE

By this stage the manager has had up to ten years of this frustrating development process. Torn from his expertise and embroiled in supervising others, he or she has lost his or her power base. And by the time the manager develops another he or she is moved again. Professional suicide may result. Donald Cole identified this phenomenon in the large division of an American aerospace corporation. He defines professional suicide as, "The process in which creative, aggressive, well educated, highly intelligent people suddenly, over a relatively brief period take steps that can only lead their careers with organisations in a negative direction". (Cole, 1981, p.xi).

He sees the symptoms as:

.   Quitting jobs to go to other jobs beneath their abilities.

.   Becoming disruptive.

.   Stopping working to capacity and retiring on the job.

.   Becoming outmoded and obsolete.

.   Developing psychosomatic complaints such as headaches, backaches. (Cole, 1981, p.1).

The causes of such behaviour are both personal and organisational. Cole's study identified several important characteristics of what work organisation contribute:

.   Unclear, unrealistic expectations and nebulous situations.

.   A management philosophy of "running lean which often meant never enough resources to do the job right but always enough to do it over". (Cole, 1981, p.2).

.   Advancement based not on task or technical excellence but on demonstrating commitment and effort.

.   Poor planning and fatigue.

.   Unwillingness to advise people where they stood on job security and promotion.

.   Poor communication of organisational goals and the individual's part in them.

.   Too little recognition of good work being done.

- A propensity to keep 'happy' by avoiding their problems.

- A reliance on charismatic leaders who are overloaded so that they fail.

- Fear of such charismatic 'superstars'. (Cole, 1981, pp.2-4).

The manager makes several mistakes which worsen the situation whenever he or she is shifted to a new job. First, he or she accepts the vague charter, enter the 'friendly and seductive honeymoon period' during which high expectations are established. Then they are tested, disillusionment is inevitable, he or she seeks formal and informal support and loses and begins to flounder in isolation. Whatever the development programme has given him it is not how to admit to, let alone cope with, failure. What is worse is that the manager has invested so much energy in the promotion game that he is unwilling to confess his or her problem. Pretence becomes essential.

While Cole tends to overdramatise the situation, it is nevertheless, the scene we have all experienced or witnessed. The competitive environment, the manager who needs help, who won't admit it and therefore does not get it and begins to falter.

By the late 30s some of the less resilient general management 'talent' had already been overwhelmed and given in. The upwardly mobile manager has been transferred from one managerial position to another; from one function to another. Each move reinforcing his dependence on the corporation while his ignorance is partially rectified by experience. Each step divorces him or her further and further from the specific discipline he or she spent four or five years at university perfecting. Yet this process is seen to be development for the manager and essential for future general managers. The power base shifts from expertise to control of resources.

For those still in the race the formal training process continues. Managerial programmes labelled stages two and three provide further insights into the world of work through an endless array of 'essential' models, theories, paradigms which are emblazoned in front of him as the latest insights into the managerial process. Each additional stage in the development programme is embroidered with additional meaning ... signs of further promotion are tantalisingly suggested as the rewards for long and faithful service to the needs of the 'system'. Indeed, it is one of the marvels of our times that such rewards of promotion, status, glory are unbelievably effective in maintaining male and female adults in suspended states of social control.

So far in this saga two important issues continue to be ignored by the controllers of the manager's development

63

process. First, his subordinates are still totally excluded
from his development programme. Management development
within a class or school is collective development;
individuality must of necessity be subjected to the needs of
the collective so personal problems with tasks or
subordinates are ommitted. Second, there is rarely any
attempt to link development back to the job situation and
his subordinates. It is true that increasingly trainers use
diaries, action plans, followup reminders to reinforce the
learning and aid the transfer process, but there is an
artificiality about this that tells grown men and women that
we are playing games.

MID-CAREER CRISIS (MCC)

By the end of his or her 30s the peak period of career
motivation is coming to an end. For one third of the
managers (Hunt and Collins, 1981) another crisis is imminent
... the socalled mid-career crisis. For the developers of
general managers, another cause of dropout occurs. Those
who suffer from mid-career problems may do so for years. In
this sense the word 'crisis' is ridiculous. Some suffer for
periods of five or more years.

   This period of a person's life is unlike other periods of
intense and sustained depression. For most other periods of
the manager's life he or she has been able to attribute
cause to effect. For the first time, for most MCC
sufferers, there is no apparent cause of their sustained
depression. They are depressed, disillusioned, drinking,
not sleeping, irritable, even violent, but they do not appear
to be able to see what has happened. What research has
shown is that the organisation, yet again, is not blameless.
The highest incidence of MCC occurs in highly structured,
large service organisations in which promotion is the major
reward and managerial mobility (laterally and vertically)
are part of a development process.

What becomes clear to the MCC manager is that not all the
talent can rise to the top. In terms of his or her
promotion, the major steps are over. He is caught,
mortgaged, pensioned in a system which has left him without
expertise and unable to begin again. Some respond in the
same way as the professional suicides ... withdrawal,
inertia, disillusionment. Whatever their reactions the
talent pool has lost some more of its stars - the numbers
are evaporating.

THE 'BIG' PROGRAMME

By his forties the manager on the 'fast track', the person
who has survived all the problems that psychologists keep
'discovering' about careers, is ready for the Advanced
Management Programme, or for public exposure. He or she has

been trained to the ultimate level of the internal programme and is seen by the training gurus to need the broadening or rounding experience ... expressions which rarely seem to fit those enthusiastic training managers who patronisingly use them about their betters.

Carefully selected business schools are chosen for the experience. The process is similar to all previous experiences ... he goes alone, not with his team, he sits and works with a variety of people from a variety of unrelated industries and he hears generalities which must of necessity, be so broad that their relevance to his situation is left unstated. The wider the range of experiences in the class, the broader the information he receives, the more the instructors are compelled to generalise about the top management role.

Nevertheless, the experience is sanctified as 'general management', or 'corporate strategy' or the macro view for future leaders of men. The more he or she suffers through long hours of work, or classroom humiliation, the more highly the experience will be regarded. Masochism appears to be essential in the race to the top.

However, by this time the real problem is already apparent. Most of the people attending such programmes disappoint the business school faculty as they are clearly not general management 'material'. (Or has the faculty so idealised the perfect manager that no one can possibly fit the model?) Clearly, idealised models are a possibility but there is also the unavoidable conclusion that the educative, career building process has already lost or not attracted or killed off, large numbers of potential general managers. The organisational world of work relies so heavily on segmentation of tasks, over zealous controls, unsuccessful reward systems, tortuous structures, contradictory development exercises that whatever spark the potential general manager had at twenty-five has been snuffed out of him? Only the extraordinarily motivated have the energy and political sensitivity to continue.

Yet the faculty of the business school is not to be denied access to the future 'stars'. Programmes are redesigned to lift the 'level' of those attending. Indeed, the circular process is well known to us all. AMP programmes attract front runners for the first and second run and then seem to slide ingloriously down the hierarchy. Programmes are revamped, renamed and repackaged to lift the level so that those elusive general managers will come.

When the general manager who reaches the AMP returns from his public management programme, the experience is often shattering. Imbued with the generalities of four or six or ten weeks luxuriating in a business school, he finds an unsympathetic environment of people who have not and will not share the experience he has had. Again, those he manages have not been involved in the development; he is completely isolated and the transfer of learning problems are inevitable. No one really wants or understands his new obsessions and in the face of opposition his obsessions weaken and disappear. From here on, the development process is usually more of the same. Another external programme some five to ten years later. The subject matter shifts closer to corporate management but the problems of re-entry and loss of learning are the same.

The consequence of this process is that little manager development really occurs. Most of what managers learn is on the job, from a trial and error process, from academically denigrated 'how to' books and from people around them (at work and at home) who share their fumbling experiences with them.

So where have all the general managers gone? Most of them have failed. Of the intake twenty to thirty years earlier, there are few who survive a development process in which those the manager has had to manage have been excluded from the learning. It is surprising that those who do reach the top are so often devoid of the managerial skills the management development programmes were designed to provide. Is it any more surprising that those who survive are so few?

THE UNDERLYING ASSUMPTIONS OF MOST DEVELOPMENT PROGRAMMES

- Management is best learnt off the job.

- The refining of experience is best achieved away from one's subordinates.

- Repeated external experiences of this sort offer a renewal process which is difficult to achieve on the job.

- Managerial development should be separated from team development.

- There are 'experts' who can tell managers the 'best' way to behave.

- Learning is readily transferred from the classroom to the work environment.

- Career progression is best enhanced through a formalised training process.

Management begins as a technical experience but becomes progressively an analytical and conceptualising process. It involves day-to-day, minute-to-minute communication with others, rather than neatness and rationality. It requires strong interpersonal links.

SOME ALTERNATIVE ASSUMPTIONS FOR DEVELOPING MANAGERS

- The best learning of skills occurs on the job.

- Most people including managers wish to learn on a continuous basis.

- Most organisations overkill the requirements for conformity by trivialising work to the detriment of producing innovative managers.

- The real art of development is to encourage learning by reducing the fear of failure, by encouraging independence or group support in the case of dependence.

- Many managers have a more varied and enriching experience away from work than they do at work as they have greater control over that experience.

- It does not appear to matter what clues, perceptual maps, models, etc the manager uses to reduce complexity to manageable terms. Common sense rather than academic rigour has provided the most persistent models, paradigms, tools, for the manager. (Indeed, it is ironic how little empirical support many of the most persistent models of man, or work, or structure or general management have).

- What distinguishes the general from the middle manager is his or her confidence that he or she can cope. Out of that confidence solutions are found, new products are discovered. Confidence can be boosted by management development but rarely in humiliating or publicly exposing courses.

- Most people learn from experiences involving joint action with peers, families, neighbours. The immediate work group thus offers probably the most relevant, confidence building, learning medium.

The irony of management development is that so many of these alternative assumptions are not part of the development process.

MANAGEMENT DEVELOPMENT THROUGH EXPERIENCE

It is true that many attempts have been made to take the findings about learning and relate them to management development. Action learning, action research, task forces, group projects, team building exercises are all based on the individual learning through experiencing with his or her peers. But for the mass of management development programmes, the ideal and reality continue to drift apart mainly because of the mass production system imposed on it.

Corporate training or development programme designs have difficulty in dealing with the peculiar needs of the individual and his or her situation. This is true even on some of those programmes designed specifically for the individual ... in that he or she is labelled, coded, classified on a series of predetermined scales so that individually tailored but mass produced and resourced learning experiences (called modules) are possible.

One complication of attempts to reconcile individual and peer group is that so many projects or learning experiences either do not include the manager's own group or are a once in a lifetime event for him and his group. We do not seem to be able to sustain the experience once the project is completed. Energy appears to wane, even in those groups which are designed specifically to encourage a sharing of ideas and a common experience.

THE WORK GROUP

There is only one way the development process can be given relevance and encourage individual development. It must be taken from the personnel function and placed with the peer group. Reconciling the needs of the individual and the collective is not easy in any organisation but it is well nigh impossible on a grand scale. Of necessity solutions and individuals have to become packaged until the very confidence and individuality we search for in general managers have been eliminated by the development process. Mass produced programmes produce mass produced and unexciting managers. It is this same reason which leads us to ask where are all the general managers? Of all the research findings on those at the top of organisations, difference rather than sameness characterise their behaviour. Yet we progressively eliminate difference through one induction process after another.

The vehicle for preserving difference within development, of permitting individuality to thrive is to bring the development back to the peer group which is small enough for flexibility and improvisation. The great advantage of the work group is that learning is relevant to the task in sight; learning can extend far beyond the immediate work situation to include activities outside work. Managers remain integrated, are not isolated in a dull bureaucratic maze.

This use of the work group has been a European answer to the inevitable compromise. It occurs in sharp contrast to the North American preoccupation with individual development. Most European literature uses the context and the group as the basis for development. Most of the redesign of jobs, of restructuring, of corporate planning has been a group process in Europe. Groups develop, members of groups develop, groups assist other groups, skills are shared. Similarly, community or village learning has had a long history in the United Kingdom and can still be watched in most rural communities.

The major obstacles to pushing learning back to a manager and his group are the personnel function's obsession with centralising development, the reluctance of experts to admit their failure in solving group problems and the long academic history of teaching by 'telling'.

Personnel managers do appear to have a universal obsession with controlling their function. Drucker's controversial question of the bankruptcy of the personnel function is as relevant in the 1980s as it was when he first published it in the 1960s (Drucker, 1954). Despite the enormous literature on the problems of developing managers we persist with the same format in development programmes. One argument is that the common language is essential for explaining an organisation's climate. If this is one objective of development, then why should language be confined to the manager?

The reluctance of the experts (consultants) to admit that they do not transfer their learning to the manager stems largely from fearing the loss of a power base should they no longer be an expert. It is in the expert's best interests to hold onto the important keys to their magnificent models such that dependence is assured. New models create new dependencies.

As academics, we have shown little imagination in varying our management development programmes, possibly because we are among the world's worst at understanding group activity. Project teams, task forces, study groups, have had a long history in industry yet the academic world is full of disasterous attempts to use group learning experiences. A panel of academics is usually the fastest way to kill a management programme.

Most of these reasons for holding on to the same sort of management programmes when we know we should let go arise from our inability to imagine alternatives. There is an alternative but it requires that training officers, academics, experts, personnel managers, become itinerant advisors, community gurus, wise old men and women whose magic is not to know but to know where to go to get the information or the skill or the technique and how to help the group to get it. Part of that counselling will lead potential general managers to withdraw, to fly away from conforming organisations to stimulating shortterm programmes in business schools or art colleges. But not to learn to manage. Most of the development process will be encouraged to be part of living in the same way that young children learn by living and experiencing.

The performance criterion of such a scheme must be, does this process lead to managerial development? It is extraordinary how rarely such a question is seen to be an important one in assessing the management development function. Yet we would have thought producing significant managers of sufficient quality was the primary objective of management development. The fact that we are (as are the personnel managers themselves) endlessly dispirited by the absence of such men and women means that the objectives of management development have been lost in a vast fog of theories, models, courses, measures of trainers' skills, etc. Add to this the contradiction of individuality and collective; of creativity and conformity of control and diversity within work organisations and it is clear we need more self directed, less dependent personnel policies for those who are to lead our organisations as general managers. Creating 'fast tracks' for those with potential is fine but ludicrous if they are then given a programme of work and training which completely eradicates the differences which made them 'fast track' people in the first place.

MBA programmes, and a host of professional higher degrees (e.g. medicine, law) were developed from the peer group model. Individuals learn to work on team problems, yet are analysed both as team members and as 'different people'. Yet even after such a confidence building experience, how many are subjected to an induction process by subsequent employers, which eliminates the gains of their business school experience.

BIBLIOGRAPHY

Cole, D, (1981), _Professional Suicide_, McGraw-Hill, New York.

Cole, D, (1981), _Professional Suicide_, McGraw-Hill, New York, p.xi.

Cole, D, (1981), _Professional Suicide_, McGraw-Hill, New York, p.1.

Cole, D, (1981), _Professional Suicide_, McGraw-Hill, New York, p.2.

Cole, D, (1981), _Professional Suicide_, McGraw-Hill, New York, pp.2-4.

Drucker, P, (1954), _The Practice of Management_, Harper and Row, New York.

Hunt, J W and Collins, R R, (1982), _Managers in Mid-Career Crisis_, Wellington Lane, Sydney.

Hunt, J W and Collins, R R, (1982), _Managers in Mid-Career Crisis_, Wellington Lane, Sydney, chapter 3.

5 Involving workers: Evidence from recent British research

FRANK HELLER AND MALCOLM WARNER

INTRODUCTION

The question of involving workers in aspects of their
employing organisation's life has received no small degree
of attention in Britain since the pathbreaking technological
changes which characterised industrialism began in the
middle of the eighteenth centry. We will not detail its
early history, but will mention a few important landmarks
(see Clark, Fatchett and Roberts, 1972, for background).
One might start with the highly innovative thinking of
Robert Owen, whose pioneering work grew out of the
workingclass upheavals of the period. For example, as a
model employer, he anticipated the 'human relations' school
of management. He helped to form the Grand National Guild
of Builders, hoping that through this organisation, the
whole building industry in Britain could be put into the
hands of workers' cooperatives. He also started an
Equitable Labour Exchange which was based on an unusual
assessment of a man's worth related to the time it took to
produce a given commodity. Both schemes collapsed, in part
because they were badly organised.

True, Owen's worker cooperatives did not find many
enthusiastic imitators; but by the end of the nineteenth
century over one hundred Cooperative Producers' Societies
were in existence. Profit sharing, too, started quite early
(about 1929), but tended not to survive for long. The
influence of socialist thinking spread in the later decades
of the nineteenth century. Britain in turn produced a
strong current of guild socialism based on the notion of
selfgovernment and small workshops supplying goods to
cooperatives.

In the nineteenth century, the growth of unions fed on the
harsh leadership practices of successful selfmade men.
Their exploitation of women and young children had to be
curbed by a succession of laws and by collective bargaining
with unions who imposed control over the jobs of their
members. Union tactics developed in opposition to
entrepreneurial claims which resembled earlier feudal
practices based on divine right. Union tactics were often
negative and restrictive and this trend has persisted over

71

the succeeding one hundred years. During the first, and
again in the second world war, unions were prepared to
relax their rigid job regulations when they agreed to
participate as equal partners in a struggle against a
common external enemy. In peacetime, however, workers
received little encouragement to share influence with
management. The Whitley Committee report of 1917
recommended that the successful wartime practice of
consultation with workers should be expanded as a
permanent feature of industrial relations. The report made
almost no impact on private enterprise but was used in the
public sector. In most respects, however, nationalisation
turned out to be a great disappointment to the labourforce.
It met none of their aspirations for a radical new deal;
they managed in much the same way as before.

The experience of the two world wars, the intervening
depression of the 1920s and the bitter experience of the
general strike of 1926, produced a radical outlook among
large parts of the labour movement. Shop stewards had
become important during the 1914-18 war as direct
mouthpieces of the workers who elected them, while
previously they were only used as a bureaucratic
fee collecting arm of the fulltime union officials.
Decentralisation of influence to shop stewards was
encouraged by several big unions later and has now been
firmly established in many industries. In this respect,
Britain has adopted a radically new stance, differing from
developments in other parts of Europe or the United States.

Possibly as a counter to this decentralisation and the
increase in workplace bargaining, possibly also as an
attempt to extend the wartime collaboration between unions
and managements, a large number of joint consultative
schemes grew up (NIIP, 1952; Somervell, 1950). Most of
them were short lived. They tended to deal with trivia and
failed to sustain the interest of the lower level employees.
Some of them were fairly open attempts by employers to
weaken or eliminate the influence of unions. But the union
movement grew in strength and in the TUC's evidence to the
Donovan Royal Commission in 1966, it began to speak
positively about worker participation in managerial
decision making. This was seen to be an extension of
collective bargaining. In 1974, the TUC took a big step
forward with a booklet on industrial democracy, which was
clearly stimulated by the 1972 EEC proposal for a Fifth
Directive (TUC 1974). This bolder thinking about power
sharing on subjects not traditionally within collective
bargaining was no doubt influenced by the apparently
successful and expanding codetermination scheme in Western
Germany and other more recent legislation in other
European countries. While the German unions started with
a third representation in the boardroom in 1952 (except for
the coal, iron and steel sector where they secured fifty
per cent), the British unions proposed a 50:50 share from
the beginning and gave evidence to this effect to the

72

Commission on Industrial Democracy chaired by Lord Bullock. We will come to this later.

Since 1970, the subject of worker participation has also received substantial attention from political parties and professional bodies or sectional interest. The Industrial Society, the British Institute of Management and the Confederation of British Industry have made statements or written booklets favourable to an extension of participation. There has also been extensive research into this subject. In a position paper for the Social Science Research Council (Heller, 1981) it was held that more scientific research into worker participation has been carried out in Britain than in any other country with the possible exception of Yugoslavia. Nevertheless, there is little evidence that this body of research, much of which will be reviewed in this paper, has found its way into action channels or has influenced policy making at the level of government or industry.

This is undoubtedly regrettable and contrasts sharply with practices in other countries. In Sweden, for instance, Mr Palme, when he was Prime Minister, arranged for a conference of social scientists to meet and advise him and he personally attended the conference for a full day. In the United States, Cornell University research on worker cooperatives under the guidance of Professor F W Whyte, has decisively influenced recent legislation on government support for cooperatives. In Germany there is legal support for companies who are enjoined to introduce practices in conformity with best available social science findings. In Yugoslavia the introduction of constitutional reforms to support stronger structural measures for worker selfmanagement was clearly influenced by a considerable amount of critical Yugoslav sociological research which had evaluated the inadequacy of previous legislation.

In Britain, the refusal to take account of serious research findings has had some curious and undesirable consequences. One is a tendency for interested parties like employer organisations, to conduct their own pseudo research. In a review of an otherwise excellent book by a very experienced journalist (Elliott, 1978) a reviewer drew attention to the fact that very little use was made of serious research, while very unrepresentative, poorly designed surveys were given much more attention than they deserved (Heller, 1979).

Another trend stemming from the same origin is for the media to ignore social science evidence in favour of publishing views from individual managers or consultants which are unlikely to be unbiased. One example of this is a recent series of articles on the socalled Japanese Quality Circles published by the Financial Times during January and February 1981. These articles purported to show that quality circles were a peculiarly Japanese method of participative decision making at shop floor level. They were being successfully introduced into Britain and other countries by a number of companies and management consultants using the Japanese model. A short while previously, the same editor had featured a similar claim. In rebuttal, one of the authors of the present paper wrote a letter which the Financial Times published on 11 November 1980. In it the writer showed that the method of participative decision making related to the quality of products "was first devised in Britain in 1944 in the textile industry and, through specialised consultants, then moved to Scandinanvia and the USA". When the paper ignored this evidence and featured the January articles describing quality circles as a Japanese method supported in the UK by a number of consultants, another letter was sent to the Financial Times. This time the letter (2 February 1981) gave evidence of the British use of this method in the 1940s by giving the page numbers of a book in which the method was described. This letter was not published and the 'Japanese' quality circle articles continued to appear. The series was later published by the Financial Times under the title "Learning from the Japanese".

The incident is important because it demonstrates our unwillingness to adopt change based on evidence from research. British management had to wait thirty years to have the ideas reintroduced - and under a false label. The final paragraph in the unpublished letter to the Financial Times makes this point clearly: "We are faced here with a phenomenon more important than quality circles; it is the vicious circle of British unused findings (innovation) which have to be tested and used abroad before they can be reimported to this country, sometimes decades later. In this inglorious process, consultants often play an important part. They follow their masters' anti-research timidty and content themselves with picking up the ideas on the long delayed return journey".

There are two reasons for making these points about the underutilisation of social science research in introducing our research summary. One is that this problem exists in many countries and should be more widely exposed by scientists and by the many bodies which finance the objective pursuit of social science research. Secondly, since this paper is an account of findings from British investigations, it is appropriate to draw attention to the possibility that one of the reasons why industrial relations problems have become so interactable in the UK is that the wrong kind of information is made available to those who could influence industrial policy and industrial relations practices.

We will return to this subject again in the concluding section.

RESEARCH EVIDENCE

This section of the paper describes results from a number
of recent studies with which the authors were involved.
The main source of information comes from a major twelve
country comparative study recently published in two volumes
by Oxford University Press (IDE, 1981a, IDE, 1981b). The
British part of this collaborative work was supported by a
substantial grant from the Anglo-German Foundation and is
published by them (Heller, Wilders, Abel and Warner, 1979).
Moreover, this section draws extensively on a report
produced in collaboration with the Social Affairs Division
of the Commission of the European Communities to whom
grateful acknowledgements are made (Warner, 1980). The
Warner report is a part of a wider study of the
participation of workers' representatives in the
undertakings, the determination of working conditions and
work organisation of member states of the community and
Sweden.

The present page does not pretend to give a complete
overview of the very extensive research published on this
subject in the United Kingdom (see for instance Abell,
1975; Batstone et al, 1977; Balfour, 1973; Daniel and
McIntosh, 1972; Guest and Knight, 1979; Hilgendorf and
Irving, 1974; Marchington, 1980; Poole, 1975; Wall and
Lischeron, 1977). Being a controversial subject, it is
possible that other social scientists would interpret the
available material differently. However, we believe that
the evidence we present and the conclusions we draw will
stand up well to public scrutiny.

Participation modalities

There is virtually no legal provision in Britain for direct
involvement by employees in decision making at their place
of work. Direct participation exists either as a result of
ad hoc collective bargaining and/or company arrangements.
Workers' assemblies are unusual in British industry.
Indeed, direct participation is less common in informal,
person to person involvement over key decisions.

The employee may encounter his superior face to face
however, or indirectly via a grievance procedure, or even
through a suggestion box. There is even so, no provision
de jure for direct influence over working conditions,
although in practice it is over such areas that workers do
have some influence (see Wall and Lischeron, 1975; Heller
et al, 1979).

There is often direct say over working conditions by the
activities of workgroups. Management often takes the
initiative and sets up such structures as briefing groups
(see Searle, 1979). Another form is familiarisation groups.
Such employee access to information is usually judged to be
necessary to support participation (Bernstein, 1976: 498).

Most frequently, workgroups elect a shop steward in their plant or office, and hence the form of participation becomes indirect. Even so, spontaneous, sometimes unrecorded, group influence is not unknown in British industry.

Work group regulation of industrial relations is often found (see Clegg, 1979, p.54), although why some groups do attempt it and some do not, is unclear. Often managers prefer to deal with convenors on site, as opposed to either the workgroup directly or the distant union official.

Various experiments in job redesign take the form of job rotation, job enlargement, semiautonomous workgroup and so on (see Klein, 1976; Birchall, Carnall and Wild, 1978; ILO, 1979, pp.32-44; Trist, 1981). They can be, more or less, regarded as 'participation' (see Bernstein, 1976).

Recent British experiments derive mostly from the early work of the Tavistock Institute. It is difficult to estimate how many major experiments there are. The Work Research Unit (a tripartite body) actively sponsored projects in the 70s. The total number of companies involved in largely minor experiments is probably higher than 500 (see Birchall et al, 1978, pp.16-17), but recent surveys tend to "overestimate the amount of significant experience in this area in the UK" (1978, p.59); "most exercises seem to have resulted directly from management initiative and to have been undertaken with largely managerial orientations" (1979, p.60).

Often big firms appeal 'over the heads' of official trade union and/or shopsteward representatives by means of employee referenda. This may be seen by some as a form of participation. Direct voting is not only confined to strike ballots (as in the case of British Steel), but may also extend to approval of a new corporate plan for British Leyland, as in late 1979.

Closely linked to such broad referenda are direct ballots for employee representatives on boards, councils and committees - although these are very limited with respect to the first, and only occasionally to be found for the others.

Even today, profit sharing exists to a limited extent, but is growing. These are now several hundred schemes, many in major companies.

Several kinds of employee profit sharing exist (see Guest, 1979):-

1. A straight bonus in the form of shares instead of cash (e.g. Marks & Spencer, ICI).

2. A deferred share scheme (e.g. Habitat, Bulmers).

3. A shareholding trust (e.g. Kalamozoo).

4. Common ownership (e.g. John Lewis, Scott Bader).

5. Cooperative shareholding (e.g. Meriden).

A survey carried out in 1976 by the CBI found that eighty-six per cent of employees believed a share in profits would boost production.

Lastly, we should note that it is often not easy to classify experiences of firms in participation. Sometimes there are mixtures of forms or practices such as <u>collective bargaining</u> plus one or two other employee involvement devices, say horizontal consultation and/or profit sharing, in the private sector, at least.

<u>Passive</u> forms of direct 'participation' may occur. Often "companies which run surveys regularly and have integrated them with their personnel policy making and planning (e.g. IBM and John Laing) should achieve, or aim to achieve, a situation without salient problems" (White, 1980, p.39). However, such approaches from the top down are no substitutes for shopfloor participation.

In a recent attempt (see Heller et al, 1979) to investigate attitudes to direct v indirect participation, results were collected from a number of British companies employing in total more than 7,000 employees. The sample consisted of 761 informants. Five plants were in the service sector, four plants were in the metal sector (high skill) and five in the metal sector (low skill). The plants spanned a size range between 100 and 1,000 employees.

Respondents were asked to assess the overall distribution of influence of various groups (i.e. workers, middle managers, etc) within their plant. In addition, key respondents (people with particular knowledge of their plant, both union and management) were asked to assess the influence of the same groups for each of the sixteen decisions (see Figure 5.1). The same study also put a similar set of questions to a random household sample of respondents, which will be noted later in the paper.

The research (1979, p.17) very clearly suggested that workers have low enthusiasm for direct participation vis-a-vis those at higher organisational levels. Often <u>no</u> information was given and just under a quarter of the company sample (somewhat more for the worker level) said it was infrequently or never offered when changes were envisaged. But nearly two-thirds felt they would take a different view from their boss, although managers and supervisors (seventy-four per cent) felt freer to express their views than workers (fifty-seven per cent).

To what extent did attitudes to representative forms of participation (e.g. trade unions, works consultative councils, etc) differ from attitudes to direct (possibly

1. Improvements in work conditions of your work group (dust, noise, safety).

2. Appointment of a new department head.

3. Establishment of criteria and procedures for hiring and selection of new employees.

4. Whether workers can follow a vocational training course (during working hours).

5. Permanent transfer of workers to other jobs within the plant.

6. Major capital investment e.g. an additional production line, a new plant, etc.

7. Whether the company should make a completely new product/services.

8. To establish who will be your immediate superior.

9. Changes in how much a certain grade (wage group) shall earn (beyond possibly existing collective bargaining agreements).

10. Replacement of personal equipment (hand tools) of workers (not trivial things like pencils, etc).

11. Changes in the way one or more departments are organised.

12. Assignment of tasks to workers.

13. Dismissal of one of the workers.

14. Whether or not work study techniques is to be used (e.g. stopwatch, MTM).

15. From when to when you can go on holiday.

16. From when to when are working hours.

Figure 5.1 Decision areas

daily) participation in plant decisions? A large number of respondents did not feel that trade union negotiating procedures were supported effectively by management in their company. While approximately a third of both supervisors and workers felt such procedures were given a real chance, forty-six per cent said that there was only moderate support.

Approximately two-thirds of all respondents felt that personal participation in plant decisions increased people's

knowledge of plant activities, enabled decisions to be more
readily accepted, improved the quality of decisions and
provided a 'better' representation of employee interests.
Slightly less than half took the view that employees had a
greater say in plant decisions as a consequence of their
personal involvement.

While managers prefer direct person to person
participation and workers prefer representative
participation, the two methods are complementary rather
than opposed to each other.

SECTOR DIFFERENCES

A number of differences between the metal manufacturing
industry and the service sector should not be mentioned as
being of importance. They support the theory that
situational requirements or historic factors lead to
substantial variations of attitudes and behaviour. Metal
sector respondents (thirty-five per cent) were more
inclined than service sector respondents (twenty-six per
cent) to feel they were not well supplied with information
on union meetings. However, the majority of respondents in
both sectors indicated they received at least some or much
information concerning such meetings. Only twelve per cent
of the total sample felt they received very much information
(N = 761).

High interest in union activities was indicated by
approximately a third of all respondents, with most
respondents maintaining at least some interest. A major
difference in the interest levels occurs between workers in
the two sectors. Only fourteen per cent of the service
sector workers, compared with forty-two per cent of the
metal workers, indicated high interest level. The low
interest of service workers is further reflected in their
willingness to become a candidate for election as a trade
union representative. Only five per cent of service
workers, compared to twenty-six per cent of metal workers,
would definitely be a candidate if asked by colleagues.
Interestingly, the interest levels of service workers in
union activities and candidature are well below even their
own managers and supervisors. This is in line with the
field experience where most representatives in this sector
were drawn from supervisory or lower management levels.
These results are almost certainly linked with the higher
proportion of women in the service sector.

Although most respondents felt they had easy access to
their trade union representatives, the metal sector rated
particularly high on such scores. It seems likely that
this reflects the organisation of work in the metal sector
where shopstewards tended to be concentrated in certain
work areas, whilst service stewards were dispersed across
the organisation.

A comparison of the actual level of involvement, aggregated over all sixteen decisions, indicated only slight differences between the two sectors. Although both sectors revealed a hierarchical decision making structure, this was less marked in the metal sector. This is a reflection of the slightly higher level of participation among supervisors and workers, and the low involvement of managers in the metal sector of the sixteen decisions compared to their service sector equivalents. These results are somewhat surprising considering the dramatic differences in the results on the flow of information, job definition and industrial relations, all of which produced less favourable attitudes in the metal than in the service sector (see later section on job description). Examination of the desired level of involvement indicated a similar hierarchical pattern to that of actual involvement (see Figure 5.2).

Service workers experience higher levels of involvement over decisions relating to hours of work; this relates to the operation of flexible hours in this sector. By contrast, hours of work in the metal sector are generally tied to the technology of production. Another example is the higher involvement of management in the metal sector concerning major capital expenditure, which probably reflects the greater autonomy many of the plants are able to exercise. Plants in the service sector tend to be linked to a centralised policy making unit covering most decision areas, whilst the main control over metal plants is by way of approval of overall budget submissions.

In the national random household sample (N = 1725) of the same survey, major decision areas were selected for further study, namely those concerning:-

    a.   improvements in work conditions;
    b.   permanent transfer within the plant; and
    c.   major capital investment.

As in the company based sample, both the respondents present (or actual) involvement and desired involvement in the respective decision areas were investigated. Two further questions were also asked; first, one concerning the extent to which the respondents' supervisors/bosses give them the opportunity to decide on their own matters concerning the organisation and planning of their work, and second, whether they take part in decisions with their superior/boss concerning their own work.

In contrast to the actual level of involvement in the respective decisions, there was a clear indication of a desire for greater involvement in each of the decision areas that present practice actually provides. Although there remained a substantial proportion of respondents not wanting involvement in capital investment decisions (fifty-three per cent), only ten per cent of all respondents did not want to be involved in decisions concerning work conditions (see

SCALE

1   Not involved at all
2   Informed beforehand
3   Can give opinion
4   Opinion taken into account
5   Take part with equal weight
6   Decide on own

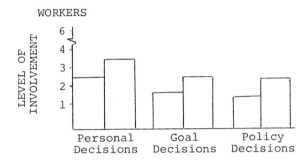

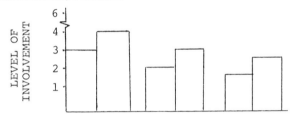

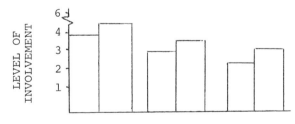

Figure 5.2 Actual and desired involvement in different types
           of decision (see Heller et al, 1979, p.10)

Table 5.1).

Table 5.1
Actual and desired involvement in respective decisions
(see Heller et al, 1979, p.26)

	Working conditions		Permanent transfer		Major capital investment	
	Actual %	Desired %	Actual %	Desired %	Actual %	Desired %
No involvement	25	10	41	21	77	53
Some involvement	52	52	41	48	15	31
'Power' involvement	23	38	18	32	9	16
(% base)	(1,667)	(1,592)	(1,483)	(1,399)	(1,606)	(1,468)

However, the contents of Table 5.1 do seem to indicate a
fairly persuasive desire for greater levels of involvement,
at least in the decision areas studied. The results in the
table need to be interpreted with some caution though as
they refer to all respondents whatever their occupation or
'level' in their place of work.

Many workers in the factory sample in fourteen companies
had reported low degrees of involvement in decision making.
The national random household survey largely confirmed the
findings of this company based sample. As with many of the
other decisions studied, workers seemed to want more say
than they already had, especially 'power' involvement.

ATTITUDES TO PARTICIPATION AT BOARD LEVEL

Unlike many other countries, Britain does not have any
statutory scheme for worker director representation on
single or supervisory boards; indeed it is the exception.
Some experiments have taken place in British Steel (see
Brannen et al, 1976), and a very small number of commercial
firms have adopted a two tier board (see Hebden and Shaw,
1977, pp.44-45); however, the law does not preclude any firm
moving in this direction if it so wants.

A random household survey (Heller et al, 1979) found that
over half of the sample of senior managers, and nearly two-
thirds of the middle managers, thought the representation of
workers on boards desirable (see Table 5.2). This, however,
contrasted with the results of another survey (Knight, 1979,
pp.52-53) which found sixty-eight per cent of managing
directors against the idea, for example.

82

Table 5.2
Desirability of board level representation
of workers in large companies, by job level
(Heller et al, 1979, p.41)

	Total %	Top management %	Middle management %	Supervisors/ foremen %	Shop floor Clerical %	Manual %
Yes, desirable	72	56	64	67	77	78
No, not desirable	28	44	36	33	23	22
(% base)	(1,508)	(118)	(294)	(203)	(239)	(654)

If workers' representatives were to be on boards, who should choose them? Two-thirds of the sample (see table 5.3) said the workers themselves should help to pick them, with forty per cent saying that only workers should choose, and thirty-five per cent wanting some mixture of workers with unions or management. Only twenty-three per cent favoured selection by management (more likely for certain top management and non unionists) (see Tables 5.3 and 5.4).

In the same study (Heller et al, 1979), the respondents were asked to choose between workers' representatives on the board or consultative committees at lower echelons of the organisation.

The data do not suggest any preference in the total sample, fifty-one per cent preferred worker directors, while forty-nine per cent picked consultative committees. Job level was again the top predictor of their preference. About two-thirds of the managers sampled chose committee rather than worker directors; and these figures were neatly reversed for the shop floor (Heller et al, 1979, p.45). Few shop floor workers opted for consultative committees, and this may be explained by a certain disillusionment with consultation in the past (see table 5.4).

Table 5.3
Who should be responsible for choosing worker directors,
by job level
(Heller et al, 1979, p.43)

	Total %	Top management %	Middle management %	Supervisors/ foremen %	Shop floor Clerical %	Manual %
Workers	40	30	35	40	44	43
Management	15	32	18	16	12	10
Trade unions	5	3	3	5	4	6
Workers and management	20	24	27	20	23	15
Trade unions and workers	3	2	3	4	4	3
Trade unions and management	3	2	3	2	2	4
Workers, trade unions and management	12	4	9	12	10	16
Others answers	2	3	3	1	1	3
(% base)	(1,479)	(116)	(283)	(202)	(235)	(643)

Table 5.4
Preference for workers' representatives on the board or
consultative committee at lower levels of the organisation
by job level
(Heller, et al, 1979, p.46)

Preference for:	Total %	Top management %	Middle management %	Supervisors/ foremen %	Shop floor Clerical %	Manual %
Worker directors	51	32	36	44	50	62
Consultative committees	49	68	64	56	50	38
(% base)	(1,170)	(71)	(215)	(162)	(175)	(547)

Joint consultation (of the traditional kind) still persists, but there is no clear pattern. As there is no law as exists say in West Germany, the works council does not have influence over specific areas such as the work environment, production organisation, as well as promotion and transfer in the British system.

In fact, in the British part of a wider study (IDE, 1981a and b), the shop steward body was defined as the main representative institution, whereas in most of the other European countries (except Italy) a works council was chosen, so the choice was (in the light of the above) presumably justified. 'Indirect participation' was very often seen by British workers as traditionally occurring via their trade union representatives.

In a study on automation and work humanisation (Jacobs and Jacobs, 1979), British workers were seen as relying heavily (as did Italian workers) on their union representatives "as a channel to gain hearing for their ideas", as opposed to the other advanced countries studied (1979, p.48). Two out of three Italians had been involved in plant committees, but only one in four British.

During periods of economic depression and extensive unemployment, collective bargaining as well as employee participation schemes are however weakened. This has been demonstrated very clearly in British Leyland (now BL Cars) which was able to dismiss the senior elected union convenor, an almost unheard of event in a highly unionised industry. BL was also able to introduce a new rule book against union opposition. The rule book gives management much wider unilateral authority where union influence had previously been the major force.

The main plant level, and often enterprise level, 'participation' in British industry is via shop stewards and their committees. However, Clegg (1979, p. 13) observes:-

> "surveys established that shop stewards operated in an overwhelming majority of manufacturing plants which employed more than 150 workers and recognised trade unions. Over half of these stewards regularly discussed and settled with management one or more aspects of their members' pay, and most of the remainder did so sometimes."

Estimates vary for the number of such shop stewards. Figures ranging from over 250,000 to over 350,000 have been mooted; around 3,500 are claimed to be fulltime (Clegg, 1979, p.52), or about one per cent of all stewards.

As one authority points out (von Beyme, 1980, p.67):-

> "The shop steward system is dominant where there are few legalised works councils or means of participation... Their power depends on de facto support from the workers

and their mobilisation activity in times of conflict."

Shop stewards are elected in nine cases out of ten (1980, p.67). The TUC is proposing to give such shop stewards' combines formal recognition in its latest plans for structural reorganisation.

RECENT AND FUTURE TRENDS

Since the Donovan Report came out a decade or so ago, the formal system is still hard pressed to cope with plant level collective bargaining. But even if 'institutional lag' is overcome, it is by no means certain that a more 'ordered' stage of industrial relations is achieveable (Goldthorpe, 1974, pp.451-452). The trade unions are too under staffed and over worked to make the formal system work effectively. The enforcement of existing rights and agreements is largely left to the unions themselves. Their success in this respect at bottom rests on their bargaining muscle.

Collective bargaining is thus very crucial. Workers' representatives who have been involved in many decision areas are not necessarily part of the formal union machinery (see Clegg, 1979). Some senior managers have taken the initiative in recent years to strengthen worker influence by ratifying closed shop agreements. The role of the shop stewards in Britain is such that they are in the front line vis a vis the extension of worker influence. For a decade at least, half the manufacturing plants with over fifty employees have taken steps to formalise the position of their shop stewards.

The classic British industrial relations example thus shows participation as almost coextensive with collective bargaining. As Clegg (1979, p.151) puts it: "Taken literally, it (participation) might be held to include the whole of collective bargaining..." The reason for this is that bargaining "gives employee representatives a share in managerial decisions" (1979, p.151). It might, in the future, once again be used for extensions to the bargaining process, but not unless full employment is restored.

Since the mid 1960s, it looked as if the recent Labour governments would not only ensure a high level of employment, but would also promote legislative safeguards for employees. Indeed, apart from the Conservatives in power in 1970 to 1974, there was a considerable extension of legal protection (see Hawkins, 1978; Clegg, 1979). Formal industrial democracy schemes and specifically the proposals of the Bullock Committee Majority Report (1977) would have constituted a clear advance. Whether or not this would merely formalise existing shop floor practices is another question.

Other social scientists are less inclined to think that a simple extrapolation of recent trends will secure for

Britain a reasonable opportunity to improve the position of the working class, their standard of living or a reasonable share in the making of decisions that critically affect their lives. They would argue that other European countries, including Scandinavia and Yugoslavia, have achieved more by using different methods.

Given the nature of the industrial relations system, however, as we have seen, we cannot see participation as entirely independent of the key collective bargaining variables in the UK system. There seems much support for the view that it is the power of organised labour in collective bargaining that helps to make up for some of the legal rights achieved by other systems. Trade unions in Britain have tended for a long time to see the process of collaborative decision making as one of bargaining, at most levels. It could thus be seen that what is happening is "merely a reconstruction of collective bargaining at new levels, although to do so would take the term beyond its presently accepted meaning". Indeed, important developments are taking place at the plant and company levels, and Britian's "industrial relations problems cannot be resolved except by giving major attention to those levels and to the mode of collective bargaining" (Thomson, 1979, pp.53-54).

It is not easy to precisely measure the relationship between those areas of worker influence gained by on the one hand statutory means, as opposed on the other hand to collective bargaining. We have seen the comparatively limited extent of de jure participation in the British system of industrial relations, vis a vis de facto reality, generally over specific issues. Britain achieves only modest scores in the listing of twelve European countries for either formalisation of participation for workers' level (rank = 11), and intensity of de jure workers' level participation (rank = 11) as reported in a recent study (see IDE, 1979, pp.279-280, see also IDE, 1981a). Britain seemed to belong to a low profile pattern which was indicated by 'relatively low scores for all groups with only minor peaks for top management and representative bodies. No one group tends to be favoured by existing rules" (1979, p.279). Yugoslavia headed the list for de jure workers' level participation, followed by Finland, Norway and West Germany.

A White Paper on industrial democracy presented to Parliament in the late Spring of 1978 was the last statutory proposal. The government at the time had already reached an impasse with both the CBI and the TUC, in any case. The proposal suggested gradual progress towards a worker director system and clearly defined statutory rights on employee consultation as well as disclosure of company information. Help was also to be given to not only producer cooperatives, but also to employee profit sharing schemes. The pressure for progress towards industrial democracy in the nationalised sector was to continue, and the White Paper amplified this. The Post Office adopted a worker director scheme (but has later dropped it). However, the momentum towards a Bullock

<u>type solution has declined, under the present Conservative</u>
<u>government.</u>

In recent years, the debate about worker participation has
become a low key issue. Worker participation is <u>not</u> for the
most part seen as a panacea to the issues of inflation, low
growth, balance of payments, unemployment and so on. It is
also <u>not</u> seen as relevant to immediate increases in wage
inflation, manning levels or redundancies, profitability or
investment. Away from the main issues, the longterm
necessity for restructuring British industry, avoiding
deindustrialisation and selfsufficiency in energy over the
medium term, seem to be priority problems. Serious
discussion of these issues has not yet adequately taken
account of the role worker participation might play.

The overall impression of British industrial relations
appears to be one of relative, if deceptive, stability, with
union membership decreasing recently. Under the present
Conservative government, unions are likely to become more
protectionist if present unemployment levels persist or
increase. All this means hanging on to what you have in
conditions of recession.

Informed opinion may, however, help to keep interest alive
in what one editorial writer dubbed "a wider agenda than
strict control of the money supply" (Guardian, 19 May, 1980).
Indeed, both Labour, Social Democrat and Liberal parties have
endorsed the case for more workers' involvement.

The proper choice for this government is to encourage a
wide range of experiments:-

"Further tax concessions, publicity and information
about 'best practices' would all help to renew interest.
The gathering recession has unfortunately provided a
convenient excuse (not only in Britain) for governments
to soft pedal industrial democracy. But that excuse
looks threadbare when reform might provide part of the
solution to the intractable problems of our industrial
relations" (op cit).

There are defensible arguments for building on existing
practices. It will not be advisable to 'import' solutions.
It seems, therefore, sensible to consolidate collective
bargaining organs, such as JCCs; to reinforce the powers of
health and safety committees; to further specify policies
relating to the introduction of new technology, for example.

A clear research consensus, for example, can be found
regarding the evidence of a strong desire for greater worker
influence and involvement at workplace level (see Hespe and
Wall, 1976; Heller et al, 1979; etc). While large
companies, according to a recent British Institute of
Management poll of 154 organisations, are now developing
employee participation programmes, this is not so for
British industry as a whole. However, many companies

reported that their managers were unwilling to share
authority and showed a lack of good leadership skills, while
their employees exhibited a high degree of apathy on the
subject and unions tended to be suspicious of both
government and company motives.

Some forty per cent of the firms:

> "opposed the idea of nationwide voluntary agreements on
> participation - the BIM's fallback position if
> legislation either through the EEC or by a Labour
> government becomes unavoidable - and only four per cent
> would accept board level employee representation."
> (Guardian, 10 July 1981).

THE INFLUENCE OF THE EEC

The de jure position thus lags behind de facto reality, but
European economic community initiatives are still being
discussed and negotiated in Brussels. Several came close to
a decision during 1982 and member countries will eventually
be expected to implement the recommendations or directives.

Two EEC initiatives were recently evaluated by a House of
Lords committee.* One concerned itself with participation
in asset formation, the other with employee involvement in
complex or transnational undertakings. (House of Lords
16732/80 and 8870/79). In both cases, the House of Lords
committee (which included members from the major political
parties) concluded that the subject of greater employee
participation will not disappear and should receive further
attention from British governments.

The major EEC preoccupation in this field is called the
Fifth Directive. It was first issued in 1972, but has since
undergone considerable changes. It now seems almost certain
that the new directive will be simpler and give considerably
more flexibility than the 1972 draft. The new draft will
not insist on structural uniformity for all EEC countries
and while there is no evidence that secret information has
been leaked through trade union channels, it will tighten up
on the provisions for confidentiality to appease the
representation of banks and other organisations. In the
intensive political infighting, the version approved by the
European Parliament in May 1982 is very noticeably less
favourable to the trade union point of view than previous
drafts. Member states will have a choice between unitary
boards or two tier structures and employee representatives
can occupy between thirty to thirty-five per cent of the
board seats. Countries with a unitary system like the
United Kingdom, can allow for a one-third representation of

---

* The subcommittee of the select committee on the European
  communities.

employees or, as an alternative, can design a representative council which would enjoy similar rights of consultation as a supervisory board. There is also provision for allowing an 'equivalent' participation system based on collective bargaining machinery. In the 1972 version, the provisions would have applied to all companies with 500 employees; now they would only apply to organisations with over 1,000. From the trade union point of view, the most serious clause is the acceptance of the employers' insistence that the board representatives can be elected from unionised or nonunionised candidates. Excluded from the proposed directive are multinationals and groups of companies. However, it is likely that multinationals will be included in another draft directive specially designed to increase the amount of information disclosure and certain aspects of consultation.*

The objective of all recent EEC initiatives in this field is to improve the climate and the reality of European industrial relations.

CONCLUSIONS

We have seen that a substantial and well documented body of evidence exists on the various dimensions of worker participation in Britain. In the introduction we lamented the fact that so little practical use is made of this knowledge, either at the level of the firm through the personnel function or at government level through a purposeful pursuit of appropriate policies.

It is only a slight overstatement to claim that a very substantial part of British companies are pursuing a traditional 'ostrich' policy. They seem to hope that by not facing the issue head on, it will somehow go away.

And yet, as long as Britain stays in the EEC, some 'accommodation' to the very much more extensive legal provisions on the continent of Europe will have to be contemplated. Only the UK and Italy lag behind the rest (apart from recent additions to the community). Most professional bodies in Britain urge companies to take bolder steps and develop schemes which suit their requirements rather than wait until more rigid provisions are legislated, entailing the uniform application of preordained structures. If the election of 1979 had returned a Labour government, something like the Bullock proposals softened by the subsequent White Paper would almost certainly have been

---

* "Proposal for a council directive on procedures for informing and consulting the employees of undertakings with complex structures, in particular transnational undertakings". (Bulletin of the European Communities, Supplement, 3/80).

enacted.

While the Institute of Directors is in a minority by opposing any form of employee involvement in decision making, the Confederation of British Industry (CBI) seems to support a very mild form of information sharing and consultation. A recent survey conducted at the behest of the CBI claims that an increasing number of the larger companies at least are developing or extending schemes of this mild kind (House of Lords, 1981, 37th Report). This evidence would, however, seem to be in conflict with most of the research we have reviewed unless very substantial changes had taken place in the last few years. Even if this were the case, it would probably do no more than repeat the unsuccessful history of joint consultative schemes which sprang up like mushrooms in the period after the second world war (NIIP, 1952, Clark et al, 1972) and then suffered various forms of deterioration, oblivion or eclipse. This forecast assumes that Britain will not continue for ever with its recent very high rate of unemployment. Once the economy of the world moves out of its prolonged depression and British industry becomes busy, the industrial relations problems will surely reappear and may even become as unmanageable as recent events in Australia (July to August 1981) where the economy had not suffered as much from stagnation as Britain's.

The motor car industry may turn out to be a barometer in this respect. Industrial relations conflicts have been reduced to hitherto unknown proportions in what was always a very strike prone industry. It would be a mistake to attribute this success to firm leadership alone. Some would, in fact, argue that it was not firm leadership so much as the rapid economic deterioration in the car industry, which severely weakened the position of the shop stewards. This gave management unusual opportunities which will continue only if the industry continues to be unsuccessful. In such a situation we find a strange juxtaposition between 'good' industrial relations indices like strikes, coexisting with 'poor' economic performance. Nobody wants to perpetuate the latter. What will happen if the economy improves?

The research findings can be summarised under three headings. The first shows support for a situational or contingency theory. This means that the various forms of influence and power sharing adjust themselves to certain situational factors. The nature of tasks, level in organisation and industrial sector are the three variables; a fourth one is competence. Without accepting that these contingencies will or should influence the distribution of power in the future in the way they do now, a knowledge of what exists is essential for planning the future. Thus, change will only be manageable if we know what determines the situation today.

The second firmly established finding shows that the actual amount of influence sharing at worker, foreman and middle management level is very low in British industry. All findings converge on this conclusion.

Finally, we have demonstrated that the pattern of
expectations or hopes for future involvement is moderate.
There is no danger that aspirations cannot be met by
relatively slight changes in decision making practices.

These findings do not exhaust our knowledge of the complex
phenomenon we have studied. Since the literature is vast,
we have not been able to draw on all of it. Inevitably we
have used our limited space by concentrating on findings
from research in which we have some personal experience.

The conclusions from our analysis are potentially
optimistic. They suggest that there is still time to adopt
a progressive stance based on sound evidence. It would be
said if, as in the case of quality circles mentioned in the
introduction, a gap of thirty years has to elapse before
British research results are reintroduced here after being
successfully applied in Japan. This warning is reinforced
from the experience of a recent international conference on
the quality of working life held in Toronto, Canada, in
September 1981. One thousand participants were expected but
1,800 registered in spite of the uncertainty and delay
created by a prolonged postal strike in Canada. The
conference attracted hundreds of managers from the US motor
industry as well as senior American and Canadian trade
unionists. We take this industry only as an example. While
General Motors and more recently Ford have introduced
extensive carefully planned schemes of employee involvement
into their large American factories, the same companies in
Britain are still fighting a rearguard defensive action on
relatively primitive schemes of informing employees without
giving them real influence (IPM, 1981).

The reason why this recent international conference is
worth mentioning in the context of the present paper on
British research is simple. The main support for the
successful developments in what is now called the quality of
working life (QWL) comes from British research. This
research started with the pioneering coal mining studies by
Eric Trist and his colleagues at the Tavistock Institute in
the 1940s (Trist and Murray, 1948; Trist and Bamforth, 1951;
Trist et al, 1963). This, and later work in the Tavistock,
and collaboratively with the Oslo Work Research Institute,
established the importance of workers' influence in the job
design process. It developed the seminal notion of
semiautonomous work groups based on sociotechnical systems
theory (Emery, 1959; Emery and Thorsrud, 1969; Davis and
Taylor, 1972; Thorsrud, 1972; Davis and Cherns, 1975; Emery
and Thorsrud, 1976). This work, with adaptations, was
successfully introduced into hundreds of Swedish firms with
the blessing of the Swedish Employers' Federation, and is now,
again with modifications, spreading in the United States.

We can have some reasonable expectation that these
successes abroad, if emulated here, could substantially

increase the extent and speed of introduction of worker
involvement and participation schemes into British industry
in the coming decade. The recent British research findings
outlined (for instance Heller et al, 1979; Warner, 1980;
Wall and Lischeron, 1977) could help to reinforce this
trend.

BIBLIOGRAPHY

Abell, P, (1975), Organisations as Bargaining and Influence
   Systems, Heinemann.

Balfour, C, (1973), Participation in Industry, Croom Helm.

Batsone, E, Boraston, I and Frenkel, S, (1977), Shop Stewards
   in Action - The Organisation of Workplace Conflict and
   Accommodation, Blackwell.

Bernstein, P, (1976), 'Necessary elements for effective
   worker participation in decision making', Journal of
   Economic Issues, Vol.10, pp.490-524.

Birchall, D, Carnall, C and Wild, R, (1978), A Study of
   Experiences with New Models for Work Organisation in the
   United Kingdom, Henley, Administrative Staff College.
   Final project report for the European Foundation for the
   Improvement of Living and Working Conditions, mimeo.

Bullock, Lord, (1977), Committee of Inquiry on Industrial
   Democracy, HMSO.

Clarke, R O, Fatchett, D J and Roberts, B C, (1972),
   Workers' Participation in Britain, HEB.

Clegg, H A, (1979), The Changing System of Industrial
   Relations, Blackwell.

Daniel, W W and McIntosh, N, (1972), The Right to Manage,
   A PEP report, MacDonald.

Davis, L and Taylor, J, (1972), Design of Jobs, Penguin.

Davis, L and Cherns, A, (1975), The Quality of Working Life,
   Volume 1 - Problems, Prospects and the State of the Art,
   Volume 2 - Cases and Commentary, The Free Press - USA,
   Collier Macmillan, UK.

Emery, F E, (1959), Characteristics of Socio-technical
   Systems, Tavistock Institute of Human Relations, Document
   527.

Emery, F E and Thorsrud, E, (1969), Form and Content in
   Industrial Democracy, Tavistock Institute.

Emery, F E and Thorsrud, E, (1976), Democracy at Work, A report of the Norwegian Industrial Democracy Program, Leiden, Martinus Nighoff.

Goldthorpe, J H, (1974), 'Industrial relations in Great Britain: a critique of reformism', Politics and Society, Vol.4, pp.419-452.

Guest, D, (1979), 'Participation at shop floor level' in Guest, D and Knight, K, (Eds.), Putting Participation Into Practice, Gower, pp.59-69.

Hawkins, K, (1978), The Management of Industrial Relations, Penguin.

Hebden, J and Shaw, G, (1977), Pathways to Participation, Associated Business Books.

Heller, F A, (1979), Review of John Elliot's book "Conflict or Co-operation: The Growth of Industrial Democracy", British Journal of Industrial Relations, Vol.17, pp.284-5.

Heller, F A, Wilders, M, Abell, P and Warner, M, (1979), What Do the British Want From Participation and Industrial Democracy?, Anglo-German Foundation.

Heller, F A, (1981), Review of Evidence Submitted to the Social Science Research Council on Worker Involvement in Britain, printed in House of Lords Report of Select Committee on European Communities.

Hespe, G and Wall, T, (1976), 'The demand for participation among employees', Human Relations, Vol.29, pp.411-428.

Hilgendorf, E L and Irving, B, (1974), Workers' Experience of Participation, Tavistock Institute of Human Relations, HRC 942.

House of Lords, (1981), Report of the Select Committee on the European Communities (Sub Committee C), relating to the Directive for Informing and Consulting Employees.

House of Lords, (1980-81), 8870/79, Asset Formation, (Session 1980-81, 36 Report).

House of Lords, (1980-81), 10732/80, Employee Consultation, (Session 1980-81, 37 Report).

IDE (International Research Group), (1976), 'Industrial democracy in Europe (IDE): An international comparative study', Social Science Information, Vol.15, pp.177-203.

IDE (International Research Group), (1981(a)), Industrial Democracy in Europe, Oxford University Press.

IDE (International Research Group), (1981(b)), European Industrial Relations, Oxford University Press.

ILO (International Labour Office), (1979), Politics and Practices for the Improvement of Working Conditions and Working Environment in Europe, ILO.

IPM (Institute of Personnel Management), (1981), Practical Participation and Involvement, 1. Communication in Practice.

Jacobs, B M and Jacobs, P E, (1979), Humanised Productivity Under Advanced Industrial Technology, Research Corporation of the University of Hawaii, Report, mimeo.

Klein, L, (1976), New Forms of Work Organisation, Cambridge University Press.

Knight, I B, (1979), Company Organisation and Worker Participation, HMSO.

Lorenz, C, et al, (1981), 'Learning from the Japanese', Financial Times, pp.24.

Marchington, M, (1980), Responses to Participation at Work: A Study of the Attitudes and Behaviour of Employees, Shop Stewards and Managers in a Manufacturing Company, Gower.

NIIP (National Institute of Industrial Psychology), (1952), Joint Consultation in British Industry, Staples Press.

Poole, M (1975), Workers' Participation in Industry, Routledge and Kegan Paul.

Schumacher, E R, (1973), Small is Beautiful, Sphere Books.

Searle, D, (1979), 'Team organisation in a construction firm' in Guest, D and Knight, K, (Eds.), Putting Participation Into Practice, Gower, pp.114-136.

Somervell, H, (1950), Industrial Peace in Our Time, Allen and Unwin.

Thomson, A W J, (1979), 'Trade unions and the corporate state, Industrial and Labour Relations Review, Vol.33, pp.36-53.

Thorsrud, E, (1972), 'Job design in the wider context' in Davis and Taylor, (Eds.), Design of Jobs, Penguin.

Trist, E L and Murray, H, (1948), Work Organisation at the Coal Face: A Comparative Study of Mining Systems, Tavistock Institute of Human Relations, Document 506.

Trist, E L and Bamforth, K W, (1951), 'Some social and psychological consequences of the longwall method of coal getting', Human Relations, Vol.4, pp.3-38.

Trist, E L, Higgin, G W, Murray, H and Pollock, A B, (1963), Organisational Choice, Tavistock Publications.

Trist, E L, (1976), 'Towards a post industrial culture' in Dubin, R, (Ed.), Handbook of Work, Organisation and Society, Rand McNally.

Trist, E L, (1981), The Evolution of Socio-technical Systems, Occasional Paper, Quality of Work Life Centre, Toronto.

TUC, (1974), Industrial Democracy: A Statement of Policy by the Trade Union Congress, TUC Publications Department.

Von Beyme, K, (1980), Challenge to Power: Trade Unions and Industrial Relations in Capitalist Countries, Sage.

Wall, T D and Lischeron, J, (1977), Worker Participation: A Critique of the Literature and Some Fresh Evidence, McGraw Hill.

Warner, M, (1980), Worker Participation: A Survey of Recent British Developments, Report to the European Commission, Henley.

Warner, M, (1981), 'The British industrial relations system' in IDE (International Research Group), European Industrial Relations, Oxford University Press.

White, M, (1980), 'Getting the drift of employee attitudes', Personnel Management, January.

6 Educational needs of managers in Australia

SURESH MUKHI

It is commonly assumed that people can be trained and developed for senior leadership roles. Indeed there is now a major industry called 'management education' which concentrates on the development of leadership skills and knowledge. However, until recently there has been little evidence to guide our activity in this field. There is need to look at the way in which people who have reached a senior management position see their own process of development. This will give us some guidelines to develop effective programmes and processes.

This paper is based mainly on data collected from senior managers in the Australian private and public sectors to determine the influences which have moulded their style of management, and what they felt was important for those who wish to emulate them. It is argued that management development programmes require major revisions in order to meet the career orientation and future needs of managers.

INTRODUCTION

Management development as an activity within organisations is on the increase. Training managers are now expected to involve themselves in the assessment of needs, design and operations of such programmes. It is commonly assumed that people can be trained and developed for senior leadership roles. However, we know relatively little about the work of these people and how they achieve their positions. The work of Mintzberg (1973) has provided some insights but it involved a study of five top managers. Other researchers such as Copeman (1971); Dalton (1959); Horne and Lupton (1965) and Stewart (1967) have developed some systematic approaches but these do not specifically concentrate on the development of managers.

The main thrust of all this work, and of course the vast range of literature on leadership (Margerison et al, 1979), is to identify theories, styles and environmental factors under which leaders undertake their job. This has led to the development of a number of useful training technologies such as that produced by Blake and Mouton (1964) and Reddin (1972).

97

The emphasis on the research work has been toward academic rather than practically oriented research. However, we need to look at the way in which people who have reached senior management positions see their own process of development and the requirements they have for managerial skills.

The present study is essentially practical in which we asked senior Australian managers questions about how they have succeeded to the positions they now occupy and what they consider are the key management development areas that should be concentrated upon to develop others to positions of senior responsibility. We looked not only at their analysis of their style of management, but also at what they felt was important to those hoping to emulate them.

THE PARTICIPANTS AND THE SURVEY

A modified version of the Management Development Survey Questionnaire developed by Margerison (1980) was used. Some changes to this questionnaire were made after interviewing twenty-five senior managers, to ensure that it was appropriate for both Australian and public sector terminology.

The questionnaires were sent to 1,000 chief executive officers on the Sydney Stock Exchange top 1,000 list of companies, and to 500 of Australia's top public sector managers. Only the department heads or people at one level below that of department heads were selected for the public sector survey. They were selected from the federal, state and statutory levels.

It was decided that follow-up letters would not be sent so that those who returned the questionnaire were those most interested. This was borne out by the fact that approximately sixty five per cent of the respondents asked for a copy of the report.

Of the 1,500 questionnaires sent out, 420 were returned in time to be analysed for this paper. Thus, overall, about twenty-eight per cent of respondents returned the questionnaire. Given that no reminders were sent out this is a fairly good level of response.

KEY INFLUENCES IN MANAGEMENT DEVELOPMENT

"What have been the major influences in helping you develop as a manager?"

This was the question which the Australian senior managers in the private and public sectors were asked to consider. To facilitate replies eighteen statements were provided which were based on personal interviews and the questionnaire designed by Margerison (1980).

Those surveyed were asked to indicate the level of

importance they attached to each item in accordance with the following scale:-

1. Of low importance in terms of helping me to become a senior manager.

2. Of fair importance in terms of helping me to become a senior manager.

3. Of average importance in terms of helping me to become a senior manager.

4. Of substantial importance in terms of helping me to become a senior manager.

5. Of great importance in terms of helping me to become a senior manager.

The results obtained in this survey are presented in Table 6.1 in rank order. The standard deviations are also shown in order to provide some indication of the scatter of the results obtained in the survey.

The top three factors in this list stand out quite clearly. In each case the average score is approximately 4 and the scatter of the results is very small, indicating that most of the senior managers who responded to the questionnaire considered that these factors were of substantial importance. The respondents saw the need to achieve results as a key factor, followed closely by ability to work with a wide variety of people and having an ability to influence and negotiate. Similarly the bottom three factors are considered by the majority of managers to be only of low to fair importance.

The results obtained show a remarkable similarity to a similar survey carried out in the UK. In summarising the results the comment used in that survey - "managers regarding their own development as a function of the kind of person they are and that in contrast things that were done to them were rated much lower (Margerison 1980)" - is equally true of the results of the Australian survey.

The results of the public sector and private sector are also very similar. Both senior managers in private and public sectors listed the same three factors as of substantial importance, and the same three factors as of least importance. But some differences do occur. The desire to see new opportunities, leadership experience early in career and family support are seen as more important influences by private sector senior managers than those in the public sector. Having more ideas than colleagues, sound technical training and a manager early in career as a model is seen as more important by public sector senior managers than those in the private sector.

These differences would seem to indicate a greater

Table 6.1

What major influences have helped you develop as a manager

| Statements | Public Sector | | | Private Sector | | |
	Score	SD*	Rank Order	Score	SD*	Rank Order
Having a need to achieve results	4.03	0.95	1	4.21	0.84	1
Ability to work with a wide variety of people	3.93	0.86	3	4.08	0.79	2
Having an ability to influence and negotiate	3.94	0.89	2	3.99	0.82	3
Early overall responsibility	3.63	1.03	4	3.68	0.70	4
Desire to seek new opportunities	3.18	1.17	9	3.62	1.07	5
Width of experience prior to 35	3.47	1.13	5	3.58	1.06	6
Ability to change managerial style	3.38	1.08	7	3.51	1.06	7
Leadership experience early in career	2.90	1.33	14	3.45	1.11	8
Stretched by immediate superiors	3.21	1.14	8	3.31	1.16	9
Willingness to take risks	3.06	1.14	11	3.23	1.08	10
Having more ideas than colleagues	3.44	1.00	6	3.19	1.14	11
Visible to top management before 30	2.92	1.26	13	3.11	1.27	12
Family support	2.79	1.22	15	3.10	1.33	13
Sound technical training	2.93	1.15	12	3.05	1.12	14
Manager early in career as model	3.14	1.34	10	2.95	1.33	15

	Public Sector			Private Sector		
	Score	SD*	Rank Order	Score	SD*	Rank Order
Having formal management training	2.10	1.10	17	2.60	1.22	16
Overseas management/ work experience **(Experience in other depts. or private sector)	2.71	1.30	16	2.36	1.34	17
Experience of leadership in armed forces	1,54	0.95	18	1.61	1.12	18

Scale of Importance

1	2	3	4	5
Low	Fair	Average	Substantial	Great

* SD refers to one standard deviation from the mean

** Equivalent question in public sector survey

influence in the development of private sector managers through challenge and initiative, and a greater influence of the need to achieve status through technical expertise, seniority and idea generation in public sector managers. The conclusion could be drawn that private sector managers reach top positions through achieving results via their own initiative, whereas public sector managers reach high positions not basically through results (this does not mean to say that achieving results is not important), but through being noticed by their superiors and having more ideas than their colleagues, and better technical knowledge could facilitate this process.

Returning to the top three factors and assuming that need to achieve results is fulfilled by achieving results through others (as a senior manager's job involves him in meeting with others at least seventy-five to eighty per cent of the available work time), it is evident that of greatest importance is to manage people. It is, therefore, important that in designing management development programmes that a considerable emphasis is placed on the behavioural aspects of management. My own experience, based on my participation in communications and interpersonal relations workshops, is that people will be what they want to be. However, we can help develop a language, skills and introduce strategies for change which will help individuals communicate more clearly and understand others. This could also help to develop personal attributes, such as need to achieve results, ability to influence and negotiate, ability to change managerial styles etc., which senior managers rate highly in their success.

MANAGEMENT DEVELOPMENT NEEDS

This was an important section of the questionnaire. There were two open ended questions in this section and the respondents were asked their views in their own words.

The questions were:-

1.   What have been the most important things you have had to learn to perform your role as a senior manager?

2.   Now that you are a senior manager, what do you consider are the key management development areas that should be concentrated upon to develop others to positions of senior responsibility in your organisation?

There was a wide range of responses but most fell into the major categories listed for each section. The data supports the earlier findings that interpersonal and motivational skills to manage people are regarded as the key to success and play an important role in learning to be a manager. The importance of managing people is stressed and is reflected in Tables 6.2 and 6.3.

Learning to be a senior manager

What have been the most important things you have had to learn to perform your role as a senior manager?

There were many and varied answers for this question, yet ninety-two per cent of responses still fitted into the eight major categories as shown in Table 6.2. Not all respondents used the exact words or phrases shown. Their answers were included, however, if they were considered to be substantially the same in intent.

Table 6.2

Important factors in learning to be a senior manager*

* Public sector results are shown in brackets.

Rank		Typical statement	% of Comments	% of Replies
(1)	1	Motivate people, get the best out of people, manage people, encourage team work	24.26 (22.41)	39.75 (31.32)
(2)	2	Patience, tact, tolerance, caution, understanding, self control, democratic style	16.2 (15.52)	26.51 (21.69)
(3)	3	Make decisions, follow through anticipate problems, accept responsibility, maintain independent judgement	13.83 (13.79)	20.18 (19.27)
(7)	4	Leadership, gain respect, maintain control, influencing others, impartiality	9.2 (6.87)	15.06 (9.64)
(5)	5	Delegate, direct work, accept help	8.6 (10.34)	13.86 (14.46)
(6)	6	Get priorities right, forward planning, set objectives	6.6 (7.75)	10.64 (10.84)
(8)	7	Understanding the system, understanding the business, product, problem	6.6 (4.31)	9.06 (6.02)
(4)	8	Choose the right people, train people, reward initiative, consolidate, promotions	6.2 (12.07)	8.18 (16.87)
	9	Others	(7.75) 8.5	

The top ranking answer, clearly designated No. 1,
contained (22.4 per cent) 24.26 per cent of all responses and
(31.3 per cent) 39.75 per cent of all respondents included an
answer for this category. Thus motivating and managing
people to achieve the best results was seen as the main
criteria for successful performance at a senior level.

The second ranking answer fits into this field as well, so
that (38 per cent) 40.5 per cent of all answers are to do
with managing people, understanding and motivating them. This
supports the earlier finding that most senior managers
consider ability to work with a wide variety of people as one
of the most important factors in their own success.

The reaction of the private sector to this question is
largely in agreement with the public sector's results. The
first three categories do receive a stronger reaction from the
private sector accounting for both a greater percentage of
total comments and included in a greater number of replies.
This indicates that motivating people and getting the best out
of them along with learning the personal skills of patience,
tact, etc. is given more weight by the private sector than
managers put on leadership functions. In the private sector
survey, this category is fourth in rank compared with seventh
in the public sector survey. So, all in all, learning to
interact with people and to manage and lead people is
regarded by the private sector as of major importance when
compared with the more functional aspects of the job, i.e.
training people, delegating, settling priorities and
understanding the system.

It has been suggested that 'getting the best out of people,
team work, patience, understanding, tact and tolerance' came
at the top of the list because those were the qualities that
the managers lacked. They therefore rated them as the prime
things they had to learn. This may be so but it also reflects
self insight and a recognition of job demands. The
higher a person goes in the organisation the more he or she
will have to take a wider view, get as much information from
many different sources and generally be open to new ideas.
All these demand the behaviour noted in the replies by the
senior managers.

Important factors in developing others

Now that you are a senior manager, what do you consider are
the key management development areas that should be
concentrated upon to develop others to positions of senior
responsibility in your organisation?

Again the responses were listed under six major categories.
The summary of the points made is shown in Table 6.3.

Human relations, interpersonal skills, personnel management,
again the people centred areas are highlighted as important
with (26.5 per cent) 49.4 per cent of all respondents
mentioning them. Technical training and knowledge rated

lower in the list.

Table 6.3

Important factors in developing others*

Rank		Typical statement	% of Total Comments	% of Replies
(2)	1	Personnel management, human relations interpersonal skills, industrial relations	28.87 (21.57)	49.4 (26.5)
(5)	2	Technical skills, knowledge of system, understanding of work, product market knowledge, commercial judgement	21.83 (5.8)	37.5 (7.2)
(1)	3	Early responsibility, mobility, opportunity	12.32 (26.47)	21.1 (32.5)
(3)	4	Problem analysis, problem solving skills, analytical training	10.92 (18.63)	18.67 (22.9)
(4)	5	Develop initiative and risk taking	5.28 (11.76)	9.04 (14.5)
(6)	6	Financial ability or understanding	4.23 (0.98)	7.23 (1.2)
	7	Others	16.55 (14.71)	

* Public sector results are shown in brackets.

There is no doubt that senior managers in the Australian public sector place experience of management far and away as the most important item on their agenda. They believe not only should people get management experience early but they should also have wide experience and be switched from one job to another.

These findings are consistent with the recommendations of the Royal Commission on Australian Government Administration (Coombs' Report) and the review of the New South Wales Government Administration (Wilenski's Report). The Royal Commission on Australian Government Administration believed that 'officers are properly and best prepared for the positions in the senior executive category through having a wide experience of different aspects of the administration.

105

To give them this experience is a more effective way of obtaining and maintaining management skills than are formal training courses. One way of ensuring that such officers can develop and maintain management skills is simply to expose them to different work through rotation to a department where their skills could for a time be used, away from the department of their choice'. Similarly, Wilenski (1977) recommended that 'the objective which the government should pursue is that of unified service. A unified service is a service in which all barriers to the free transfer of employees between the public service and statutory authorities are removed and an individual employee has the opportunity to transfer from organisation to organisation'. The public service board encourages interdepartmental mobility as a necessary means of executive development (Wilenski, p. 131), which is consistent with the findings of this survey.

There are some major differences between senior public sector managers and their counterparts in private industry. The former placed heavy emphasis on early responsibility, mobility, opportunity followed by personnel management, human relations, interpersonal skills and industrial relations. Combined, these two categories accounted for almost half of the total comments made. In the private sector, early responsibility, mobility and opportunity only ranks third, with personnel management, human relations, interpersonal skills and industrial relations in first position, having been commented on by almost half of the responses. The replies to this question appear to reinforce our observation that private sector managers put more weight on the need and acquisition of behavioural and people related skills.

OVERVIEW OF RESPONSES

When looking at an overview of these responses it is evident that these senior managers tend to recommend to newcomers their own methods of development. Personnel management, human relations scores well in what the new man should be good at. This factor has shown up in all dimensions of the research To be successful one has to be able to establish effective relations with others.

Motivation was seen to be very important. The need to achieve results ranked first in the list of factors generated by senior managers. Further, according to senior managers there is no substitute for experience. Early responsibility and mobility was ranked first by public sector managers as the key management development areas that should be concentrated upon to develop others. They argued that it is vital to have width of experience early in their careers and also have early overall responsibility for important tasks.

Overall, to be successful in the Australian private or public sector one needs to be motivated to achieve results, to be able to establish effective relations with others, to have a width of experience early in one's career and to have sound technical skills.

Today we need a much better understanding of management development so that people are moved to positions within the organisation in order to obtain the experience. This research has given several guidelines as to how this should be done with particular reference to moving people between their functions early in their career. It also gives guidance on the nature of experience in terms of providing people with overall responsibility for specific sections of the organisation's business. Finally, it indicates the prime importance of providing potential senior managers with early responsibility and all the challenges that go with bringing together a team of people to work on given tasks and objectives.

WHAT CAN WE DO TO DEVELOP MANAGERS

On average there is an eight year gap between reaching senior management and being appointed chief executive. The period during the thirties is, therefore, a critical time in a person's career. Typically, if they are to reach high executive office, they must be learning the job during their early thirties, with a view to taking on the top jobs in their early forties.

To what extent, therefore, do the management development programmes in large Australian organisations facilitate people gaining this sort of experience? In a number of large organisations with which I have worked, the entry into senior management roles is often delayed until the ages of thirty-seven to forty. This means that there is a critical five year period when valuable experience is being missed. It is this factor of age related to experience that we must look at very critically in developing the leadership talent within organisations and in particular enabling people to gather wide experience across functions such as marketing, production, personnel and finance prior to the age of thirty-five. I believe there is a career cross over point between the technical and the managerial aspects of work occurring at this time.

Crossing over from technical to managerial aspects can be difficult for some as they are leaving the work they know best for something which is more ambiguous and less definable. Most technical jobs have defined parameters and people are trained to perform to given standards.

While it is important to learn from the experience of crossing over into a mainly managerial job it is important that it is supported with the knowledge and skills that are fundamental. In this case, the educational organisations do have an important role to play in helping people understand the essence of accounting, financial reporting, developing and assessing marketing plans, basic principles of scheduling, budgetting and planning.

However, leadership involves more than knowledge and skills. The higher one goes in the organisation the more one is dealing with intangibles. The senior manager is involved in trying to get sufficient information to not only plan the future but 'invent' entirely new approaches. Moreover, as the problems of communication become greater the senior manager needs particular skills in understanding people and mobilising their energy. Indeed the senior manager needs not only a deep understanding of the business, but a particular insight into his own and other people's behaviour.

CONCLUSION

The key issues emerging from this research have major implications for management development policies and training practices.

The responses of the senior manager about their own experience points to the vital importance of early development. Assuming a manager has a sound technical training, it is too late to wait till he or she gets into the forties before developing him or her as a top manager. Our work has given a clear indication what chief executives regard as important if people are to develop management skills and abilities.

.   The process of management development must begin early in one's career. If you are forty and still at a junior level then your chances of rising to any height are slim.

.   It must involve people who have sound technical training.

.   It must involve exposure to different positions to gain width of experience.

.   It must involve being in a position of responsibility.

.   It must involve selecting people with a high degree of motivation.

.   It must involve people who have the ability to work with, manage and motivate others.

Above are the main points stressed by the Australian senior managers. Given their own path to the top and given the fact that these managers will be recruiting future senior managers means that people with potential must be developed in the above key areas.

BIBLIOGRAPHY

Blake, R, and Mouton, J, 1964, The Managerial Grid, Gulf Press.

Coombs, H C, 1976, Royal Commission On Australian Government Administration, Australian Government Publishing Service.

Copeman, G, 1971, The Chief Executive And Business Growth, Leviathan House.

Dalton, M, 1959, Men Who Manage, John Wiley.

Holland, J L, 1973, Making Vocation Choices: Theory of Careers, Prentice-Hall.

Horne, J, and Lupton, T, 1965 'The work activities of middle managers: an exploratory study', Journal of Management Studies, vol.1, no.21.

Margerison, C, 1980, The Chief Executive Management Development Survey, Management and Organisational Development Research Centre, Cranfield School of Management, England.

Margerison, C, Hunter, N, and Drake, J, 1979, Management and Organisation Development Bibliography, 3rd Edition, MCB Publications.

Mintzberg, H, 1973, The Nature Of Managerial Work, Harper and Row.

Reddin, W, 1970, Managerial Effectiveness, McGraw Hill.

Stewart, R, 1967, Managers And Their Jobs, Macmillan.

Wilenski, P, Direction For Change, Review of New South Wales Government Administration.

Part II
Applications in organisations

7 Making management education work in an organisation

ALAN BARRATT

This chapter is a potpourri of unrelated issues of concern,
activities, that appear to have significance in improving
and developing the management resources of an organisation.
You are all aware of the less obvious but vital
organisational characteristics that impact on the personal
growth and development of managers in any organisation.
Most of these characteristics will not be new to you. My
intention is to place sufficient weight and emphasis on these
to provide managers with strategies to effectively behave and
cope with a variety of forces that exist within the
organisation. Let me outline a number of these
characteristics which I will explain in greater depth and
later provide you with a diagnostic instrument that will help
your thought processes. The following characteristics will
be emphasised, organisational neurosis, getting commitment,
TV training for executives, consulting skills for
practitioners and management education implications.

ORGANISATIONAL NEUROSIS

In the majority of organisations in my experience, there
often appears an issue or factor that takes on a grossly
exaggerated form in comparison with its rational contribution
it makes to the organisation. Let me explain further with a
couple of examples. In one manufacturing company the
organisation was well managed, profitable, and growing
dramatically in an expanding market. Whenever a review of
profitability and productivity was established, the ratio of
direct to indirect employees took on neurotic proportions
which usually resulted in the direct staff of technical
support to the production facilities being reduced.
Following this regular event, management and supervision in
the company began to unquestionably accept this regular
event.

A second example is in a multinational organisation. When
reviews of productivity and performance take place or action
plans in the area of cost containment, the first key area to
come under the microscope is the issue of headcount and
improvements usually can emerge by reduction in the level of
headcount. The point I am making about these two

organisational characteristics is that organisational
neurosis exists in most organisations and the issue whether
direct or or indirect ratio or headcount, becomes
unrealistic and out of all proportion to the tasks and
problems facing the organisation at that time. Where this
exists, it is very difficult to cure as it is ingrained in
the thinking and orientation of all levels of management.

PUBLIC AND EMPLOYEE RELATIONS

A further characteristic that appears to be influencing the
1980s is the very high sensitivity called for in the fields
of public affairs and employee relations. In recent years
I carried out a formal survey of senior managers about their
concerns and the issues that were mainly on their minds that
led to anxiety on their part. If this could be summarised,
senior managers in major organisations are fundamentally
concerned with the interface of the organisation externally.
Sometimes this is, particularly in European countries,
concerned with coming to grips with government intervention
in organisations and dealing with the huge amounts of
legislation affecting organisations today. Today's
environment of being socially responsible as well as
profitable is key. This particularly shows itself in the
way local press and media are interested in the way
organisations impact on the community, environment and thus
the visual and moral awareness of senior executives in
organisations to these sensitivities. Senior managers are
very concerned that the local radio station or television
network can knock on their doors and seek an opinion on many
possible issues that will have newsworthiness. This
organisational characteristic to me means that during the
next decade those of us involved in the education and
training of management will need to place considerably more
emphasis in the field of communication internally and
externally. It is important what to know, when to say it
and how to say it, and to whom you should say it. I want to
explore these areas in a little bit more depth and share
some of the experiences in the last few years which have
been in various forms for our organisation. These
organisational characteristics I have mentioned so far need
to be focused and spotlighted to a much greater extent than
we have in the 70s. If our management education and
management development is to be operationally relevant and
have a level of creditability among our captains of
industry, action needs to be taken.

GETTING THE APPROPRIATE COMMITMENT

As was mentioned previously, communications plays a very
important part in the chief executive's time now that we
have arrived in the 1980s. I think it is fair to say that
often management development advisers, amongst others, avoid
being proactive with the executive right at the top of the
organisation, chairman, general managers, etc, but prefer to

take on the role of being reactive to their perceived needs for management training and development. I argue that if you are serious about getting total commitment from the decisionmakers in your organisation, the place to start is with them and more importantly attempting to problem solve their key concerns.

There appears a fundamental question that practitioners involved in management development should ask, "What is the level of commitment required to achieve the success of your plan or programme?"

To me there seems to be three basic levels that can be used and the appropriate level for the task in hand needs to be clearly and accurately established. I see the levels this way.

Level 1 - Top management involvement including participating in the design and implementation of an action plan.

Level 2 - Commitment and visible support from the chief executive for the programme or plans being pursued.

Level 3 - The chief executive's permission to carry out the programme or action plan.

Obviously top level management is not always needed to give its blessing and support to a variety of programmes and action plans, as your key client can facilitate the successful implementation without the top level of involvement. However, it seems vital, before too greater investment is made in the design or resourcing of any planning programme, an appropriate level of commitment is obtained to get the job done.

TV TRAINING

Many of you may ask where does TV training fit into this potpourri. It is based on purely my experience and the experience of other colleagues in different organisations. The background is this. If as a management developer or organisational consultant you wish to be fully effective, you must make every effort to ensure that you have the professional respect, level of commitment, and the ear of the decision makers in any organisation or unit. Let me share my experience in attempting to achieve this. The story begins when a regional president asked me to identify the training needs and the actual training involvement of managers at a very senior level in several countries. Regardless of the amount of training that occured within each manager's field of responsibility, the key issue was to identify what actual training or development the managing director or chairman of the local board had personally received over the last seven years. Having established that, which as one would expect with the exception of the occasional seminar did not amount to much, we went on to raise questions and concerns of the senior executives in the carrying out of their current day to day work. It appeared that chief executives spend forty per cent of their time on activities that can be loosely categorised as employee relations, people problems, or public relations including government interface. On probing this to a greater depth, chief executive officers are concerned about social responsibility and live with the fear at the back of their minds that a situation will occur that will cause the local or national press to knock at their door. Their blood pressure increases dramatically with the thought of a major fire or catastrophic accident when a television crew may turn up on site or alternatively the chief executive is requested to be interviewed on television at the studio.

Therefore, it seemed to be a useful development programme for these chief executives to reduce this blood pressure and anxiety and as a result we embarked on a programme, the object of which was to give confidence in meeting the media.

Why is it important? Organisations make provisions in their budgets for considerable sums of money allocated to public relations, community relations, improving their company's or industry's image. An appropriately ill chosen word, uttered by the chief executive, and reported by the media can often obliterate that budget. Furthermore, a chief executive can rapidly curtail his career by being ill prepared to effectively deal with the press.

The skills involved are different to that of public speaking because the television media is an unusual phenomena in the normal working day of a chief executive. How did we go about developing these skills? We decided with the managers involved to run two or three seminars to give practice and develop skills in being interviewed on television. Peter Tidman, Television Interview Training Ltd in the UK, was the consultant that has worked quite extensively with us since those days and we owe a great deal to the contribution he has made. Executives were taught to communicate effectively through the lens of a camera by obtaining the viewing audience's interest and getting their attention, then attempting to engage their minds to the issues in question. Which means that you do not speak the boardroom language or the language of your industry but you communicate to the average television viewer young and old. Finally, you attempt to leave the viewing public with something to remember. As we all know, practice makes perfect, and while our goal was not perfection, we did want to stimulate a series on hostile interviews that would give our chief executive officers the experience of facing a television interviewer. I could spend a considerable amount of time discussing in depth the details of how we went about this training but I believe it is suffice to say that this experience was very effective for our executives. Secondly, it gave the management training function a significant boost in creditability that indicates to me that if you assist personally chief executives in their own growth and development, it ensures a sympathetic hearing, and hopefully, concurrence to other training and development projects that are proposed to him at a later date. To complete this gaining creditability through this television training story, we provided an opportunity as a diverse organisation to brainstorm and identify the vunerable areas of any organisation as far as newsworthy issues are concerned. This in turn enabled us to think through possible responses that could be made in the unlikely event of one of these vulnerabilities becoming real.

CONSULTING SKILLS

Many professionals in our business come to realise the significant contribution that our personal effectiveness plays in being successful with the development of management. We have trained many internal consultants and some of the skills we feel are appropriate to be successful in management development are listed. It goes without saying that the course alone is insufficient, however, a continuous exchanging of ideas, practices and results between the internal consultants enable effective growth to take place. We usually start this process of development skills by a six to eight day crash programme, the content of which appears as follows:-

1. The consultant's role, internal versus external.

2. Approaches to organisational diagnosis.

3. Building your own diagnostic model.

4. Methods of data gathering.

5. Intervention technology.

6. One to one consulting.

7. Conflict management skills.

8. Team building skills.

9. Data feedback and action planning methods.

10. Managing the consulting process.

It would be fascinating to survey the number of people in the field of management development that glibly call themselves consultants to determine just what skills of consulting they have acquired over the years. I believe that developing the right client relationship, particularly as an internal consultant, is an essential ingredient for the success of any project or assignment you undertake. I referred earlier to the level of commitment that is necessary. If as with an OD programme a contract is vital, it has equal significance in the installation of a management development programme. Most contracts attempt to:-

1. Clarify and define the relationship of the consultant and the client,

    and/or

2. Clarify with the client where the client is personally, where he and she would like to be (mission, goals, objectives), and alternative ways (strategies for getting there).

Making the assumption that the management training consultant adviser has all the necessary skills and an interesting programme for his client, then it is worth taking stock in the early stages of proposing a new development and review your chances of success. It might be helpful for you to try my profile of success to see what your chances really are.

A PROFILE OF SUCCESS (FOR ORGANISATIONAL/MANAGEMENT DEVELOPMENT PRACTITIONERS)

In Figure 7.1 it shows a profile of three levels of success, and by establishing the specific profile for each project it may indicate the criteria that need to be further improved to move you from say a medium to a high level of success. I believe the profile is self explanatory but what appears important is that each time you make an intervention or develop a programme workshop you quickly albeit 'on the back of a cigarette packet' take stock of the relative chances of success that you might enjoy with this particular activity. Management development advisers often have many different activities in the air at one time and it seems good business sense to put your efforts in:-

a. the highest payout areas, and

b. those areas where your success probability is highest.

The important tasks and objectives will be apparent through the support and commitment of your executive management. Therefore, you will have an obvious picture of those most visible projects which will direct your work.

118

Figure 7.1

Success profile
(A tool for organisational consultants)

Success Dimensions	Rank and scale 1-9		
	1 2 3	4 5 6	7 8 9
1. Involvement of client	. . .	. . .	\ . .
2. Level of commitment	. . .	. . .	. > .
3. Credibility (self)	. . .	. . /	. . .
4. Acceptance of methodology	. . .	. < .	. . .
5. Availability of human resources	. . .	. . .	> . .
6. Quality of human resources	. . .	. . /	. . .
7. Budget availability	. .	< . . .	. . .
8. Orientation to project goals	. . .	. . ~	. . .
Level of success	Low	Medium	High

Let me explain Figure 7.1. The profile is very simple.
You simply rank on a one to nine scale a number of criteria
or dimensions that appear to be important. These dimensions
are as follows.

Involvement of client

Obtaining involvement prior to the start of the project is
vital. The client may be the chief executive, the general
manager, or just a line manager at any specific level within
the organisation, but they have one specific commonality and
that is his involvement and continued support is vital to
the success of the programme.

Level of commitment

The second factor to consider is the actual level of
commitment obtained from the client and as I mentioned
earlier, one is to think of this in three distinct levels
and within each of those levels honestly evaluate what score
you feel is appropriate. In establishing the level of
commitment you should review not just your client but all
the other persons that could add to its success or take
away (sabotage) its success and make a general judgement as
to the level of commitment.

Creditability (self)

A third factor to review is consultant creditability. That

119

is the leader of the project, an internal consultant or a
management development adviser's personal power and
creditability. This is a self assessment of our level of
creditability in respect to the nature, scope and complexity
of the project. It is fair to say that each of you feel
more comfortable with some projects more than others,
therefore, a little heart searching is necessary to rank
this particular dimension.

Acceptance of methodology

We have all seen and can recall the speed of which 'in
techniques' come and go. With management teams and
organisations it is often the case that they reject the
technique as being flavour of the month. For instance, this
month it was quality circles, last month it was action
research. Each organisation has its favourite and more
acceptable approaches to the issues involved. A residential
programme for the management team may be acceptable to one
organisation where a plan for one to one consultation might
be more appropriate to another. In order to score this
particular dimension, you need to seek an understanding of
the client and ensure a genuine orientation has taken place
of the methods and approaches that will be used on this
particular method of the project. A personal experience of
mine has been that if the legitimate title for the
methodology is likely to cause ineffective reaction by the
client, then some other generic title can be used to
describe the activities. I find myself increasingly saying
to clients, "let us work out a plan of action for this" or,
"let us establish an organisational improvement programme".

Availability of human resources

Of human resources you need to make an honest, accurate
assessment of the availability of selecting and bring to bear
the appropriate resources for the project. In scoring this
you need to consider the psychological maturity of those
persons on your team and the relevant experience with the
scope and dimensions of this project.

Quality of resources

Previously we looked at the availability of support staff
for such a project, but this dimension deals with the
practical experience and appropriate data base that the
resources you are using can bring to bear on the project.

Budget availability

This dimension is a realistic assessment of the budget
availability including the necessary contingency plans that
could emerge. I am sure we all have experienced ambitious
projects embarked upon that due to budget restrictions and
cost containment programmes have prevented the success, or at
least the total success, of any particular project. Just
another one of the issues that can go wrong.

120

Orientation to project goals

The final dimension to review is orientation to the project goals. This is a subjective view that the project leader makes of the level of understanding than those associated with the project may have.

When projects move from the original contract and either expand or occasionally contract, it is inadequate to assume that everyone understands such a move even if initially the orientation level of those involved is high. In scoring this final dimension, you must attempt to identify how satisfied you are that every key player in the project has a clear understanding of the objectives and proposed results.

Go through the eight dimensions and score your perception of the relative weighting on each of the eight. If you have other professionals on your team you may independently ask them to conduct the same exercise. You will see from Figure 7.1 that by the example of joining up the numbers you can develop yourself an individual profile and from the scale at the bottom decide whether you have a low, mid or high chance of success. In Figure 7.2 I attempt to develop a simple strategy for improving the low scores on the success profile and simply state what action you are going to do it, and say by what date. Therefore, if you just use Figures 7.1 and 7.2 as a very quick and ready method of taking stock of the probable success of your intervention, then it is my belief that you will at least have a realistic view and a clear understanding of anticipated results.

Figure 7.2

Profile improvement plan
(A tool for organisational consultants)

Action plan	Strategy	Completed by
SD		
7 Improve budget availability. (In light of current cost containment programme).	Review estimated costs. Look for cost savings. Discuss with client effects of budget limitations on quality, etc.	In writing before 1 May (start project 15 May).

As with all self completed data collection tools, the key is what action is going to result from the data you have established. Furthermore, I find it gives a certain confidence and support to you as project leader in realising the optimum opportunities for the project.

CONCLUSION

As you have discovered, these potpourri items are unrelated,
yet they have a significant bearing on the success of
developing management and organisations. If you look hard
enough you will find the issue I will call organisational
neurosis exists in your organisation. You will also find
that ensuring the right level of commitment from the
organisation is vital for all projects. Using television
training or some other method that involves management of
the top of the organisation will certainly enhance the ease
of your work. The message I would leave for all of us
involved in management development education is to consider
some of these issues. It is my gut feeling that managers in
the next decade will need to have much greater emphasis
placed on their effectiveness as quality communicators. The
willingness and experiences related to obtaining personal
feedback on their own effectiveness and the effectiveness of
their subordinates is going to take on an enhanced role.
Organisation's social responsibility and internal and
external behaviour is going to be an increasingly more
visible ingredient in our business lives. Therefore, it is
my conclusion that we may need to reorientate our training
and development more towards the direction I am indicating.
But whatever happens, it seems that in our profession we
have a major task ahead of us into the 80s and onwards to
ensure that our top management have the skills and abilities
to cope with their changing role.

8 Ethics of interventions: A political perspective

ANDREW KAKABADSE

In a paper I recently wrote (Kakabadse, 1982), I made the point that simply doing a 'good job' and hoping that promotion is likely, or at least the sack is unlikely, is an unrealistic hope. For people with some ambition and certain survival instincts, attaining professional competence is only the first step. To achieve high office relatively rapidly requires skills in negotiation, skills in forward planning, skills in making projects work, skills in getting on with people, in fact, skills in being different and yet ironically in being able to fit with superiors, colleagues and subordinates. The reality of working life is that a substantial number of individuals spend their time at work vying for limited resources, competing for limited status positions, attracting the attention of senior executives, producing competent task work, assisting others and paying attention to home life. The working situation induces a wide range of experiences.

With so many different forces operating in any work situation, what behaviours should a third party interventionist enter into and what ethical standards or guidelines should he/she adopt? In this paper an attempt is made to explore the position of the third party interventionist. The experiences and views of a process oriented consultant (works with the client on his problems rather than trying to impose predetermined solutions) are explored. His activities in one intervention are discussed. It is indicated that the consultant considered it necessary to act 'politically' due to the circumstances of this particular case. The intervention is still currently active and whether the consultant will eventually be 'successful' is open to conjecture.

It is concluded that perceived political interactions are a natural everyday experience for most people in any organisational setting. Whether attempting to resolve open conflict or to introduce changes in an organisation, third party interventionists should be aware that certain 'political strategies' need to be adopted to try to reach some sort of mutually acceptable solution.

THE CASE

A police organisation in the USA has recently faced
substantial criticism for its handling of various community
problems. In response, the organisation has attempted to
examine how and why certain problems have arisen.

As part of the examination process, the director of the
police department decided to initiate a study of career
development and motivation within his organisation. The
brief to undertake the study was passed down to the
Assistant Director Personnel who decided to call a meeting
of the various interested parties in the organisation.
After a limited number of meetings, the interested parties
decided to form themselves into a steering committee. They
recognised that they neither shared the expertees or
insights to conduct a study of motivation and career
development in their organisation. They obtained the
assistance of a consultant (to be known as John), but he
could only offer a limited amount of time as he was fully
employed as an internal consultant by a large multinational
company. John and the steering committee met on a number of
occasions for a period of a year but made only limited
progress. Eventually, John suggested that a project team
should be formed to carry out an indepth study of career
development.

The steering committee agreed and formed a project team
consisting of three senior officers, two middle ranking
officers and one sergeant who acted as the secretary/
administrator to the team. The steering committee decided
that a second consultant should be hired to act as adviser
to the project team. A second consultant was eventually
hired. The intervention described below is centred on the
activities of the second consultant (to be known as Steven).

THE INTERVENTION

A number of individuals were approached to see whether they
would be interested in acting as consultant to the project
team. A favourite candidate was eventually identified. He
is an academic who had been used as a visiting speaker at
the organisation's police training college. He had already
established a reputation as a good lecturer on their senior
management programme and his experience as a researcher and
consultant made him attractive to the organisation. In
addition, both the manager of the training college (a senior
police officer), who was shortly to be promoted to a top
management position in the organisation, and the senior
management programme tutor favoured the individual and
argued for his acceptance.

The chairman of the steering committee, a senior police
officer and an exceptionally influential individual, invited
the academic (Steven) to act as second consultant to the
project team. Steven agreed, if the fee was right. The

director of the police department found Steven's fee
acceptable but did not have the authority to issue payment.
A central servicing unit could only authorise payment.
They stated that they would have to be convinced that the
money was to be spent wisely. This proved embarrassing for
the client. Both client and Steven recognised that the
central servicing unit were unlikely to make a quick
decision. In addition, the director of police was
demanding results and had already indicated a deadline for
the project team, one year hence. The central servicing
unit could well have delayed the proceedings for up to six
months. Steven indicated that he would do the job on the
understanding that he most likely would eventually receive
his fee. The chairman gratefully agreed, thanking Steven
for taking the risk and organised separate meetings of the
steering committee and project team in order to introduce
him to the parties involved.

At Steven's first meeting with the project team, the
atmosphere was tense. Steven gave a brief resume of his
past work experience and indicated that he looked forward to
working with the team. The most senior man on the team
welcomed Steven but stated that the team did not expect as
many problems as they currently faced when they first
agreed to take part in the project. As the conversation
developed, it became clear that the project team had had no
real guidance, nor had any real experience of working on
people and manpower oriented problems. The members of the
team shared an additional anxiety. Recognising their lack
of knowledge and experience in the area, they questioned
whether they could produce any meaningful results and if
that happened, would that be to the detriment of their
careers? Steven listened and agreed with the team that at
this early stage, a number of meetings would have to be
held to identify what direction the team should take.

A number of meetings were held between Steven and the
project team. Steven stated that he would not wish to work
with the team if they established any processes of
formality such as an agenda. Protests were pushed aside by
Steven, who stated that he was taking over the running of
the team and anyone who felt they could not continue would
always be free to leave. Steven knew that no one dare
leave because of career implications. The meetings quickly
became brainstorming sessions, exactly as the consultant
desired.

The team influenced by Steven's view, decided that simply
examining career development systems in operation in other
public service and private organisations was insufficient.
A study would have to be conducted examining the existing
career development system in the organisation. Some
members of the project team were against the idea, stating
that the study could uncover views held by members of the
organisation that would be highly critical of senior
management. How could the project team feed that
information back? Steven advised them not to concern

themselves with the results of the study before they had even planned the structure of the study.

The chairman of the steering committee approached Steven enquiring as to progress made. He indicated that the other members of the steering committee would wish to meet Steven, and even if it was early days, be given a brief report of developments to date. Steven readily agreed, stating that he would wish to meet John before the steering committee meeting. The two consultants arranged to meet.

The meeting between the consultants was polite but tense. Steven concluded that John would probably be in favour of a study. It also became clear that John had not really identified the direction the intervention should take. If John could be given some role in the study, then he would argue in favour of the study at the steering committee meeting. By probing John, Steven concluded that various members of the steering committee were anxious about the results of the whole intervention. The senior managers on the steering committee also felt their careers to be potentially in jeopardy if the eventual results produced were considered unsatisfactory. The two consultants agreed to support each other at the steering committee meeting.

Before the steering committee meeting, Steven decided that the intervention had to be concerned with substantial changes in the organisation. Steven also recognised that he had began to behave in ways that could be considered, if not unethical, at least on the borderline. The values of working with your client at his pace in his territory, being open and sharing information were unrealistic in the situation. The only clear policy the consultant could identify, was to pursue the diagnostic study of career development in the organisation, whether the client wanted it or not. Steven concluded that change was needed at the subsystems level in the organisation. To accommodate that, some form of data was required.

Steven's first meeting with the steering committee was uneasy. The consultant was introduced by the chairman of the committee and then asked the consultant to address the members. The consultant offered his view of his role in the intervention and went on to explain the various ways of examining career development in any organisation. He indicated that the various approaches had been fully debated by the project team and that they only sensible direction to take would be to undertake a study of career development in the organisation. It would not make sense to develop policies for the future without understanding how people felt about their jobs, their level of work satisfaction, their views on promotions and methods of appraisal. At this point, both Steven and chairman sensed that the other members of the committee seemed restless and anxious. The chairman confronted the group by stating that if others were peturbed about what was said or just wished to ask questions, they should feel free to do so. Steven agreed stating that

that he preferred this to be an open and honest meeting and that the members should feel free to ask any questions.

Certain minor questions were asked concerning how such a study could be conducted. After half an hours discussion, one member stood up stating that he was not in favour of such a study. What use would such information be to the organisation? Steven responded by asking what alternative approach could be undertaken, bearing in mind the organisations director's demand for results. The member (a senior and influential police officer) stated he did not know but there must be some other way. However, he could not remain to discuss the matter as he had other meetings to attend. He added that this one seemed to be a waste of time. Steven thanked him for his valuable input and when he had left the room, the consultant asked the others whether they could offer any alternative suggestions to examining career development.

Another member stated that Steven was right. The only way to begin to examine career development would be to analyse peoples' views about their jobs, work, promotion prospects and management styles adopted by their superiors. With the one member leaving the meeting, and the other seemingly in favour of some sort of study, the other members seemed to visibly relax. Steven capitalised on the pro study contributions by asking the others for their suggestions on how they would go about organising such a study. Numerous contributions were made and even the most nonesensical was warmly praised by the consultant.

After one hours discussion, Steven felt confident that he had managed to turn the mood of the meeting in his favour. He dramatically stopped the conversation and turned to John (who had remained silent throughout) and asked him to give his expert opinion on whether a study on career development should be undertaken. John stated that he could see no alternative. Steven dramatically turning to the other members asked whether anyone was in favour of the one dissenting voice that had left the room. No one was, and in fact considered his objections to be destructive. The meeting unanimously concluded that the study be carried out.

Reflecting on the meeting, Steven decided to take the following steps:-

a.   reduce the level of anxiety amongst the members of the steering committee and project teams,

b.   isolate and reduce the level of influence of the steering committee member who objected to the study,

c.   develop a warm and positive relationship with each senior police officer in the organisation.

Steven became more proactive with the project team. He

paid less attention to their needs and issues and more to the mechanics of conducting a study. Steven organised a series of workshops on research methodology and interviewing techniques. In addition, more brainstorming sessions were held exploring how to conduct the proposed research. During this time, one of the members of the project team was identified by the consultant and the other members of the team as being unsuitable. Steven approached the chairman of the steering committee to discuss the unsuitability of the one project team member to the study. To the approval of all (including the project team member), the individual was transferred out. The consultant wanted him replaced by the senior management tutor currently at the training college. After a number of phone calls and informal one to one discussions with influential senior officers, the senior tutor was appointed to the project team. Steven agreed that once the senior tutor was in post, he would spend substantial time coaching him into the project at no extra cost.

Steven, together with the senior tutor, agreed that a pilot study was necessary. The pilot study should be conducted as a series of semi structured interviews. A sample was identified and members of the project team were each given particular sample populations to interview. Steven stated that only he would interview only very senior officers as he would be seen as least threatening.

Steven used the opportunity to develop friendly relationships with the senior police officers that he could arrange to see. Some of the managers sat on the steering committee. Not only did they offer information about their job, task activities and motivation, but were encouraged by the consultant to discuss the project at length. Fears and anxieties that individual senior officers held were reduced through discussion with the consultant. The one member of the steering committee who objected to the study refused to be interviewed. His superior also refused to take part in the study. In discussions with the chairman of the steering committee and his superior, the consultant emphasised the cooperation he had received from most members of the organisation, except from the one who objected and his superior. Slowly the word got round that only one group in the total organisation were difficult and uncooperative in a project that was now recognised as important to the future of the police organisation.

Throughout this time, the members of the project team met to discuss the data being gathered in the pilot study. In the opinion of all, the data was more valuable than originally expected. A steering committee meeting was held to discuss progress to date which both the consultants and project team members attended. It was agreed at the meeting that the pilot study results were valuable and that the main study should be started. The individual who had originally objected to the study was not present, nor had he attended the last few meetings. Steven, at the end of the

meeting, invited the steering committee members and the
members of the project team to his university for lunch to
celebrate the successful completion of stage one of the
study. Most of those invited attended the lunch, which
turned out to be a success. By now Steven was viewed as
acceptable to the organisation.

IDENTIFYING THE POLITICAL STRATEGIES

The project team are ready to embark on to the main study.
The actual results of their studies so far, or even what
they intend to do, are irrelevant so far as this paper is
concerned. What is of importance is to identify and
examine the strategies adopted by Steven in the
intervention.

The strategies

1. Identify the stakeholders. It is imperitive in any
    intervention to identify those individuals who have
    an interest or stakeholding in the situation. Whether
    their interests are compatable or incompatable with
    those of the individual, all the stakeholders have to
    be approached so as to identify their intentions in
    the situation. In the case above, Steven identified
    all potential stakeholders. Any whose views were not
    acceptable, attempts were made to isolate them from
    their colleagues and hence reduce their capacity to
    influence others.

2. Working on the comfort zones. In order to
    effectively influence anyone, work on the other
    person's comfort zone unless it is absolutely
    necessary to do otherwise.

    An individual's comfort zone consists of those
    behaviours, values, attitudes, drives and ideas that
    the person in question can accept, tolerate and manage.
    The reason the comfort zones are emphasised is that
    every individual has developed a range of values and
    behaviours which they find acceptable and wish to put
    into practice. The range of values and behaviours is
    their identity. The person concerned may call it his
    personality. Something unique that is them.

    Hence, people will pay attention to the concerns of
    others as long as their own are not threatened. Once
    an interaction with another concentrates on the issues
    important to only one party and is threatening to the
    other party, that interaction is likely to be
    terminated. And why not? People meaningfully
    interact only when they have sufficient interest in a
    situation.

    People hold two interests in any situation:-

-   the final objective i.e. what is in it for them,

-   the manner in which the final objective is achieved
    i.e. the process.

People are as much concerned with both processes and
outcomes. By handling the interactions so that the
process feels comfortable to the receiving party,
outcomes can be managed so as to satisfy most parties.

Steven used this strategy more than any other. At
this moment in time, he is generally recognised as
being a friend to most of the stakeholders.

3.   Networking.   Organisations are a mixture of various
     cultures and group identities. The group identities
     may or may not coincide with the hierarchical
     structure of overt objectives of the organisation. In
     terms of what really does and does not get done, the
     network may often be a more powerful force than
     superior/subordinate relations. For any outsider
     entering a situation that they wish to influence, it
     is necessary to identify the networks that exist and
     the individuals who are generally recognised as
     upholding the values of the network.   These
     individuals are then influenced by working on their
     comfort zone. Steven identified a number of networks
     and gained access to most. He plans to utilise his
     access to the key stakeholders in the networks in part
     two of the study.

4.   Making deals.   Making a deal with other individuals
     or groups is common practise in most large
     organisations. Whether resources are limited or not,
     different individuals or groups may agree to support
     each other to achieve a common purpose as long as
     there are benefits for them. It is realistic to
     expect individuals and groups in the organisation to
     wish to promote their own goals, which may be at the
     expense of others. Consequently, coming to some sort
     of agreement about common policies, or at least not
     disturbing each other's aims, may be necessary.

Two deals were made by Steven. First to continue on
the project without fully agreeing the financial side
to the contract. For his own career ends, Steven
wanted the contract and was therefore willing to take
a risk of doing work which may have gone unpaid. By
making such a deal with the chairman of the steering
committee, it was hoped that the chairman would argue
forcefully to have Steven's financial terms accepted.

The second deal was to coach the senior tutor, who
was a latecomer to the project team, for no extra
payment. Apart from the fact that the tutor and
consultant were personal friends, the tutor also
possessed substantial knowledge and experience in the

'people management' type subjects which made him the most important member to the project team.

5. Withholding and withdrawing. It is impossible to satisfy the needs of all parties in any large, diverse organisation. One way of ensuring that certain groups do not overreact to issues which they recognise as important, is to withhold information. By preventing certain information from becoming common knowledge, the manager is able to achieve whatever objectives he has identified without facing opposition that could destroy his plan. In such circumstances, the manager should be fairly convinced that his plan is valuable. It is that others have not or will not recognise its worth. However, to constantly withhold information is not recommended, for such behaviour is indicative of a manager who cannot confront certain problems. Continuously withholding information is a means of protecting the manager and not the policy.

Withdrawing from a situation is at times necessary. There are times when the presence of a manager in a dispute or negotiation is of no help. To withdraw and allow the different factions to negotiate their own terms, or for management to withdraw an unpopular policy and shelve it for the time being, are common practises. The larger and more diverse an organisation becomes, the more important is the timing of actions. When to introduce or withdraw plans and information are important considerations for policy implementation.

Steven used the strategy of withholding information and withdrawing from potentially difficult situations, on numerous occasions. Criticisms of particular individuals or of the organisation which the consultant felt would be unacceptable to the project team or members of the steering committee was withheld. In fact, the project team have no knowledge of the data the second consultant gathered in his interviews with senior management.

Throughout the intervention, Steven was consistently not presenting to the senior officers he met, the full picture. Each was told a slightly different story to the other as to the objectives and expected outcomes of the study, according to what the consultant considered would be acceptable. In addition, if a slightly unpleasant situation required attention, Steven would approach one of the senior officers, offer him information and advice on how to handle the situation and then withdraw so that he would not be implicated in the outcomes of the interaction.

6. If all else fails. By practising any one or more of the above strategies will not guarantee success. It's necessary to identify some fallback strategy if all

else fails. Each person concerned would have to identify his own fallback strategy according to the demands of the situation and what he could personally handle. In this intervention, the second consultant identified two fallback strategies.

First, if this particular intervention failed, or if the consultant was not chosen to work with the project team, then at least Steven had negotiated warm and friendly relations with important people in the organisation who could call him in at a later date on other projects or refer him to other organisations where he could get work.

Second, Steven had only just begun to work on the comfort zone of the boss of the chairman of the steering committee. This person was the former manager of the training centre and now promoted to a senior position in the organisation. It was predicted that the individual would be the next director but one. Whether these rumours turn out to be true in the future is unimportant. The fact that he was currently considered as important and influential was sufficient reason to nurture his favour.

REFLECTIONS

Certain questions arise out of this case. What of developing trust, trying to establish a common understanding and treating others as human beings instead of levers for self betterment? In fact, for anyone holding a third party role, whether it be an intervention into an organisation or a conflict resolution situation, should questions of ethics ever arise? From this case in this paper, three ethical issues are identified:-

1. When is sharing feasible? Sharing of information, opinions or even anxieties is only feasible when people identify with certain common elements in the situation such as tasks, team identity, traditions and personal interdependence. However, concerns as having ones policies adopted and developing long term organisational plans are unlikely to be comfortable shared experiences. When a number of individuals are involved in the process of generating and implementing longer term plans, it becomes as much a trial of strength and wit as to whose predominant values will eventually be accepted. Senior organisational personnel may sit in the same room debating issues, but that is all they share. For any third party involved in such a situation, how much information and opinion to disclose is dependent on what is feasible in the situation.

2. Who is your client? Developments in any intervention

132

may bring both client and consultant to a different point than they had first expected. Not only may plans and expectations have changed, but further, the very need for the client and consultant to work together. Certainly any intervention that concentrates on the longer term strategic issues in an organisation may well lead to rapid changes of expectations for both client and consultant. From the consultant's point of view, the client he first started with may not be the client with whom he should interrelate.

Changing clients in the same organisation may not be easy. By switching clients, the consultant could damage his original client's position, his own position or may even leave both parties exposed to other vested interests in the intervention. The ethical issue is to what extent can the change practitioner be open, sharing or even feel responsible for his original client whilst knowing that client and consultant may have to part because the situation may change.

3.   When eclectic; when humanistic? In any organisation, there is always an uneasy balance between outcomes and process, between achieving objectives and the way in which they are achieved. In my recent paper (Kakabadse, 1982), I indicate that third party resolution technologies have arisen out of the OD (organisation development) movement. OD seems to have concentrated on processes, the way things are done and has only really entered into outcomes in particular areas such as job redesign or data feedback surveys. As a consequence, third party strategies for handling longterm strategic change have been left relatively unexplored. Approaches to OD and third party intervention/conflict resolution have only been developed to cope with the micro side of change.

This case, if nothing else, indicates that macro change requires both a new philosophical base as well as alternative strategies for action.

BIBLIOGRAPHY

Kakabadse, A P, (1982), 'Politics in organisations: re-examining OD', Leadership and Organisation Development Journal, Monograph, Vol.3, No.3.

* I would like to thank H.R.D.International for allowing me to publish substantial extracts of this paper, previously published in H.R.D.International, volume 4, number 1, pages 5 - 8.

9 One company's experience with performance appraisal

MAURICE HAYES

INTRODUCTION

Nicholas International arose from a merger in 1969 of Aspro
Nicholas, a UK based multinational company, with Nicholas
Proprietary, the original Australian company which had
previously been a separate company. The resulting company
was small by multinational standards, having total members
at the time of the merger in the region of 5,000 world wide,
but was widely spread with manufacturing plants in twenty-
five different countries.

Both companies had been progressive in their personnel and
training philosophies. Each had developed appraisal systems
in the early 60's which were typical of that time. The
appraisal documentation invited appraisors to rate their
subordinates on twenty-two different factors, on a nine
point scale, ranging from poor to outstanding. In addition,
they were expected to describe in detail the person and
their potential.

The arrival of appraisal documentation on an executives
desk caused dismay as it was seen to have no relevance to
the problem of doing the job. The personnel department was
forced to spend a great deal of time in chasing executives
to get them to complete the chore. As a consequence, the
completion of the documents tended to be mechanical and in
most cases simply a repeat of what had been said the
previous year. Many parts of the company had not cooperated
and were regarded as fortunate in not being involved.

The writer decided on joining the company that the
establishment of the performance based system should become
one of his first priorties. The first stage in this was to
persuade senior management of certain important aspects of
philosophy. The first point was a quotation from Professor
Jim Hayes, President of the American Management Association.
The statement was, "management development is management".

The point here is that managers develop by managing. As
in any other activities, managers improve by practising
their skill. We developed a saying that training takes
place in the classroom, whilst development is in work. We
persuaded people that training is only of value when it is

134

applied and practiced in a work situation. We established
what we called 'the needs of the subordinate' which were:-

The subordinates' needs

1. Tell me what results you want me to achieve.

2. Give me an opportunity to achieve them.

3. Tell me how you think I am going on.

4. Give me help and guidance if I need it.

5. Reward me for successful or outstanding
   performance.

The next point we had to get firmly established was that
the responsibility for training and development was not a
specialist function but was part of line management
responsibility. Training specialists are facilitators, but
the responsibility is clearly between the executive and his/
her boss.

We were able to establish in advance what senior
executives and middle executives of the group regarded as
being the characteristics of a good management development
programme.

CHARACTERISTICS OF A GOOD MANAGEMENT DEVELOPMENT PROGRAMME

1. It will help managers to do today's job better and
   more profitably.

2. It will help to coordinate personal and company
   goals.

3. It will prepare managers to do tomorrow's job
   better and more profitably.

4. It will recognise that responsibility for
   development must be in the line organisation.

5. It will accept that the only person who can
   develop anyone is the person themself.

The first of these characteristics is the most vital
because unless the management development scheme is oriented
towards helping managers for the present job, it is unlikely
to get off the ground and maintain any kind of momentum.
The coordination of personal and company goals if often very
difficult and is not as obvious or automatic as most senior
managers would like to believe. Most management development
programmes are conceived with the objective of preparing
managers to do tomorrow's job better and more profitably.
The responsibility for development being in the line has
been discussed previously. We believe that it must be based

on the person/boss relationship.

Finally, there is no point or mileage in any scheme or programme trying to develop people who don't want to develop.

Accordingly, the 1970 appraisal documentation caused something of a sensation in its apparent simplicity. It asked only three questions:-

1. How does his/her performance compare with his/her objectives?

2. What training or development is proposed?

3. What potential do you envisage for this employee?

Executives found these questions to be more meaningful, though more searching and in many cases very difficult to answer. The documentation led to requests for training on establishment of objectives and on counselling.

Having established an active interest in appraisals and its relevance and relationship to work, the writer then preceded to introduce a new form of job description which superseded the previous lists of duties, responsibilities and authorities. The job descriptions were written under the headings of:-

a. scope,

b. resources,

c. relationships, and

d. key result areas.

All executives were trained in writing their own job description which they then agreed or modified in discussions with their boss. In general, the specific objectives for the upcoming period should reflect the key results that the person was expected to achieve. The next stage of training activity was on writing objectives and we used the nemonic PRAM; standing for practical, realistic, attainable and measurable, as being the characteristics of good objectives. The appraisal documentation for 1971 contained advice to both appraisor and appraisee on how to prepare for and conduct the counselling interview. We suggested that at the interview the first step should be to review the job description to ensure that it still reflected the job being done. The next stage was to create objectives and both parties were advised to prepare their proposals before the interview. Great stress was laid upon the method by which performance would be measured. It was also recommended that they regard the documentation as being a working document between them to be used regularly so that the summary interview at the end of a full year should not contain any surprises.

THE SYSTEM

Our appraisal documentation starts with the following statement:-

> "Appraisal embraces all the actions a manager must undertake when assessing a job holder's performance against agreed standards of measurement and communicating that assessment in such a way that it will result in an agreed clear plan of action for performance improvement".

We then explain the documentation and the fact that two copies of a coloured sheet are enclosed which record the outcome of the interview.

A copy of this coloured sheet is the only documentation that comes out of the interview between person and boss.

We next go on to outline the corporate purpose of appraisal, which we see as being:-

1. To improve the job holder's performance and effectiveness.

2. To improve and/or promote the job holder's personal development.

3. To ensure that the job holder knows and understands how he/she is viewed by the company.

4. To provide the company with information on the job holder's views of personal development.

5. To provide meaningful information, as an aid to optimising compatibility between performance and remuneration.

6. To provide, at a point in time, a snapshot of the company's executives.

7. To aid corporate human resource planning and development.

The coloured sheet then requires the immediate manager to answer a series of questions relating to the individual job holder:-

1. How does performance in the job compare with agreed objectives?

2. What areas have been identified for personal development to make the job holder a more

effective manager?

3. What specific action has been agreed and will be taken by the job holder or immediate manager?

4. What recommendations or proposals are made for assistance by a third party?

We then follow through with some advice on preparation of the interview. We suggest that the appraisor reads the documentation carefully and fills up the section headed "Past Performance" which relates to the performance during the period under review. We recommend they take into account the following criteria:-

1. Were objectives agreed by job holder and immediate manager?

2. To what extent was achievement or otherwise within the job holder's full control as opposed to external influences over which there was no power of control?

3. To what extent can achievement or otherwise be used as a benchmark for improved performance in the future?

We then go on to propose the way in which the interview should be conducted. We suggest that the first thing to do is to review the job description:-

1. Does the job description mirror the job holder's function?

2. Do stated responsibilities reflect actual responsibilities?

3. Are authority levels commensurate with responsibilities?

4. Do current and proposed objectives fall within the stated parameters of accountability?

5. Does the job holder have the required skills, essential knowledge and desired attitudes to meet his or her various responsibilities?

We then suggest that the appraisor, having made an assessment, as to how performance compared with objectives, should then discuss these with the job holder and reach agreement. Where particular circumstances prevented full attainment of objectives, should be recorded and agreed. We then suggest that future objectives for the upcoming period, together with the measures of performance, should be agreed. We stress that a meaningful discussion is essential to both the job holder and the manager. Therefore, the immediate manager should give due consideration to future objectives

138

prior to the meeting. As a consequence, specific training and/or development requirements may become prerequisites to the achievement of agreed future objectives. We then recommend that the appraisor and appraisee have an open and candid discussion on the future envisaged for and by the job holder:-

1. What contributions can and will be made to achieve a higher degree of effectiveness?

We regard it as important to explore such questions as:-

1. Are the job holder's ambitions and aspirations compatible with his or her personal abilities and the company's needs in the short and long term?

2. Does the job holder have obvious or latent skills, experience or talents, not wholly used in the present job but could be used to the benefit of both individual and company in another, specified area?

Having planned and completed the appraisal interview, and recorded the conclusions and agreements on the main documentation and on the coloured sheet, we recommend that the immediate manager retain the documentation in order to monitor progress and advancement from the next period.

We then state explicitly that it is a fundamental of good management that our people are aware of how they are getting on during the course of the year. Regular meetings to discuss progress, facilitate advice and assistance towards achievement of agreed goals are essential and as a consequence the formal appraisal becomes neither a surprise nor an occasion to be approached with undue anxiety.

The next page of the documentation records what has gone before i.e. job description review, past performance review, and agreed future objectives. On the back of the documentation we give some guidance on the general principles of appraisal interviewing as follows:-

1. Notify people well in advance. And in such a way that it doesn't cause unnecessary anxiety. Give sufficient time and advice so as to allow job holders to prepare themselves.

2. Ensure no interruptions. By communicating non availability of involved personnel and, if possible, arrange for the venue to be on 'neutral ground' and behind a closed door.

3. Remember the purpose. To appraise performance against AGREED standards and not evaluation of an individual as a personality. When presenting facts, invite opinions, pose brief questions which allow the job holder to respond at greater length,

and do not interrupt. Be senstive to things which are left unstated and be aware of underlying strain or emotion. A summarising remark at an appropriate time shows understanding, suggests a willingness to listen and may well help the job holder to see problems more clearly.

4. Plan the interview. Consider how to put the job holder at ease, establish the facts to support your assessment, envisage likely reaction and the questions which may be needed to discover feelings and attitudes. Establish success criteria for an effective interview.

5. Decide interview objectives in advance. Isolate job holder's obvious strengths and weaknesses which it is proposed to draw out from the job holder during the interview, but which you are prepared to modify in the light of the results of the interview.

6. Adopt the right attitude. The aim is to seek agreement on evaluation of past performance, an action plan for greater effectiveness and concensus on realistic objectives for the future. Browbeating or manager v subordinate attitudes will prevent meaningful appraisal and objectivity.

7. Maintain the right atmosphere. An appraisal interview is a meeting of two minds, its purpose – a review of past (known) events and/or achievement, exploration and agreement on individual action to improve future performance with the minutes of such a meeting written on the coloured sheet. The atmosphere should be calm, relaxed but businesslike with adequate time. As a general rule it is inadvisable to attempt more than two appraisals in any one day.

8. Be prepared for criticism. It is a natural reaction to apportion blame. A subordinate who fails to achieve goals will not infrequently seek to implicate others, and the manager is frequently seen (in the eyes of the job holder) as a contributory factor. Do not jump to an immediate defence – ask for specific examples. Irregular and/or too infrequent reviews can be justifiable grounds for criticism.

9. Build up on strengths. This tends to be far more rewarding to both parties than attempting to concentrate on and eliminate weaknesses.

10. Identify improvement areas. Allow the job holder to see a range of possibilities from which to

select what will or can be done. Having agreed priorities, commit these to paper - decide what contribution each can make, what assistance can be sought from a third party, and again commit this to paper. Subsequent discussion along these lines would be the drawing up of personalised action plans with related acceptable measures of performance.

11.   Close on an encouraging note. Aim to leave the job holder with the feeling that it has been a satisfactory interview. An open meeting with a simple theme - the immediate manager's concern for the job holder's continual personal development and the need for both parties to commit themselves to specific, measurable and realistic action to achieve this.

In implementing this system we have found that training in the different aspects of the programme has been essential and has been ongoing. Different parts of the group have recognised the value of job descriptions written in this form as an aid to identifying essential skills, developing profiles and using this data in constructing meaningful advertisements when positions have to be filled.

Similarly, the framework has been extended to include job evaluation characteristics at some of the larger establishments. We have found that though managers readily grasped the importance and characteristics of objectives, they have nevertheless found discussion groups, short seminars, and workshops to be of great value.

In more recent times some excellent films and video tapes have become available to stimulate further discussion. Similarly, training in appraisal interviewing and counselling have proved to be a skill which creates its own demand for further development. In our opinion, the programme would have had very little chance of success without this very substantial training input.

THE RESULTS

In company with many other organisations, Nicholas have found the external environment throughout the 70's to be a difficult one, particularly compared with the 50's and 60's. It is felt that the performance appraisal system has made a very significant contribution to helping Nicholas weather these very stormy economic times. The use of the methodology has not turned out to be what was originally hoped and envisaged. We had hoped that the 70's would have been a period of rapid expansion, via new product launches, geographic expansion of existing products and acquisitions. The decade started out in this manner and by the beginning of 1974 the group was employing some 6,500 people. Then with the inflation in oil prices, the famous wages explosion in Australia, and general downturn in trading, it became necessary to become more efficient. Consequently, it became necessary to go in for increased mechanisation and, consequently, reduction in staff employed. There is little doubt that the performance appraisal system assisted managers in these difficult times "to do todays job better and more profitably", and it certainly helped in coordinating "personal and company goals".

At the same time the system pointed out some essential modifications to our personnel policies, if we were going to be able to shed labour and still enjoy good employee relationships.

During the period 1974-1980, the group reduced the staff employed from 6,500 to under 3,000, without industrial unrest in the Anglo Saxon, African and Asian countries. We did have a strike in France in early 1966, and we were able to manage our way through this and reconstruct good relationships, primarily as a consequence of the discipline and methodology involved in our performance appraisal system.

During this period, the profitability of the Nicholas group increased steadily, not only in measured dollar terms, but also in real terms after allowing for inflation. The performance appraisal scheme has been central to the style and technique of managing the group from through the very top down through all the regions.

It is often suggested that it is relatively easy to run performance appraisal systems when people are concentrated on one site. We have found that provided adequate training has been given, the results in diverse situations can be just as effective. For example, the use of this kind of objectives setting in sales force situations is readily accepted. However, one of our main regions is the Africa - Asian region and the manager of this region is based in Nairobi with territories as far apart as India, Nigeria, Middle East and South Africa. He has found the clear establishment of objectives and regular reviews against them to be invaluable. When he visits his territory managers during the course of a financial year, their first task is to review performance against objectives, identify potential problem areas where help can be given or where because of circumstances beyond our control there is likely to be a short fall, or alternatively, where new opportunities have been created. In this situation performance appraisal and budgetary control provide comprehensive control methodology. This particular manager attributes a great deal of the success of this region to the performance appraisal system.

As well as its function in aiding the management of the business, the other major benefit that comes out of the system is a clear individualised and tailor made training and development plan for each person. The reasons why we ask for copies of the coloured sheet are to help arrange training and development activities, provide suggestions as to how the training needs can be fulfilled, and when appropriate, mount internal courses to fulfill these needs. Thus training has become oriented towards fulfilling felt needs of the staff, rather than whatever happened to be either fashionable or consistent with the training skills of the manager.

THE FUTURE

Over the next few years, many companies will adopt a methodology similar to the one outlined earlier in this chapter. Many will give inadequate attention to the training needs which are inherent in such a programme and will suffer disappointment, as has happened over the past few years. Some companies will recognise that there is no short cut and that training and full comprehension of the system and acquisition of the relevant skills are essential. These companies will obtain considerable benefits from performance appraisal.

Many people are looking to build on the foundation of performance appraisal to bring a sharper focus to bear on its objectives. The writer is working to develop a methodology which incorporates subordinates in evaluating the performance and training needs of their boss. Many readers will remember with an extensive study conducted by Harvard Business School published in the early 70's indicated that subordinates were better forecasters of executive success than their peers, bosses or staff observers.

Mr Malcolm Kerrell of Nicholas is working to bring the skills components of managerial work into sharper focus and develop methods of identifying individual training needs under nine headings. They are:-

1. Interpersonal communication.

2. Interpersonal influence.

3. Interpersonal decision making.

4. Group communication.

5. Group relationship or influence.

6. Group decision making.

7. Intergroup communication.

8. Intergroup influence/negotiation.

9. Intergroup collaboration/decision making.

Development of this technique has been used successfully with selected individuals and will be refined and developed over time for wider use.

Another interesting development is the work of Mr Leon
Noone of Discern Pty. Ltd., who is focussing attention on
work teams rather than simply managerial subordinate
relationships. In a private communication he described the
basic concept as follows:-

> "The conventional performance appraisal focusses on
> manager and subordinate. My proposed system recognises
> that work occurs in a social setting. The individual
> doesn't and cannot work in a vacuum.
>
> Each employee is part of a team and contributes to (or
> hinders) team goals. The team, in turn, affects the
> individual's performance. Cooperation, or its lack, the
> efficiency or competency of every team member, team
> goals and the relationship with the individual and
> organisation goals, the communication systems in
> operation, and general factors such as morale and
> motivation, all affect performance, they are intimately
> connnected to the work situation and the job performance
> of each member of the group".

Noone has gone on to develop the implementation stages and
documentation around these ideas and is in process of
experimental work in applying the system.

It is clear that many practitioners in the field of
human resource development are looking to performance
appraisal and development there from to assess managerial
problems of the future and identification of training needs.

144

10 Using OD to improve managerial productivity: The case of Culver City

JAMES BOULGARIDES AND DAVID JAMIESON

PREFACE
Our purposes in developing this paper are:

- To highlight the stages and activities in a unique seven year organisation development effort, and

- To identify insights, questions and considerations for longer term OD.

By necessity, our approach here will be brief but should provide the framework for further discussion and analysis. Since the initial efforts in the first two years provided the foundation, game plan, consultant client relationship, and initial 'unfreezing' of the organisation, we will discuss these initial activities in more depth, while subsequent steps will only be described briefly. Following the programme discussion, we have raised and briefly commented on some of the insights, questions and considerations we have experienced.

INTRODUCTION

In these times of accelerating change, cities are often faced with the need to respond to new and increasing demands with the method and practices of previous decades. Such situations make it even more difficult to effectively deliver services to meet the changing needs of citizens and create growing frustrations among city officials and citizens alike. Out of these frustrations and the desire to continually improve the city's effectiveness, an increasing number of cities are initiating programmes to introduce and manage change.

One such programme has been underway since the summer of 1973 within the city of Culver City in California. Culver City, incorporated in 1915, is a charter city of approximately 38,000 people.* The early history of Culver

---

* The following historical highlights are drawn from Edwin I. Rudd, Jr., "Municipal Reorganisation in a California Medium Sized Jurisdiction", an internship report, Department of Public Administration, U.C.L.A. (Spring 1974).

145

City was dominated by the movie industry with up to twelve studios in operation during the first four decades. In the early 1940's, additional expansion occurred when specialised aerospace contracting firms began to locate in the city and by 1947, when the original charter was adopted, the population, number of businesses, and services required had greatly increased. Since that time, the population has more than doubled and changed in ethnicity, crime and other problems of urbanisation have been on the rise, the movie industry has slowly declined, and the construction of multiple unit dwellings, highrise buildings, and shopping centres has accelerated. These changes have had significant impact on the need for the city's resources and services. In 1973, the original charter was still in operation, in spite of three charter revision attempts. The charter established a five person Council with authority to appoint a Chief Administrative Officer (CAO), and department heads. The city clerk and treasurer were elected officials and most employees were under civil service. The Council was involved regularly in day to day matters and there were many instances of direct council department interaction and bypassed channels. There had been few changes in the basic structure of the city, and a number of key administrators were now nearing retirement. In short, the city had changed relatively little internally, while externally their world had begun to change rapidly. It became increasingly apparent that there was an urgent need to plan and introduce changes and develop new practices to plan for, coordinate, and manage this increasingly complex municipal organisation.

Although the CAO and Council had concluded that external consulting resources were needed, considerable concern was expressed regarding the type of firm and approach that should be engaged, especially in light of negative past experiences. Culver City had previously utilised numerous resource consulting firms. The consultants would determine the nature of the problem, make recommendations relating to how to solve the problem and the city would then attempt to implement their recommendations. This 'resource consulting' approach worked well when related to 'thing oriented problems' such as traffic patterns, redevelopment alternatives, compensation studies or the type of equipment required to meet a specific need. However, this approach had not worked well when related to changes that more directly affected the organisation's members, their interaction, problem solving and communication patterns.

The city was more interested in a 'process consulting' approach in which they would jointly work with external consulting resources in identifying areas hindering their effectiveness, exploring alternatives, developing action plans, implementing desired changes and responding to varying needs over time. They were not interested in buying answers, but in obtaining assistance in their process of developing a more viable organisation.

After interviewing several consulting firms, the city

decided to engage the services of MRG Associates to assist
them in planning, initiating and managing a comprehensive
programme of organisational and operational change.

MRG Associates utilises a methodology known as the
Management Responsibility Guide (MRG) Process to help
organisations and their communities understand more clearly
their goals, the job to be done, who is accountable to whom
for what and how they can interact and communicate more
effectively. In short, they help organisations to first
manage accountability so that they can more effectively
initiate and manage change.

The MRG Process systematically gains involvement and input
from multiple levels of the organisation in establishing
accountability and communication networks and enhancing
management practices. The process focuses on identifying
operational practices and organisational concepts that are
at variance with the basic purposes of the organisation and
can be used as a primary tool in facilitiating organisational
analysis, operational and/or organisational changes.

THE INITIAL CHANGE PROGRAMME

At the outset, the MRG Process was utilised in a
comprehensive change programme in Culver City. The
programme began with a study of the capabilities and
resources in those departments more affected by the growth of
the city. Following this endeavor, the key administrators
were involved in MRG Process to systematically define the job
to be done, highlight and resolve issues and problems,
clarify roles and relationships, and decide how they could
work together most effectively. Subsequently, the Council's
perceptions of how they should relate to the job to be done
were obtained and the entire management group participated
in identifying charter and code sections and city policies
needing revision. Throughout this period of time, a city
employee worked closely with the external consultants, being
trained in the use of the process and general consulting
skills, so that the city could continue to work with this
methodology at other organisational levels and in future
years with little external support.

Phase 1. In June, 1973, a study was initiated to gain an
overview of the operational, organisational, and staffing
capabilities of the Public Works department in light of its
central role in meeting the growth needs of the city.
Interviews were conducted with the Public Works department
and division heads, the five councilmen, the CAO, and key
administrators from the Parks and Recreation and Planning and
Community Development departments. These interviews
produced a wealth of information related to the purpose of
the study and other operational concerns. The findings were
presented in the form of a discussion paper reflecting the
desire of the process consultants to raise questions and
considerations for the city and begin joint dialogue around

147

those issues. In that report some issues were raised and
some background information, an initial assessment, and some
alternative considerations were presented. Some of the key
questions raised were:-

- Should engineering remain a part of Public Works? If
  not, should it be a separate department supporting
  both Public Works and Planning, or should it be
  organisationally re-located within Planning?

- Should the Building division be separated from Public
  works and allied with Engineering or should it become
  a part of Planning?

- Should all maintenance activities with the exception
  of those relating to streets and sanitation be
  combined into a single division or should a partial
  reorganisation be considered at this time?

- Should an Environmental Protection Division be formed
  which would be accountable for all enforcement of
  fire, health, zoning, building, weed abatement codes
  and ordinances?

- What can be done to utilize the expertise and know
  how of current administrators while simultaneously
  injecting new blood into the management group?

- How can present administrators and employees be given
  new experiences so that their value to the city and
  their growth potential is increased?

- Should Culver City continue its current policy of
  developing internal capabilities for meeting the needs
  of its citizens or should more subcontracting and use
  of external resources be considered?

- Should one department be accountable and be given the
  necessary authority for integrating all operational
  and long range plans and decisions affecting the
  total community development programme?

- How can the Council have more time to play a greater
  role in relation to the long term planning
  activities?

- Do the respective roles and relationships of the
  Council, CAO, Assistant CAO, and department heads
  need to be clarified?

This phase of the project resulted in: the generation of
new discussions around the above topics; some immediate
shifts in operations, such as the integration of electrical
and building maintenance functions; and the highlighting of
the need for greater involvement from a broader selection of
city officials in taking a future oriented look at the
changing job to be done, their current organisation design

148

and accountability patterns, and how they interrelate,
communicate, and problem solve together.

Phase II. In the fall of 1973, a city wide organisational
effectiveness project commenced, utilising the MRG Process
as the central methodology. The scope of this project
included the CAO, those reporting directly to him, the City
Attorney, City Clerk and City Treasurer. In addition,
approximately forty other city employees at various levels
were involved in the initial data gathering. A city
employee in the administration office was chosen for training
in the MRG Process and began working closely with the
consultants during the initial planning sessions. A meeting
was held with the project participants to discuss the
purposes of the project, to surface their expectations and
concerns, and to describe the MRG Process and the
methodology to be used. Participants also received some
literature describing the steps in the process and a set of
focusing questions to be used in the interviews.

DEFINING THE JOB TO BE DONE

The focus of this project included the total scope of city
operations. Consequently, over fifty city employees were
interviewed, some many times, to ascertain the key elements
of the job that should be done and the operational practices,
organisational concepts, and role and relationship issues
that hinder the effective accomplishment of the city's
purpose. During these interviews, problems and issues were
surfaced and alternative solutions explored.

   After analysing the data from the interviews, a
'configuration design' was developed. This design is a
framework or set of categories for organising the job to be
done into logical functional modules, i.e., not necessarily
how the job is currently organised and accomplished. The
following design was used for Culver City:

   -   Administration and General Management
   -   Legal
   -   City Clerk
   -   Financial Management
   -   City Treasurer
   -   Personnel
   -   Support Staff
   -   Community Planning and Development
   -   Redevelopment
   -   Environmental and Zoning Enforcement
   -   Community Compliance and Enforcement Services
   -   Inspection and Code Enforcement
   -   Engineering

- Maintenance
- Public Safety and Protection
- Civil Defense
- Paramedic
- Police
- Public Services
- Human Services

Using the interview data and experiences from other organisations, approximately 450 task descriptions which highlighted the job to be done and the issues needing discussion and resolution were developed. Some examples of task descriptions are:

- Develop goals, plans and priorities to meet changing needs of city.

- Develop annual operating budget in light of financial resources and established goals, plans and priorities.

- Provide guidance and direction pertaining to and process applications for state and federal grants and serve as primary liaison with granting agencies.

- Identify and evaluate social services and leisure time needs and resources of city in order to provide appropriate and relevant services.

- Develop affirmative action policies, programmes and controls, monitor to ensure compliance, evaluate effectiveness and initiate corrective action when necessary.

The 'configuration design' and task descriptions were reviewed and discussed with the participants, modified as needed, and finally approved. The tasks were then placed in a linear charting matrix with the positions of the participants and other key personnel listed across the top.

Defining the job to be done establishes a task oriented framework for problem solving, surfaces the issues, and provides the opportunity for the consultant and client to jointly clarify all aspects of the operation and its structure and explore alternative operational and organisational designs that might be more effective in facilitating the organisation's mission.

In the Culver City project, a different organisational concept did emerge. A new arrangement for top level accountability, the 'Office of the CAO' with two AAO's, was introduced and approved by the Council. Basically, this concept established a three person Office of the CAO, with

150

one AAO accountable for administration and internal affairs, one AAO primarily responsible for community development and related functions, and the CAO operating as primary liaison with the Council and having direct responsibilities over some city departments, such as police and fire.

DETERMINING HOW THE PARTICIPANTS PERCEIVE RELATIONSHIPS

One of the most perplexing role and relationship problems is determining how members throughout an organisation perceive their own and other's relationships to the job to be done and to each other. Differing frameworks, styles of communication and semantics often get in the way. It is therefore important to find a common basis from which members of the organisation can communicate with one another about their respective roles and relationships.

The MRG Process meets this need by providing a common 'responsibility relationship' language that is divided into seven different aspects of accountability. The first three codes relate to who is accountable to whom for what:

A - General responsibility

B - Operating responsibility

C - Specific responsibility

The remaining four codes of the language specify types of relationship and pertain to how individuals and groups work together to get the job done:

D - Must be consulted

E - May be consulted

F - Must be notified

G - Must approve

A second briefing of the participants was held to review the new organisational concept, describe how it would operate in terms of work flow and reporting relationships, describe what the next steps were, and to review the MRG Process 'language'. The participants were instructed in how to use the codes to enter their perceptions of how they should relate, under the Office of the CAO concept, to each of the task descriptions in the matrices. The titles of all the participants, as well as, key external individuals or agencies were entered across the top of the matrices. In this phase, the direct participants were limited to the CAO, two AAO's, the department heads, City Attorney, Clerk and Treasurer, so that accountability for the total job to be done could be clarified among that top management group before the involvement of additional organisational levels. However, each department head was encouraged to work with his subordinates in determining what their response should be.

IDENTIFYING KEY ISSUES AND PERCEPTUAL DIFFERENCES

The individual perceptions of the participants were compiled
to form a composite set of matrices. Upon analysis, it was
found that significant differences did exist as to who should
be accountable to whom for what and how they were going to
interact and work with one another. Some one-to-one follow-
up sessions were held to ensure that each participant
understood the language and the responses he or she had
recorded. Issues and differences surfaced throughout the
matrices, but were most pronounced in relation to:

(1) The relationships between the Administration office
     and the accounting and financial functions in the
     Clerk's and Treasurer's offices.

(2) The fragmentation of the city's inspection and code
     enforcement programmes.

(3) The relationships of the Engineering, Planning and
     Building divisions.

(4) The excessive approvals desired by some
     administrators.

(5) The ambiguity in the City Attorney's role.

(6) Some common areas of endeavor between the Parks and
     Recreation and Police departments.

(7) The apparent organisational independence of the
     elected city officials.

CLARIFYING AND RESOLVING DIFFERENCES

The composite matrices were distributed to each of the
participants and over a six month period a series of problem
resolution session were held, including a one and a half day
retreat, in which the identified issues were discussed and
differences addressed. In these meetings, the external
consultants served as facilitators to the group as they
discussed their various perceptions, how operations relating
to a specific task were currently operating and how they felt
it should operate in the future. As the sessions progressed,
issues were resolved, communications became more open and
decisions began to be made concerning how they were going to
interact in the future. Through these meetings and some one-
to-one discussions, almost all of the differences were
resolved, the Office of the CAO concept was accepted and
understood and the management group established an open
forum for surfacing and resolving complex and controversial
issues.

152

The entire inspection and code enforcement area generated many perceptual differences concerning accountability and much confusion as to how the city should perform their various inspection and enforcement functions. An internal task force was created, composed of those involved in various inspection activities (planning, building, public works, business licences, fire), to conduct a more detailed analysis of the inspection and enforcement requirements and develop some solutions and future recommendations. The work of this group resolved many of the differences in the MRG matrices, cleared up much of the existing confusion, helped to design the job of a new code enforcement officer, and established some new coordinative and interaction patterns.

Structurally, most of the units having any involvement in inspection and code enforcement activities were subsequently pulled together under the jurisdiction of the AAO for community development. As a result of this move, all enforcement endeavors had top level coordination and direction for the first time.

CONVERTING WHAT 'SHOULD BE' TO OPERATING REALITY

Many changes in organisations fail in the transition between planning and implementing. All too often, people assume that because something had been decided or announced it will come to happen. In reality, the implementation phase requires constant attention to assist people in new roles, iron out 'bugs' that arise and support and encourage new behaviours and interaction patterns. In later management group meetings, key administrators focused on operational changes they wanted to make, how the changes would improve effectiveness and what would be required to effect the changes. In addition, the external consultants met regularly with the CAO and AAO's to review key issues and discuss their patterns of interaction and communication with each other, with the city's department heads, and with the Council. Some of the decisions agreed to during problem resolution sessions were simple to implement and were soon operating. However, some of the issues being discussed and resolved had policy implications, required charter changes or needed some additional study before proceeding. These additional areas ultimately became the focus of attention during the ensuring years.

SUBSEQUENT CHANGE ACTIVITIES

Following the city wide reorganisation and MRG programme, subsequent change activities fell into four basic categories: organisational structure refinements, departmental operational and role clarification, training and planning and team development. In addition, additional consulting assistance began to accelerate in other areas of endeavors (eg, redevelopment, data processing and training).

During the next six years, the following occurred in

roughly the depicted sequence:

(1) Training for city management personnel in basic
     communications, human relations, supervision and
     other management topics.

(2) A review and update of tasks and roles in the MRG
     approximately eighteen months after the initial
     programme.

(3) A study and the movement of the building inspection
     function to the Fire department.

(4) A study and the movement of Public Works inspection
     and the survey crew to the Streets department.

(5) A productivity study and consolidation of positions
     in the Streets and Maintenance department,
     representing significant labour savings.

(6) A planning, sharing and team building session for
     city department heads.

(7) Clarification of the personnel, records and payroll
     functions between Personnel and the City Clerk.

(8) Establishment of the Community Development department
     with Engineering, Planning and Redevelopment.

(9) Internal role clarification with the Police
     department.

(10) An administrative practices audit reflecting needed
     changes in budgeting, accounting, record keeping and
     other areas.

(11) An internal clarification of City Accountant, City
     Clerk and City Controller roles and operating
     practices.

(12) Expansion of traditional Parks and Recreation roles
     to a Human Services department charter.

(13) Establishment of a Municipal Services department
     including separate Streets and Maintenance
     divisions and integrating all park and landscape
     maintenance.

(14) A Council, top and middle management retreat that
     helped to open up issues, plan future goals and
     build relationships.

(15) An interdepartmental clarification of all traffic
     management tasks.

(16) A shift in the AAO administration function to a
     primarily data processing orientation.

154

(17)   A shift in Personnel to report to the CAO.

(18)   Additional training in management and interpersonal styles.

(19)   The establishment of an internal change and monitoring team (MERT).

(20)   A 1980-81 update of tasks, roles and relationships.

(21)   A programme of sequential interdepartmental conflict and perception resolutions.

Today, the external consultants have less involvement in the ongoing problem solving and development and are used more as specialised resources on specific assignments.

ISSUES, QUESTIONS AND CONSIDERATION FOR LONG TERM OD

In this section, we would like to raise some questions related to our learning and concerns in the Culver City case and briefly respond.

How do the change programme activities in Culver City relate to managerial productivity?

Improving producitivity among management personnel has long been an elusive topic. Basically, we are talking about how people get done what they need to get done in the most effective and efficient manner. At management levels, what needs to be done is often more difficult to define than at technical work levels since the role of many management personnel involves looking ahead, reviewing, and influencing others to complete their task.

Consequently, one avenue for improving managerial productivity involves clarifying the job to be done among managers and their respective roles and relationships. In this manner, the what and who are less ambiguous so more attention can be focused on how to do it better. Another avenue for improving productivity is the division of work load among managers. Each needs enough work and challenge to keep motivated and active without giving one individual too much of one task or too great a diversity of tasks. In the latter case, managers often get overwhelmed and do not provide appropriate concentration on all tasks. Consequently, the use of organisation development methodologies in Culver City addressed managerial productivity particularly through restructuring the top management and subsequent organisation shifts, role clarification, interaction and team building, and group participation in the identification and resolution of problems and future planning.

How do you deal with changing aspects of the job to be done?

You can use the MRG matrices as a tool to focus attention on new or changing tasks through periodic reviews and updates. In Culver City, this was particularly true in redevelopment, human services, traffic maintenance, engineering and data processing. As the nature of the job to be done in these areas changes or grew, attention was paid to identifying the tasks and how people should interact to get them done.

How do you deal with changing personnel?

Changes in the City Council and key staff can either help or hinder a project. In Culver City over fifty per cent of the key personnel changed and key changes occurred in the Council (Figure 10.1). By taking the time to brief and discuss current activities with new personnel and reviewing their MRG relationships, the transitions went smoothly. With each change, new people were integrated quickly and the team began to break old norms and function more effectively together.

How do you deal with naturally occurring changes during the change period?

You go with them. You use them to strengthen flexibility, to change roles and to build interaction. A new shopping centre, changing demographics and many of the retirements all triggered important discussions and changes in management structure or practices.

When is change most feasible?

-   When the environment changes.

-   When personnel change.

-   When problems are severe.

-   When an organisation's demands are growing.

-   When top management (CAO and Council) supports and encourages it.

All of these were able to be used in Culver City.

When do external resources become 'crutches'?

-   When decision makers stop making decisions or rely too heavily on 'outside advice'.

-   When key players do not get personally involved in the change process.

-   When everybody 'wants the consultant to do it'.

Each of these issues occurred at times during the overall project. As internal and external resources build close,

	1972	1979
CAO	H Dale Jones	H Dale Jones
City Clerk	A Christensen	*P Dolce
Treasurer	L Herrera	L Herrera
Attorney	D Austin	*R Ogie
Police Chief	J Menning	*T Cooke
Fire Chief	Kendall	*W Sweeny
	W Harris	W Harris
	W Phelps	W Phelps
City Engineer	L Molnar	*J Lathrop
Park	R Wells	*J Mabrie
Sanitation	F Machado	F Machado
Street Maintenance	P Angel	P Angel
Maintenance		*W Spry

*Changes (over 50% of key personnel changed).

Between 1972 and 1979 the changes occurred for the following reasons:

City Clerk	Retired in mid term
City Attorney	Retired disability
Police Chief	Terminated, court suit
Fire Chief	Retired
City Engineer	Retired
Park Superintendent	Retired
Maintenance Director	New (1979) position as a result of consolidation

The city council

With the elections held each two years, the city council as the policy making policy body underwent change.

1970	1972	1974	1976	1978
Lotz	*Lotz	Lotz	Brundo	Brundo
Pachtman	*Pachtman	Pachtman	*Jacobs	Jacobs
*Astle	Astle	*Perkins	Perkins	*Perkins
*Brogdon	Brogdon	*Alexander	Alexander	Alexander
Botts	Boulgarides	Boulgarides	*Boulgarides	Boulgarides
Change	20%	40%	40%	0%

157

1970	1972	1974	1976	1978
Cum Change	20%	60%	100%	100%

* Indicates year of election or re-election.

The same city council has held office from 1976 to 1979. In 1974 and 1976 two new councilmen were seated each election.

Figure 10.1 A comparison of key personnel between 1972 and 1979

collaborative working relations, it is important to remain cognizant of the different roles each should play.

How important are changes in organisation structure for generating and implementing change?

Most important! It unfreezes the status quo, provides shifting (perhaps more appropriate) responsibilities, often opens up new opportunities and directly addresses the organisation and division of the job to be done. The initial restructuring with subsequent shifting of functions, while traumatic for some, has truly facilitated the change and development of the city and many individuals.

How important is an initial 'road map' outlining future organisational changes?

Very important! If you are thinking long term, then you can outline a game plan and move systematically towards your goals. In addition, a 'road map' helps you to plan in conjunction with naturally occurring changes and to have patience.

How critical are multiple interventions?

We believe they are necessary in long term changes. The mixture of re-organisation, role clarification, management training, participative planning and team building was important in solving complex problems, winning acceptance and helping different individuals and departments to develop.

How important are the roles of elected officials, top city administrators and consultants?

This three way network was very significant. The Council alternately were initiators, reviewers, decision makers and political liaisons. The CAO and his AAO's became stronger, guided the projects and made more decisions as the programme progressed and the Council roles changed. The consultants were alternately facilitators, experts, analysers, confronters and counsellors. Over time the Council became less involved in actual project activities, but began to be informed or asked for decisions by the CAO. Project steps and assignments were planned by the office of the CAO and

the consultants. Increasingly the direction of the project
moved from Council - consultant, to consultant - CAO to CAO.

How important is a trained internal resource?

A city employee was trained in the beginning, but
subsequently left the city. At first, his role was helpful
in follow up and implementation, reducing the need for
outside resources. After he left, the consultants were asked
to be more involved in many follow up steps, but could never
be present often enough to provide the type of assistance an
internal consultant can.

Finally, five additional questions, common to most OD
projects, are raised without comment for your discussion.

1. How do you deal with resistance to change?

2. How important is the mix between process and
    resource consulting in order to effect organisation
    change?

3. How important is the mix between addressing
    interpersonal and structural role issues?

4. How fast or slow should an OD programme proceed?

5. How can you evaluate outcomes from many activities
    over many years?

11 The practice of management education within a company

DAVID BARRON AND JOHN ROBERTS

INTRODUCTION

This case study describes a joint venture in management
education between a leading international telecommunications
organisation, Cable and Wireless plc, and the Cranfield
School of Management. The joint venture began early in 1977
and continues to the present: it has been evaluated
rigorously throughout this period by a variety of methods,
including a full scale research project leading to the award
of a doctorate to the researcher. In scale it is believed to
be one of the largest ranging collaborations between industry
and a business school ever, covering a wide range of managers
from all locations in which the group operates.

CABLE AND WIRELESS

The Cable and Wirless group of companies is one of the
largest international telecommunications operators in the
world, employing approximately 10,750 staff in more than sixty
countries. It operates high technology communication systems
on behalf of governments and private organisations, and
relies heavily on technological skills to maintain a
commercial competitiveness. Staff are located in four major
areas: the Far East especially Hong Kong, the Middle East,
the West Indies and London. Many operations are run in
partnership with national governments. This is so in the
case of Bahrain and Hong Kong for example, but the group
retains control of operations through its London head office.

  At the beginning of the joint venture the group's turnover
was £177 million: in 1982 turnover had increased to £354
million. Earning per share rose in the same period from
3.50 pence in 1977 to 6.60 pence in 1982. Staff numbers
however grew slowly, from 9,700 to 10,750. The growth in
turnover is largely due to the explosive growth of the world
telecommunications market, which in certain fields grows at
the rate of thirty per cent per annum. The relatively slow
growth in the number of staff is an aspect of the rapidly
changing technology employed in international
telecommunications which copes with greatly increased
traffic without a proportionate increase in the number of
staff.

160

Accompanying this growth in turnover have been many crucial changes in the group's markets and its methods of meeting the demands placed on it. These changes will be underlined in the body of the text, but one important change which underpinned the need for the joint venture with a business school had taken place in the early 1970's: this was the realisation by senior management (mainly concentrated in London) that although the business was prospering, the growth in revenue was built on a shrinking base. In many of the countries where the group operated, local pressures to nationalise expatriate posts and in time the whole operation, would be hard to deny. The long term (i.e. into the next century) forecast was that this 'concessional' business, which at the time accounted for more than ninety per cent of group revenue, would decline, and an alternative source of revenue was necessary. (Concessional business was the term the group used to describe long term contracts with governments which allowed it to operate telecommunications services within that country). An effort to integrate vertically its business into manufacturing in the early 1970's as a response to this threat had been a failure, yet the need remained to find new sources of business.

This was not a question of immediate corporate success or failure: the concessional business looked from the standpoint of the mid 1970's, and has proved to be, a continuing success. The group's response to the likely long term decline in concessional business was to move into private telecommunication systems, offering project management combined with technological skills in the 'nonconcessional' field. Typically this business could be the specification, procurement, installation, operation and maintenance of sophisticated radar and radio systems at airports, or providing radio links for oil companies between operating units and drilling rigs in areas of the world where local systems were not able to meet the specialist demand. One major market identified for attack was the United States of America: there the 'concessional' market was not completely open, but the provision of specialist services such as network management were a possibility and a substantial investment in the United States has resulted. This 'nonconcessional' business was seen to require staff who had skills in the technology, as before, but also more commercial awareness, more knowledge of finance, greater man management capability and more sense of business than the traditional 'concessional' business demanded, i.e. all those factors which could be called general management skills.

Cable and Wireless therefore saw the need to change the skills of many staff: the view of the corporate future held by many senior staff made this imperative. It was also a radical departure from its previous mode of operation. The culture of the group was that of a career company: many staff particularly outside the UK, had joined straight from school and envisaged having no other employer before retirement, rising gradually through the ranks on merit and service. This culture was of course highly compatible with the long term

centralised concessional business: it seemed largely
inappropriate for the more competitive private business now
being developed. This view of the future was therefore a key
concept in the decision to link with a business school and to
retrain the group's managers.

THE LINK WITH A BUSINESS SCHOOL

In 1976 a start was made in the process of researching the
means by which these training needs could be met. The group
did not possess a management training college, although it had
four technical training centres world wide which were a
potential resource. However the teaching staff in these
centres were exclusively technical and could not be released
from existing commitments, and it was decided not to expand a
technical training institution into a technical cum
management centre. An option to open up a new training
centre dedicated to non technical training was also discounted
as too expensive given the size of the group and population
of managers to be trained. A third alternative was to buy off
the shelf training available from one of the management
centres in the UK,: this was also rejected as likely to be
inefficient and unlikely to meet the objectives of the
training programme. Much more could be done than a simple
investment in general management training programmes,
reputable though these were at many institutions.

    The option chosen was to devise, in partnership with an
institution which was willing to cooperate, specific general
management training programmes which met the needs seen by
the organisation for now and for the future. The joint
venture concept was not new: it had been successfully
pioneered by Manchester Business School in working with
clients. But the scale of the venture proposed here was
something not attempted before: over £250,000 would be
invested in a three year period, and 600 managers would pass
through the training programme. The work would be monitored
by a steering committee of senior representatives from the
group and the business school, and the venture was to have the
enthusiastic support of the directors.

    Given these circumstances, the choice of the Cranfield
School of Management as the partner in this venture was
crucial. Cranfield was approached, along with other business
schools and commercial training institutions, by the training
staff of Cable and Wireless, to gauge their interest and
likely enthusiasm for such a venture. Of all the major
schools, Cranfield appeared to be most aware of the overall
nature of the project: it had a reputation for able staff
who featured in a wide range of public courses, and had
recently appointed a Professor of Management Development.
Additionally it was used to working with overseas clients and
to dealing with service industries. The school had recently
moved into purpose built teaching accommodation and needed to
grow. The combination of all these factors seemed
overwhelming and the Cranfield School of Management was chosen

and agreed to become, Cable and Wireless' partner in a joint
venture in management development.

Initially, the brief which was agreed between the partners
can be summarised as:-

1. Working to identify specific problems associated
   with change and growth, and discovering how best
   they could be resolved.

2. Acting as a catalyst in the development of
   thinking and new skills among managers at all
   levels.

3. Designing and providing training courses that prove
   to be needed to equip staff for new and different
   work.

4. Providing a forum for discussion of subjects of
   concern to the business.

5. Supplying specific skills and building these skills
   into Cable and Wireless managers.

6. Enabling managers to mix with their peers from
   other organisations. This last point was
   important, for the career nature of Cable and
   Wireless led to an inward looking tendency which
   needed to be dispersed.

This then was the initial brief agreed by the training
staff of Cable and Wireless and the Professor of Management
Development at the Cranfield School of Management. Largely,
it was the perceptions of a limited number of people in each
organisation. These views now needed to be tested among a
wider group of managers who would confirm their validity or
add their own to the original concept.

DIAGNOSING TRAINING NEEDS

The brief agreed with the Cranfield School of Management was
the starting point for a lengthy series of interviews with
senior staff designed to test the accuracy and validity of
the perceptions already fed to the staff at the business
school. Interviews, conducted by the Professor of Management
Development and the researcher who was later to gain a
doctorate from the project, largely verified the views
already put forward, but substantially added to the
understanding which was developing between the two partners.
Formal identification of training needs came from systems
already in use in the group, including discussion of the
business plans, the annual operating budgets and longer term
forecasts: manpower plans were available to show the trends
in staff utilisation and likely shortfalls or surpluses.
Managers had appraisal data for their staff to guide them,
and succession planning was beginning in many areas. Putting

163

all these together revealed a pattern of training needs which
confirmed the first discussions held in 1976 with training
staff. More diffuse data were available from the group's in
house organisation development specialist who was closely
involved in the work - both at its inception and follow
through. A clear structural distinction existed between those
responsible for management development and the OD specialist:
the latter's position was firmly outside the personnel
department, with no responsibility for the management of
programmes. His role was as a catalyst or agent for change
rather than executive, although his support and experience
were called on continuously during the contract, and his
input into many programmes was extensive and well received.
Having agreed the scope of the venture and validated the
needs of the organisation so far, it was clear that the
partners needed some form of on going body to direct the
venture, providing feedback on operations and setting
guidelines for future activities. This body was named the
Steering Group, consisting of a small number of senior
respresentatives from both partners, but with Cable and
Wireless members in a majority. It was to be one of the most
successful areas of cooperation between the two partners, as
it operated to senior level, provided a continuous channel
for the updating of training needs and roused some initially
sceptical managers to participate in an undertaking which
they could see was aimed at promoting the better conduct of
the business, both now and for the future. Meeting at
quarterly intervals at alternative locations, the steering
group continues its role at the heart of joint venture
activities.

A summary of the investigative work described above was fed
back to a large group of managers in head office before the
venture began its first programme. This meeting, attended by
the chairman, directors and a large group of senior managers
launched the venture into the group, acting both as a
publicity medium and feedback mechanism.

INTERPRETATION INTO AN EDUCATIONAL PROGRAMME

Given the data described in the previous paragraphs, it was
clear that the main population to be trained were at middle
and upper middle/senior management level. Many staff had
reached their respective levels of seniority on the basis of
their technical rather than managerial skills and had had
little or no exposure to those concepts of management skills
and knowledge which could make significant improvements to
their own performance and the performance of staff reporting
to them.

Nevertheless, the managers had specific expectations of
management development: initially they expected taught
programmes, conversely a loosely structured experiential
development programme would have been rejected. Equally, they
recognised that the most valuable learning took place while
doing the job itself. Putting these two proposals together,

three levels of programme were created: the Middle Managers Course, the Manager's Refresher Programme (later called the Experienced Manager's Course) and the Senior Management Programme - each dealing with an increasingly senior level of staff.

The Middle Management Course

This began as a five week general management course, incorporating three weeks taught at the School of Management covering general management themes; one week researching projects in London head office, and a final week preparing reports and recommended actions for the clients. In later courses reports were videotaped, entailing considerable presentation skills work in the final week.

The middle managers attending this course were usually staff in their thirties, often with engineering qualifications to degree level as their starting point, but very little exposure to management principles. They consistently rated this programme highly, as for many it was their first chance to spend time in the company of others looking at problems which they had met in their work as managers: to understand concepts such as discounted cash flow or analysing organisational behaviour; or to have the opportunity to query senior management on plans which affected their own future. Acting on their feedback, the course ran twice yearly in its five week format for three years, and in 1981 was thoroughly revised to become a three week programme lacking the in company projects but incorporating a visit to another organisation, for comparison. The key feature of a mix of Cranfield specialist and Cable and Wirless senior manager contributing to the programme has been retained throughout, and commitment to the course by both institutions has remained high: indeed its success has been one of the most outstanding achievements of the joint venture.

The Experienced Manager's Course

This two week general management programme was designed for a specific population: those upper middle level managers, usually in their forties who formed the backbone of the organisation, but had little formal management training and were not best suited to the Middle Manager's Course. Wrongly treated this level of management can delay improvements or stifle the organisation: properly motivated they are a key asset to the business. Recognising their importance, a general management course was created for them, covering similar ground to that of the Middle Management Course, but in a more concentrated format while retaining the dual inputs from Cranfield and Cable and Wireless staff. In the longer term it is recognised that the nature of this course will change, and it will become a booster for those staff who attend the Middle Management Course some years earlier: for the moment it attracts a population with little or no management training. Its results have been good, as measured by the resarch and feedback received - these points are taken up more fully in the paragraph on research results.

Senior Management Programme

This was again devised as a two week general management programme for groups of up to a dozen senior managers, taught jointly as in the earlier two programmes. It has however a different outcome from the other two courses: despite hard work by both partners the course was never a success, and after four programmes had been run the course was discontinued. This experience was a setback for the joint venture, but useful lessons were drawn from the reasons for the failure. With the benefit of hindsight it was seen that the course was misconceived from the outset: at senior levels it was almost impossible to bring together a standard programme which met the diverse needs of participants, who themselves brought to the programme experience of many different facets of the business. The number of common needs was too small for the programme to meet any but a fraction of the total needs of the group, and a modular approach of specific topics taught by leaders in each field is now being investigated as the chief training method for this group.

RESEARCH

Given the scope of the activities described in the previous paragraphs, the end product of this investment in training must be of great significance. The activities were assessed by the usual methods of during and post course evaluations completed by participants, but course members were followed up in an uniquely thorough manner by a researcher attached to the joint venture. The research set out to answer two basic questions:-

(1)   To what extent do managers apply what they have learnt in the classroom to the jobs they subsequently do?

(2)   What are the important factors affecting this process of transfer?

In summary the researcher found that the answers to these questions depended on:-

The type of programme attended and the category, age, seniority, personality type, length of service and professional background of the manager himself.

In all cases, transfer depended on having learnt something worth transferring: on having the opportunity and support to attempt transfer, and on having the energy, enthusiasm and insight to try.

Within these groups of managers however, large differences emerged in the success of their efforts: clearly middle managers were the most satisfied with their training,

166

experienced managers least satisfied and senior managers
rather mixed in their feelings. Factors the research
highlighted in producing these conclusions were:

- the different priorities of managers: senior
  managers were more interested in the business
  environment; experienced managers in their specific
  jobs and middle managers in the people with whom they
  worked,

- perceptions of the climate in which managers attempted
  to transfer their new skills and knowledge differed
  little between the level of manager where a
  difference existed. National staff from overseas
  branches in particular found the climate of their
  work environment more conducive to change.

The overall result was that the value of the programmes
were consistently defined as having been firstly theoretical,
secondly personal and thirdly practical. Theoretical in this
sense meant a theoretical understanding of situations and
events, not abstract academic work for its own sake.
Undoubtedly managers perceived the programmes as having been
valuable, the climate essentially facilitative and
colleagues supportive.

The aims of the joint venture were shown by this research
to have been largely achieved: although many difficulties
were apparent during the progress, the brief agreed between
the two partners had been fulfilled in all six aspects.
Questions posed by such activities are inevitably: did it
work and is it continuing? The answer to both is a strong
affirmative, although it is not the same creature five years
on. Most emphasis, as the venture progresses along its own
learning curve now shifts to workshop style, shorter
sessions building on the groundwork achieved in the first
five years. Whether this will be equally successful may well
be the subject of further research.

167

Part III
Future of management education

12 The practice of management education and training

KEN HALL

The writer acknowledges his indebtedness to the companies, the training managers and the managers who took part in the survey. And he is especially grateful to Joyce Drimatis, whose competence and dedication as research assistant made light work of a demanding task.

PART A: MANAGEMENT DEVELOPMENT - AN OVERVIEW

INTRODUCTION

Few management issues have grown in importance as rapidly as that of management development. There may have been a 'golden age' for managers when a compliant workforce seldom if ever questioned the manager's competence, although this is highly improbable. But there is little doubt that today's manager cannot expect to manage as of right - he has to establish his authority time and again by proving that he has kept up to date in a rapidly changing economic, technical and industrial relations environment. Further complexity is added by the fact that management theory is not constant. Yet management theory and management development are closely related in that management development is frequently made to fit the theory of the day. Thus in comparing today's widely differing approaches to management training with the attempt to train for the 'one best way' in the early part of this century, one has to understand the changes in management theory which have taken place in the intervening years.

The growth of scientific management in the early part of this century sought to rationalise management by attempting to provide one correct way to approach management training. Yet it was precisely from that period onward that attempts to define what constituted effective management was becoming increasingly difficult in a complex and changing environment. As a consequence, some management specialists began to argue for a situational view of management, i.e. that effective management was contingent to the situation in which the manager was located. Research by, for example, Joan Woodward (1965) and Burns and Stalker (1961) demonstrated the wisdom of this approach. Search for one

171

universally applicable best management style, whilst not wholly aborted, is no longer pursued with the vigour with which it once was. Most management specialists now take some kind of a contingency view.

Contingency theory proposes that there is no one single best management style or one organisational structure which is applicable and effective for all situations. It is now accepted that the effectiveness of an organisation is complicated by a host of demands and constraints (Joyce 1979). Contingency theory, moreover, suggests that managers should analyse their situations in order to devise their own effective approach to management, or that alternatively their situation should be analysed for them by management training specialists. Ashton et al (1975) sees management as a function within an organisation and that each organisation has a different pattern for this function. The authors developed this view on the information gained from three case studies which led them to argue for a contingency approach to management development.

According to Glube and Margerison (1976), management training should consist of the following steps:

(a)   find out what people really want (i.e. what they need);
(b)   involve participants in the training design;
(c)   get the programmes agreed to by the senior people;
(d)   make training relevant to organisational rewards.

Glube and Margerison's suggestions add to, but accept the normal methodology of a successful training programme as commonly quoted by most training specialists (Barber 1968), viz:

1.   The identification of training needs
2.   The formulation of training policy
3.   The implementation of this policy (i.e. the training process)
4.   The assessment of training effectiveness

Glube and Margerison suggest that training is likely to be supported if it is associated with one or more of their above points, and that this support will be less readily forthcoming if training is seen as a remedial exercise or an organisational procedure that everyone habitually undergoes. There is general consensus in the literature that organisations must constantly examine their own specific needs as well as those of its managers.

The findings of a project conducted by the European Foundation for Management Development which had as its purpose the development of a better insight into the ways in which organisations select between internal and external training, provides further support for the above notion. That project revealed that generally the objectives as well as the perception of individual managers, their organisations and the training institutions themselves tend to differ and the overall conclusion to a study by Berger and Nixon (1981) was that it is essential for training programmes to be integrated with job requirements and organisational demands.

Unless there are specific learning goals and a close connection between the training and the work setting, then transfer of learning is unlikely. Therefore as much time and energy needs to be put into the activities which build a 'learning system' within the organisation as into the training itself.

In an earlier study, Berger (1981) set out to evaluate the effectiveness of management training. The main results of this were that:

1. Transfer of learning was greatest when participants went to the training course with clear learning and personal development goals and worked in jobs where they had autonomy to introduce change.

2. Transfer of learning was much greater when on the job projects were included as part of the overall training design than when these were absent.

3. Training often fails to produce change because the course design does not take into account the unique situations and demands which managers have to cope with. (Berger and Nixon 1981).

Funch (1981) views management training as allowing a manager to consider various management concepts while assisting the acceptance and application of those which he perceives as necessary or useful to the work environment. Beyond that, management training requires specific skills and techniques that are necessary for the maintenance of the individual, the group and the work associated with the manager's particular expertise. Funch proposes that management development is aimed at maximising the potential of managers through the processes of management training, management coaching and management education.

MANAGEMENT TRAINING INSTITUTIONS

In the following discussion on location of training, little emphasis is placed on the training process itself. Taking the four-step training methodology, viz: (1) needs identification, (2) policy formulation, (3) policy implementation and (4) effectiveness assessments, the third point (policy implementation) will not be analysed in any depth here. It is the intent of this paper to consider

how training needs are identified, policy is formulated and
how the new skills are integrated into the work situation.

Management training has been one of the real growth
industries of the last twenty years or more. A whole host
of individuals and institutions now offer management
training, including individual consultants and consultancy
groups, professional institutions and business schools. The
efforts of consultants will not be described beyond the
obvious comment that in common with most other such
enterprises, consultants vary greatly in quality and know
how and that, whilst consultants do offer training courses
open to the general public, their real value lies in their
ability to concentrate on tailor-made in-company training
programmes.

Regarding professional associations, a great variation of
philosophies can be observed. Some professional
associations perceive themselves primarily as 'qualifying
associations' and learned societies, providing their
members with paper qualifications after examination (or
exemption) and offering a forum for debate, but allowing
others to undertake much of the (routine) training. Other
professional associations perceive themselves as being
primarily a voice for their professional membership,
granting qualifications to suitably qualified persons as
part of that process, and any training offered is perceived
as an important, but not prime, function. They often act as
a counteracting force to trade unions, yet fulfil many of
the criterion of trade unions themselves. Yet other
professional institutions perceive themselves primarily as
training organisations. In the field of management
education and training some of these latter bodies have
proved to be major innovators and have acted as a spur to
both consultants and to the business schools.

MANAGEMENT DEVELOPMENT - THE PLACE OF BUSINESS SCHOOLS*

Business schools are costly enterprises to establish and to
maintain. Whilst many have gone through a phase of
'organic' growth, some have been established in order to
meet the specific purpose of upgrading the management skills
of their particular community and a number are intended to
act as an international catalyst for change and improvement
of management practice.

---

* The writer has over the last few years visited a variety
  of business schools in a number of countries, including
  the United States, Canada, Britain, France, Switzerland,
  Ireland, Australia, New Zealand and S E Asia. The
  description of business schools does not apply to any
  particular school but is the writer's perception of the
  situation in many of these institutions.

Most business schools provide higher degrees* of the MBA
and MSc type. They also offer short executive development
programmes. Skills can usefully be divided (Becker 1962)
into 'general skills' and 'specific skills'. Using this
categorisation, MBA programmes are in the main oriented
towards general skills while MSc-type courses aim towards
the specific skills end of the spectrum. Thus, for example,
operations research or finance courses are aimed towards
specific skills training.

A number of issues which are of importance to business
school educators appear to be barely recognised by 'the
customers', while other issues are considered as fundamental.
Thus, business school deans are inclined to vigorously
debate the orientation problem of whether business schools
should be 'academic' or 'professional' in their direction
(1980). The evidence appears to suggest that course
participants (and their organisations) are not particularly
enamoured with academic elegance or an academic approach to
management development, but desire to acquire directly
applicable skills and hence appear to support the notion
that business schools should aim to be professional in their
orientation. A purely professional direction, however, may
not be appropriate for business schools operating in
academic institutions, so this then becomes a question of
making certain that the 'centre of gravity' is inclined
towards the professional end of the spectrum.

Course participants are vitally interested in learning
methods. There is obviously a place for 'talk-and-chalk'
but the trend towards gaming, role playing, the case study
approach and other 'non-instructional' methods would appear
to find growing support. In broad terms, the view of
companies and of individual managers undertaking training is
that the more practical, applied and immediately useful a
course, the better. Business schools would be wrong to
throw out good educational methods with a long-term
development advantage in order to meet the wishes of
participants and organisations who inevitably have a
shorter time-horizon and who usually understand learning
methods less well than do the instructors, but business
schools would be equally unwise not to heed the wishes of
their 'customers'.

Among other issues which have been debated in the business
schools is the importance of a 'quantitative' versus a
'qualitative' approach to management training and the
emphasis which should be placed on 'general' as opposed to

---

* Pre-entry training, as for example for first degrees, is
not being considered here excepting where undertaken by
practising managers as part of their general management
education.

'specific' skills acquisition. Some business schools are
reputed to be heavily oriented towards a 'quantitative'
approach to management training whilst others take a more
descriptive, analytical and 'qualitative' direction. Some
years ago a number of business schools felt that in order to
safeguard their academic integrity (as well as presumably
meet the needs of their outside constituents), they should
direct their teaching towards the 'quantitative' study of
management. Possibly the introduction of the newer
generation of computers played some part in this process.
More recently there has been a swing, albeit possibly of
limited magnitude, towards a more 'qualitative' approach to
training - elegant mathematical models are of little use in
practice if the assumptions on which they are based are
flawed. The past few years have demonstrated the difficulty
of accurate forecasting, given the turbulent economic and
social environment in which industry now operates and this
has led to a measure of disenchantment with a highly
'quantitative' approach. Perhaps the succinct statement -
'If practical outcomes are so uncertain, why bother with
crunching numbers to the Nth degree', provided by a North
American business school dean to the author, is a case in
point. The respondents to the study described in this paper
were more interested in following a 'qualitative' approach
to management training and especially in gaining some
insight into the problems of man-management. And the
importance of 'specific skills' training should not be
minimised. Thus as early as 1966, the UK Association of
Teachers in Management (Pugh 1966) suggested that the content
of a good management programme should include such topics as:
accounting, finance management, marketing, O & M, O.R. and
industrial engineering as well as the more general topics of
communication, behaviour analysis, management theory and
business policy.

Thus it would appear that if management trainers wish to
meet the perceived needs of their constituents then they
should not over-emphasise the quantitative approach in their
general management training, should pursue a broadly
'professional' orientation and should provide both general
and specific training. The following pages describe a study
specifically undertaken for this paper and which provides
some evidence on these and other issues.

PART B: THE MANAGEMENT DEVELOPMENT SURVEY

A number of research projects have been undertaken in recent
years with the purpose of establishing what management
really wants from management training. Not surprisingly
management trainers, whether working in universities and
colleges, in professional associations or in consultancy
companies have sought data on training needs in order to
produce better courses. As the body of data has grown so
researchers have been encouraged to analyse the training
needs of their constituents. Thus for example Attwood

(1979) quotes Digman's work 'How Well-Managed Organisations Develop Their Executives' as the stimulus for his own study.

Attwood's research methodology utilised postal questionnaires. He sent out 515 questionnaires and received 119 returns of which 110 were used in his statistical analysis. Crockett (1979) also used the postal questionnaire method and obtained a satisfactory response rate for this method of thirty-one per cent. More recently Saul (1981) of Chandler and McLeod Consultants in a mixed interview/telephone/postal approach generated additional useful information. These studies provide invaluable insight into the management development process. Yet the twin problems of non-response and consequent possibility of bias, and of the quality of response from mail surveys led us to undertake an intensive study of face to face interviews. The fact that many of the other surveys had concentrated in large part on the manufacturing sector acted as an additional stimulus for undertaking yet another survey.

Twenty Western Australian organisations representing the various sections of the primary, secondary and tertiary sector of economic activity were contacted. It was intended to achieve one hundred per cent response rate of this small but carefully stratified sample, and this was obtained. The twenty companies included mining, metal, building materials and foodstuffs manufacture, retail stores, financial institutions and other sections of the tertiary sector, government departments and government instrumentalities and so forth. In broad terms the data so obtained supports that of other surveys, thereby indicating that the postal survey and various other methods with all their imperfections in terms of response rates provide us with excellent results. But there is little doubt that to obtain rich, qualitative data requires 'permissive face to face' interviews. Fine nuances which are missed in a postal approach are noted and shed additional light.

The object of the survey was to gain answers, *inter-alia*, to the following questions:

1. What are the organisations' managerial training needs?
2. How are managers identified for training?
3. How are their needs established?
4. What training methods and designs are used for management programmes?
5. How is training evaluated?
6. What changes can be made to the present training system used by the organisations?

After careful negotiation with each company's senior management, altogether sixty eight managers were given one or more in depth interviews. Forty-eight represented those who have or could have had management training and twenty were training/personnel specialists responsible for the implementation, coordination and evaluation of training programmes. A structured interview schedule was used in order to assist in the uniformity of information gathered but additional unsolicited information was also noted. Absolute confidentiality was guaranteed. As suggested in the survey methodology literature, the quality of information thus obtained was significantly richer than that which would have been obtained by mailed questionnaire, or by mailed questionnaire allied to a 'phone interview. During the course of interviews, rapport and trust is established between interviewer and interviewee which provides the interviewer with a deeper insight than would otherwise have been the case. Probing is possible which gives greater confidence in the results obtained. And despite the availability of techniques which provide us with measures of statistical reliability, there is still no substitute for high response rates.

RESULTS

The average length of time that had elapsed since our managers had completed their major or basic qualification was sixteen and a half years and seventy one per cent of the managers had completed that qualification at least ten years previously. In a period of technological and environmental changes of unprecedented magnitude, it may not be unreasonable to assume that such a period is excessive unless regular refresher courses are undertaken. Hence some form of continuous management education and training to assist managers to keep well informed and up to date would appear to be mandatory.

The fact that the better part of three quarters of our managers had completed their tertiary qualification at least ten years previously is in itself an indication for the need for further training. Yet the situation proved even more complex. Fifty per cent of our managers had not acquired any management qualification at all. Hence their tertiary qualification, in another discipline, may have been useful to them when they worked, for example, as engineers or chemists, but may not be particularly helpful now that they are managers - this was brought out time and again in conversation. Of those who had some management qualifications, fifty four per cent acquired them as part of their earlier professional training and a mere twenty three per cent of all the managers surveyed had acquired some form of management qualification apart from their original tertiary degrees or diplomas. So any suggestion that the management force is highly trained and qualified in management techniques would be open to serious dispute.

MANAGEMENT POTENTIAL

Both managers and training managers gave similar positive responses concerning the operation of a management

succession plan within their organisation - forty per cent
of both groups indicated that the organisation did operate
a formal management succession plan. The remaining sixty
per cent of the managers stated that there was definitely no
such plan in operation, whilst the sixty per cent of the
training managers who had not confirmed the existence of a
succession plan were not anything like as firm in the view
that there was no such plan - many *suggested* that some kind
of *informal* plan did exist.

Perhaps disappointing but not surprising to management
educators and trainers, management education is in the main
not the most important criterion for promotion. Sixty seven
per cent of the managers maintained that 'performance on the
job' was the most common approach used by their organisation
for the promotion of managers. This was followed by
'potential' with a forty eight per cent response rate.
'Education' rated a mere forty per cent and education here
is not limited to management education but can encompass
functional disciplines such as engineering or chemistry.
But any suggestion of Australian anti intellectualism is
hard to maintain when Attwood's (1979) British survey is
considered. He found that the promotion criterion
consistently used by his organisations were:

Performance	99%
Previous management experience	80%
Previous industrial experience	61%
Education	35%

Hence for the UK sample, performance was evaluated even
more highly than for our Australian sample and education even
more lowly. Attwood argues that the low percentage of
promotions gained by 'education' is an illustration of a
recently recognised phenomenon of managerial careers - that
on entering management, a person begins in fact a second
career - that is, a change in direction from his/her
original career path. It may perhaps be pertinent to reflect
whether one reason for the frequently suggested poor quality
of man management in both countries may be partly due to the
fact that management is entered by people who in large
measure are unprepared for that particular career.

Sixty per cent of the organisations used the 'performance
appraisal' as a procedure for identifying managers for
management training. An informal approach using 'observation
of performance on the job', was used according to thirty
eight per cent of the managers and these figures correspond
to those given by the training managers who were interviewed.
In Attwood's UK sample, the appraisal system was used in
combination with internal advertisement, referral and
interviews but only two of his organisations used the
appraisal out of 110 companies.

MANAGEMENT DEVELOPMENT POLICY

There is a broad consensus among management trainers that
management training should be conducted by the organisation's
training specialists as well as by external agencies - the
decision on who should train being based on training needs.
External agencies, it is suggested, have expertise gained by
training a broad spectrum of managers from a variety of
organisations whilst the organisation's special needs are
best known and frequently best met through the efforts of its
own training specialists. Fifty per cent of our managers
responded that the organisation's training department and
external agencies were both used to plan and conduct
management training programmes; forty per cent responded
that external agencies alone were used - which did not
correspond with the twenty per cent agreement rate from
training managers on this question. Only twenty per cent of
the managers reported that management training was
conducted by the organisation alone. These figures appear
to suggest that only in a minority of the organisations is a
formal in company management training programme in
operation.

THE DESIGN AND CONTENT OF MANAGEMENT TRAINING PROGRAMMES

Sixty per cent of managers and seventy per cent of training
managers suggested that participants of management training
programmes were able to influence the design and content of
the programme. More significantly, a mere twenty three per
cent of managers stated that participants were able to
influence the programme prior to its construction, whilst
forty per cent of responses indicated that participants were
able to influence the programme only after having actually
participated. These figures could be compared with the
Australian survey conducted by Saul (1981) which found that
in management training programmes seventy three per cent
of management training participants were unable to influence
the design and content of training programmes. If influence
here means influence prior to programme construction, then
for our sample the corresponding figure was seventy seven
per cent.

    Perhaps not surprisingly, ninety two per cent of the
managers felt that it was very important for participants
to be able to influence the design and content of management
training programmes. Training specialists would maintain
that they are best able to assess training needs but a
relatively often quoted reason (by twenty seven per cent of
our managers) given as support for the need to influence
training programmes was that 'management training should
develop the manager's needs and the manager is the one most
aware of his own weaknesses'. Whilst it is certainly true
that most people are unable to be wholly objective in
matters of self analysis it would be difficult to mount a
logical argument going totally against that particular view.

TRAINING DECISION MAKERS

The survey indicated that between seventy and eighty per cent of the organisations trained their managers at all levels. This should be compared with Attwood's figure of sixty one per cent. Responses by our managers as to who should make the decision on participation in the management training programme were:

Management and immediate superior	45%
Divisional Manager	45%
Manager's own decision	10%

Responses here also indicated a clear understanding of the time and money involved in off the job management development. There was broad agreement by managers and by training managers that the higher the cost and the greater the length of time involved in the programme, the higher the level at which the decision is and should be made.

IDENTIFICATION OF TRAINING NEEDS

Sixty seven per cent of the managers interviewed reported that their organisation had a system for identifying managerial training needs: this compares to a seventy five per cent response rate given by the training managers.

The most common ways of identifying training needs appear to be as follows:

Performance appraisal	56%
Observation of performance	30%

Only twenty five per cent of the managers reported that manpower planning was part of the organisation's system used to identify managerial training needs. This figure should be compared with a fifty per cent response rate supplied by the training managers. This finding is supported by Cole (1981) who also established that training for change is the fastest growing area in management training and most common here is training to improve job performance. He suggests however that training for personal development is the most neglected area in management training.

Forty two per cent of managers as compared to twenty five per cent of training managers reported that the system of management training does not extend to those at the very top of the organisation. These figures provide additional support for the findings obtained by Crockett (1979). Senior managers felt less in need of more exposure to training than did middle and junior managers. Management literature is full of examples of senior managers who feel that their subordinates require training but perceive themselves as being above such mundane activities to require any further comment here. Cole (1981) found that in the UK, directors and senior managers feel that they have reached

181

a level where training is not necessary for them. But we found exceptions - senior managers (i.e. chief executives) who perceived a personal training need and undertook regular training. In general, their organisations were among the most training conscious of all those surveyed.

Forty eight per cent of managers stated that the system covered the training needs of the individual as well as reflecting the organisation's own perspective, whilst thirty three per cent of these correspondents reported that the system reflected the organisation's perspective alone. This should be compared to the figure of sixty six per cent of training managers who replied that the system reflected both individual and organisation needs, whereas thirty per cent reported that the system reflected the organisation's perspective alone. Of all the organisations surveyed, one half identified training needs annually, fourteen per cent at least bi-annually and fifteen per cent only as the need arose.

The managers felt that the most important aspects in systematic management training are as follows:

Assist the growth and development of managers	19%
Important for developing man-management skills	19%

Training managers on the other hand felt overwhelmingly that it is a means of assisting managers to improve their performance on the job.

SUGGESTED CHANGES WHICH COULD BE MADE TO MANAGEMENT TRAINING PROGRAMMES

(a) Managers

Implement a more systematic management training programme   33%

Programmes should be designed to meet the needs of managers   19%

(b) Training managers

Organisation needs to implement a systematic management training programme   10%

Management training at present is far too general and programmes should be oriented to the specific needs of managers   35%

Only ten per cent of the training managers suggested that a systematic management training programme should have an evaluation component embracing post training procedures. That management training specialists, imbued in the philosophy and techniques of good training should be so happy to ignore one of the fundamental steps of good training programmes as enunciated in the literature is perhaps surprising.

TRAINING METHODS

Training managers reported that training occurs in a
locational sense:

Internally	15%
Externally	55%
Both	30%

The skill areas in which managers said they had recently
most often been trained were:

Man management	50%
Planning	40%
Finance	38%

The skill areas in which training managers said training
had recently most often been given were:

Man management	85%
Personnel	70%
Accounting	65%
Planning	65%

The perceived need for more man management training was
emphasised by many of our managers. The urgency of this need
may in part explain the difference in the responses on this
criterion between the managers and training managers.

The results support Attwood's (1979) survey in the UK in
that he found that finance, man management and general
management have maintained their position as being areas of
continuing educational need, reflecting the way in which
management continues to recognise two of its most important
resources - capital and manpower.

TRAINING UNDERTAKEN BY MANAGERS INDEPENDENT OF THEIR
EMPLOYING ORGANISATIONS

Thirty eight per cent of the managers interviewed had not
attempted to undertake any training independent of their
company. Fifty four per cent had made attempts to acquire
some units of management education or had gained a
qualification in this area, for example by completing a first
degree, by taking units towards a management course or by
undertaking post graduate studies. Of those managers who had
participated in internal courses, all felt that the subject
matter had been highly relevant, whilst seventy eight per
cent of managers who had participated in external courses
agreed that the subject matter had been highly relevant.
These figures would appear to support the notion that the
managers had a positive attitude towards training generally.

183

TECHNIQUES USED BY THE ORGANISATIONS FOR MANAGEMENT TRAINING

These are in descending order:

(a) Managers' responses

On the job training	77%
Seminars	65%
Understudying/assisting senior management	48%

(b) Training Managers' responses

Seminars	85%
On the job training	75%
Understudying/assisting senior management	70%

These findings support those of Crockett who established that seminars and understudying/assisting senior management were among the most popular techniques used by organisations in Western Australia and similarly Burack (1981) found that the most effective approaches, considered the most potent for training and development practice by training managers in the USA, were coaching, workshops and on the job training. Cole found that managers prefer -

- involvement and participation linked to realism
- active learning rather than passive learning
- diagnosing business problems and proposing solutions (i.e. cases)

They disliked -

- games and gimmicks
- lectures
- theory

Given these results, it would be difficult for business school academics to maintain that business schools should have their primary focus in the 'academic' rather than 'professional' area. Those business school deans who are attempting to move their schools into a more professional direction, away from a purely academic approach, appear to be supported by the practising manager in need of training. But as suggested elsewhere, care must be taken not to go too far here. Throwing out the baby as well as the bathwater is poor strategy.

OPPORTUNITIES FOR SELF DEVELOPMENT

It is often argued that organisations should give their managers as much assistance as possible in the furtherance of their own self development. Many organisations are not large enough to maintain a specialist training department, in which case some concessions to the managers, encouraging them to develop themselves through formal education, may be one way of overcoming this lack of in-company training opportunities. This notion is supported by a study carried out in the USA on the 'Effectiveness of Training and Development Methods for Managers' (Burack 1981). That study found that formal education was considered next in importance to company training as a 'major source of skills development'.

Of the organisations taking part in the survey, in forty five per cent of cases, seventy per cent of managerial staff were trained annually, thirty per cent of the organisations surveyed train between thirty per cent and forty per cent of their managers annually whilst one quarter of the organisations only train as the need arises and fifteen per cent of the organisations do not train managers at all. A more extensive survey (Crocket (1979) revealed that of the 441 executives who responded, 37.8 per cent had not attended any formal in company programme during the previous three years and another 38.8 per cent had averaged less than one day's attendance per year at in company programmes. A similar pattern of responses was found when executives were questioned concerning attendance at external programmes.

This survey has shown that organisations predominantly use external agencies for their more formal training - the extensive use of seminars by the organisations provides a measure of support for this expressed view-point.

EVALUATION OF TRAINING

Evaluation of management training occurred in the following manner:

	Managers' views	Training Managers' views
Informal feedback from staff	54%	40%
Written reports	52%	70%
Change in performance (improvement)	40%	35%
Regular reviews	23%	35%

Saul (1981) in his research for Australia's National Training Council has suggested that effective training should be viewed as a three stage problem-solving process, viz:

    Stage 1   -   planning
    Stage 2   -   training
    Stage 3   -   follow-up

As Saul subsumes the 'identification of training needs' and the 'formulation of training policy' under the heading of 'planning', his methodology is standard for manpower training as given in the literature. Saul suggests that most organisations give inadequate consideration to planning. In our survey, the majority of managers had the opportunity to influence the design and content of programmes only after they had been completed, through the evaluative process.

According to Saul, training is often undertaken as a cure for a problem which has been incorrectly defined and could better be overcome in some other way. Remarks made to us appear to support this conclusion.

TRANSFER OF SKILLS

If the purpose of training is to provide the manager with skills which he will use in his daily work, then it is not unreasonable to assume that most companies will take great care to give the manager the opportunity to actually practise his newly acquired skills. Sixty per cent of the managers in the sample stated that they could implement the skills they had learnt on management training courses. Yet when it came to the assessment of training effectiveness, training managers suggested that:

Organisation does not formally assess to what extent a participant on a management training programme has applied the skills he/she has learnt.	35%
Organisation only uses an informal approach by observing the performance on the job.	35%
Organisation uses performance appraisals.	15%
Organisation has formal validation procedure.	5%
Organisation uses post training test procedures.	10%

PROBLEMS AFFECTING MANAGEMENT TRAINING IN THE FUTURE

Not surprisingly, many of the responses suggested that the future was unlikely to be problem-free. Some of the suggested problems were:

1. Forty per cent of training managers felt that problems may occur as a result of money allocated to training being tied to organisation growth and development.

2. Twenty five per cent of managers responded that more suitably qualified training managers would be required in the future if training of adequate quality is to result.

3. Twenty five per cent of managers felt that the conservatism of senior managers inhibits the

successful implementation of management training
programmes and hence a change in attitude at this
level was required.

Ninety five per cent of the training managers stated that
they had access to those who have the final say on decisions
concerning management training, but only sixty per cent were
satisfied with the resources available for management
training programmes. It is of course not unusual for
managers in any functional area to feel their budget to be
inadequate to meet their objectives. Yet if a country's
future depends on its human resource and if the quality of
its management is seen as one of the crucial variables in
the success or failure of a country's economy, then lack of
financial resources for management training could have very
negative consequences.

But before taking a bleak view of the future it is worth
noting that sixty five per cent of training managers saw
their organisations as progressive.

PROFILE OF TRAINING/PERSONNEL MANAGERS

If training is to be effective then the budget is not the
only cause for concern. At least as important is the
quality of trainers - and much else. It is therefore
gratifying to note that eighty per cent of the training
managers interviewed had some tertiary qualifications and
fifty per cent had attended short courses on how to train.
Forty per cent had a first degree and at least one training
manager possessed an MBA with a major manpower development
content. The average age of the training managers was
forty three years, but sixty per cent were over the age of
forty years and the average length of time that they had
spent in training was 14.35 years. So the average quality
of training managers appears to be highly satisfactory.

SOME GENERAL POINTS

There is no doubt that certain activities undertaken under
the 'management training' umbrella have little, if any,
practical outcome beyond allowing training departments,
organisations and course participants to be seen to be
'doing something'. They can of course also entertain - or
bore - and they help provide the management training
industry with employment. By the same token, badly needed
training frequently just does not take place, to the
disadvantage of individuals, organisations and the economy
generally. And thirty years or more after its formulation,
good training methodology is often being ignored. But
overall, great strides have been made in the quality and
quantity of management training, which does give cause for
satisfaction.

187

A RESEARCH NOTE

The methodology of seeking a one hundred per cent response
from the selected organisations and utilising face-to-face
interviews was in part an attempt to establish if the more
normal mailed questionnaire approach produced biased results.
This did not prove to be the case - and such an outcome
should give more confidence in data obtained by the less
expensive method. The location of our survey may also
warrant comment. Western Australia is an isolated community,
with an atypical work sector mix. Yet the management
training problems observed were similar to those which
researchers in other locations, with quite different
industrial and commercial mixes, have noted. It would be
presumptuous and premature to form firm conclusions from
this - but it would appear that despite the great difference
which managers in different locations face, there are
significant similarities in management training needs in
advanced industrial societies.

PART C: SOME LESSONS FOR THE MANAGEMENT EDUCATOR AND TRAINER

It is easy to understand why in a highly competitive and
turbulent industrial and commercial environment, in which
management decisions almost invariably have direct
consequences for the well being of the organisation, the
search for better management skills is pursued with such
vigour. Whether the challenge has been successfully met by
the management training specialist is open to question. Not
surprisingly, an area like management training in which
there is frequently no immediate and clearly defined fool
proof measure of success or failure, has encouraged many to
take advantage of the buoyancy of the market whether or not
they had much to offer. Among consultants, the poor as well
as the excellent have been able to charge high rates for
their services. Professional associations too have provided
their constituents with training courses which have at times
been well below that level which the organisations minimally
required if management skills were to be enhanced. An area
of special concern here has been that of man management,
with its often contradictory theories on motivation and
leadership, many of which have proven of doubtful validity
in a variety of situations.

   In business schools the explosion of demand has on
occasions led to careless recruitment and has meant that
so-called 'management experts' have occasionally lacked both
experience and insight. Moreover, the attempt by certain
of the business schools to maintain a high 'academic'
profile in order to be accepted by their peers from other
disciplines as academically respectable, has at times been
to the disadvantage of those who expected relevant and
practical training and education. In another direction the
dilemma which business schools face in this context is
readily understandable. There is not only the necessity to
educate and train the practitioner, but also the urgent need

to research in order to help establish a body of knowledge
pertinent to the needs of those who require educating and
training.

It is accepted that in any discipline in which the
behaviour of people is of major importance there will be
areas of doubt and room for dispute, yet unless there is a
solid core of proven and readily understood knowledge, then
training can barely commence. In so far as one is able to
assess the evidence, there have been considerable
achievements, aided by the efforts of the better consultants,
professional associations, and business schools. One would
reasonably expect further advances which will help to remove
areas of uncertainty and doubt and hence management education
and training should become more relevant with each
succeeding year. The evidence of our survey, as described
in this paper and supported by the work of others, suggests
that training managers and management trainees are in large
measure satisfied with the training available. Via pertinent
evaluative processes, both groups are already in some measure
able to identify those trainers and courses which use
unsuitable methods and less useful subject matter and hence
avoid such enterprises, concentrating their scarce financial
resources rather on those areas and trainers where a useful
outcome is reasonably assured.

Recent research has shown that approximately three-quarters
of management training 'events' take the form of short
courses, seminars and workshops - relatively little attention
appears to be focused on planned work assignments or other
forms of management training. There are many obvious
administrative and political advantages to having management
training which is comprised of short courses, run by training
specialists, not least of all because management is thereby
seen to be committed to training and development. Saul
(1981) concludes that management trainers are skilled at
running training events which have good 'face validity',
but suggests that there is a need for data to be collected
which would enable the 'content validity' of the programmes
to be evaluated. For many companies the whole process of
course evaluation requires a serious rethink.

One theme throughout this paper has been the importance
of company-promoted training for specific skills. Whilst
it was not part of the purpose of our paper to consider
formal education for first or higher degrees in any
substantial sense, the value of this avenue for skills
acquisition should not be minimized. One of our assumptions
throughout has been that 'general skills' are in very many
cases best acquired via formal education and hence the value
of undergraduate and postgraduate management courses. Much
of 'specific skills' training is best approached through the
organisation's own training specialists, acting either as
trainers or as direct facilitators of training.

Perhaps one of the most satisfactory outcomes of the
survey was the high quality of company training managers.

A survey by the author in the North West of England in 1963 provided results which indicated a different and less satisfactory situation. At that time many training managers were barely skilled in the training function and often badly educated. Whilst it is difficult to compare the situation in Western Australia with that of the North West of England over a nineteen year time-gap, it may not be unreasonable to assume that the quality of training specialists has improved throughout. This in turn should lead to better training and manpower development.

The conclusions which arise out of our survey suggest that:

1. Managers do require some form of training/education, when the length of time that has elapsed since the attainment of their original qualifications is considered.

2. The identification of managers in need of training usually occurs through a combination of performance appraisals and observation of on-the-job performance.

3. Management trainees are in the majority of cases only able to influence the design and content of management training programmes after the course has been conducted. This is in the main due to the use of external agencies or pre-packaged training courses.

4. Very many of the managers are keenly aware of their lack of certain skills and do attempt to improve these by self-development through management education.

5. The most often felt need for skills enhancement is in the area of man-management.

6. In the majority of cases managers appear to have a positive approach towards training.

7. The majority of organisations which have in-company training appear to follow a traditional line, leaving innovative training to external agencies.

8. The evaluation of both internal and external agencies is for the majority of the organisations carried out in an informal way.

9. The successful implementation of a management training programme depends to a great extent on the commitment of senior management and on good planning.

10. Many of the most senior managers do not consider that training applies to them and one negative outcome of this is that organisational change which is frequently necessary if newly acquired skills are to be practised does in many cases not take place.

11. The assessment of training needs as an initial

process prior to training itself, or of the
evaluation of training after the completion of the
process, leaves much to be desired. If better
training is to ensue both will require real
enhancement.

So finally when one views management education and training
as it is practised in this penultimate decade of the
twentieth century, there appears to be room for major
improvements in a variety of directions, yet there is also
room for considerable satisfaction. Much progress has been
achieved and consequently management skills in companies are
generally of a higher order than they have ever been. The
reasons for this are many and varied, but there is little
doubt that the quality of company training specialists and
of trainers generally, as well as the perceived need for
training by senior managers and the consequent positive
attitude to training by such persons, has played a major role
in this change. The improvement amongst management trainers
in the various institutions has no doubt played its part and
hence it is possible to end this paper on a clear note of
optimism. If management training and education are nowhere
near perfect, it is much better than it used to be. Although
there is room for major improvements, much progress has
already been made and success is normally built upon success.

BIBLIOGRAPHY

Ashton, D, et al, (1975) Management Development - Theory
  and Practice , Journal of European Training monograph
  vol.4, no.6, MCB Publications, Bradford.

Attwood, L T, (1979) 'Management development in British
  companies', Journal of European Industrial Training,
  Monograph, Vol.3, No.8.

Barber, J W, (Ed), (1968), Industrial Training Handbook,
  ILIFFE, London.

Becker, G, (1962), 'Investment in Human Capital', Journal of
  Political Economy (supplement), Chicago. NB: The terms
  'general skills' and 'specific skills' are used in this
  paper in a somewhat different manner to that suggested by
  Becker.

Berger, M, and Nixon, B, (1981), 'Management development that
  works', Journal of European Industrial Training, vol.5,
  no.3.

Berger, M, (1981), 'Training and the Organisational Context',
  cited in Berger, M, and Nixon, B, 'Management development
  that works', Journal of European and Industrial Training,
  vol.5, no.3.

Burack, E H, (1981), 'The effectiveness of training and development methods for managers', Training and Development in Australia, vol.8, no.3.

Burns, T and Stalker, J, (1961), The Management of Innovation, Tavistock.

Cole, G, (1981), 'Management training in top companies', Journal of European Industrial Training, vol.5, no.4, pp 1-8.

Crockett, G V, (1979), 'Executive training and development in Western Australian enterprises - Part 1', Work and people, vol.1, no.3, AGPS Canberra, September.

Funch, C, (1981), 'Management education in Australia', Training Development in Australia, vol.8, no.2, Sydney.

Glube, R H and Margerison, C J, (1976), 'Managerial leadership - implications for training and development', Journal of European Training, vol.5, no.1.

Hall, K, (1980), 'Business schools - an international perspective', Gazette WAIT, vol.13, no.2, Perth.

Joyce, L, (1979), 'Management training: developments and trends', Journal of European Industrial Training, vol.3, no.6.

Pugh, D, (1966), The Academic Teaching of Management, ATM Occasional Papers no.4, Blackwell, Oxford.

Saul, P, (1981), Management Training in Australia, Research Report to the National Training Council, Canberra.

Woodward, J, (1965), Industrial Organisation: Theory and Practice, Oxford U.P., Oxford.

13 Developing professional managers

PETER FORRESTER

There is no field of education, and probably no field of human endeavour, which is so healthily self critical as that of management education. The last twenty years or so have seen a plethora of reports, commentaries, monographs, etc. criticising, usually constructively, the current provision. Outstanding examples are the Gordon and Howell (1959) and Pierson (1959) reports, the Mant report (1969), and latterly a thought provoking symposium edited by Cooper (1981). Nor must we forget the long and effective campaign for action learning waged by Revans in many books and papers, e.g. (1980) and the sytematic studies emerging from the University of Lancaster, e.g. Binsted and Snell (1976). A consideration of future needs is given in a recent AACSB/FME report (1981).

Certain common themes are apparent. Management education is often said to be too 'academic' in character and insufficiently related to real life. It has become constricted and warped by an irrelevant educational system and shibboleths developed in another age and for other fields. Managers learn by doing, not by being told. Noncognitive skills, such as those of effective negotiation, communication and leadership are more important than analytical techniques. The world is changing more rapidly than ever before, and the job of the manager of the late 20th and early 21st centuries will be very different from today. Few, least of all the present author, would deny the value of this continuing self criticism and debate.

This article has two main themes. First that side by side with the need for rigorous attention to quality and relevance of management education, there is an at least equal need for a vast increase in quantity (except perhaps in the USA). In most of the world, management is the last refuge of the amateur, gifted or otherwise. This position will not be rectified by managers being sent on a few days or weeks of courses, or involved in a part time action learning exercise. Whatever the style and pattern of management education it must be as rigorous and complete as that of a doctor or engineer.

Secondly, that management education must at all costs avoid becoming stereotyped and constrained into a limited number of

narrow moulds. Its structure must reflect a great diversity
of needs.

PROFESSIONAL EDUCATION FOR MANAGEMENT

Management is now the world's most important profession. The
vast majority of the world's population is now to a greater
or lesser extent dependent for survival on the goods and
services provided by organisations large and small, public
and private, and the effectiveness of these organisations
rests more than anything else upon the quality of management.

In all professions the quality of performance depends upon
a number of factors, including particularly the innate
abilities, basic education, and experience of the individual
practitioner. It also rests upon the potentiality for each
generation to stand upon the shoulders of the previous one.
If we all have to discover the wheel for ourselves there is
no chance of progress. Each generation needs to have
available the knowledge and understanding gained by its
predecessors, as a foundation and springboard for further
development and improvement. Professional education has a
number of purposes, but two are paramount - the imparting of
the current state of the art, and the development of ability
to apply and advance it.

In these respects management is closely analogous to other
major professions such as medicine and engineering. All
three rest upon innate ability, knowledge, acquired skills
and experience. The oft quoted half truth that 'managers
are born not made' is equally applicable to medicine and
engineering, though in the latter cases it seldom leads to
the conclusion that systematic training is unnecessary. The
medical and engineering professions have developed systems
for professional development which ensure that their
practitioners have both a sound knowledge base and practical
training in its application.

This is not to say that the preparation for these
professions is universally regarded as perfect, and indeed it
is under frequent criticism and review, but the need to
combine knowledge and experience is never questioned. It
seems to the author to be transparently obvious that
managers capable of handling the extremely complex tasks of
the future need, in addition to innate ability and
experience, a knowledge base which is as sound as possible.
As Gordon and Howell put it twenty years ago "Systematic
knowledge is the first ingredient of professional competence".

The analogies with medicine and engineering, while
valuable and instructive, cannot be pushed too far. There
are important differences between these professions and that
of management. In particular:-

    a.   Their knowledge base is much more limited and clearly
        defined than that of management. There is hardly any

194

field of human knowledge which can confidently be described as irrelevant to the practice of management. This poses a much greater problem of selection and distillation of the essential from the merely desirable. This problem is enhanced by the fact that the systematic study of management is relatively new, and the core body of knowledge much less well developed.

b.   In engineering and in medicine, the concepts of their underlying sciences can be experienced and illustrated in the laboratory. For most fields of management the only 'laboratory' is real life. The aspiring engineer can, in a laboratory, take of piece of steel, machine it to the required shape, apply a known stress to it and observe what happens. The aspiring manager cannot, on the other hand, apply a stress (such as a change in the market) to an organisation and see what happens. This places much greater emphasis on the need to blend theory with practice throughout the development process. Somehow or other the management student must be enabled to relate classroom theory to the complexities of the 'real' world.

The problem facing the management educationalist can be summarised thus - how can the aspiring manager be enabled to gain the knowledge and skills necessary for his or her task, together with the practical ability to apply them?

WHAT IS MANAGEMENT?

Numerous definitions of management can be found in the literature, but none provide a boundary definition. All embrace the concept of the application of resources to some specific objective - but this applies to all human work. Brown (1960) does put forward a boundary definition of 'manager', namely the occupant of a role having the authority to select, 'deselect' and differentially reward subordinates. One limitation of this approach is that it relates only to one aspect of the managerial task - achieving results through other people. In many roles generally regarded as part of 'management', this part of the role is minimal or even absent altogether. Examples of such roles are management development adviser, corporate planner and systems analyst. It may well be argued, as Jones and Lakin (1977) have done, that such roles have multiplied excessively in relation to 'real' line management, but it is difficult to imagine that they could be eliminated altogether.

As the author sees it, 'management' education should be concerned with all roles involved in the planning and monitoring of collective work - a high proportion of those above shop or office floor level. The point must be made that the process of management, and therefore the need for management education, arises in all work organisations, whether they be concerned with manufacturing, commerce, policing, health services or whatever. This point is regrettably obscured by the practice of describing themselves as 'business schools'. The term 'business' is even less precise than that of 'management' - (the shorter OED includes for example 'mischievous or impertinent activity'), but it has an undoubted, if unfortunate, connotation of manipulating money, rather than efficiently creating wealth. This paper is concerned with management skills, which include many, but not all, business skills - e.g. shorthand and typing.

It is also necessary to recognise a fourth source of complexity. Many managerial roles require expertise of a technological character, such as engineering or chemistry. Obvious examples are Chief Engineer, Chemist or Metallurgist, but the need for technological expertise is not limited to specialists. The production and marketing managers in high technology companies are, to say the least, at a considerable disadvantage if they do not possess a basic understanding of the underlying technology. The educational implication is that technological and managerial knowledge and skills must be acquired, in parallel or in sequence.

WHO ARE THE MANAGERS TO BE EDUCATED?

Taking the broad definition of management here assumed, the range of qualities and skills needed in different managerial roles is very wide. In line manufacturing management or general management, the skills of leadership are of prime importance. In other functions such as marketing or accounting, such skills are important, but no more so than more specialist expertise. At top levels the ability to formulate and deploy an overall strategy appropriate to the environment becomes of supreme value. Indeed there are probably only three kinds of skill and knowledge required by all managerial roles:-

    a.   The ability to conceptualise work - in Jaques* (1976) terms, to work at rank II or above.

    b.   Basic economic literacy - the recognition that the purpose of work is to produce added value.

---

* Jaques, on the basis of extensive research, concludes that there are discrete and qualitatively different levels of work, each requiring a corresponding level of conceptual capacity for satisfactory performance. Rank I relates to concrete work (e.g. shop floor), rank II to 'removed concrete' - e.g. first level of management, etc).

c.   Interpersonal skills, and particularly the ability to coordinate and take responsibility for the work of others.

It follows that managers will come from a wide variety of educational and experiential backgrounds. A few may have set their sights on management from an early age. The majority are likely to discover their ability and motivation for management work only after other kinds of work experience.

The development of managers is not thus a matter of identifying a potential managerial elite at an early age and putting it through a standard educational procedure. Instead it requires a flexible system for identifying and supplying the educational needs of a wide variety of people at different stages of their careers.

CURRENT SYSTEMS OF MANAGEMENT EDUCATION

a.   At school

While a relatively small proportion of school children will become managers, in democracies all will have the opportunity of influencing the economic affairs of their country and, to an increasing extent, those of the organisations in which they will work. Furthermore, school leavers need to make decisions about their careers, and it is essential that they should have some basis for assessing the opportunities which industry and commerce can offer.

It is a valid criticism of school education, at least in the UK, that little, if anything, is done to develop economic literacy or any understanding of how the goods and services which people require are actually provided. 'Business studies' are now finding their way into schools, but at a disappointingly low pace. It is highly likely that one reason for the disappointing economic performance of the UK owes a good deal to traditional educational attitudes - a point stressed by Nind (1981) among others.

b.   First degree in management and equivalent courses

The limitation of undergraduate management education were dealt with in some detail by Gordon and Howell (1959) and are frequently echoed today. These include the relative immaturity and lack of seriousness of purpose characteristic of many undergraduates. The need for managers to have a broad foundation of general education is also emphasised. Gordon and Howell concluded that "for most students with the motivation, ability and other qualities which promise a successful career in business, graduate training in business is better than undergraduate ... undergraduate years should

197

be devoted to a broad education with emphasis on
English, natural science, mathematics, history and
economics and other social sciences". On the other
hand they also concluded that "Undergraduate business
instruction can, if improved, serve a useful purpose
for those students strongly motivated towards a
business career who are unable or unwilling to take the
better, but longer and more expensive route", (i.e.
first degree plus experience, plus postgraduate degree).

There are few management educators or businessmen who
do not share this view, that first degree courses in
business (and their equivalents) are a useful but by no
means optimal form of management education.
Nevertheless, in most countries they are a large, and
often dominant sector. This is an interesting example
of the inflexibility of national educational systems.
In the UK, for example, the rapid growth of first
degrees as compared with the relative stagnation of
postgraduate courses is due to one simple factor - that
of student support. The undergraduate student receives
a mandatory grant, whereas the support grants available
for postgraduate courses are derisively small in number.
More generally, first degree education is convenient to
the system - it fits in neatly with the pattern of
education for other disciplines. The concept indicates
that education should continue without break from school
through university and then come to an abrupt halt.

c.   Postgraduate management education

This title is used to cover all forms of systematic
postgraduate study leading to degrees and diplomas of
universities and equivalent institutions.

When, as is frequently the case, such studies are
pursued immediately after a first degree, then, in the
author's view, the advantage over a first degree in
business is marginal. Probably the major argument for
immediate postgraduate courses is that they can bring
into the profession of management a number of very able
people who might otherwise tend to be attracted into
other fields.

Most of the major graduate schools in the USA, UK and
many other countries recognise clearly the advantages
of practical experience inbetween a first degree and a
postgraduate course, and give preference to experienced
students. Very few, however, (of which Cranfield
School of Management is one) make such experience an
absolute requirement. The practical problems are
formidable. At the ideal age, probably around twenty-
eight to thirty, most able men and women are well
launched in their careers, experiencing their first real
management responsibilities and often with family
commitments. A break of one or two years is something
which many feel difficult or impossible to undertake.

This accounts for the growing popularity of parttime postgraduate courses, long a feature of the American scene and now developing rapidly in some other countries. But the problem such courses pose are also very significant. To combine demanding study over several years with an onerous and responsible job is far from easy. On the other hand there is, or at least should be, valuable synergy between work and study. The day to day problems of work give relevance and motivation to learning. The new understanding developed in the learning process aids and gives added zest to work.

d.   Company controlled management training

This is a vast and still growing sector with a huge range of style and effectiveness. At one end of the scale there are a few companies who run what is virtually a modular MBA programme using their own training centres. Only in very large organisations can the cost of such an operation be spread over sufficient numbers of students to make it worthwhile and, of course, it carries the danger of excessive inbreeding. At the other end of the scale, there are still companies whose involvement in management training and development takes the form of sending a few managers on external programmes on a 'whose turn is it next' basis.

In the main, however, in career management development has become a much more professional process in medium and large scale companies. A new breed of specialists has arisen who have the understanding and experience to make discriminating use of internal courses, external courses, action learning, etc. This is a fertile field of cooperation between business schools and business (and other) organisations which brings considerable benefit to both parties. Such exercises can provide a valuable mix of manager development and organisation development. The growth of this kind of cooperation is perhaps the most outstanding advance in management education over the last few years.

There are, however, in the author's view, two dangers. One is obviously the inbreeding problem, due to lack of crossfertilisation between people with experience in different organisations. The other is less obvious but perhaps more serious. Only very rarely do such activities seek to provide the basic managerial literacy which is, in the author's view, essential for managers of the future. Accordingly, most forms of company controlled management training should be seen as a complement to rather than a substitute for thorough initial education.

The principal strengths and weaknesses of these four main types of management education are listed in the following table:-

Form of education	Strengths	Weaknesses
First degree in business	Fits into conventional education structure. 'Captures' some able people for industry. Provides time for thorough theoretical study.	Difficulty in relating theory to real practical problems. No experience basis for selection of students. Immaturity of students.
Immediate postgraduate degree or diploma	As first degree, plus can build upon sound first degree foundation.	As for first degree.
Postexperience MBA or equivalent	Builds upon, illuminates and structures experience. Thorough study. Makes selection on basis of track record practicable. Provides sound foundation for future learning.	Breaks into career – may necessitate change of employment. Family commitments may make difficult or impossible.
Company controlled management training	If well designed can be relevant to company and individual needs. Enables learning to be reinforced by immediate application. Can incorporate organisation development. Promotes effective business school/organisation cooperation of benefit to both.	Rarely provides thorough basic education in management. Usually costly. Danger of inbreeding.

This analysis points the way to what should be the main stream approach to developing managers for the future:-

a.   Selection of potential managers should follow significant work experience and when aptitude and motivation have become apparent, usually twenty-five to thirty.

b.   Candidates should come from a wide variety of educational and experiential backgrounds. Many will have first degrees (in a variety of disciplines) or professional qualifications, but this should not be an absolute requirement.

c.   Within the next few years candidates should engage in systematic studies totalling to the equivalent of at least one year fulltime.

d.   This study should be aimed at providing basic management 'literacy'. The basic discipline functions and skills required are already well documented, but need to be complemented by an understanding of the changing environment in which managers must operate.

e.   These studies must be reinforced by the opportunities to practice, refine and develop learning and skills in demanding and responsible roles.

f.   There should be a variety of forms of alternation between educational and experiential elements, e.g. the educational element could be either a single fulltime period, as in a conventional MBA programme, in modules, or in parallel with work, as in a parttime MBA programme.

g.   As managers are promoted into more senior roles, and as the environment changes and the state of the art develops, further short periods of study or action learning should be provided.

h.   The design and conduct of this management development progress should be the subject of continuous monitoring and review, by practising managers and educators working in partnership.

I would like to conclude by emphasising the concept of partnership. Management must develop into a singly fully competent and dedicated profession. This can only be achieved if educators and practising managers play a full part.

BIBLIOGRAPHY

AACSB/FME, (1981), International Conference, American Association of Collegiate Schools of Business and European Foundation for Management Development.

Binsted, D and Snell, R, 'An Investigation into the Development Requirements of Management Teachers in the UK', University of Lancaster.

Brown, W B B, (1960), Exploration in Management, Heinemann, London.

Cooper, C L, (1981), Developing Managers for the 1980's, McMillan, London.

Gordon, R A and Howell, J E, (1959), Higher Education for Business, Columbia University Press.

Jaques, E, (1976), A General Theory of Bureaucracy, Heinemann, London.

Jones, R S and Lakin, C F, (1977), 'The four orders of administration', Management Decision, Vol.15, No.4, p.367.

Mant, A, (1969), The Experienced Manager - A Major Resource, British Institute of Management.

Nind, P, (1981), See Cooper, C L.

Pierson, F C and others (1959), The Education of the American Businessman, McGraw Hill.

Revans, R W, (1980), Action Learning, Bland and Briggs, London.

14 The functions and organisation of university business schools

TOM LUPTON

PREAMBLE

In 1965 the British business community through the
Foundation of Management Education and the British
(Labour) Government jointly, equally and generously
funded the establishment of two post-graduate centres of
excellence in management education, one attached to the
University of Manchester and the other to the University
of London. A number of special requirements distinguished
these schools from other university-attached graduate
schools, and have strongly influenced their subsequent
development. First, they were to be financially
independent of the universities to which they were
attached. A government subsidy was to be granted
annually directly to both schools so as to leave them free
to develop independently, outside the budgetting
constraints of their own universities. Second, the
Government budget (which was channelled like all
university finance through the University Grants
Commission) was to be initially only half of what was
required to meet those running expenses of the schools
that were related to masters and doctoral programmes.
Third, there were generous government scholarships and
bursaries to support candidates for those programmes, and
some sponsorship from business firms. Fourth, and very
significantly for their subsequent development the schools
were required to earn the other half of their income by
charging economic fees for such Executive Development
Programmes as they could find a market for and to break-
even year by year. With the passage of time and the
reduction of government budgets for university education,
the schools have had to raise more and more from fees to
compensate for the falling off of government funding for
capital and recurrent expenditure, and for scholarship
income. Manchester Business School in 1982 is funded
one-third from government sources and two-thirds from its
own earnings, and the government share is still falling -
fairly rapidly.

I mention all this partly by way of background for those
who are unfamiliar with management education and the
funding arrangements for university education in the UK,
but mainly to emphasise the point that continuing

education for business managers has been from the beginning a very large part of what Manchester and London business schools have done. The same can also be said of the other university-attached schools in the UK.

Manchester and London provide a variety of residential short programmes ranging from one day to ten weeks, and from the very general to the very specific. They cater for managers at every level in organisations both public and privately owned, and from the very small to the very large. These courses take place in the same buildings and residential facilities and at the same time as the graduate and doctoral work, of the school, and are taught by the same faculty members. In any week of the year of these year-round schools, a member of faculty could have been engaged with the first year MBA class, the second year MBA class, a middle management group on a 10 week general programme, a group of very senior executives on the three week up-dating seminar, a supervision of a doctoral student and so on. He could also be engaged in other weeks, on other days, with managers on a programme specially designed for a particular company.

This has meant and still means that there is continuing and persistent pressure on the schools and their faculty to be relevant in all they do to the development needs of managers and the problems of their organisations. The criteria of relevance are applied to programme design, to the material presented, and to the method and style of presentation. Because fee income is closely connected to success in all those things, no-one who wants job security is foolish enough to ignore them. The funding of research and the provision of facilities for management learning, such as computers and audio-visual services, depend also on fee income, as indeed does financial support for MBA students as government finance diminishes.

However, the schools also have a requirement to be rigorous. That is to say, they must as university institutions promote the scholarly virtues. The research and publications of the faculty must stand-up to the established canons of judgement in fields of academic knowledge in the universe of free enquiry and their teaching must reach high levels of technical competence and objectivity. Like all university teachers, their careers depend to a large extent on how well they shape up to these requirements.

THE ORGANISATIONAL REQUIREMENT

Given a mission to become more deeply involved in continuing education on a larger scale how can (should) graduate business schools organise themselves to combine rigour and relevance fruitfully, economically, and flexibly? And what kind of people does one need to do it

effectively? These are not rhetorical questions. In
Manchester we have been seeking an answer to them for 16
years, and we are still changing in response to changes
in markets. Although my analysis of the problem will be
general, my references, naturally enough, will refer to
my own school. That is as it should be. Manchester has
notably been more adventurous and innovative than most
European schools in tackling the problem.

Let me put three questions and propose an answer to
them.

1.   What is (should be) the job(s) of a post-
      experience university based business school?

2.   How could (should) business schools be organised
      to do the job effectively?

3.   How shall their effectiveness be measured?

The short answer to question 1 is that the job of a
business school is to link reciprocally and fruitfully,
<u>fields of action</u> with <u>fields of knowledge</u>. This means
that the activities that go on in the schools and those
that faculty get involved in outside the schools e.g.
research, consulting, should all be directed to that end,
and that the schools should be organised so that the job
is done effectively.

FIELDS OF ACTION

I define fields of action as the settings in which
managers do their work (i.e. organisations large and
small, public and private, industrial and commercial) and
what goes on in those fields, i.e. what managers do, why
they do it and with what outcomes. How many business
schools see it as their job to be involved in 'fields of
action'? How many business school faculty could give a
convincing answer to the naive critic who says "Why don't
business schools teach about what managers do, rather than
what management professionals do (as professionals not
managers) and what academics prefer to teach"?

There is a pat response, namely that it is not and should
not be the job of a university school to be as practical
as all that. From such a perspective, the job of a
university is to train young minds to think straight and
to provide a protected setting where the young can
experiment with values and ideas, generally position
themselves in society and prepare themselves for
responsible citizenship and professional work. When one
thinks however of mature graduate students in their
mid-twenties already committed to a career in management
it is surely difficult to hold on entirely to such a
belief. It is even more difficult to justify it to, say,

205

a divisional managing director aged 45, attending a senior
executive programme. There are still some who would say
that university business schools ought not to get
themselves involved with such people. I cannot see how
we can escape involvement. Indeed I believe that we
should actively seek it.

This implies that we should address ourselves to such
questions as what managers do, what they ought to be doing,
what skills and competences they need so as to carry out
their tasks effectively? As it happens, there is some
systematic general knowledge about those questions.

Henry Mintzberg in his book "The Nature of Managerial
Work" collated the published results of all the systematic
observations he could find of managers at work, and added
some of his own. He concluded that there are ten
managerial roles, all of which can be found, in any
manager's job; weighted and proportioned differently from
job to job. Most managers recognise these easily. I was
one of the authorities cited by Mintzberg, (Horne and
Lupton 1965) and the middle managers I studied in
Birmingham, England in the early sixties were involved
in all the roles. I can recognise the roles myself in the
work I do as Director of a business school. The curious
thing is that when one compares the curriculum of MBA
programmes and the design of executive development
programmes with the work managers actually do, the problems
they encounter and their needs for skill and competence
to resolve them, one always feels a certain unease at not
seeing as many connections as there might reasonably be
expected to be.

In Mintzberg's list of ten roles there are three
interpersonal roles, three informational roles, and four
decisional roles.

Interpersonal	Informational
Figurehead	Monitor
Leader	Disseminator
Liaison	Spokesman

Decisional

Entrepreneur
Disturbance handler
Resource allocator
Negotiator

These are, of course, abstract general ideas derived
from empirical observations of activity. Some of the
characteristics of these activities are that they are made
up of episodes of relatively short duration, have great
variety, and exhibit no obvious regularity and continuity.

"Managers must shift moods frequently and quickly, fragmentation and interruptions are commonplace - especially for those managers closest to the action". (Mintzberg).

I have never ever seen even in my own school an MBA syllabus or an Executive Development Programme which gives instruction on how best to perform the ten Mintzberg roles, or how best to cope with managerial job characteristics such as variety, fragmentation, brevity, although the design of our programmes and projects give some opportunities for learning to cope. One thing is sure, that managers in their jobs do not usually require a skill of listening to lectures, making notes, and analysing cases. Most programmes are overweighted with these activities, with the resource allocation role, and to some extent the informational roles. Sometimes practice in management skills is included, e.g. in Manchester we use 'live' realtime consulting projects - but it is invariably the economics, the behavioural sciences, the finance, the accounting, the marketing, and the business policy; in short the fields of knowledge - that are the building blocks of classroom bound curricula, and not the learning of managerial competences.

THE FIELDS OF KNOWLEDGE

University business schools are commonly peopled by specialists; economists, sociologists, psychologists, accountants, financial analysts, operational researchers; marketing, personnel and production specialists; and they are marked off from each other by the boundaries of discipline departments - representing distinct fields of knowledge, each with their journals and jargon, and their own canons of judgement of published work; on the quantity and quality of which preferment so largely depends. When in the late 50's the US business schools were somewhat concerned about their image they were advised to make sure that their research outputs were as good as, or better than, those coming out of single discipline departments in universities (Gordon and Howells 1959). Some would say "and rightly so"! The Charter of my own university says, for example

"the object of the University shall be to advance learning and knowledge by teaching and research".

There is nothing there about fields of action, and there are many fine scholars at Manchester to whom the idea that what they are doing in research and teaching might or should be of fairly short term relevance to anyone, is unacceptable. It was in a Manchester laboratory that the atom was first split by Rutherford and his team.

He was asked afterwards in the first flush of his triumph or so the story goes, whether he could think of any practical uses to which his discovery might in future be put. He looked astonished and said that nothing came immediately to his mind.

The model that many academics work with is one in which fields of research are deliberately insulated from fields of action because of the possibilities of value contamination. The problems for research are therefore derived from the fields of knowledge and the findings are put back there to be criticised and improved upon. If others wish to turn the findings to practical use then so be it, but it is not the researchers job. I do not see how medical schools and business schools can be like that. They must derive the questions for research from the fields of action, and the results of research should be used and tested in fields of action so as to define more problems for research. If we look at it like that then our problem of business school organisation is defined. We must be organised not just to respond flexibly to shifts in the fields of action but positively to influence them - via teaching, action research/consultancy and in other ways to be described in a moment: we should also be sensitive to what is going on in fields of knowledge and positively to influence them too. Our faculty should however be orientated to task and problem rather than to discipline.

BUSINESS SCHOOLS AND THE ENVIRONMENT

But consider the business school in a changing environment as illustrated in Figure 14.1.

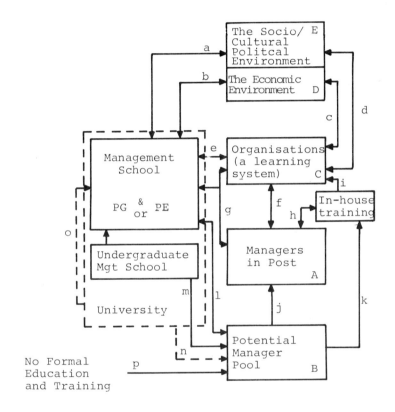

Figure 14.1 - The environment of management schools

There is no need to emphasise the speed, novelty and magnitude of the changes occurring in the general environment, e.g. the shift of emphasis in international trade from the Atlantic rim to the Pacific rim, the internationalisation of business, the energy crisis; and the changing political, cultural and ideological climates in which business had to be conducted; e.g. the resurgence of Islam, the political turbulence in the Middle East and in South America, and the awakening of China. The organisations responding to these same environments are (formally and informally) learning systems themselves for the managers and potential managers they recruit from universities and elsewhere. If the business schools do not respond adequately to their needs i.e. to supplement those learning processes, then organisations will do the whole job of management development themselves, which would isolate them from direct access to fields of knowledge and business school faculty from fields of action.

It is noticeable already that many large European and American companies are moving in this direction, or have already created their own business schools to serve their own management development needs. As Figure 14.3 indicates, there is a stern logic behind such decisions which links manager development to the wider corporate aims. From this standpoint the business school can be seen as a peripheral resource, a place where occasionally a company-trained manager can meet briefly with managers from other companies to broaden his perspective. Some companies regard the schools as sources of possible faculty in company programmes designed by company trainers. This can be a profitable sideline for faculty of business schools. In my view, this is not a healthy development. What is needed instead is a partnership which will join the strengths of company management with the strengths of business school faculty. In this way both enhance their competence via joint diagnosis and resolution of company problems. In Manchester we have developed a flexible vehicle for accomplishing this which we describe as the Joint Development Activity (JDA).

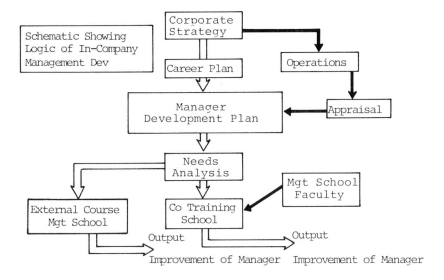

Figure 14.2 - Screens management schools from direct access
to company as environment for learning

A JDA begins when the senior managers of a company and
senior faculty of a school agree that it would be a good
idea to combine organisation development and manager
development in the company by mobilising business school
faculty and facilities as resources. Then, typically
there are four stages in the JDA process.

Stage I   In company:

             Company senior management working closely
             with senior business school faculty define
             a list of salient company problems. The
             company selects a group of younger
             managers to join the JDA.

Stage II   At business school - 4 or 5 days:

             Senior managers discuss the problems they
             have selected with the younger managers
             chosen for the programme.

             The company managers then explore the
             resources available in the business school.

211

Stage III   The problems are then shaped into projects
which small groups can work on. Business
school resources are identified and
attached to the groups.

Project plans are drawn up.

Stage III   At the company - 3 - 6 months:

Young managers return to the company.

They meet to work on their projects
perhaps one day a week in company time,
and they are given access to the data they
need. They also know that they can
telephone the business school for help and
can use its facilities as they reasonably
wish.

(During stage III there may be a short
project review sessions of one or two days
at the business school or in the company).

Stage IV   At company (one day):

Project findings and recommendations are
presented to the senior management of the
company during which the contribution of
business school and its faculty are
frankly assessed.

Every JDA is an essay in combining rigour and relevance,
a development experience for all concerned and a
contribution to the better performance of the company.

The costs of such projects are usually assessed and
agreed stage by stage, and the stages themselves might be
re-designed as the JDA progresses and experience is gained.

Question 2: Organisation of business schools

Business schools that are organised in traditional ways
find it difficult to conceive or set up and carry out JDA-
type projects. This is one reason why we in Manchester
have been seeking new organisational forms to facilitate
interchanges across the boundaries of business schools and
other organisations. Figure 14.3 shows (in only slight
caricature) the traditional business school organisation.
The significant interfaces are those between departments
of specialists and the fields of knowledge that those
specialists cultivate and harvest. Courses of lectures
and cases are made up of building blocks from single
disciplines, and in the teaching programmes the building
blocks are the discipline themselves. Students come in
directly from other schools and universities where this
form of activity is familiar, and graduate later into

212

fields of action. The modes of learning in fields of
action are very different indeed and in the carry over the
ex-student has to find practical ways of joining the rigour
with the relevance fruitfully, a task for which his
previous training gives him few skills. Some say that the
case study performs this function. I believe it to be on
the contrary a brilliant device for isolating the
classroom from problems in real life and real time, and
for distancing the teacher from the students.

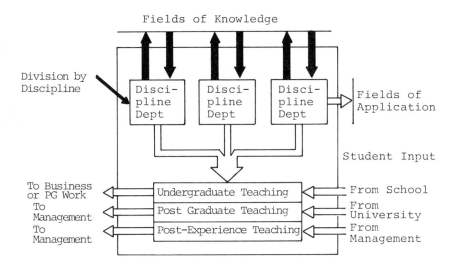

Figure 14.3 - Schematic of university-based management
            school (pre 1980)

In the traditional structure the links with fields of
action can only be through the individual consulting work
of faculty, or by using organisations as sources of data
for cases or for field-of-knowledge research. Sometimes
practitioners are invited into the classroom, where for
the most part they are not very much at home nor very
effective because the rules of the game are written by and
for the scholars.

Our solution at Manchester to the organisation structure
problem evolved and is still evolving from our innovative
style of discovering and organising processes for learning
such as the live project and the JDA. Sixteen years ago
we set our faces firmly against establishing discipline

departments as the main organising principle of the
School. We organised by task instead, and we derived the
tasks in the process of relating to fields of action. The
faculty and other resources to pursue the tasks are
enlisted by personal negotiation between programme
directors (who are faculty on job rotation) and individual
faculty members. All faculty members are encouraged to
start and direct new programmes. With a lively faculty
all this is a recipe for generating variety and that is
what has happened. To handle the variety we started to
group activities of similar kinds into Centres, each
relating to its own <u>fields of action</u> and each with its own
Director with a high degree of autonomy. At that point
it occurred to us that if what we were doing were further
developed it could be a general answer to the problem of
linking rigour and relevance. These general ideas were
set out in a paper I presented to Deans and Directors of
European Schools at Nijenrode in Holland just over a year
ago and are illustrated by Figure 14.4.

Section C

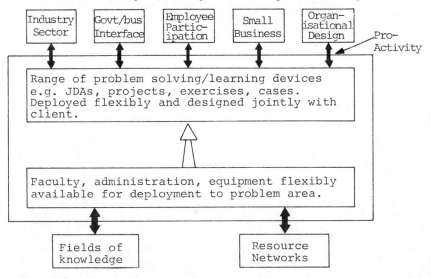

Figure 14.4 - Schematic of any management school post
1980

214

At the top of Figure 14.4 are some possible types of interface with the fields of action. The units of organisation (our Centres) are shown as pro-actively relating each to its own part of the field of action, and, as the double-headed arrows show, developing its own materials and methods for doing that job effectively. The materials and methods are also derived from fields of knowledge as faculty are deployed flexibly to the changing tasks deriving from fields of action, and as resources for the tasks are enlisted from outside the school through "knowledge networks" wherever they may be.

Since last year we have moved rapidly to consolidate an organisation pattern based on that general idea. We have six 'centres' now. Our International Banking Centre is related to a particular industry and companies in it. Our Small Business Centre deploys expertise about new enterprises and small ones; our Executive Development Centre meets a particular need for residential courses for managers drawn from many sectors. The Language Learning Centre at MBS was set up to meet an urgent current demand in international operations. The Graduate Centre is devoted to the task of preparing young people for managerial careers via Master and Doctoral Programmes. Finally, our Development Centre is devoted to experimentation with ways of linking fields of knowledge and fields of action.

The teaching faculty are all located in the Graduate Centre, and are a cost to that centre. Other centres negotiate faculty into their programmes of work at a transfer price and all faculty are available to all centres. All centres are cost centres, and are normally expected to earn a surplus year upon year which is transferred to a central fund to finance the general facilities which service them all - audio-visual, computer, printing, library etc. The central fund also supports faculty research of a fundamental kind. Research specifically directed to particular fields of action is funded from the centres' own earnings.

The variety that such a system generates demands an open, democratic and flexible set of co-ordinating procedures and styles, and ways of defining acceptable strategic and tactical directions. Like most organisations, we are better at dividing things up than getting them together, but we are aware of it and are working hard at it.

THE EFFECTIVENESS OF BUSINESS SCHOOLS

The answer to question 3 - how is effectiveness to be measured? - is by now fairly obvious. If the efforts of schools and their faculty are directed to fields of action then the criteria of success must be how those efforts contribute to the resolution of the problems that have been jointly defined and tackled in those fields of action, as in the JDA and the live project - where outcomes are known. The test must also be how well the research in fields of knowledge can be deployed in problem definition and resolution, as for example in action research, where the researcher is concerned with solving his clients' problems, and adding to scholarly output at the same time. The sole criterion can never be in a business school the volume of papers published in refereed journals, although that can be one measure amongst many.

CONCLUSIONS

I personally believe, therefore (amongst other things):

a)   that business schools are bound increasingly to become agents for continuing education for those working in public and private organisations.

b)   that such moves entail an active concern to link fields of action with fields of knowledge fruitfully for both, and to join rigour and relevance.

c)   that our traditional business school structures and styles are not well suited to do that job, especially in turbulent and volatile environments.

d)   there are structures and styles which could be appropriate, and that our Manchester experiment offers an example.

e)   that to change to such structures and styles is not easy; it might in fact be even more difficult in some societies than it is in others because the structures and styles needed predicate a degree of openness and adaptability that might not be easy to come by.

There are many problems about careers and rewards involved in the organisational "tilt" towards fields of action that we have made in Manchester. We are still trying to solve them. To describe what they are however, and how they might be resolved would take me beyond the limited scope of this paper, and they are probably more specific to the British academic labour market than the other issues I have addressed.

216

BIBLIOGRAPHY

Gordon, R A and Howells, J E, (1959), Higher Education for Business, Columbia UP.

Horne, J H and Lupton, T, (1965), 'The work activities of middle management' - an exploratory study, Journal of Management Studies, vol.2, No.1, p.14.

Mintzberg, H, The Nature of Managerial Work, (1973), Harper and Row, New York.

15 Management education for real

ROGER BENNETT

MAJOR DILEMMAS

Management education today seems to be in a quandary. Few
people would deny (and many indeed have proclaimed) the
importance of effective management in the development of
profitable enterprises and a sound economy. Many people
recognise the contribution that management education can
make in helping to develop more effective managers.
However, the current economic situation in many countries,
particularly the UK, has brought about drastic cuts in the
financial support available for management education.

In addition, many people have criticised the value and
contribution of management education (see, for example, the
reports by Mant, 1969 and Platt, 1970). The criticisms
have been varied: too academic in approach, poor standard
of instruction, remoteness from the real world of
management - as evidenced in a number of research reports
(London RMC, 1978; Thames Valley RMC, 1977). Lupton (1980)
reflects the criticism that graduates of business and
management education programmes are not always well suited
to take on senior management roles in large manufacturing
organisations. He feels, too, that many companies find
such programmes too broad and general to be of much use in
specific job situations. Yet companies still persist in
sending people on management education programmes!

This conflict between the need for management education and
the value and effectiveness of current management education
programmes has been with us at least since the 1960's and no
doubt will continue to be with us. This does not detract
from the requirement placed on both clients and providers of
management education to regularly examine what is happening
and whether it fits the needs of managers in organisation as
well as society as a whole.

There is another dilemma - a dilemma of approach or
philosophy. It is related to the conflict between need and
value but is to some extent separate from it. This dilemma
has been well articulated by Handy (1975). He described it
in terms of a continuum with instrumentalist approaches at
one end and existential approaches at the other. The
instrumental approach or philosophy sees the manager as a

218

person to be shaped and fitted to undertake those activities and purposes for which he is suited. It often results in management education approaches which are subject based and teach things to people. The existentialist approach sees the manager as a person who is able to develop his own purpose and activities in management. The manager is able to exercise choice and self determination. This approach sees the manager as an individual. The method used will be in terms of teaching individuals rather than teaching things to individuals. The management educator is a coach and tutor who helps facilitate the learning of the manager.

Thus, for any given agreed management education need, there may be quite different approaches to the education of managers depending on the philosophy or approach held by the management educator. The dilemmas involved here cannot be resolved simply by debating the virtues of one approach versus another. It seems to me that we can only tackle those issues when we have understood the requirements placed upon management education that stem from the needs of effective managerial performance. It is the purpose of this chapter to examine the needs of effective management and to attempt to establish a general framework within which effective management education can take place. Before we can do this, we must be clear as to what is meant by the term 'management education'.

WHAT IS 'MANAGEMENT EDUCATION'?

Management education is used in this chapter in a specific way. Many people will use the words education, training and development in loose and interchangeable ways. This may be because little thought has been given to their meaning or because it is held that there is no difference between them. On this issue I have to express a personal view. It is my contention that there is a significant difference between them, although the edges will be blurred and there will be some overlaps. For me, training is a process that is concerned with the acquisition and development of specific skills to do particular activities or jobs. Thus, management training will be geared towards helping a manager carry out a particular function or set of activities within that function.

Management education can be contrasted with this in that it is a process concerned with the acquisition and development of knowledge and skill which fits a manager to take on a role in management. It is thus more general and broad based than management training yet may be concerned with the development of certain skills. It therefore overlaps with training. Development is seen as a means of fitting and helping an individual to take on jobs at different levels or in different spheres of management in general. It may thus embrace both training and education activities. This chapter is concerned with management education as defined above. There will be implications for management training and development but the main thrust will be on provisions and programmes for helping managers to take their proper place in management.

In working towards some form of consideration of 'management education for real' we shall need to look at the requirements of effective management, the needs identified for the education of managers through various research studies, and how these come together, if at all, in shaping a framework for management education for the future. Although I shall in part be arguing from research based findings, my main argument will be a personal one. Whatever biases and prejudices show through, will have been developed over a period of nearly fifteen years as management educator, consultant and researcher. These biases and prejudices will have been remoulded and reshaped through experiences with national bodies in the UK concerned with the validation and funding of management education programmes. I hope that, above all, a streak of reality will glimmer through the clouds of bias and despair, generated by the very real warm and friendly relationships I have enjoyed with managers on a variety of management education programmes. It is they who must share at least some of the responsibility for what I say in this chapter.

THE AIMS TO BE ACHIEVED

But what are the aims of management education that must be taken into account by its providers? In specific terms, the aims of any management education programme must be related to the managers and problems for which it has been designed. Their needs and requirements have to shape the nature of the educational experience offered. It should, according to Koudra (1975), improve the specific knowledge or skills of individual managers. This was a view of external courses commonly held by companies. Whilst Koudra was referring to management 'training' courses, the emphasis on the individual is, if anything, more pronounced in educational programmes.

Thus, for example, Lupton (1980) appears to see the aim of such programmes being to prepare men and women with the necessary values, skills and ideas for careers in management and to be introduced to the necessary parts of the various disciplines relevant to management.

In general terms, the major purpose of all management education programmes must be to make a contribution to the improvement of the effective performance of managers, wherever they may operate. This was the key purpose ascribed to the business schools by the Franks Report (1963) and evident in many management education programmes more than ten years later, as demonstrated by Higgins (1977).

The requirements of 'management education for real' must therefore be consistent with the requirements of effective management in general. We need therefore to look at what we know about effective management.

REQUIREMENTS FOR EFFECTIVE MANAGEMENT

That 'management education for real' has to be related to the requirements for effective managerial practice is hardly contentious. Indeed, the work of the Centre for the Study of Management Learning at the University of Lancaster in the UK is very clearly based on this assumption. The view is that before effective management learning can take place, something must be known about what it is that makes for an effective manager. Whilst, no doubt, a good number of management educators have firm, if not fixed ideas or assumptions about the nature of these requirements, we should draw upon the available research evidence. The past ten years have seen a growth in studies of managerial effectiveness and of the publication of views based on experience and conceptual analysis. I shall be selective in presenting some of this material simply because a complete review is not necessary in this chapter and indeed would not be possible.

It is important to establish what we mean by effective management. Although opinions differ widely, as illustrated by Brodie and Bennett (1979) there does seem to be a degree of support for a view of managerial effectiveness which is goal oriented. I, therefore, am disposed to consider managerial effectiveness as the relationship between what a manager does and what he is expected to achieve within the constraints imposed by the manager himself, his position, the organisation and the socio-economic environment.

An increasing number of UK writers have put forward their views and research findings on managerial effectiveness. For example, Stewart and Stewart (1976) found in their research that of a range of factors and characteristics relating to effective managers, only about one third applied across different managerial jobs. The bulk were very specific to the work of managers. They established nine characteristics of the generally effective manager and these were:

self management

individual decision making

group decision making

relations with peers and superiors

management of subordinates

221

attitudes to change

social skills

communication, and

specialist skills/knowledge.

If such characteristics were to hold good across the majority of managerial situations, then it would seem that the Stewarts have presented us with a ready-made agenda for management education. Such an agenda would include the learning of self management techniques, decision making techniques, how to manage people and get on with people, how to manage change, how to communicate, and the acquisition of specialist skills and knowledge related to management in general. Later on we shall assess the extent to which this is possible.

Another UK study, carried out by Margerison (1981) concentrated on the requirements for success as a top manager. In this study a number of senior executives were interviewed and subsequently a larger number circulated with questionnaires. One set of findings had to do with things that senior managers felt were important to them in achieving success. There were five factors which were overwhelmingly endorsed as being of great importance. These were:

1. The ability to work with a wide variety of different people in different situations.

2. A need to achieve results.

3. Early overall responsibility for important tasks rather than trivial delegation.

4. Early experience of leadership.

5. Wide experience in many managerial functions before the age of thirty five.

These findings, and others stemming from Margerison's work, suggest that management education has an important but minor role in contributing to effective management. Many of the activities and experiences which his group of senior managers felt were important were those that, in the main, could not be adequately dealt with in the classroom. This view seems to be supported by Foy (1979) who argues in part for the need to move learning out of the classroom. That is, to set up a better relationship between the management education programme and the job being done by the manager. This could be interpreted as a move away from management education and more towards management training, or alternatively, the means of making the education more real.

A rather different set of requirements is put forward by Pedler, Burgoyne and Boydell (1978) who list what for them seem to be the qualities of a successful manager. These are grouped into three categories

1. Basic knowledge and information.

2. Skills and attributes.

3. Meta-qualities.

In the first category come the command of basic facts and an understanding of the relevant area of work. The second category is the biggest and is concerned with continuing sensitivity to events; analytical/decision making type skills; social skills and abilities; emotional resilience; and pro-activity (an inclination to respond purposefully to events). The third category is concerned with creativity, mental agility, balanced learning habits and skills, and self knowledge. These latter qualities are inherently necessary for the others to be put to good use. An interesting aspect of this classification is that it is general insofar as it can be applied to any manager and any managerial job. Yet it comprises elements which can be tackled through educational programmes and skill development programmes as well as those which are really part of the individual's make up. Perhaps 'management education for real' is all about distinguishing between such aspects.

A rather different formulation is that by Bennis (1981) who suggests five key traits for successful chief executives. These are:

1. Vision - that is a capacity to create a compelling vision of the desired state of affairs which the executive wishes to achieve.

2. Communication and Alignment - that is a capacity to communicate that vision to people in the organisation in order to gain support.

3. Persistence, Consistency and Focus - that is a capacity to maintain the direction of the organisation, especially when the going is tough.

4. Empowering Others - that is a capacity to create environments that can tap and harness the energies and abilities necessary to bring about the desired results, and

5. Organisational Learning - that is a capacity to find ways in which the organisation can monitor its own performance, review past activities and establish future ones.

These traits are consistent with an Organisation Development (OD) view of management and management development but do not immediately suggest an agenda for management education programmes. They do, however, suggest a set of criteria against which we might evaluate the effectiveness of particular programmes. In other words it might be possible to assess the extent to which a programme has made a contribution to each of Bennis's categories. This might be difficult, especially in separating out personal characteristics and qualities from those acquired through a management education programme.

Other research, such as that by Sank (1974) in the US, and Bennett and Langford (1979) in the UK has sought to determine the criteria for assessing managerial effectiveness. The work at Thames Valley RMC led to the establishment of six key criteria, supported by an analysis of the work of twenty three major writers and researchers on management performance. The resulting criteria were:

general effectiveness (e.g. goal setting, planning)

decision making

delegation

communication

job knowledge

relationship with subordinates.

These also suggest an agenda for management education programmes.

These studies seem to imply that management education must be concerned with improving the knowledge and awareness by managers of a small number of factors conducive to managerial effectiveness. Of the contenders, my list would contain the following, which are not in any order of importance:

managing the behaviour of oneself and of other people

tapping one's innate skills and abilities

making, implementing and controlling the effects of decisions

communicating with enthusiasm what is required to be done

knowing the job, the organisation and its components

managing change

drawing on previous experience.

224

Some of these (such as behavioural studies) can to an
extent be taught in the conventional way. Others (e.g.
managing change) require an experiential approach. Certain
of them (e.g. communicating with enthusiasm) cannot be
taught, but their importance can be established through
example and debate. One major omission from the list - and
one that is not often referred to - is 'politics'. All
organisations are political systems, and the effective
manager recognises this and is able to cope with it, even
using it to advantage. Politico-behavioural skills can be
acquired through debate and practice. They cannot be
gained from a textbook.

THE NEEDS TO BE SERVED

Establishing a realistic base for management education
requires an understanding of the needs it must serve.
Clearly, one important need is to meet the requirements for
effective management. But there will be other needs that
must be met. There have been many reports published which
have sought to identify these needs. For example, Reynier
(1982) has identified over thirty major reports and reviewed
their contents. Some of the reports - for example Pocock
(1977) - portray the views of small committees as to what
constitutes the need for management education in the future.
Others are based on research studies, such as Taylor (1967).

   The emphasis too has varied: in some reports it has been
placed upon the perceived needs that should be met or on
the demands for management education, whilst in others the
concern has been with resources and provision. Whilst these
reports are not comparable either in terms of their
conclusions or the methods used or the focus (some have been
regional studies, others have looked at sectors of industry
whilst some took an international view) they do provide some
interesting thoughts on the needs that management education
should serve. Here we shall briefly describe some of them.

   An important study in the late 1960's was that by Mant
(1969) who looked at the ways in which and the extent to
which, management education programmes met the needs of
experienced managers. He concluded that many educational
and updating programmes could not be justified. His studies
led him to the view that managers were developed more
successfully through 'on the job' training, projects and
collaborative consultancy work than through external
educational programmes. He thought there was a need for
better links between the academic and business communities.

   In quick succession, Rose (1970) and Leggatt (1972) also
produced reports on management education. They had a major
impact on the management education scene and helped
highlight some of the needs it might serve. For example,
the Leggatt report identified that many companies felt the
courses that met their needs were those in finance,
organisation and method, marketing and systems design. The

225

major needs identified had to do with managing people and updating technical knowledge. For senior managers, planning and decision making were found to be of importance.

In a more recent study Foy,(1978) suggested, among other things, that production management, industrial relations and small business management would require much greater attention in management education in the 1980's. A year later, a study by Attwood (1979) found that courses in finance, managing people and general management were most frequently used by his sample of 110 companies of the Times Top 1000. The least used courses were in production, data processing and purchasing. To some extent, this seems to go against Foy's findings.

There have been a number of studies of different sectors of industry. Most of these have been carried out by various Industry Training Boards. The report of one such study (CAPITB - 1975) suggested that the needs management education should serve would be those concerned with the requirements of organisations and their managements. These were seen to be the need for more adaptability, better productivity, paying greater attention to managers understanding their own behaviour and attitudes, better planning and the elimination of waste, and becoming more legally competent.

In the Iron and Steel Industry (1980) three key aspects of the role and training of supervisory management were identified: technological change, organisational change and interpersonal relationships. Communication was also thought to be important. Some core competencies were established and included technical know how, organisation and control of work, and the management of systems. Many of the ITB studies, however, have had more to do with identifying the nature of managerial work and the types of managers employed rather than specific needs that management education should be trying to satisfy.

A unique study of financial institutions is reported by Taylor (1977). He concluded that better links were needed between academic institutions and financial institutions, that more use should be made of tailor made in-company programmes, and that secondments of academics to the institutions should be considered. A claim was made for systematic use of OD and team building and for a change of style from paternalism to participative management. The topics that management education should cover were identified as those being specific to financial institutions: they included such things as manpower planning, corporate finance, marketing financial services, and strategic planning.

There have also been studies of an international and comparative nature. One of the earliest examples is that by Lowndes and Payne (1975) who reported on a study of supervisory training and development in Holland and Denmark. More recent examples have sought to review management education and training on a wider basis. For example, Pocock (1977) in his report for the European Foundation for Management Development reported on the views of a committee of nine people from education and industry concerning the education and training needs of European managers. The views were characterised by a mainly multi national and top management perspective. They saw the major concerns of managers in the future having to do with social, political, economic and technological environments. They also saw continuing education to be of importance. A recent study by Kanellopoulos (1980) found that management centres in Greece, Germany, the UK and the US anticipated a continued move towards more in company and job related programmes with the trend being more pronounced in the UK. This study is of interest since it reflects the perceptions of staff in management education institutions rather than those of managers in industry or organisations generally. To this extent it is portraying staff perceptions of their clients.

A very broad ranging report was published by the International Academy of Management (1981). Based on the deliberations of an experienced committee together with contributed papers, it sought to establish a world view of experience and needs in management education. The report quite rightly treats each region of the world separately - the needs and experiences do vary. For the 'Western' manager, admininstrative skills, interpersonal skills, intellectual ability, stability of performance, work motivation, values of the business, and entrepreneurship are seen to be important. The report gives an extensive listing of factors and sub factors in the operating environment likely to affect management and their related areas of knowledge. These range across political, economic, resource, ecological, technological, social and international factors. It provides a pretty exhaustive agenda for management education.

In addition to the national studies, there have in recent years been a number of studies of regional and local management education and training needs in the UK. An early and important example was that of Taylor (1967), which adopted a marketing perspective. Whilst this study set the stage for many later studies its conclusions are now reasonably dated. There have been several more recent regional studies of management education needs. In 1976, for example, the Welsh Regional Management Centre published a report of their study of the Perceived Need for Management Education in Wales. It went well beyond specific needs and embraced trends and demands. They established that management education programmes must be more closely linked with the real needs of the region. Those were to help organisations survive in fairly hostile commercial and industrial environments. They found too that many companies needed help in assessing their management problems. Advice on problem solving was seen to be required rather than panaceas.

A few years later a major report on the education and training of managers in the London region was published by the London Regional Management Centre. This looked at many aspects of management education and training including the numbers of managers to be trained, the trends in training and the use of particular sources of management training. As with a number of other studies, including those at the international and national levels, it found that many firms expected to do more of their training internally because it was cheaper, more convenient, easier to control and could be made more relevant to specific requirements of managers. External programmes were used where they were relevant to the needs. This is further evidence of the need for management educators to get more closely in touch with their markets and clients.

This latter point is a theme of a recent report on a number of studies of management education and training requirements in the Thames Valley area (Reynier - 1982b). The Thames Valley Regional Management Centre has, in addition to carrying a regional study of needs and provision, encouraged and initiated a number of local studies. Nearly 500 organisations have taken part in this work, which sought to identify size of the market, the business climate now and in the future, training practices, training organisations used, awareness of provision, attitudes to provision, trends in management training activity, and key training needs. Again a trend towards more in-house on-the-job related training was identified. The perceived needs varied from one location to another although there were some common strands. For example, industrial relations or industrial legislation figured in four of the studies: general management was thought to be important in two of the studies and finance in a further two studies. Computing and the use of micros was also an important perceived need. In terms of skills, it was found that interpersonal relations and communications skills together with financial skills were seen to be in demand. Of particular importance was the need for people to work effectively as groups.

Taken together, these reports throw out an impossible challenge to management educators. The range of needs to be met seem unending. However, some (more or less) common themes emerge. These have to do with the needs for

more in-company and job-related educational activities

closer links between the providers and clients of management education

improved knowledge and skill in managing people, interpersonal relations and industrial relations

better awareness and understanding of the technical
aspects of managerial work (including job knowledge,
finance, decision making, systems management, and
planning/administrative skills).

greater knowledge and understanding of the operating
environments within which management takes place.

These confirm and extend several of the requirements for
effective management derived from our limited review of some
of the research evidence. We now have some useful pointers
regarding the form and content of management education.

A DESIGN FRAMEWORK FOR MANAGEMENT EDUCATION

It seems clear that management educators and the courses
they design have to get closer to the real world of
managerial work. Their role cannot simply be to educate -
it must be to educate with a clearly identified purpose in
mind. That purpose has to be the improvement of effective
management. This is not to say that management educators
have not needed these requirements in the past. They have.
The pity is they have not gone far enough. Management
educators must continue to become more related to, if not
integrated with, their clients and other organisations, in
focussing their activities and efforts on organisational and
managerial problems, as pressed for in a number of reports
(see for example Mant, 1969; Owen, 1971; and Foy, 1978).

Achieving this is much easier said than done. There are,
as we have seen, many different needs and requirements that
can be placed upon management education. These can be met in
a variety of different ways through different lengths, types
and design of programmes, based on different learning
philosophies. It seems to me possible, however, to
establish a common framework for designing management
education that will provide the necessary links between what
Binsted (1980) has called 'temporary learning environments'
and 'work learning environments'. Temporary learning
environments are those which are created specifically to
facilitate learning outside the work situation, such as the
classroom or training laboratory. Work learning
environments are clearly those related to the context and
activities of the managerial job. All too often management
education takes place in temporary learning environments in
such a way that it can be difficult for course members to
relate the learning to the work situation. This is
particularly true of the full time programmes.

There seem to me to exist three major elements of a design
framework for management education that effectively links
temporary and work learning environments. All are concerned
in one way or another with enhancing or developing an
individual manager from a particular existing state of

learning (see Binsted 1980, section 4 for a further discussion on this). The first element concerns the existing level of knowledge and awareness of the manager. As we have seen previously, part of the aims and intentions of management education programmes is to improve this level of knowledge and awareness. However, different participants will be working from different starting points. An important consideration is how to bring to a common level the knowledge of all participants. Typically, we make those with a reasonable level of knowledge and awareness endure unnecessary repetition in the classroom whilst those with a lower level are brought up to date.

We could and should more effectively use in our design framework self study and possibly distance learning approaches. We can assess the learning requirements through preprogramme interviews with the participants and their bosses. It would then be wholly realistic to expect to be able to identify the type and extent of self study that would be required to reach the determined common starting level. We have the necessary technology and resources to do this: books and journals abound; many radio and TV programmes address managerial issues; learning packs of one form or another exist or can be designed and developed; all and any of these can be used by an individual to improve the initial knowledge, ideas and so on that are required to bring him up to acceptable level. A normal tutor course member relationship can still exist and assessments of the course members' progress can be made using essays, multiple question type assessments and other devices. The overall assessment would not lead to judgements about whether the course member had passed or failed but rather whether that course member had reached the required level of knowledge and awareness. Where that level had not been reached, then further self study would be needed.

The second element would extend the temporary learning environment from an individual basis to a group basis. This would be a conventional classroom approach to learning. It would use to the full the benefits and advantages of those classroom techniques which not only lead to the acquisition of knowledge and increased awareness, but generate debate and discussion on issues which are important to managerial work as seen both by tutors and course participants. This part of the design framework would be concerned less with acquisition of knowledge and more with generating an awareness and understanding of the problems and issues that managers face generally.

It would in effect be concerned with two phases of the learning cycle described by Kolb and Fry (1976). These are 'observation and reflection' and 'formation of abstract concepts and generalisations'. It would however draw upon a third element of the learning cycle, that is 'concrete experience'. This experience would be of two forms: one would be the work experience of the participants from which they would draw the problems and issues that are of concern to them whilst the other would be the concrete experience of their own self study. This latter is just as real an experience as any work day activity. The observation and reflection required would concentrate upon the relationship between them. It is hoped this would lead to the formation of useful and relevant concepts and generalisations. Conventional continuous assessment of assignments and essay papers can be used to evaluate performance. The ultimate requirements would be to test these notions in new managerial situations - as implied by the fourth stage in the learning cycle.

This testing phase represents the third element of our design framework. For the most part it can be achieved only through activities that are either part of or based upon managerial or organisational problems. It seems to me, therefore, that this third element should be based on some form of action learning approach. This approach seems to fit neatly with our previous elements. As Revans (1971) and others - particularly Body (1981) - have pointed out, action learning is based on a process which sees action leading to reflection then on to understanding and then back to improved or further action in an unending cycle. What is required now in our design framework is an opportunity for bringing together the increased knowledge and awareness through the self study programme with the increased understanding of issues and problems from the classroom programme in thinking about and taking action on managerial problems.

Many management education programmes lead to a qualification of one sort or another. This design framework will enable a more flexible approach to be taken to the achievment of such qualifications. In particular, there are two attractive features: one is that management education can be developed on a modular basis to fit the work, career and life patterns of managers doing the programme. The second is that a credit based assessment and award scheme becomes practical. This would allow, for example, credit to be given for satisfactorily completed self study assignments for undertaking a relevant short educational course, or for the project work in the action learning phase. Such considerations are by no means new - there are examples of modular schemes and credit based assessment (for example the Open University, the Cranfield School of Management and the Anglian Regional Management Centre). The view adopted here is that more management education programmes can achieve greater flexibility and relevance using such a design framework.

A SUMMARY VIEW

It is always risky to attempt to put forward a simplified view of a complex matter. Management education is such a complex matter. As we have seen, there are many demands

231

placed upon it - many needs and requirements to meet. Yet
we have also some common strands emerging, and have
considered the elements that might comprise a design
framework for management education. It seems to me worth the
risk of omitting some interesting side issues in order to
focus on the main requirements. We must adopt a view of
management education if we are to make progress toward
improving managerial performance. The view I am putting
forward draws on the findings of some useful research, yet is
essentially personal. It recognises the complexities of
modern management education and practice, yet sees in it
opportunities for simplification. It seeks to integrate
temporary and work learning environments yet accepts that
each is important in its own right.

This view is shown in summary form in the following diagram.
This shows the three elements of our design framework, under
each of which are listed those aspects of management that I
view as important. These have been derived from the review
presented earlier in this chapter.

The individual based self study must afford opportunities
for the manager to improve his knowledge and understanding of
the key subject areas that influence management. This will
form the pattern of the group based classroom learning on
issues which are central to performance in organisations and
which increase the managers' understanding of their work.
The action learning phase is primarily concerned with
application. The problems and issues to be addressed cannot
be spelt out in advance of a particular group coming
together. It is proposed that the learning set take the form
of a properly constituted 'learning company', operating as a
management team would in the best run organisations. The
clients would be the manager's bosses. If the client doesn't
like the actions proposed or taken, the 'learning company'
must address this as the next stage in its development. In
this way, continuing management education becomes real.

Some of the work to which this chapter relates has been
carried out by my colleague, Paul Reynier. I am grateful to
him for the opportunity of drawing upon his studies.

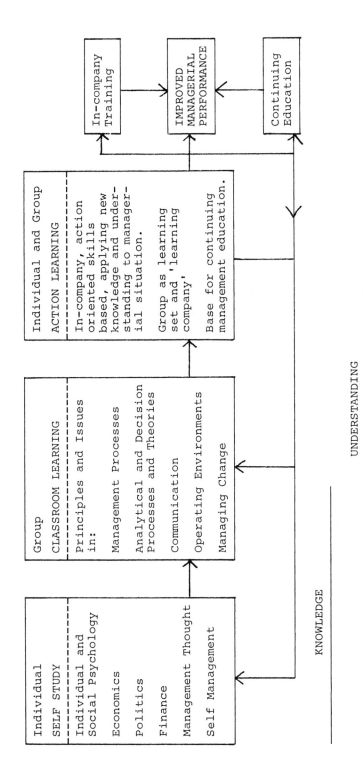

BIBLIOGRAPHY

Attwood, L T, (1979), 'Management development in British
companies', Journal of European Industrial Training
Monograph, Vol.3, no.8.

Badawy, M K, (1978), 'Design and content of management
education - American style', Managment International
Review, Vol.1, no.8, pp.75-81.

Bennet, R and Langford, V, (1979), 'How to measure managers',
Management Today, December, pp.62-5, 122.

Bennis, W, (1981), 'The five key traits of successful chief
executives', International Management, October, p.60.

Binsted, D, (1980), 'Design for learning in management
training and development - A view', Journal of European
Industrial Training Monograph, Vol.4, no.8.

Boddy, D, (1981), 'Putting action learning into action',
Journal of European Industrial Training Monograph, Vol.5,
no.5.

Brodie, M and Bennett R, (1979), Perspectives On Managerial
Effectiveness, Thamesman Publications. See also Chapters
9 and 10 of Bennett, R, (1981), Managing Personnel And
Performance - An Alternative Approach, Business Books,
and Bennett, R and Langford, V, (1982), 'Exploring
managerial effectiveness', Williams, APO - Using Personnel
Research, Gower, for further discussion on managerial
effectiveness.

Chemical and Allied Products ITB (1975), Some Indicators for
the Development of Management and Organisations Over the
Next Decade.

Foy, N, (1975), The Missing Links: Management Education in
the 80's, FME.

Foy, N, (1979), 'Management education - current action and
future needs', Journal of European Industrial Training
Monograph, Vol.3, no.2.

Franks, Lord, (1963), British Business Schools, BIM.

Handy, C B, (1975), 'The contrasting philosophies of
management education', Management Education and
Development, Vol.6, no.2, pp.56-62.

Higgins, J C, (1977), 'Management schools and industry',
Management Education and Development, Vol.8, no.1, pp.28-38.

International Academy of Management, (1981), Management
Education - A World View of Experience and Needs.

Iron and Steel ITB, (1980), Supervision - Now and Then, Deighton J J.

Kanellopoulos, C, (1980), 'International comparisons in management training and development', Journal of European Industrial Training, Vol.4, no.4, pp.22-5.

Kolb, D A and Fry, R, (1976), 'Towards an applied theory of experiential learning', Theories of Group Processes, Cooper, C L (Ed.), Wiley.

Koudra, M, (1975), Management Training - Practices and Attitudes, BIM.

Leggatt, T W, (1972), The Training of British Managers - A Study of Need and Demand, HMSO.

London Regional Management Centre (1978), Education and Training of Managers.

Lowndes R and Payne J, (1975), Supervisory Training and Development in Holland and Denmark, Anglian Regional Management Centre.

Lupton, T, (1980), Business schools in the 80's and beyond, Working Paper No. 49, Manchester Business School/Centre for Business Research.

Mant, A, (1969), The Experienced Manager - A Major Resource, BIM.

Margerison, C, (1980), 'How chief executives succeed', Journal of European Industrial Training Monograph, Vol.4, no.5.

Owen, T, (1971), Business School Programmes - the Requirements of British Manufacturing Industry, BIM.

Pedler, M, Burgoyne, J and Boydell, T, (1978), A Manager's Guide to Self-Development, McGraw-Hill.

Platt, J W, (1968), Education for Management - A Review of the Diploma in Management Studies, BIM.

Pocock, C C, (1977), Educational and Training Needs of European Managers, EFMD, Brunel.

Revans, R, (1971), Developing Effective Managers, Praeger.

Reynier, P, (1982a), Management Development in the Thames Valley: A Study of Congruence Between Needs and Resources. M.Phil. Thesis CNAA.

Reynier, P, (1982b), 'Management educators look to their market, Journal of European and Industrial Training, Vol.6, no.1.

Rose, H, (1970), Management Education in the 1970's - Growth and Issues, HMSO.

Sank, L, (1974), 'Effective and ineffective managerial traits obtained as naturalistic descriptions from executive members of a super corporation', Personnel Psychology, Autumn, pp.423-44.

Stewart, V and Stewart, A, (1976), Tomorrow's Men Today, IPM.

Taylor, B, (1967), 'A seller's market for management education in Britain', Management Decision, Summer 1967.

Taylor, B and Ryan, J, (1977), Management Training for Financial Institutions, Administrative Staff College, Henley.

Thames Valley Regional Management Centre (1977), Management education, training and development requirements in the Thames Valley Region, Working Paper No.2.

Welsh Regional Management Centre (1976), The Perceived Need for Management Education in Wales.

16 Where is management education and development going — some key questions

CHARLES MARGERISON

In this article I want to raise some important questions about management education and development. These are questions which I have asked myself as a result of talking with a large number of persons from many organisations and different industries. The answers provide my personal view on the state of management education development as it is at the moment and gives indications of where I believe it will move to in the coming years.

WHY HAS MANAGEMENT EDUCATION AND DEVELOPMENT BECOME AN IMPORTANT ISSUE?

Until the mid 1960's, there was little formal management education available. It was assumed that people would be trained in particular professions and they would then graduate by experience to become effective managers. In many companies loyalty and long service was the key factor in the management development process.

The conditions following World War II created many opportunities, and people with any level of managerial skill had the chance to come to the fore. However, it was recognised that people who were promoted under such conditions had to learn through practical experience. Little opportunity was provided for off the job education. For most it was a case of sink or swim.

By the 1960's many factors had pointed to the need for a more planned approach to management education. It was recognised that there needed to be educational organisations who specialised in the study and tuition of management topics. Many companies began to recognise that the traditional process of developing managers on the basis of experience needed to be supplemented by a more comprehensive approach to manpower planning and the development of people.

These moves were not based upon the charitable notion that education is a good thing. They were responses to the hard logic and challenge of the business environment. These challenges are still with us today, providing even more forceful pressure for us to develop more effective approaches to management development. Let us look at some of these pressures.

The professionalisation of management

The growth of large organisations has meant that people can
now make a career in management. Moreover, the day to day
operations of organisations are increasingly in the hands of
professional managers, and there is a market for their
services. It therefore becomes important that systems are
established to ensure that people are promoted according to
their ability and that the process is seen by others to be
fair. The old process of paternalistic selection has had to
give way to a more acceptable democratically based form of
promotion. Alongside this, therefore, it has been essential
to build up a total process of management development
involving manpower plans, objective setting, appraisal and
performance review ratings, followed by training and
development facilities and increasingly a planned approach
to organisation development.

Education demands more education

People coming into the management ranks since the 1960's
have typically had more formal education than their
predecessors. Therefore such people recognise the value of
training and are not content to rest upon the basic
qualifications that they have obtained. This is particularly
so in the field of management where considerable changes are
taking place in the economic environment and also in the
research that has generated new thinking and techniques
related to the management process.

The result has been a continuing pressure from staff for
management education in order that they can keep up to date.
Large organisations have therefore responded to this, not
only to maintain the overall knowledge and skill within
their organisation, but to ensure that managers have not
left to seek such opportunities elsewhere.

My observations lead me to believe that the modern manager
does have a view that the organisation is responsible for
providing him with continuing education, not only so that he
can do his present job well, but in order to keep him up to
date in the profession of management.

Pressure from below

Today's manager has to explain to his staff what is
happening and why it is happening. The days of the
unquestioned authority of the manager have gone in the major
industrialised countries. Educated, unionised staff demand
that their leaders listen to their views and give them
information as well as instructions.

It is therefore crucial that managers are sufficiently
knowledgeable to do this. Experience in the previous job is
in itself no guarantee to help one not only manage the next

level up, but to explain issues to staff. Of course it goes
beyond explanation. Shop stewards are elected not only to
represent but negotiate.

Therefore the pressure from below for managers to develop
their knowledge and skill is considerable. Too often
managers feel exposed because the shop steward knows more,
is better trained in negotiation and is more skilled at
presentation. In such circumstances the manager as a leader
is undermined. It is therefore clear why management
education has become important in the area of industrial
relations. Such pressures will continue at a greater speed
and intensity as we move into the 1980's with the
proliferation of consultation practices and more
professional union representation at all levels.

Fear of unionism

There can be no doubt in my view that one of the key
influences in stimulating the tremendous growth in
management education and development is the concern that
senior managers have that middle and junior managers might
join unions. In this sense management education and
development is, I believe, a political response to this fear.
In essence, senior managers are saying to people at lower
levels of management that they do not need to join an
outside body in order to obtain better opportunities for
advancement. By establishing a total process of management
education and development, senior management, I believe, are
signalling to other levels of management that they can 'look
after' the career needs of their staff, and by implication
also their salary and other compensating needs.

This is an important point as unions have been gaining
considerable ground in the white collar field. Indeed the
growth in the union membership has been far greater amongst
blue collar areas. Already large sectors of the white
collar labour force is unionised, notably in the civil
service, teaching and local government. Recently unions have
begun to record substantial numbers in junior management
levels such as foreman surpervisors within industry and
commerce. I believe there is now considerable concern that
middle and subsenior managers could join unions and therefore
management education is seen as a response to this challenge.
There is a concern in most large organisations that if
middle and senior managers do join unions, there will be a
question mark over their loyalty to the organisation and
they may seek their vocational interests not through the
direct executive line but through the channels of
negotiation. Therefore at the political level management
education is a strategic response not to the individual
needs but to ensure a collective approach to maintain
managerial identity and solidity.

My own view is that such fears are exaggerated. However
there are trends which indicate that the manager of
tomorrow will be a person of multi loyalties and will not

just be the servant of the organisation. He will typically
have loyalties to his profession, his own career, his
family, and I believe also to his union, which may well
transcend his loyalty to any specific organisation.

The pressures of competition

It has always been said that there is room at the top for
good people. Equally, it has been true during the last
fifteen to twenty years that with the expansion of industry
and commerce there has been a shortage of trained managers
who can cope with the demands of wide ranging business.
There has therefore been a very active market in managerial
talent. A whole new profession, indeed an industry, of
selection and recruitment consultants has grown up. Within
this specialised breed, a management selector, called the
head hunter, has emerged. It is a lucrative business and
indicates the state of the management market.

Organisations are very aware of these pressures and
therefore wish to ensure that their own staff get the best
opportunities within their organisation without being
tempted elsewhere. An essential part of this clearly is
providing first class management education and development
facilities. Therefore it comes as no surprise that
considerable amounts of money are being made available both
for internal and external education programmes. In
addition, considerable time and energy has gone into
designing appraisal and performance review mechanisms.

STANDARDS FOR PERFORMANCE AND PROMOTION

It is quite easy to see a tradesman or an unskilled worker
as doing a poor job. The result is usually there in a
visible form. However, it is usually more difficult to
assess how well a manager has done. A lot of his work is
intangible. Typically, if you ask several managers how they
are judged, they will refer to 'being in the black' or
'having a good bottom line'. Such terms have become
virility symbols of modern management.

However, as organisations get larger and more complex, it
is vital that standards are set and that people are promoted
for achievement. Moreover, this needs to be done not only
on the basis of personal whim, with one manager doing it and
another manager not, but on the basis of company policy.
Therefore, management development has been a way in which
improved managerial standards have been sought. All sorts
of methods have been tried, and currently there is
considerable concern in many organisations to establish
effective performance appraisal meetings so that overall
policy can be translated into action at all levels.
Moreover, such performance appraisals are often used not
only for resetting objectives, but as a basis for both
promotion and compensation. Therefore, a considerable

amount of the work of the personnel specialist is now devoted to management development in designing, implementing and monitoring the management appraisal process.

LEGAL BACKING IS A GREAT STIMULUS

In Britain at least, there has been considerable stimulation to management education through the various laws that have been passed. In 1964 the Industrial Training Act was a prime factor in setting up industrial training boards who could exercise a levy tax on companies to ensure that training was done. Although this has now been changed to a levy exemption system, the overall effect has been to get companies to spend money in the field of training and this has had a considerable effect on the field of management education.

Indeed the work of the industrial training boards has recently singled out the field of management education for special attention. This comes at the same time as initiatives from the Manpower Services Commission in this field.

In other countries there have been similar developments. In France, for example, companies have to give a specific percentage of their payroll costs to the training and development of staff. On a wider basis, the European Economic Commission has laid aside considerable sums of money for research and also for training, not only in technical fields, but in the management field also. Therefore, it is not surprising that management education development has grown, given the considerable governmental support that it has had. It is likely that given the present state of unemployment and the trends that are predicted for increased unemployment in the 1980's, that further support will be forthcoming. Rather than have people idle, governments prefer to have people in training. A very important form of such training will be management education. The dangers are clear. We may well raise people's expectations as well as their skills and knowledge, but if no jobs are available we shall have a very well educated, dissatisfied group of people.

MANAGEMENT EDUCATION AS A BUSINESS

Along with the trends that we have described, a number of specialist organisations have grown to service the demand. Management education is a commercial proposition. There is now a major consulting industry in the field. There is considerable competition between both large and small consulting organisations to provide not only the knowledge, but also the educational programmes. In my view, many of these organisations have come into the market without sufficient resources, and there is a danger of oversaturation.

In addition, the educational institutions have developed rapidly to provide courses and programmes. The universities, polytechnics and technical colleges over the last fifteen years have flourished as an integral part of this new market. Typically they have had problems in separating out their commercial and their research functions. We shall say more of this later. However, it is clear that the major state funded tertiary organisations are now part of the commercial market place and need to manage their operations as effectively as they instruct others.

There can be no doubt, however, that the money which has been put into developing business schools in particular as prestige places for research and education has provided considerable impetus to management education as a whole. We now have literally thousands of people applying their minds to the problem of industry and commerce, and research publications serve not only as knowledge but as a form of marketing.

Industry and commerce, of course, has supplied a lot of the funds, particularly for business school operations and is now demanding practical return. However, many business schools would prefer to go the way of academic rather than commercial interests, and here lies a fundamental conflict. Nevertheless business schools have made a considerable contribution to the prestige marketing of management education and development, and, as we shall see later, are increasingly at the forefront of new approaches to developing the field with particular regard to continuing education.

The move of educational organisations into the management development field is, however, only a response to the opportunities created by the various pressures that have been outlined. My view is that these pressures won't go away. During the next few years we shall see managers demanding more management education as their professional awareness grows. The fear of managerial unionism will continue, while the competition for good managers will speed up. Governments will continue to put pressure on for more management training at all levels and staff groups will exert increasing pressure on managers to keep them up to date. Internally organisations will further recognise the need for sound and fair management development systems, and externally the marketing of educational and consulting services to meet such concerns will increase. The future for management development as an area of activity is indeed bright. There are too many pressures on everyone for it to decline in popularity.

HOW SHOULD WE HELP MANAGERS LEARN?

There has been considerable experimentation in the area of educational tuition for managers. Clearly experienced managers do not like to sit for long hours behind desks

242

listening to lecturers pontificating about the latest theories and research. As managers, they are men of action and have a very varied, usually exciting, but invariably demanding job. The traditional way of tuition invalidates all these factors associated with management. The lecture makes the student into a passive person in the education process and it assumes that the lecturer has the knowledge and that the student has little to contribute.

The people who come to management programmes are usually very experienced in the day to day problems of managerial tasks. Moreover, they are usually well educated in one specific field, whether it be engineering, accountancy, personnel or some other professional background. In addition, they come for a particular purpose. Their reason for attending is associated with particular problems and opportunities that they see in their business. They therefore wish to contribute to the agenda and to have particular issues which concern them discussed. They do not wish to be taught in the formal sense, but rather engage in a dialogue on how new ideas and methods can be applied to their particular work situation. Over the last few years we have seen, therefore, a number of innovations in educational method and these will continue into the 1980's at a rapid pace.

The introduction of computer assisted learning systems will speed up the process from a technical point of view. However, in addition to this there are major initiatives being taken to help managers engaged in self development. All this goes way beyond the other traditional educational method of the case example.

The case approach has stood test of time and proved very valuable in getting managers to look at specific examples and the way in which techniques could be applied. However, the weakness of the case method has always been that it deals with other people's problems at a time and place removed from the present. In a sense it is learning by analogy rather than by direct example.

Whilst the case method will continue, I believe that its real value in the future will be in developing real life cases based upon the contributions made by participants in a particular programme. This is to say they will bring with them their own cases. Moreover, they will consult with each other on how to tackle these particular cases. In doing so they will not only gain practical interest into their specific problem, but develop the skills of consultation and help.

Alongside this development there will be a continuation of the move towards experiential learning. This has already taken many forms, such as getting managers to work on simulated tasks and developing particular experiences so that participants can learn in a practical way without too many risks. At one level the old outward bound system of

learning is a classical form of experiential development.
However, this has been brought into the classroom by
developing small scale management exercises which can be
tackled within a relatively short period of time. This has
made an enormous impact, but really needs in the future to
be reinforced by better feedback systems so that people can
really understand what it is they have done.

Alongside this development there have been major advances
in business games ranging from the sophisticated computer
applications through to small scale paper and pencil tests.
I believe these are invaluable in giving people an overall
idea of how the complexity of business revolves around
integrating financial, marketing and production policies
together with manpower policies. However, they have not been
too valuable in my view for helping people learn about the
behavioural aspects of business. Invariably the computer, if
used for such a purpose, has a seductive element which rules
out consideration of how one achieved ones results in favour
of having yet another go for the jackpot.

Behavioural training, however, has grown apace and is one
of the, if not the major sectors of management education
today. The range of programmes goes from the highly
structured managerial style and problem solving course,
right through to the relatively unstructured encounter groups
and T groups. However, the latter have fallen into
considerable disfavour in the last few years as research
results have shown little transfer effect to the business
operations.

Instead we have seen a move towards more specialised
behavioural training programmes with special courses on
things like negotiating skills, interviewing skills,
communication presentation skills. In this the television
facility has played a very important role and will continue
to do so into the 1980's. Managers want to learn how to
perform better, not in general but in specific areas, and
the television gives very powerful feedback of performance.
Again we need to improve our feedback systems and processes.
It is a time demanding activity and requires very skilled
staff to assess the learning process.

This leads to what is in fact the major development that I
see occurring in the 1980's. Essentially we will move from
emphasis on the teacher to emphasis on the learner. We will
move from external inputs to internal reflection. We will
move from impersonal analysis to personal exploration.

What does this mean? It means in essence that the most
important person in management programmes will be the
managers themselves. They will be expected to bring with
them to programmes issues which they wish to discuss and the
teachers will be expected to build their contributions
around the agendas of the participants. This will demand
far more flexibility from the teachers than we have seen
previously. Secondly, the managers will be asked to learn

244

far more by looking at their existing personal way of operating rather than looking at someone else's way of operating. Positive introspection will therefore be very important for learning. Thirdly, we shall see far more of the personal audit apprach through checklists, questionnaires and managerial style indicators. This will range over all functions of the business and in the area of leadership which has innovated in this particular respect. Fourthly, we shall see far more learning by interpersonal consultation and practice rather than didactic exposition. Fifthly, I believe that the management programmes of the future will be spread out over a period of time on a modular basis so that managers can learn, then implement, then learn again before going back to implementation. This process of reinforcement, as we know, is the most effective form of learning.

This is not to say that the management teacher should not teach. What it does say is that the management teacher must become more flexible in the way he teaches. He will have to build upon the agendas set by participants rather than just teach his theories based upon historical cases with only the vaguest form of discussion about the current particular problems brought by members. In future the management educator will be expected to take the initiative in setting the area for discussion, but then relate his contribution to the specific requirements of the participants.

In addition, we shall therefore see much closer relationship between management education and the role of the teacher as an organiser of learning. In this sense the teacher will have to become a manager. Equally, the manager will have to become a teacher. As we all know, it is the teacher who learns the most. In this sense, future management programmes will have to be organised so that the managers can become active learners about their own situations in the context of new theories and methods, but worked upon in a practical way using both teachers and fellow students as resources.

We shall, therefore, move more towards management education as a resource concept. No longer can we begin to think of dispensing knowledge and skills. Instead we must see education establishments as resource centres. This means the teachers will be resources as well as other participants. Their job is to provide an environment within which people can work and take an active part in acquiring what is required to improve their managerial abilities. This will take some time to develop, but the beginning has already been made. What it essentially means is that the management teachers must take a lead and set up opportunities where people can learn from each other. It is in this sense they must become managers of learning.

HOW WILL MANAGEMENT DEVELOPMENT LINK WITH ORGANISATION
DEVELOPMENT?

It is clear that there is an emerging area of
professionalism within management which we can call
management development. However, it is an integral part of
the management function, not something separate.

Therefore, let's start at the individual level.
Management development is very much an individual thing.
For anybody who is going to succeed in managerial work, he
must take the responsibility upon himself to seek the
initial basic training and have the drive and motivation and
discipline to pursue it. Although opportunities can be
provided, it is the individual who must plan his own personal
development. This means taking probably at least a three
year perspective and drawing up specific action plans and
having a five to ten year plan of one's career within which
to shape these specific developmental activities. If one is
working for an organisation of any size, one should therefore
look to the facilities that they have in the structure for
developing one's career.

During the 1980's, people will increasingly judge a
company on its approach to management development. Some of
the questions they will raise will hit at the key issues of
work and employment. Is the aim to try and develop people
from within, or always go outside and look for talent.

Secondly, one should look at the selection policies for
both external and internal people. Are the selection
criteria well laid out and is selection based upon fair
principles and practice. It is important that an
organisation does select people upon merit and it is
therefore a good first step to look at the way in which a
company goes about selecting both new staff and people who
are to be promoted from within.

Thirdly, it is important to look at the ongoing assessment
that a company makes of its managers. What sort of an
appraisal system, if any, is established? How far is the
appraisal an active system rather than one which just
involves passive form filling. If the performance appraisal
system is really working, then you will find that people are
promoted on the basis of their record.

Therefore, management development does imply a great deal
of the relationship between managers and their bosses. It
means that the manager should be looking all the time towards
the overall development of his staff and being encouraged
through the policy and resources of the organisation to help
them do their job better and develop themselves for future
positions.

However, the prime factor is usually trying to improve
people's performance in their existing job. This is where
management development can make its biggest impact. It is

not courses or training events which can really make the improvement. It is day to day management. The manager subordinate relationship is the key in successful management development. If this is not working, well, then courses and educational activities will not improve things in any significant way. The motivation and energy that needs to go into improving performance must come through the interactions that managers have with their staff. For if the management development system in your organisation does not seem to be working, first of all look at the policies and then see whether individual managers are carrying these out. It may well be that they do not feel sufficiently knowledgeable about the policies, or have the skills to conduct the appraisal and the development process in the proper way. At this stage, then managerial conferences and training programmes may well be one answer. However, the fundamental fact is that we need clear policies and the desire to implement them at all levels of management if the management development process is to take off.

Now what I see happening in most organisations is that at the policy and resource level, the management development process is being taken seriously. For all the reasons that have been listed above, major organisations are now bringing a considerable amount of energy into developing their staff. Many organisations are employing specialist advisers in the field and devoting a considerable amount of time so that people can prepare themselves to do their existing jobs better and plan their careers for the future. The real problem, as I see it, is in the implementation of these policies.

Typically people don't have sufficient time. I hear, as I go through most organisations, that the cares of the day take up the available hours and people have little time to sit down and discuss how the job has been done or should be done in the future. In most cases, people are too busy playing the game to blow the whistle and discuss how the game should be played.

This indeed carries over to the performance appraisal process. Many managers indeed say there is no need for this as they are continually appraising their staff and do it on a daily basis. However, there is no doubt in terms of its overall effect on the work process, there is a need for a disciplined approach. This will usually mean conducting a regular review, at least annually, and often biannually if not quarterly, to make sure that the work which has been assigned is being done and that people's development needs are being taken care of in order that the objectives can be met.

In this sense the appraisal process is no more and no less than an audit. Just as one would audit the books of the company so it is important to audit the personal and managerial development of people. This, however, should not be done in an inspectorial way. The aim is to facilitate

247

development rather than to check and inspect. To this end the performance appraisal process should be a continuing thing. It should be a positive thing. Unfortunately it is often seen as a once a year phenomenon having little relevance to the business and day to day work. Moreover, it is often seen as a negative thing whereby the boss is seen to be publicly criticising his staff. Clearly, if this is so, then the foundations of management development in the organisation will not get very far. The important thing is that managers must feel that they are working together, not only to develop their own competence, but that of the organisation.

Therefore, it is important that we look at the organisational aspects of management development. One clear feature is the importance of doing effective manpower planning. All organisations in the process of change need to make projections on the need for various levels of skill and ability. This clearly involves an understanding of the managerial requirements for the next three to five years. Too many big organisations go in for new plans without realising the need for managerial talent and, therefore, failure is often a result of not having sufficient people with managerial skill at the time it is required. To a large extent this can be overcome through careful assessment and looking at the talent within the organisation on a regular basis. Therefore, the appraisal process can play a vital role in this as well as helping at the individual level.

Further, on the organisational side, it is important to recognise that many of the management development issues cannot be resolved at the individual level. It is not just a question of giving people more knowledge or more skill. Moreover, it is not just a problem of helping understand their job better. The issue relates to the way in which people work together in an organisation. Therefore, management development needs to be seen very much in the context of organisation development.

A clear example of this involves team building. One manager's job may well depend heavily on the success of another's manager's work who is working in the same team. If they don't work together, neither can win. It is important therefore, that in looking at the plan for individual management development activity, that one also looks at the plan for having effective work teams. Considerable work has now gone on to develop strategies and methods to get teams to work together more effectively. It will, however, be a major thrust in the 1980's to link management and organisation development together.

The whole issue of organisation development is one of bringing people together so that they can thrash through problems and issues in order to come up with solutions which will enable people to tackle problems both collectively and individually. Organisation development essentially means helping people within the organisation who have different geographical places of work, to share information and negotiate contracts and agreements on how they can achieve the tasks and objectives. This is easier said than done. It often requires the intervention of external people who can bring together people to discuss issues openly. In this, the business schools have increasingly taken an active role along with consultants and individuals who are skilled in process consultation work.

All these areas will continue to flourish. As organisations get more complex, what we need are people who can cross boundaries and bring together people from different functions, speaking different languages, so that we can get some common approach to the way in which we should work. It is the intangible area of management. We will see tremendous growth in people who are skilled at the interface areas. Management development will increasingly link with organisation development. At the moment there seems to be separation of the two, with management development placing more emphasis upon training and education of individuals. However, the second major phase which will emerge strongly in the 80's is to link together these two functions so that wherever there is educational training of individuals, there is an integration into the way teams work and the way these new ideas and methods can be spread throughout the organisation at all levels of management. In essence this means that management education must link much more firmly in to the central tasks of individual organisations. This means that management education will become more specialised in dealing with particular organisations rather than with particular topics.

Management development will become task based rather than knowledge based. This fusion of management and organisation development will in itself produce a major field of research study in the 1980's and be one of the main advances that I foresee in the whole area of managerial work.

WHAT ROLE WILL EDUCATIONAL INSTITUTIONS PLAY IN THE FUTURE OF MANAGEMENT DEVELOPMENT?

The fundamental role of educational institutions in industry and commerce until about fifteen or twenty years ago was concerned with apprenticeship training and specialised instruction for particular professions such as accountancy or engineering. It is true that there were earlier initiatives, particularly in America, to develop management educational training, but these were limited in size and confined in the main to the American scene. It is only recently that management education has become a world wide phenomenon with specialised institutions such as business schools and other organisations providing wide spectra of education activities.

Indeed, until recently it was assumed that anyone who was

249

sent on a management programme was inadequate at his job.
In some organisations today there is still a suspicion that
if people have to go on a management course it is indeed a
remedial programme rather than a development programme. I
am pleased to say that this is fast disappearing and will,
by the 1980's have disappeared entirely. Indeed, the
reverse situation will occur. If people are not sent on
management development programmes, it will be assumed that
they are not performing appropriately and that they will not
be advancing in their career. Already we see that one of
the preconditions for promotion is that people should attend
management programmes and keep up to date with current ideas
across many subjects and understand developments in other
industries and countries.

This augurs well of course for the educational
institutions. However, there has been a lot of competition
in this particular area over the last decade and such
competition will increase. For the moment I shall confine
myself to the business schools and talk about the work that
they have done. Business schools have been somewhat elitist
in their approach. They have gone for the top and senior
ranks of management, charged high prices and put on
programmes which are more strategic in their level rather
than technique based. There is now, I believe, a move
towards being less elitist and more broadly based in the
material that is offered. However, business schools will
tend, I think, to be the market leaders in price and should
always be at the forefront, putting forward the new ideas,
while trying to do so by using methods which are practical
and relevant to the day to day working of managers.

Unfortunately one of the major criticisms of business
schools is that their teaching methods fall far short of
what is required. Often the topics chosen are of interest,
but academics tend perhaps to still teach the way in which
students on other courses are taught. Essentially what the
businessman needs is a practical guide rather than a
theoretical discourse. This means that business schools
have got to look much more closely to their educational
methods and this, I believe, could be the biggest area for
research and development and application that they could
invest in in the next decade.

There is no doubt, however, that the business schools have
given a lead in many areas in indicating what can be done.
The Master of Business Administration programmes probably
form the cornerstone and provide the basis for a
professional group of managers across many industries.
Already, in Britain alone, about one thousand people with a
Master of Business Administration degree, or the equivalent,
qualify each year. If we add the graduates from the United
States, Europe and Australasia, we find that each year
throughout the world we are now training a vast army of
people who will have the basic conceptual understanding of
business, together with many of the technical skills that
are required. This in itself won't guarantee success in

business but it does provide the foundation within which people can get experience.

There will therefore be a massive change in the management development structure of organisations. I believe we now have the basis for an educated corps of managers, equivalent to those which we would find in medicine or any of the other major professions. I am not saying we have similar standards as yet, but with the numbers of people who are being trained with the basic qualifications there is no doubt that a vast change is going to occur in most large organisations. We shall have people who speak similar languages at technical and commercial levels. They will expect high standards. The competition for places in organisations will be considerably increased.

Alongside the indepth work with the Master of Business Administration, we have the short programmes which managers attend to bring themselves up to date, whether it be in marketing, finance, human resources, or business systems. These provide the opportunity for experienced managers to refresh their knowledge and ideas and keep up to date with current events. They don't provide in indepth foundation, but for people who have considerable experience in business they do provide an integrative framework.

I believe we now have, as we go into the 1980's, a most interesting situation. Most of the postwar managers have had little formal management education. They gained what they knew by experience. Therefore we are getting a meeting of two cultures. It is important that the new educated group of managers learn from the experienced managers. It is equally important that the older group are willing to learn from the younger qualified group. To this end it is vital in the management development process that opportunities are provided for the sharing of ideas and experience. This can be done interally within organisations and can provide tremendous energy in improving the overall level of management if it is done well. However, I find little attempt is made to engineer such meetings and I think it is important in the 1980's that this interface between the experienced group and the newly trained group should be facilitated as an integral part of both management and organisation development.

My feeling, however, is that business schools and similar organisations have concentrated far too much on courses and training events. There has been insufficient attention to the interface between the organisational work that goes on in business and commerce and the way in which business schools can contribute to that on a regular basis. There have been some notable exceptions such as the joint development activities at Manchester Business School and the action learning projects initiated by Revans. My colleagues in the Management and Organisation Development Research Centre at Cranfield have also made major contributions in this difficult area.

During the 1980's we shall see more of this interface work and an extension of the current initiatives. Project work from students in industry and commerce as part of their formal study will grow. Reciprocally managers will recruit for temporary periods on their projects special help from educational bodies whose interest is in researching new developments while contributing to existing problems. However, such moves need to be seen in the context of changing approaches to educational methods.

A particular facet of this will be the move towards continuing education in the management area. Already we have seen the Open University succeed in providing opportunities for lifelong education. We shall shortly see similar innovations in the particular field of management. Attempts have already been made to launch the open business school. Current work at Cranfield School of Management is exploring a major initiative centred on the concept of distance teaching, using film, video tape and educational packages to help people develop their knowledge and skill in their own time without necessarily having to enter a classroom.

Alongside this also at Cranfield, the provision of credits for people doing work in continuing studies has now been established. That is, managers can acquire credits over a period of time by doing a variety of courses in educational work. These credits will enable them to be eligible to sit for higher degrees in management studies.

Within the companies and organisations there will be a much more coordinated approach towards management education. Increasingly, careers will become more planned. For people who wish to advance it will become important to have had a series of work experience linked by both internal and external educational programmes.

The manager's role as a management educator will therefore become more prominent. It will be seen as a line manager's job to provide the basic management training and development. We shall move to some form of human asset accounting and staff development will increasingly become a major issue for all managers.

Alongside this we shall see considerable changes in organisational structure. More organisations will work on a horizontal as well as a vertical system. The matrix form of organisation centering itself upon project leadership will become more appropriate, given the complexity of tasks and the different professional skills required.

Therefore we shall see considerable advances, not only in individual development, but in team development. We should expect a lot of attention to be paid to new theories and practices in the area of organisation development, particularly given the pressure for consultation and communication, as well as negotiation from all levels. These changes will place considerable pressures on management development specialists both within the organisation and in the educational organisation. There will be an emergence of a professional identity amongst such people and the formation of networks of professional bodies to facilitate the assuring and preparation of ideas.

The 1980's represent a major challenge for both managers and educationalists who are concerned with management and organisation development. It is a field which is one of practice and pragmatism but demands considerable research. So far this has been noticeably in short supply. We shall see, however, within the next five years, considerable amounts of money set aside for specific projects and it is important that these are conducted within the action research frame of reference.

Management education and development has a bright future if those involved can keep up with the pressure for change and the complexity of the world in which they have to work.

17 The outdoor development factor

JOHN BANK

"When I doubt myself, I remember the rocks. If I could do that, there is nothing at this company that I can't do."

a manager

"We came home more willing to take risks, more trusting of each other, and more aware of the special abilities of the people we work with."

a salesman

"When we left the mountain it looked changed. No difference. None of us could say the same about each other."

an executive

"Sure the company benefits. You get something like this from the company, ... and you feel like giving it back."

a shopfloor worker

It was the moment of truth, like the hand on the shoulder in a parachute jump. After hours of work, the executive students had finally rigged a rope and pulley system that would carry members of their team across a wide chasm over a hundred feet deep. The first man in the queue confided to me nervously, "I'm so afraid of heights that it took me a week to work up to standing on the top of a twelve foot ladder to paint the ceiling of my lounge." He leapt off the edge of the ravine into the void. As the harness and pulley took his weight and started to swing him over the waterfall he amazed everyone by removing one hand from the harness to take a camera from his jacket pocket to photograph the scene below. From the opposite side of the ravine a TV film crew followed his progress as he was being hauled on to solid ground, a reporter thrust a microphone at him and put the abrasive question: "How will this help you <u>manage</u> back at work?"

Bordering on parody, the event encapsulates the outdoor

development factor in management education. There was the difficult task on the rock face to be accomplished by team work, imaginative planning and leadership. An element of danger and risk sharpened the moment, although since the activity was carefully supervised by a trained mountain instructor, it was more an illusion of danger than real jeopardy.* Fears had to be coped with. Bad judgements and their consequences caused delays and difficulties. Yet a sense of community developed and shared achievement and a certain 'joie de vivre' marked the experience. And after it all, even before the critical debriefing where much learning takes place, there was the intrusion of the outside world in the presence of the film crew to ask the nagging questions about the relevance of the experience to the manager's job.

Whatever its relevance, outdoor development has staying power. Media coverage of the phenomena may be in or out of fashion. Yet over the decade there has been a continuous growth in the outdoor management programmes on both sides of the Atlantic. It is a sprawling and difficult area of management education to research, especially in evaluating the relevance of the courses in the work life of the managers who participate in them. The task of the researcher is not helped by the distortions of the media presentations of the concept (a good learning session on the rock face does not necessarily make good TV), nor by the cynical attitudes of the doubters who dismiss the whole idea as a lark or company perk.

I have been at the edge of the development of outdoor development for managers for seven years, in the first instance as a visiting lecturer at the London Business School, where I accompanied executive students on short programmes at the Outward Bound Mountain School at Eskdale, Cumbria. Later I introduced the idea at the Cranfield School of Management and watched it slowly gather momentum. I have designed outdoor development modules, attended the courses as participant or staff member helping with on the spot feedback and evaluating the experiences afterwards. I have surveyed several forms of the outdoor development training, noteably the Leadership Trust, and have discussed the ideas and concepts with outdoor development staff, company trainers, academics involved directly with the field, and with Chris Bonington who draws on his own rich experiences as a world class mountain climber, to find some lessons in leadership for managers. Finally, I have made a study of the data available from the American experiments with this type of management pedagogy.

---

* During over forty-two years of Outward Bound courses in thirty-two schools in seventeen nations, over half a million people have gone on courses and there have been forty fatalaties. In Britain there have been six fatalaties out of 200,000 people on Outward Bound courses.

At the outset of this chapter, I discuss objectives for
the courses, which are fairly common and international. I
turn next to various programmes designed to meet the
objectives. I then undertake the orienteering task of
relating the subject matter to the real life role of the
manager.

OBJECTIVES FOR THE COURSES

Outdoor development courses can be used to achieve the
following six goals:-

    1. Selfdevelopment through personal audit.
    2. Developing team building skills.
    3. Attitudinal change in the assessment of self and of
        others.
    4. Developing leadership.
    5. Increasing communication skills.
    6. Learning to deal with change and uncertainty.

Selfdevelopment: To conduct one's own audit of personal
resources

Given a set of novel and demanding exercises, the participant
will dig deep into his own resources to find hidden strengths
and uncover weaknesses. The aim is to effect a confidence
building experience based on extending oneself. In the
dramatic outdoor scene, the course member begins to realise
that many of the limitations he feels are artificial and
selfimposed. Quite naturally he takes stock of his own
level of health and fitness measured against his peers and
staff members. It can be a salutary experience for an over
indulgent executive to abseil a rock face with an amazingly
fit climber or for a timid manager to brave the white water
of rapids with a fearless colleague.

    In this area of selfdevelopment, the physical environment
is used to stimulate personal risk taking, exposure and the
exploration of one's own rules, habits and constraints.
Selfdevelopment is seen as the unearthing of personal
abilities and capacities which makes the person as manager
more autonomous. (Radcliff and Keslake, 1981).

    The experience can also be an antidote to burn out. New
research in America has broadened the categories for burn
out to go beyond the 'helping professions' such as doctors
and mental health workers, soldiers, policemen and airline
personnel. 'Burn out' is a state people find themselves in
when they have made intense efforts with few or no visible
results. As a consequence, they feel angry, helpless,
caged and spent. Many managers are subjected to this sense
of exhaustion and futility and to a higher level of stress.
(Levinson, 1981). The results of the new technology alone
should put more pressure on managers in the coming years.

Outdoor development programmes with their combination of

of physical challenge and personal reflection can be apt
prescriptions for coping with stress and burn out.
Freudenberger (1980) recommends that companies deal with
these problems by sending managers to workshops and
seminars and other off site physical activities where they
have opportunities to release pent up frustrations and
renew themselves.

Just as selfdevelopment need not be a solitary quest and
can be strengthened by relationships with others,
counteracting burn out need not be a solo activity. Here
again the mutual support established on outdoor development
programmes and the sense of community can be beneficial.

One of the personal objectives in this area is developing
a commitment to better physical fitness. There is an
underlying belief in the real link between physical fitness
and mental alertness, high morale, motivation and general
effectiveness. It is felt that the outdoor experience may
prompt a participant to develop a regime of regular
exercise which is tailored to his personality, lifestyle,
age, current level of fitness and personal motivation.
There is a potential payoff for both the person and his
company, here in all areas of work, particularly in
stressful and demanding situations.

The communion with nature opens up reflections on a
deeper interior life. As Henry David Thoreau put it:

> "I went into the woods because I wished to live
>   deliberately,
> to confront the essential facts of life and to see
> if I could not learn what it had to teach, and not,
> when I came to die, discover that I had not lived."

Team building

Team building has always been an objective of successful
organisations. It is well known that one of the strengths
of the Special Air Service Regiment (SAS), is rooted in the
way that organisation builds it teams, carefully maximising
each persons strengths and compensating for his weaknesses.
Companies also make appeals to team work. One of the more
bizarre examples of team building occurred when the manager
of a US based IBM sales unit with 100 people rented a sports
stadium in New Jersey for an evening. In front of their
spouses and children, and some top executives, all members
of the sales team ran through the player's tunnel onto the
field as their names were flashed on an electronic
scoreboard while the crowd cheered.

Another approach to teamwork appeared in an Outward Bound
brochure.

> "The anchor is weighed, the sails unfolded to catch the
> wind and the vessel sets out to meet the challenges of
> the open sea. It is outward bound. The success or

failure of its voyage rests not only on the skills of
the individuals and the crew, but also on their ability
to work together as a well motivated and stable team
through routine manoeuvres and moments of crisis."

The parallel is then rather simplistically drawn between
sailing and business activity.

"Such team work also plays an integral part in the
success of the modern business enterprise but is often
obscured by the familiarity, pressures and stress of the
working environment.

Outward Bound creates the opportunity for individuals
to learn to work together as a team and to meet the
challenges presented by the outdoors.

What participants learn is more than seamanship, rock
climbing or canoeing, they learn that each of these
activities is a shared experience which depend on
cooperation and the assistance of others for success.

They learn that being part of a team is as demanding as
leading it and that individual achievement can be
magnified through team work."

In less dramatic ways, most successful companies devote
some time to team building, team leading, team working and
team maintenance. Yet managers at all levels can easily
feel lost in the organisation and isolated from others.
The team work celebrated in 'Theory Z' (Ouchi, 1981) is
often sorely lacking in British and American firms. Two
consultants in a new study of forty-two of America's best
run companies, In Search of Excellence, argue that the best
managers value action above all else, a spirit of 'do it,
fix it, try it' (Peters and Waterman, 1982, p.13). The
writers draw heavily on the work of social scientist Ernest
Becker who documents the essential 'dualism' of people; to
want both to be part of a team and to be recognised
individually (p.80). Outdoor development training focuses
on the first need, while companies must tend to both. The
Leadership Trust, for example, states as one of its four
overall objectives: "to develop the ability to build and
harness cohesive teams to achieve common objectives."

Assessment

Assessment is an ethical issue in management education.
Business schools as a policy do not provide companies with
specific feedback on individual management student
performance. Such feedback could compromise lecturers and
would certainly be regarded as a threat by executive
students. By setting to one side such assessment, the
business school creates a protective environment where the
management student feels safe to explore issues, techniques
and skills without the feeling that his company's personnel
director is lurking somewhere in the background, waiting to

258

talk with the lecturers to take a measure of his performance, to compare him with his peers, to weigh his promotion potential.

This ethic should also be adopted by the organisation doing outdoor development, particularly when such activities are joint ventures involving, say for example, an outward bound school and the department of business studies of a university. Assessment should remain an internal company matter. Hence the assessment that goes on during outdoor development courses is not to help the sponsoring company's personnel department size up particular managers, but rather to foster selfassessment and a safe environment where course members are free to evaluate each others performance to offer helpful appraisal of behaviour, as two experienced trainers in this field suggest:

> "Our objectives for the programme were severalfold. For the participant as manager we would provide a series of opportunities for him to take a complete view of himself as a resource and to extend his capacities to meet a complex variety of managerial situations. We would provide him with opportunities to see himself as others see him and to reflect upon those views, adapting his own behaviour if he so chooses." (Radcliffe and Keslake, 1981, p,88).

Whether the course participants are undertaking a management course with an experience based outdoor learning module, or are on a contract company course, there is bound to be reassessment of others. The sudden change from the classroom or company offices or factory floor to the rockface or the rapids, forces participants to evaluate each other in new role sets with entirely new demands.

The development of leadership

The latest company based research in America argues convincingly for an exploration of leadership by managers. (Peters and Waterman, 1982). The chief executives of the most successful US companies require leadership skills "a strong leader (or two) seemed to have had a lot to do with making the company excellent in the first place." The great leaders leave behind a legacy that their successors must protect. The leadership task of the chief executive is "to manage the values of the organisation." They demand high quality in their product and employee participation in their operations. They ask for their employees' ideas and "treat them like adults", allowing talented people 'long tethers' for experimenting.

Most experience based outdoor training for managers has the development of leadership as one of its objectives. The Leadership Trust, for example, in its promotional material sets out its philosophy of leadership, which is quite presecriptive.

"Leadership is both a science and an art. The scientific or 'head' aspect refers to its principles, methods and functions. It involves problem solving, establishing objectives, planning, organising and decision making. The art or 'heart' aspect refers to the intangible human factors. These are personal qualities, personal power, morale, motivation and the vital areas of human relations such as trust and integrity. <u>Leadership starts with knowing and controlling onself so that one may approach and handle people and situations right</u>. This means learning to use both one's 'head' and 'heart' positively to win the commitment and involvement of people to achieve a common purpose.

Leadership development therefore begins with defining individuals' innate leadership abilities and then enhancing them with the knowledge, skills and selfconfidence to be able to apply them effectively. Our courses enable people to <u>learn from practical experience</u> which recreates the real and similar problems, pressures and situations that confront us at work. The essential learning comes from the constructive feedback and skilled tuition provided in the reviews after every practical session. The Leadership Trust provides an environment where managers can <u>practise</u> leadership, make errors if necessary, gain constructive feedback and learn without threat to their selfconfidence or career." (Gilbert-Smith, 1983).

The objective of giving people the experience of leadership in a practical way, where there is minimal risk to those being led, is akin to efforts which have been a part of military training for decades. Work in training for leadership, undertaken at the Royal Military Academy, Sandhurst, and the Royal Air Force, demonstrates that to improve the effectiveness in any organisation, five areas must be carefully studied. The first of these is the structure of the organisation, which should allow many opportunities for the practice of leadership under varying degrees of supervision. Likewise, a tradition of good leadership should be part of the organisation's value system. Secondly, formal courses on leadership should be developed to the highest standards. Thirdly, such course work should be tied in with subsequent practical leadership training in the officer's training programme. Fourthly, staff members should be given the opportunity to continually study and improve their performance in leadership training. And fifthly, a small research and advisory team should be created to maintain and improve standards. (Adair, 1968).

Interestingly, outdoor development programmes give attention to all of these areas in establishing course objectives and in setting objectives for their own staff development. This is one of several areas for reciprocity between outdoor development organisations and management schools. Business schools use the skills of mountain

260

instructors to create experiential learning for their management students. In return they might offer to the mountain instructors experiences of the business school environment where they may learn more about the theory and practice of management in a classroom situation for their own development and a further enhancement of their dealing with managers on the rock face.

In describing its leadership development programme, the Colorado Outward Bound School says the course is:

"Offered in the fall and spring with the outdoor as the teaching medium for leadership skills. While the course focuses upon leadership within experiential education, leadership skills taught are applicable to any walk of life. You will participate in teaching, leading, following, project presentation, planning and organising activities. In the end, you'll develop the knowledge, experience and sense of purpose to act effectively. In addition, you'll learn, general mountaineering, backcountry first aid and emergency procedures, how to deal with wilderness hazards, group dynamics and counselling skills. You'll explore the moral, social and spiritual dimensions of leadership."

(The objectives are many and perhaps there is more than a touch of oversell in the description, but it does take 3½ months).

Communication skills workshop

The work 'communication' comes from three Latin words, the prepostion 'cum' meaning 'with', the word 'unus' meaning 'one' and a corruption of the verb 'facere' meaning 'to make'. In its root it means 'to make one with'. Not surprisingly improving communication skills is one of the objectives espoused by most outdoor development training courses. The Brathay Hall Trust, in Ambleside, Cumbria, which runs 'Management in Action' courses, is so committed to the communication objective, they have a specific drama department which adds this type of communication to the hard tasks of mountaineering and canoeing.

The Leadership Trust, the Outward Bound Mountain School (Eskdale) and the South West Regional Management Centre use transactional analysis in their development training. The Leadership Trust employs transactional analysis as an aid 'to selfawareness and selfcontrol, for handling and approaching people and situations properly and to develop leadership skills." Some outward bound courses employ a TA consultant who helps design the courses and plays a leading role in debriefing the adventure exercises and group dynamics using transactional analysis. The South West Regional Management Centre use transactional analysis as a conceptual framework for use by course participants in dealing with leadership experiences.

261

Dealing with change and uncertainty

The coming shakeup in the industrial world due to the
widespread use of the microprocessor and the impact of new
technology will make the role of the manager more critical.
The so called 'third wave' (Toffler, 1980) will bring on
massive social upheaval as 'things fall apart' and entire
new systems of automation and industrial organisation emerge.
The manager will have to cope with uncertainty and change on
a scale which is unprecedented. To carry people along with
him during such dislocations will take leadership, team
work and new ways of coping and prevailing in uncertainty.

Finding new ways to develop an understanding of change and
skills for coping with uncertainty seems imperative for
educators and trainers of tomorrow's managers.

"Much management education has fallen down in failing to
relate theory to the hard, practical world of managing
resources and people and taking the consequences of
decisions. No business game, no simulation, no case
book study can ever approach the reality, because the
inevitable emphasis is on the intellectual framework of
a problem, and not on living inside a world which
contains unpredictable personalities and events, in
which the basis of management may change from minute to
minute ... and in which the only thing certain is that
nothing is certain." (Mansell, 1975, p.64).

Managers, when placed in the training situation created by
an outdoor development programme, are uneasy about the
unfamiliar scene. They are not comfortable with projects on
the rock face, the assault course or the canoe route.
Decisions are called for in a context of great change and
uncertainty and the physical and emotional effects of these
decisions are felt immediately, and at times painfully.

The Food, Drink and Tobacco Industry Training Board in its
several years experience with outdoor development, has
emphasised the objective of managing change and uncertainty.

"Managers apply their skills to a range of tasks which
are quite different to those they face at work, but
which are challenging and real"

stated a seminal report on outdoor development from the
Training Board (Creswick and Williams, 1979, p.3).

"The results of their action are immediately apparent,
providing clear evidence of their performance and a
basis for feedback, questioning and experiment.
Although the outdoor tasks are not normal they are
inescapably real. Managing an outdoor situation is like
managing life - it is full of unpredictable events and
people, a result has to be achieved and there are only
limited resources and time available. Because the tasks
are so different to the normal work situation, the

262

underlying management processes are laid bare."

Chris Bonington is a believer in the potentiality of the outdoors to sharpen managerial action. Executive decision making, participative leadership, team building, the management of uncertainty, motivation, dealing with industrial relations (a threatened strike by the Sherpas) are all part of the life and death reality of a major mountain climbing expedition. These aspects of management are as real as the logistic planning and stock control for which Bonington used computer programming (Bonington, 1976). He feels that in climbing Everest in 1975, he encountered nearly "every type of management problem one could think of". His many Himalayan expeditions have all been an extreme confirmation of the power of the outdoors as a vehicle for managing uncertainty.

THE COURSES: MODELS FOR OUTDOOR DEVELOPMENT

Comparisons which appear in the media of outdoor development courses to army training are gross exaggerations. They have neither the rigour nor the 'selection intent' of military courses.

The selection course for the British Parachute Regiment, for example, which sorts out two-thirds of all candidates who attempt it, gives the men less than two hours to complete a ten mile battle march, carrying 30lb packs, 20lb of webbing and a 10lb rifle.

After struggling through mud and water and hillsides, the men are kept awake all night digging trenches, doing exercises and fending off instructors who creep up on them and attempt to steal weapons and equipment. At dawn the candidates run a 6½ mile stretcher race across difficult country in teams of eight, each man carrying 175lb on his shoulders. They then must go round the assault course three times in under 7½ minutes and complete the steeplechase within eighteen minutes. Finally, they have to carry telegraph poles over rough terrain in less than fifteen minutes and do a 14 mile march over harsh landscape. The Para leadership maintains they are not out to break men but "to make them", to find the man "who doesn't quit, who has the robustness of the mind to keep going when everyone else falls."

Outdoor development courses, by contrast, are designed to meet the manager where he is and to help him to 'stretch' himself while the staff and other students provide support. There is an element of 'action learning' in the model, whereby managers "learn by doing the thing." (Revans, 1980). The principles of 'action learning' were taken up by the EEC's Foundation for Management Development (FMD) when it stated that:

"New approaches in educational technology for large

audiences, action research and action learning ...
should be broadly experimented with and promoted."
(EFMD, 1978).

These principles can easily be applied to outdoor
development for managers. At the heart of 'action learning'
is the ability to extract from the new task itself a
sustainable desire to know what one is trying to do, what
is stopping him from doing it and what resources can be
found to get it done by overcoming the obstacles. Usually
the process requires the help of a small number of people
who are also on the same quest.

To the people who summed up his work with the too
simplistic phrase "learning by doing", Professor Revans
said that it was rather "learning to learn by doing with and
from others who are also learning to learn by doing" (Revans,
1980, p.288). The focus is then not on the knowledge of the
teacher, but rather on the experiences and the needs of the
learners. In particular, the outdoor development programme
emphasises one of the options of action learning whereby an
unfamiliar problem is studied in an unfamiliar setting.

The physical tasks that are at the core of outdoor
development courses, whether they be abseiling a rock face,
or climbing a mountain peak or navigating rapids in canoes
are real tasks which present real problems to real people in
real time with real constraints. Unlike simulations and
case studies, the physical tasks are so designed that the
manager will experience the practical outcome of his own
actions or decisions thereby creating a learning process
which could lead him to modify his behaviour or opinions.
As such the physical tasks of the outdoor development
courses, dependent as they are on small group work,
constitute action learning experiences which stand on their
own.

All outdoor development courses include various physical
tasks to be achieved individually and collectively. Not
surprisingly the various outdoor organisations have
differing approaches to the physical demands of the
courses. Most make the physical tasks tough enough to
'stretch' the students and dramatic enough to excite
challenge and awaken them without overtaxing their
abilities. Many programmes include an 'all night' exercise.
The Outward Bound School at Eskdale offers a number of
'night exercises', one called 'Muffit', in which the
participants impersonate secret agents working with
partisans to steal a consignment of plutonium. The
exercise involves orienteering in the dark in harsh
weather trying to elude the enemy police. In the manner of
Le Carre's Smiley's People there are codes and rendezvous
in the forest and a deaf mute guide. There can even by
humour in the gruelling eight hour exercise as when a senior
executive in a balaclava, while looking for a 'contact',
disturbed a courting couple. He rapped on the roof of their
car parked in the midnight dark of the forest and put a

coded message to the shaken driver, "Are you the jungle king?"

The Leadership Trust, which once employed such all night activities, has moved away from them because they exhausted the students and made subsequent learning more difficult.

Three outcomes of an effective outdoor development course are personal development, team development and manager development. In such a course the outdoor tasks are the focal points where there is a convergence of inputs from management training, which include managerial principles and skills and inputs from the outdoor environment (see Figure 17.1).

Across the spectrum, the physical activities can range from simple rock climbing where groups achieve goals to survival exercises where individuals are left on their own to find routes while living off the land. It is quite obvious that the physical activity must be suited to the designed outcomes.

For example, one of the desired outcomes of the Leadership Trust's management training is to help a student learn ways of handling and controlling himself effectively, even under pressure. The training is reinforced by a tutor attached to every six to eight students who in effect provides a model example of such control in his own behaviour. The tutor also holds the safety of the group and establishes the integrity and boundary of the group in which the member can become freer and freer to express himself. The tutor creates a membrane of safety and support for the group. He makes sure that each person has at least one, usually two, opportunities of leading the group and experiencing support.

Each group, in turn, tests itself out in three physical activities, namely subaqua diving, rock climbing and canoeing. The physical activities themselves comprise only eight per cent of the course content, but they are crucial because they are used to wrenching people out of their normal patterns of behaviour and mind sets. As Michael Price, Executive Course Director of Leadership Trust explained:

> "The physical activity is a powerful vehicle. It is important that it be totally real because then you get real emotion, real fear, high anxiety, high on low morale, real aggression and real learning."

In the Leadership Trust approach, one goal is to "improve the ability of people to lead teams effectively", which is different from simply personal development. The course is designed to build bridges back to their places of work.

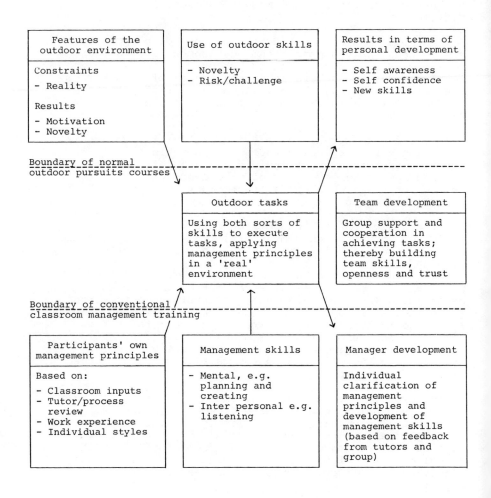

Figure 17.1 Linking the outdoor environment with management
development - a basic model
(See Creswick and Williams)

DEBRIEFING

An essential part of outdoor development is the debriefing
which is built into each activity. During the debriefing
some of the experiential learning is articulated, peer group
evaluations of performance take place and the inputs from
the outdoor staff, company trainers or academic staff are
made. Discussions during the debriefing often focus on two
aspects of the physical activity - task and process - which
are separated out to facilitate the analysis. For example,
it is helpful when debriefing a 'mountain rescue' activity
to distinguish what aspects of the group's performance
related to the way they want about the rescue task -
responding to the squawking radio and the call for help,
organising the stretcher team, orienteering to the place
where the injured climber lay, administering first aid and
carrying the person back to base camp. Another discussion
would focus on process issues - how the leader emerged (or
failed to come forth), how an inventory of expertise in the
group was taken, how decisions were made, etc.

Debriefing periods are the best times to draw out the
personal, industrial and organisational relevance of the
physical experience. In a night exercise, for example, two
groups arrived at a small mountain hut in the middle of a
forest to find that the hut could accommodate only half their
numbers. The first to arrive began preparing a meal with the
raw ingredients they found in the hut. Later the leaders of
both groups joined the cooks inside the hut to plan strategy.
Meanwhile, the remaining members had no choice but to stay
outside standing in a cold, unrelenting rain. As the
leaders argued loudly at great length, they never thought to
establish a communications link with the troops in the rain,
whose resentment grew as they remained literally and
figuratively in the dark. Reflecting on this experience, one
manager said:

> "Standing out there in that cold, midnight rain, without
> anyone telling us what was happening, although we were
> within earshot of the leaders' meeting, made me feel
> like shop floor workers must feel when managers fail to
> inform them of decisions made around them that directly
> affect them."

At debriefings, the essential role of the tutor emerges.
Some of the group dynamics and physical tasks can bring out
explosive conflict between members of a group. The tutor,
charged with maintaining the safety of the group, must be
skillful at allowing painful learning to take place without
permitting a group to veer onto a destructive course. While
conducting their courses, the Leadership Trust keeps an eye
open for potential tutors. When they find a manager on the
course who controls himself especially well and has the
gifts they require in their approach to leadership and team
building, they write to his company and invite him to
volunteer for training as a tutor. After a day of testing,
the selection of the manager as a tutor trainee is usually

267

confirmed. He then attends two three day tutor's workshops
to learn some basic skills. Next he is invited to attend
an open course as a novice tutor working with a mature
tutor. Each year he is invited to tutor's workshops and
asked to do the odd course. The Leadership Trust now has a
roster of 180 tutors who augment their fulltime staff of
fourteen.

FEEDBACK AND EVALUATION

Most outdoor development courses end on a natural 'high'.
It is important when getting feedback that a researcher
allows the froth to settle before handing out questionnaires
or holding feedback sessions, or at least to have a two
staged evaluation - one immediately after the course and one
several weeks or months later.

   A typical evaluation of an executive outward bound course,
based on questionnaires, occurred in October 1977. Forty-
four members of the London Executive Programme (London
Business School) out of a class of fifty-eight, chose to go
on the Outward Bound Programme, at the Mountain School in
Eskdale. They took the train from London to the Lake
District and woke to a day of training that seemed more
suited to commandoes rather than desk bound executives. They
swung from cables strung from trees sixty feet in the air at
high speeds, climbed fourteen foot high walls, attacked rope
ladders, wire bridges and rock faces with determination.
They leapt from a simulated parachute jump, abseiled a cliff
and practised carrying a stretcher down a rock face. They
were divided up into four groups of eleven men each and
engaged in competitive group dynamics. At night each group
chose a campsite in preparation for an assault on a major
peak the following morning.

   The small group I was with as a faculty adviser, pitched
two man tents above Burnthwaite in the Wasdale Valley. In
the morning, with a cold rain falling, we followed a pony
track to the corridor route and climbed the Skew Gill. As
the cataracts fell around us, we made our way up the
slippery rock to the summit of Great End (2,987 feet). We
then followed the ridge via Broad Crag and climbed Scafell
Pike (the highest peak in England at 3,206 feet) in a
hailstorm. At the summit, as we huddled and sheltered
behind some huge rocks and ate bread and cheese, a park
ranger with a dog emerged from the mist and hail to ask what
on earth we were doing there in such foul and dangerous
weather. It was a question we had all been asking outselves.

   Later, forty-three out of the forty-four men filled in the
three page questionnaire evaluating the experience. Their
ages ranged from thirty to fifty, with an average age of 36½.
Of the forty-three men, thirty found the course relevant to
the London Executive Programme (LEP) and thirty-six men felt
that the module should be included in the next LEP, six
said it shouldn't and one man was uncertain. Throughout the

questionnaire they indicated the strengths and weaknesses of the outward bound module for managers. One executive student had an extreme reaction against the whole affair. In his evaluation form he argued that the London Business School, as "his surrogate employer" was in "violation of the Health and Safety at Work Act (1974) in its failure to supply details of hazards in advance of requiring such dangerous involvement." It was a minority opinion of one, in fact the business school had arranged for medical exams for the men beforehand and taken out insurance on their behalf, which is standard procedure.

Questionnaires evaluating a five day course at the same Outward Bound Mountain School five years later in the Autumn of 1982 for members of a parttime MBA course at the Cranfield School of Management were very positive about the experience. Twenty-two out of thirty-five members on the course volunteered to attend. The response rate on the questionnaires was nineteen out of twenty-two. All but one of the students found the outward bound course "personally valuable" and everyone felt it should become a regular feature of the MBA course. Surprisingly, the most gruelling activity of the course, the "night exercise" was singled out as "the most enjoyable, valuable or rewarding". These management students ranked the stated objectives of the course in terms of which were most important to them in the following order:-

1. Personal audit.
2. Communication skills.
3. Team building.
4. Leadership.
5. Confidence building.
6. Reassessment of roles.
7. Training potential (for others like their subordinates).

The Cranfield MBA candidates explained the relevance of the outward bound course to their managerial activity, and to their own interaction as MBA students, in an open ended question. One student said:

"For the first time, we as a group ceased to be analytical observers and became operants. It thus became possible not only to explore the impact on other people of your decisions, but also to identify your own reaction to other peoples' decisions. As this was done in a demanding environment, the decision made had a direct and sometimes painful impact upon you. Hence it made me realise the extent of the power of the decision maker and how callous he can become if he fails to appreciate the effects his decision will have on the operants. It 'humanised' the classroom theories."

Another MBA student explained:

"When people are under stress they react differently than

269

in ordinary circumstances. The course accepts and magnifies these reactions, which would develop more slowly in an office environment."

A testimony in support of the course was made by an MBA student who said:

"I felt that by putting us in 'real life' situations as opposed to classroom simulations, concepts such as direction, leadership, decision making and just plain listening, became much more readily understood."

A fifth MBA student observed:

"By appreciating that feelings under the surface may be quite strong and ready to reveal themselves, the course illustrates the need for me to understand that others have different levels of commitment and different perceptions, which may cause interpersonal problems. It helped to underline to me the frustrations of working with others with those different levels of commitment and different perceptions and the need to approach those frustrations more positively and less defensively. The course also raised the problem of competitiveness and the friction this creates between individuals, who may have, in the past, been on good terms. There is an obvious trade off between achievement and antisocial, aggressive competitive behaviour. This was exaggerated in some instances on the course, but is entirely relevant to a business situation."

In a sentence, another managerial student summed up his experience:

"The important thing in this for me is that I have learnt how valuable and essential trust is between the leaders and the followers."

An American company, Martin Marietta Aerospace, created a Career Development Course in collaboration with the Colorado Outward Bound School to help train their managers, technicians and professionals, clerical and support staff. The company hired an outside consultancy firm to do an evaluation of the course. The major finding of the outside consultancy firm was the course's effect on employee turnover. Normal turnover for the company was about 8.4 per cent of the work force per annum. However, for those employees who took both the Managing Personal Growth (MPG) two day incompany course and the four day Outward Bound Career Development Course, was only 1.7 per cent. For employees who have taken the incompany course only, the MGP, the turnover figure is six per cent, an improvement over the base line figure of 8.4 per cent, but falling far short of the 1.7 per cent rate for those who did the incompany course and then went on the outward bound module. The consultants sum up their findings by saying:

"The impact of the programme on Martin Marietta Aerospace Corporation and its employees has been positive. While most of the benefits defy precise quantification, we found increased employee enthusiasm and loyalty, traditional indicators of increased employee productivity." (King and Harmon, 1981).

Myra W Isenhart attributes much of the success of the Colorado Outward Bound School to the eductional methods employed, which are based:

"on a learning model which acknowledges that we assimilate and use information which is available in our daily lives, rather than delivered in the classroom. That is, the assumption is that people climbing peaks and running rivers develop insights about leadership, selfreliance, team work and risk taking ... Learning through an outward bound experience is not adding bits of information, but a catalytic process through which the learner integrates his/her experience and interprets them with wider meaning." (Isenhart).

THE LINK TO THE PRACTICE OF MANAGEMENT

President John F Kennedy gave an executive order in writing to have US missiles removed from their silos in Turkey in 1962. His decision was made after examining alternative strategies and the recommendations of the Joint Chiefs of Staff, the State Department and the National Security Council. Several months later, at the height of the Cuban missile crisis, President Kennedy was amazed to learn that his order had not been carried out and that his control system failed to report this breakdown in his executive authority. (Allison, 1971).

From presidents to heads of multinationals to middle and frontline managers, the manager's job remains a complex one which intermingles interpersonal, informational and decision making roles. Data based research reveals that the task of the manager is far from the classic model of a person who plans, organises, coordinates and controls. (Mintzberg, 1975). The pace and pressures of his position, as Mintzberg points out:

"drive the manager to be superficial in his actions - to overload himself with work, encourage interruption, respond quickly to every stimulus, seek the tangible and avoid the abstract, make decisions in small increments, and do everything abruptly."

The multiplicity of the manager's roles requires skills as well as knowledge. Hence it is the task of management education to attempt to incalcate in its students skills as well as cognitive learning. Yet while lectures and books can be used to transmit knowledge, skills can only be

learnt by practice with feedback from tutors and fellow
students. The catalogue of requisite skills for managers
include the skills of negotiation and communication, of
motivating others, of sorting out conflicts, of networking
and channeling information, of coping with uncertainty and
ambiguity, of decision making and of dealing with totally
new situations.

Business schools, according to Mintzberg, should enhance a
manager's entrepreneurial skills "by designing programmes
that encourage sensible risk taking and innovation."
Outward bound staff maintain that they are providing
managers with the experience of risk taking. Testimonials
from managers highlight the risk element in the course.
Arthur Levitt, Jr, Chairman of the American Stock Exchange,
Inc said:

> Our first confrontation with the rapids was a terrifying
> experience. But we had our game plan. Each crew had
> scouted the turbulent waters from the shore and
> discussed the route they wanted to take. Suddenly we
> were doing it, flashing by angry looking rocks,
> maneouvering our raft by ugly patches of swirling
> water, paddling furiously first one way then another
> through the white water turbulence ..." (Levitt).

On a 100 foot abseil down a rockface in New Mexico,
Katherine Slobe, manager of personnel planning and
programmes for Xerox, misjudged the position of her feet and
let out too much rope. She ended up hanging upside down
from the top of the sheer cliff while an instructor told her
how to right herself to get out of serious trouble. She
surpassed herself and did it. She said of the course:

> "It was a great personal experience. I learned what I
> always suspected, that you can do a lot more than you
> think you can if you're willing to try it."

Katherine Slobe's words sum up the simple philosophy of
the outward bound approach. The first outward bound schools
were established by Kurt Hahn, a German/Jewish educator, who
earlier developed the Salem School in Germany in 1920 as an
antithesis of the authoritarian German schools of the time.
His opposition to the Nazi regime won him a prison sentence
in 1933, but influential friends got him released and out of
Germany. He went to Scotland where he founded the
Gordonstoun School in 1934. His philosophy of education
stressed the development of a student's inner resources as
well as intellectual challenge. He trained his school boys
in mountain and ocean rescue. At the outbreak of World War
II, Hahn helped to set up a school for British Merchant
Mariners at Aberdovey, Wales, specialising in survival
training. The school was named "Outward Bound" and that
became the name for a movement that now has thirty-four
schools in seventeen countries dedicated to Hahn's philosophy
of education. The Aberdovey School is now one of the
leading outward bound schools in management education and in

the rough economic climate of Britain in the 1980s is still in the survival business.

Outward bound has always concentrated on courses for youth and has funding from industry for such work. Its involvement in management education, according to Ian Fothergill, Director of the Outward Bound Trust, and formally Principal of the Outward Bound, is a long term commitment. Roger Putnam, Principal of the Outward Bound School at Eskdale, has carried the commitment to management education far enough to purchase a stone mansion near the School's entrance for the education of managers. "Personal fulfillment and character building can only aid to the managerial role" said a Cranfield MBA student making the link between the course and his job.

The Managers in Action course run by the Brathay Hall Trust turns out managers "who are able to act more positively and flexibly as managers of groups, communicators, decision makers and team members." The Trust's seven day course has a skills focus for practising managers. The course follows the theories of John Adair, the founder of action centred leadership, which has enjoyed wide application through British industry. According to the action centred leadership model, an efficient manager needs to have:-

1. Technical competence to manage the technology of the job.

2. Knowledge of the functional area of management.

3. A cluster of management skills required to motivate people to work for corporate goals. (Adair, 1982).

The skills area is most relevant to outdoor development. What then are the specific managerial skills which can be practical and reinforced through outdoor activities? A list of these skills would include:-

1. Observing.
2. Selecting pertinent data.
3. Diagnosing problems.
4. Formulating solutions.
5. Deciding.
6. Communicating.
7. Motivating.

Some participative methods are better than others at giving a person practice in these managerial skills. For example, field studies are best for promoting observing skills and case studies are best for developing diagnostic skills for problem solving (see Figure 17.2).

The strength of the outdoor development pedagogy is that it can encompass elements of all the methods and thereby

Management
skills:

Effectiveness:

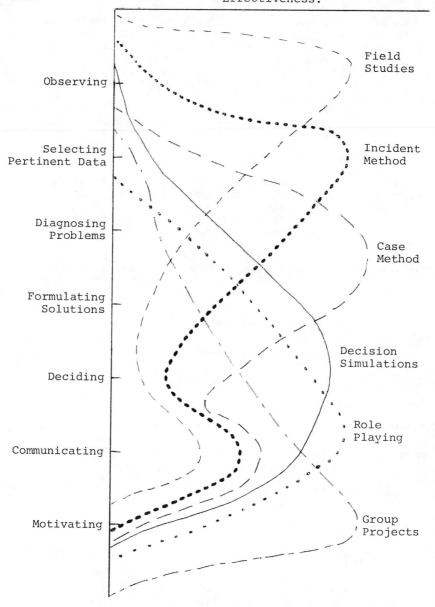

Observing

Field
Studies

Selecting
Pertinent Data

Incident
Method

Diagnosing
Problems

Case
Method

Formulating
Solutions

Deciding

Decision
Simulations

Communicating

Role
Playing

Motivating

Group
Projects

Figure 17.2   Effectiveness of Participative Methods
(See Hawrylyshyn, 1977).

274

provide effective practice for the whole range of managerial skills. The Leadership Trust, for example, sets up small factories on the Wye River where the management students are required to produce products and distribute them through a warehouse to a railhead within budgetry constraints. Critical incidents are set up by the tutors to create real pressures on the men in their various production and distribution roles. The entire project is designed to bring to light the real behaviour of the men and their true managerial styles. The experience provides the raw material for working on managerial skills.

There is a great difficulty in assessing the relevance of outdoor development to managerial performance with hard data. This is due to the fact that part of the impact of the programmes is felt quickly and directly. The rest of the impact is distributed in indirect ways over a long period of time. Long term consequences would include employee's improved health, higher morale and more efficacious attitudes. To survey these long term benefits would require longitudinal studies. In such studies it will be extremely difficult isolating the variables and demonstrating causality, given the complexity of the managerial roles and the indefinability of some of the benefits of outdoor development programmes. But it is definitely an important research area for the future. Pilot outdoor development training courses, like the ones launched by the South West Regional Management Centre, should flourish and help provide the data for research into such learner centred activities. (Beeby and Rathborn, 1982). As this area of management education expands, more sensitive instruments will be developed for feedback and better strategies for ongoing research.

The focus of it all is the manager whose roles will grow more complex in the new millennium. The manager will continue to be "the dynamic, life giving element in every business" and he will rightly expect those who claim to teach and train him to use a dynamic and life giving pedogogy. In view of the uncertainty and ambiguity that lie ahead for manager and education, both might well explore the reality behind the outward bound motto - "to serve, to strive and not to yield."

BIBLIOGRAPHY

Adair, J, (1982), Action Centred Leadership, Gower.

Allison, G T, (1971), Essence of Decision: Explaining the Cuban Missile Crisis, Little, Brown.

Beeby, M and Rathborn, S, (1982), "Incorporating use of the outdoors in development training courses', Journal of European Industrial Training, Vol.6, No.6.

Bonington, C, (1976), Everest the Hard Way: The First Ascent of the South West Face, Hodder and Stoughton.

Creswick, C and Williams, R, (1979), Using the Outdoors for Management Development and Team Building, p.3, The Food, Drink and Tobacco Industry Training Board, Gloucester.

Drucker, P F, (1968), The Practice of Management, p.13, Heinemann, London.

EFMD, (1978), European Foundation for Management Development, Management Education in the European Community, p.38, Office for Official Publications of the European Community, Brussels.

Freudenberger, H J, (1974), 'Staff burn out', Journal of Social Issues, Vol.30, No.1.

Freudenberger, H J, (1980), Burn Out: The Melancholy of High Achievement, Doubleday, New York.

Hawrylyshyn, B W, (1977), L'éducation des dirigeants - aspects méthodologiques, Peter Lang.

Isenhart, M W (undated), An Investigation of the Interface Between Corporate Leadership Needs and the Outward Bound Experience, published by and available from the Colorado Outward Bound School.

King, P and Harmon, P, (1981), Evaluation of the Colorado Outward Bound School's Career Development Course Offered in Collaboration with the Training, Education and Employee Development Department of Martin Marietta Aerospace, pp.4-5, Harmon Associates, San Francisco.

Levinson, H, (1981), 'When executives burn out', Harvard Business Review, May/June 1981, pp.73-81.

Levitt, A Jr, (undated), 'Corporate survival ... on a raft, Chief Executive, No.11, pp.34-38.

Mansell, C, (1975), 'How GEC learns action', Management Today, May, p.64.

Miller, J, (1982), 'A wilderness challenge for corporate brass', The American Way, February.

Ouchi, W, (1981), Theory Z: How American Business Can Meet the Japanese Challenge, Adison-Wesley, Reading, Maryland.

Peters, T J and Waterman, R H, (1982), In Search of Excellence: Lessons from American's Best Run Companies, Harper and Row, New York.

Radcliff, P and Keslake, P, (1981), 'Outward bound?', in Boydell, T and Pedler, M (Eds.), Management Self Development, Concepts and Practices, pp.85-98, Gower.

276

Revans, R W, (1980), Action Learning New Techniques for Management, p.288, Blond and Briggs, London.

Thoreau, H D, (1981), 'What I lived for', Walden, Vol.2, AMS Publishers.

Toffler, A, (1980), The Third Wave, William Collins & Co, London.

For the history of outward bound see: Wilson, R, (1981), Inside Outward Bound, Douglas and McIntyre, Vancouver.

18 Management learning processes and multiple value systems

CARY COOPER AND JOHN BURGOYNE

DUALISTIC MANAGEMENT LEARNING PROCESSES

Over the years there have been numerous attempts in the behavioural sciences to examine the process of influence between change agents (e.g. teachers, or clinicians, or parents) and the objects of their influence (e.g. students, patients, children). There has not been a concomitant effort to do the same in the field of management education, that is, to systematically explore the learning mechanisms between a management educator and a manager, although the parallels with behavioural science theory are obviously there. In this chapter we hope to highlight some prominent social science theories with a view to extracting concepts that may be useful in helping us to develop a working model of a learning theory applicable to the management education process and to explore the multiple value systems impinging on the individual through social influence learning processes.

Behavioural science theories of learning

As early as 1913, McDougall (1913) wrote about the processes of mental interaction and learning, emphasising two main concepts; "suggestion" and "imitation and sympathy". In the former, the change agent (e.g. teacher) 'suggests' the possible conditions or alternatives of change to the influence (e.g. student), whereas in the latter the influence learns by assimilating his actions and affective state to those of the agent. For the most part these fundamental concepts were lost until their reemergence and refinement in the early 1960's. Slater (1961) outlined a learning theory of 'identification', describing two influence mechanisms; personal and positional identification. In personal identification, the ego identifies with the actual person of the alter, that is, the qualities inherent in the agent as a person who creates conditions that maximise change of learning, whereas in positional identification the role of the change agent is that of the desired model and this provides him with a major source of influence. Winch (1962) utilised a similar dichtomy in describing situation centred or actor centred influence. Situation centred influence is similar to positional identification in that it refers to behaviour acquired by the identifier, which is interpreted as corresponding to one or more of the roles involved in a particular influence situation. Actor centred influence corresponds to personal identification in that behaviour acquired in this process is orientated to the model as a person. He further highlights this distinction by positing 'product' and 'process' dimensions. Situation centred influence is product orientated, that is, the influence changes his behaviour or disposition to behave in relation to the agent's behaviour. On the other hand, actor centred influence is process orientated, that is, the influence learns to behave in some manner as a result of environmental conditions, related to the agent's behaviour and yet independent from it, which provides various opportunities to learn.

Raven (1965) and French and Raven (1960) also emphasise concepts similar to the above in their conceptualisation of the five bases of power: reward power (based on ability of the change agent/teacher to mediate rewards for the influence/learner), coercive power (based on possessing the means of punishment), legitimate power (based on influence/ learner's perception that the change agent/teacher has the right to influence his behaviour), referent power (based on attractiveness of the agent to the influence), and expert power (based on influencee's perception that the agent possesses detailed and special information). The concepts of referent and expert power are reminiscent of the product/ process differentiation. In referent power, the influencee or learner is amenable to influence when the agent or teacher is perceived to be an attractive or desirable model, whereas in expert power it is dependent on the learner's perception of the agent's attributes and how meaningfully these attributes are related to the goals of the particular influence situation. Raven and French have also added another important dimension, namely, compliant influence. This is expressed in terms of reward and coercive power. In these concepts, the crucial determinant of influence is the anticipated reaction of the agent. In compliance, the learner does not react to the content of the induction but rather to the agent's ability to mediate rewards/punishments (Kelman, 1961).

Lazowick (1965) has posited a trichotomous theory of influence, which emphasises the concepts of pseudo identity, imitation, and introjection. A pseudo identity influence relationship is present when the learner behaves as if he and the model were one and the same person. Imitation, however, is described in the strict Symonds sense of one person copying another (e.g. the management trainee modelling a favoured senior manager). Both of these concepts refer to a relationship in which the learner takes over behaviour associated with the teacher, because it allows him to gain the satisfaction that goes with defining himself as identical to the change agent or in pursuing a satisfying reciprocal role relationship. In contrast, an introjective influence relationship is one that emphasises the environmental conditions that activate change. In this

279

process, the agent is seen as possessing characteristics that aid the establishment of an environment that encourages change in the person structure. Schein and Bennis (1965) suggest that any change adopted through an identificatory or modelling relationship will not bring about either lasting effects or the integration of the change within the ego system. Response readiness, in the deeper layers of the personality, can occur only through an introjective approach that provides the learner with selforientation. Bradford (1958) also emphasises the introjective or internalising approach to influence in the teacher learner relationship. He suggests that learning can be internalised in a relationship which develops and maintains a supportive climate and encourages selfexploration rather than a 'relationship of safety' (traditional teacher learner role relationship).

Kagan's (1958) concepts of prohibition learning and vicarious affective experience also seem relevant to the discussion. 'Prohibition learning' he defines as the "adoption and practice of the prohibitions of the parents and parent substitutes". This concept follows directly from the Freudian ideas of the father as the agent of aiminhibited sexual impulse in the primitive prototype of the family. In this sense, the learner (in Freudian terms the son) sees the influence agent (i.e. the father) as an idealised model, as a result of the earler prohibitory relationship, and is willing to be influenced by him. Kagan's concept of 'vicarious affective experience' approaches the 'climate creator' paradigm. It "refers to the experience of positive or negative effects on the part of the person (or influencee) as a result of an event which occurred to a model". Rather than the influence being agent orientated, as in prohibition learning, it is the learning event created by the behaviour of the change agent and the way in which this is perceived that provide the influence.

The various ideas outlined above suggest an influence approach to learning wherein the role of the change agent seems twofold.

On the one hand, we have influence that is dependent on the change agent as an external source, that is, the teacher as a role model, exemplified by the concepts of positional identification, situation centeredness, referent power, pseudo identity and imitation, and prohibition learning. On the other hand, we have the private acceptance of influence in which change is independent of external support, the motivational significance of which attaches itself to the change agent or teacher more as a person and less as an object, exemplified by the concepts of personal identification, actor centeredness, expert power, introjection, and vicarious affective experience.

Dualistic paradigm of theories of change agent influence

Theorist	The person of the influence agent	The influence agent as a learning model
McDougal (1913)	Suggestion	Imitation and sympathy
Lazowick (1955)	Introjection	Pseudo identity and imitation
Kagan (1958)	Vicarious affective experience	Prohibition learning
French and Raven (1960, 1965)	Expert power	Referent power
Slater (1961)	Personal identification	Positional identification
Winch (1962)	Actor centred	Situation centred
Schein and Bennis (1965)	Scanning orientated	Identification orientated

In view of the overlap and theoretical ambiguities of the above concepts, we were reluctant to review them in the way that we have. However, it is this coincidence of attention, in fact, that makes them an appealing focal point for examination. We shall attempt, from this point on, to relate our use of these concepts in a more systematic way.

DUALISTIC THEORY OF THE PROCESSES OF MANAGEMENT LEARNING

It seems from an historical review of the social influence literature that there is widespread theoretical agreement (Kelman, 1961) as to the presence of at least two basic learning processes; identification based learning or using the educator as a learning model, and selfdirected learning where the educator (as a person) helps to create the conditions for the individual to choose his own learning style or approach. It is the intention here to highlight Cooper's (1976) dualistic theory of management learning, and then to explore multiple value systems in the context of this theory.

	Antecedent	Consequent	
		Short Term	Long Term
Learning by modelling	Attractiveness of management educator) Salience of management educator)	Change consistent with expectations and behaviour of model	Transferability of learning limited
Selfmanaging the learning process	Openness/congruence of management educator) Learning community climate of trust) Awareness and avoidance of dependent learning styles)	Change consistent with own needs	Learning transferable to variety of management settings

Figure 18.1 Dualistic Theory of the Process of Management Learning

Modelling as a process of learning

Modelling and imitation occur when an individual observes
and copies attitudes and/or behaviours from someone else
(Bandura, 1977). As Bandura (1966) has suggested:

> "Informal observation of the process of social learning
> as it occurs in naturalistic situations reveals that
> the behaviour of models in one form or another is
> utilised to some degree in facilitating learning
> regardless of whether the subject is being taught the
> responses necessary for playing golf, swimming ... or
> for conducting psychotherapeutic interviews".

In the context of management education, this process of
learning takes place by an identificatory process with a
management educator or indirectly by modelling the behaviour
of one's boss, colleagues, and subordinates. Managers
learn, therefore, by modelling management educators as well
as significant others in their work environment. The model's
influence is based largely on his attractiveness as perceived
by the 'learning manager'. The model is seen to possess
characteristics that the manager would himself wish to have,
in a sense, his ego ideal. The individual's desire to
approach his ego ideal and the salience of the relationship
for him provide the antecedent conditions for learning and
for his willingness to accept the model's influence. The
learner accepts influence "to share vicariously some of the
positive goal states which the model commands" (Kagan, 1958).
Change is adopted as a part of an active attempt to
establish a desired selfdefining relationship with the model.
The learner's concern here is not simply measured in terms
of the model's attractiveness but with the salience of this
attractiveness for him.

Identification based learning

Identification based learning can be defined as the
acceptance of influence in order to establish or maintain a
satisfying selfdefining relationship to the management
educator. Therefore, the attitudes and behaviour the
learning manager adopts in the process must be associated
with and required by a role that he wishes to enact. Thus,
much of the learning gained through a modelling process
remains tied to the external source and dependent on
external support. Learning is not likely to be integrated
into the trainees internal system. As Schein and Bennis
(1965) suggest:

> "When he identifies himself with a model once he has
> chosen the model, he limits the new information he
> acquires to what the particular model makes available to
> him. This process is more likely to lead to new
> attitudes which will be reinforced by the model but
> which may not fit as well into the rest of the
> personality".

Thus, in an identificatory modelling process, the management educator serves as a model whom the management trainees wish to resemble with the resulting learning tied to the model and in the direction of the model's attitudes and behaviour.

Although an individual's managerial attitudes and behaviour can change in positive directions as a result of a process of learning based on modelling, this change tends not to be generalisable or long lasting since it is tied to a particular model or management educator. Transferability is only likely in subsequent working situations which closely resemble the context of the original learning environment where the modelling took place.

In summary, a modelling or identificatory learning process is likely to take place if the management educator or significant other (e.g. boss, personnel officer, etc) is seen as attractive or possessing the attributes the management learner or trainee desires for himself. The learning manager accepts influence in a modelling process because the management educator is salient for him, thus by doing what he does and believing what he believes, the manager gains the satisfaction that goes with defining himself as identical with this salient figure. Change produced by this kind of learning process may not, however, be generalisable to a variety of management contexts because it is essentially tied to the resources offered by the one model.

Selfdirected learning

Another major process by which management learning can take place is by the management educator creating the conditions for selfdirected learning. Both research and experience in the field of psychotherapy, particularly client centred, have demonstrated that personal, idiosyncratic, and internalised change is facilitated when the change agent (i.e. therapist) provides the conditions for patient self growth by being open, discouraging dependency, and creating an atmosphere of trust. In management education (Cooper, 1981), there is a growing interest in encouraging 'learning managers' to diagnose their own needs and design selfhelp programmes of change and development. This can be achieved if three basic antecedent conditions can be offered by the management educator:-

1.   Openness/congruence in his relationship with learning managers.

2.   The ability to create the conditions of trust in the learning community.

3.   Awareness of and avoidance in encouraging 'dependent' learning styles.

The first two conditions are inextricably related. The

284

more open and genuine the management educator or significant others in their relationship with the learning manager(s), the more likely he is to help lay the foundations of trust which inevitably create the climate where self management of learning can take place. The management educator is not asked to model 'openness' but to actualise it, as Rogers (1961) suggests "openly being the feelings and attitudes which at that moment are flowing in him". Only when this kind of sharing of 'real' information occurs can we begin to form trusting work and learning environments. The third condition of avoiding dependent learning styles is quite different from the previous two. The onus here is on the managerial change agent to be aware of his own needs in attempting to create dependency relationships with learning managers. As we have already suggested identifying with or modelling the management educator may help the trainee in learning new managerial styles and approaches in the short term, it may also create an unnecessary high level of dependence on this change agent, hindering the transfer of learning to some backhome work environment. To be able to create the conditions for the self management of learning, the managerial change agent or educator must be sensitive to 'learner dependency' and be able to confront it. As Argyris (1966) suggests, some mechanisms must be introduced in the learning process to act as a "springboard to get away from him (the educator/trainer) as the sole criterion for effective behaviour and look to themselves and one another as important resource people". In the selfmanagement of learning, the trainee or learner has two major responsibilities for his own development; first, to develop the skills to diagnose his own strengths and weaknesses, and second, to plan a programme of change to utilise the full range of learning resources available to achieve his/her needs.

Two main consequences of encouraging selfdirected management education are:-

1.   Any change that occurs will be linked to meeting the needs of the particular individual.

2.   It will tend to be transferable to a variety of contexts, since it is not tied to one resource and since the learning or change programme selected will more closely fit his subsequent work environments.

Issues arising from the theory of management learning

There are several short and longterm management and organisational training implications of the theoretical constructs outlined above, which we would like to briefly discuss here. First, in many management education contexts a modelling or identificatory relationship between educator/change agent and manager does take place and is likely to be an important element in the learning process, primarily, as Bolman (Cooper, 1976, p.41) argues, because the "trainer

frequently appears to be powerful, if not always attractive".
All too often trainers are not aware of this dynamic, which
has several consequences:-

a.   they encourage and foster a dependency learning
     style that prevents the transfer of learning back
     to the work environment,

b.   the trainer does not appreciate the potential
     educational value of modelling and therefore does
     not utilise it to the best advantage.

One can minimise the consequences of a. by doing as Bolman
(ibid, p.43) suggests "what is essential, I think, is that
the identification process be publicly discussable and its
effectiveness publicly tested". If the modelling process is
publicly discussed, the individual can evaluate more
accurately the direct and indirect consequences of modelling,
the problems involved with the transfer of learning
associated with it, etc. In this way dependency can be
avoided, acquired behaviour can be examined, and the whole
dynamic of the teacher/student relationship can be advanced
by opening it up for exploration.

There are also longterm consequences of examining the
dynamics of modelling in management education. It has long
been suggested by managers, for instance, that they learn
most from other managers. That is, that there is a subtle
and less than conscious educative process that develops, on
a day to day basis, where managers observe the consequences
of the behaviour of their colleagues, internalise those that
lead to successful outcomes, and discard (from some of the
effective behaviours) those that are not adaptable in the
particular circumstances of that particular manager. This
learning sequence is essentially a modelling or
identificatory one. It may be possible in the future,
therefore, to try and harness this natural process as a tool
of management development. The natural modelling dynamic
could be the focal point for an approach to management
centred learning, where teams of managers come together to
share their perceptions of the behaviour of their colleagues
they perceive as 'modellable', in the context of that
particular work situation. This will not only provide
managers with an enhanced awareness of effective and
ineffective behaviours, but also will begin to create the
antecedent conditions of openness, trust, and interdependence
which are necessary for selfmanaging the learning process.

Second, and finally, if we consider it desirable for
managers to selfmanage their own learning experience, then we
must take steps to ensure that top management are adequately
prepared to allow this kind of development to take place.
As Argyris (1966) suggests, "each trainer behaves in ways
that create the conditions for both psychological success
and failure, which is related to his own needs and
psychological makeup". The management trainer can exploit
his role in the pursuance of his own needs, particularly in

his desire to be liked or to exercise power. As Schein and
Bennis (1965) emphasise in discussing change agents
generally, "the possibilities for unconscious gratification
in the change agent's role are enormous and because of their
consequences, for the health of the client as well as the
change agent, they must be examined". If we accept the
desirability of encouraging the manager to structure to some
extent his own learning environment, it will be necessary to
develop management teacher/change agent development
programmes which focus on the teachers motives and how these
may enable or prevent the student manager from learning in
his own way.

Figure 18.1 summarises the antecedent and consequence
conditions of Cooper's dualistic theory of management
learning described in the last couple of pages. It is hoped
that this conceptual model may stimulate further thinking
and research in the area of the processes of management
learning. We have not attempted here to comprehensively
examine the whole variety of learning dynamics in management
education or to establish an airtight theoretical structure,
but rather to make explicit two processes of learning which
have been a concern for many writers in the fields of social
change and influence, and which might have applicability to
management learning processes and management educators in
particular.

MULTIPLE VALUE SYSTEMS

As we have seen, there are two major aspects of the learning
process as it occurs in management education and development.
On the one hand, there are those processes of social
influence by which people are socialised toward the norms,
practices and behaviours of the organisation, professional
grouping or specialism for which they are being prepared.
On the other hand, there are the processes of 'autonomous'
learning in which the person develops his or her own
understanding of their situation, their own ways of coping
and achieving goals, and their own values and personal
ideologies (Cooper, 1981). Burgoyne and Stuart (1977) have
separated out a number of 'schools of thought' about the
learning process, which can be seen as the implicit theories
underlying various management education and development
practices. These can be divided into two broadly similar
categories, those that see the person as shaped by the
environment, either by a mechanical process as in
conditioning theories, or by social processes as in more
sociopsychological theories of learning. In contrast, those
schools of thought about learning that have their roots in
cognitive psychology, humanistic psychology, or
phenomenological, experiential or existential views of the
nature of the person, emphasise personal autonomy, choice and
responsibility, and interpret learning as the process by
which the person comes to exercise these effectively.
Possibly only those theories with their roots in
psychoanalytic, psychiatric and clinical psychological views

of the world cannot be so easily classified, interpreting learning as a change in the dynamic balance between inner drives, personal will and socially derived forces. The aim of this part of our chapter is to consider some of the possible different forms of context of the learning process in management education and development, and in particular the thesis that in many situations there are multiple rather than unitary value systems impinging on the individual through the social influence learning processes. A number of implications that follow from this will be explored.

Dominance of social influence or autonomous processes of learning

An obvious question to explore is whether some management education or training situations work principally through a social influence process and others by creating the condition for autonomous learning. At first sight this dualistic theory seems an attractive approach. As a broad generalisation those events that are more naturally labelled 'training' (which does imply semantically shaping to a preconceived form), seem to correspond to social influence, while those approaches more normally called 'education' (with the literal meaning of 'leading out' what is naturally within the person) seem more to do with autonomous learning.

Thinking in terms of specific events, it seems attractive to envisage, say a company induction training programme where all kinds of procedures and norms are taught, status labels learnt, 'correct' organisational behaviour modelled, etc as social influence events. On the other hand, personal growth orientated workshops carried out under the banner of management development may at first sight appear to be entirely in the autonomous learning category.

Although this simple picture may capture some aspects of reality, there is, however, a danger that it is too simplistic. In practice, it seems that application of one model always seems to include substantial elements of the other model. Thus, it is usual in 'educational' programmes for there to be some concept of a 'core' or foundation of concepts, technique, skills, etc that has to be 'trained in' as a basic necessity (like reading, writing and numeracy in schools). Furthermore, it is often argued that all education has a socialising function (Morrison and McIntyre, 1971) in which some set of values, attitudes, ideologies are inculcated.

On the other hand, even the 'tightest' and most structured form of training events have their informal sides, and participants in them talk in terms of learning and double guessing the roles of the game, and hence, in effect, preserving, exercising and developing their personal autonomy. Given that management, like the military, are perpetually trying to hold the balance between discipline and initiative, it can be argued that the latent function of many highly structured training events may be, in part at

least, the development of the ability to exercise autonomy
(initiative) in a discipled (bureaucratic) environment.
Tightly structured training events may in effect implement a
hard nosed 'in the deep end' educational philosophy for the
development of autonomy: participants have the individuality
and independence put under pressure so that they either give
it up (sink) or find effective ways of protecting,
preserving and exercising it in a hostile environment (swim).
The folklore that trainers in this kind of context rate more
highly participants that stand up to them (provided they do
not overstep some invisible mark) than meek conformists,
support this general interpretation.

The notion of multiple value systems

The image developed so far has been one of the individual
autonomously pursuing his own development in the context of
strong attempts to shape him or her into the norms, values,
and behaviour patterns of some organisation, profession or
occupational grouping. This implies that such organisations
or groupings have relatively clear cut and unitary value
systems into which they socialise newcomers. Commonsense
again suggests that this is a simplistic picture. It seems
more realistic to think in terms of organisations and
groupings having continuously changing multiple value
systems, with different points of view dominating in
different parts at different times. It is hard to think of a
professional body in which there are more or less continual
debates about the nature of the profession, its function in
society, and appropriate standards of conduct for its
members. Similarly, very few organisations when viewed
closely, have a universal and unquestioned set of rules,
procedures, attitudes and values. Most are made up of
various factions with changing membership, beliefs and
relative power.

These phenomena are no where more clear than in the context
of management development programmes. Within professional
bodies it is in decisions about criteria for membership, and
the kind of training to enable people to meet them, that the
difference of opinion emerges. Similarly, in organisations it
is issues about the graduate intake or the management trainee
induction programme that bring the views of different
factions to the surface. This is because, we would argue,
everyone involved recognises, at some level of consciousness,
that it is the values and ideology into which the next
generation of managers is socialised that will become
dominant.

This is a speculative interpretation of the management
development situation, but we will offer as supporting
evidence two observations that we think will ring true for
many people actually involved in such situations.

Firstly, the setting up of a specific management
development programme often seems to be much more complex,
time consuming and illogical than many people feel it has any

right to be. Viewed as a technical process, such designing should proceed through steps of defining learning aims and objectives to the choosing of appropriate teaching and learning approaches, to formulating ways of implementing these both in training activities and administrative arrangements. The experience is rarely like that. Such processes seem more typically to involve repeated consultation with an ever broadening network of people, the gradual formulation of approaches and their sudden overthrowing, sudden decisions and reverses about resources, scale, 'official' support and the like. Such a process is better accounted for as the surface phenomena of a deeper 'political' process in which different factions are seeking dominance, coalition, compromise, selective advantage and so on.

The second and closely related observation is that those whose job it is to manage, coordinate, and administer management development tend to find the definition of their own roles problematical, and the main nature of their activities as essentially political. This common experience is totally consistent with the interpretation that everything to do with management development, including its own definition in a given situation, is not clear cut and well defined, but is in fact a kind of arena in which representatives of different factions interact to arrive at balances of power, coalitions, compromises that allow joint action to proceed. Thus the role of anyone centrally concerned will be a focal issue for such a process, and much of the activity of a person in such a role, will be that of a rather powerless gobetween trying to keep channels of negotiation open, to identify and exploit juxtapositions of interest amongst different factions.

Implications of multiple value systems

If processes of social influence in management development represent multiple rather than unitary value systems, then this has some implications for the individuals on the receiving end.

Rather than being influenced towards one relatively consistent and enduring set of beliefs, values and norms, the individual is likely to be exposed to influence that may both contradict each other at any one point in time, and change over time. In this situation individuals may, and probably do, react in a number of different ways, depending, amongst other things, on the extent and nature of his autonomous learning processes.

One possibility is that the individual may internalise the contradictory and changing values, thus making what was our external conflict, internal to the individual. It is easy to see how at best this is likely to render the individual indecisive and ineffective, and at worst, leave him in a state of stress with the various psychological and physiological consequences that might entail.

Another possibility is that the individual, in noticing the
multiple influences impinging on him, becomes firstly aware
that they are different value systems, secondly that there is
no definitive 'truth', or 'one right attitude' to various
issues, and therefore renders himself less likely to be
'taken over' by any one view or internalise the conflict
between them. If the process goes this way, then the
multiple value system, in a sense, serves to create more
space for autonomous learning, as compared with a unitary
situation.

A third possibility, which is an extension of the second,
is that the individual will realise, at some level of
consciousness, that the conflicting influences impinging on
him reflect an image of the organisation, profession, or
occupational grouping he is in or moving into. The
influences can then be exploited autonomously, as a learning
opportunity for acquiring a good understanding of the
different factions and points of view around, their
relative significance and power, and the process by which
they interact and change. Furthermore, the individual may be
able to experiment with allying himself with various factions,
or trying to exploit the differences between them. Thus, such
a person may use such a management development programme as a
natural laboratory for the development of political
managerial skills.

Latent functions of management development

The notion of latent functions - that activities and social
institutions serve important purposes other than those which
are their normal publicly stated purposes - can be applied to
management development. The argument so far has suggested
two major latent functions for management development:-

1.   To serve as an area or forum in which different
      factions, values, points of view, are negotiated,
      reconciled, compromised, and generally maintain
      some kind of shifting balance so that cooperative
      work can proceed. Such processes take place to a
      lesser extent within formally set up courses,
      conferences, workshops, etc and more in the often
      complex processes by which such events are planned
      and arranged.

2.   To serve as a 'political' training ground for the
      more naturally astute course participants, as a
      rough and ready 'sink or swim' approach to the
      development of such astuteness, and as a natural
      selection process for such people.

The notion that management development serves significant
latent functions can be supported to some extent by
observation. Those concerned with management development are
prone to worry about the 'evaluation' issue from time to time,
and consider the evidence, or more often lack of it, that
their efforts increase managerial performance in any cost

effective way. Decisions are also made from time to time about the scale, the nature, and the resources devoted to management development. The observation is that in practice there is not much correlation between such decision making and the evaluation of the achievement of manifest functions. This suggests that other considerations might be shaping such decisions, which is at least consistent with the idea that significant latent functions are operating.

Implications

The implications of this analysis, by its nature do not take the form of a number of 'technical' implications of specific things that could be done if the theoretical analysis is right.

The implication is more that management development is part of some rich, complex, semihidden, and valuable processes in organisational and individual life. The kind of conclusions that follow are that we should at least take care not to destroy these valuable hidden processes, that we may even be able to help them along a little, and that we may be able to save some resources and worry by not pouring more and more effort into turning management development into a straightforward technical function, which is futile, and which would destroy management development in the unlikely event that it succeeded.

Being more specific:-

1.   It may be appropriate to accept that the complex processes of arranging and 'setting up' management development activities are necessary, are part of the necessary 'action' rather than a regrettably necessary precursor to the action.

2.   Furthermore, if handled with skill and sensitivity, the 'planning' processes can be helped to have constructive consequences in their own right.

3.   That at least some programme participants can and will pursue some important but less visible learning goals, particularly developing political astuteness, which can be helped and tolerated, and that care should be taken not to 'purify' out of the situation the features that make this possible (by, for example, hiding differences of opinion, feeling it necessary to forcefit a single party line into the programme).

4.   There may be some not too obvious individual 'casualties' of management development who internalise too much external conflict. It is likely to be worthwhile developing sensitive strategies to help them.

5.   That of necessity management development may have to

be messy and volatile, and can be damaged by well
meaning attempts to tidy it up with systematic
procedures and technological solutions.

6. That 'doing' management development may inherently
    involve living with ambiguity and uncertainty, but
    it may help to be aware of some of the more latent
    functions which it serves. If management development
    continues to serve as a viable 'arena' for the
    organisations, and as a 'laboratory' for individuals
    to develop organisational political awareness, then
    it should survive and prosper.

7. Latent functions have, by definition to stay latent
    and be pursued with discretion and tact. It is not
    good logic to think in terms of bringing latent
    functions into the open, and then plan systematically
    for their achievement.

BIBLIOGRAPHY

Argyris, C, (1966), Explorations and Issues in Laboratory
    Education, National Training Laboratories, Washington DC.

Bandura, A, (1966), 'Social Learning Through Imitation' in
    Jones, M R, (ed.), Nebraska Symposium on Motivation,
    University of Nebraska Press, Lincoln, Nebraska.

Bandura, A, (1977), Social Learning Theory, General Learning
    Press.

Bradford, L P, (1958), 'The teaching-learning transaction',
    Adult Education, Vol.8, pp.135-45.

Burgoyne, J G and Stuart, R, (1977), 'Implicit learning
    theories as determinants of the effects of management
    development programmes, Personnel Review, Vol.6, No.2,
    pp.5-14.

Cooper, C L, (1976), Developing Social Skills in Managers,
    Macmillan, London.

Cooper, C L, (1981), Developing Managers for the 1980s,
    Macmillan, London.

French, J R P, and Raven, R, (1960) 'Bases of Social Power'
    in Cartwright and Zander (eds.), Group Dynamics,
    Tavistock, London.

Kagan, J, (1958), 'The concept of identification',
    Psychological Review, Vol.65, pp.296-305.

Kelman, H, (1961), 'Processes of opinion change', Public
    Opinion Quarterly, Vol.25, pp.57-58.

Lazowick, L M, (1965), 'On the nature of identification', Journal of Abnormal and Social Psychology, Vol.51, pp.175-83.

McDougall, W, (1913), An Introduction to Social Psychology, Methuen, London.

Morrison, A, and McIntyre, D, (1971), Schools and Socialisation, Penguin, London.

Raven, B, (1965), 'Social Influence and Power' in Steiner, I D, and Fishbein, M, (eds.), Reading in Contemporary Social Psychology, Holt, Rinehart and Winston, New York.

Rogers, C, (1961), On Becoming a Person, Houghton Mifflin, Boston.

Schein, E H and Bennis W G, (1965), Personal Learning and Organisational Change Through Group Methods, Wiley, New York.

Slater, P E, (1961), 'Towards a theory of identification', Merill-Palmer Quarterly, Vol.7, pp.113-26.

Winch, R F, (1962), Identification and its Familial Determinants: Exposition of Theory and Results of Pilot Studies, Bobbs-Merrill, New York.

Footnote   Some of the material used in this article was originally published by the authors in MANAGEMENT DECISION journal. We would like to thank MCB Publications for permission to use this material here.

19 Training for change: The value of data feedback

ANDREW KAKABADSE

In this chapter, I examine the value of data feedback as a means for introducing change and problem solving in organisations. In particular, a model of data feedback is offered. I argue strongly that because of the changes taking place in society which will directly impact upon work organisations and that because the more traditional approaches to management education have substantial limitations, approaches to data feedback should be considered an essential element of the services offered by any management education institution.

CHANGE, INNOVATION AND DECLINE

Innovation

Andre Piatier (1981) states that the western world has extended into the third industrial revolution due to innovations that have already taken place - new energy sources, new means of transport and new means of communication. Most of us are aware of the increasing pace of technological change, yet few of us are aware of its enormity. For example, did you know that:-

a. in the USA, 6,000 new food products are generated each year,

b. it is estimated that seventy per cent of the consumer goods to be sold in 1988 have not yet been invented,

c. knowledge had doubled between 1800 and 1900; it doubled again between 1950 and 1960; it doubled again between 1960 and 1966; since then it has been impossible to keep track of its growth,

d. ninety per cent of all scientists that ever lived are alive today (estimated five million),

e. in 2000 AD it is estimated that there will be at least twenty-five million scientists,

295

f.   in California, a group of scientists are
      developing ways of utilising solar energy to the
      extent of providing all the power and energy the
      USA needs. Coal, oil and gas are likely to become
      redundant. The scientists estimate that by using
      the hydrogen in solar energy to generate controlled
      nuclear explosions, this in turn will produce
      sufficient power for domestic and industrial
      requirements. Energy on such an enormous scale
      could become a viable proposition within the next
      five years,

g.   developments in micro-electronics, robotics and
      tele-communications will have far reaching effects
      over the next fifteen years. The information
      revolution has already introduced new, cheap and
      easy to use methods of data storage, retrieval and
      analysis. Automation is now in our offices with
      word processors, desktop VDUs (visual display units)
      and facsimile transmission.

The end result will be that head office will become
more unimportant whilst branch offices will increase
in importance.

Only just around the corner are the telephone linked
view data systems whereby the individual in his
house will not only be linked with other individuals
both by sight and sound but also with information
systems, hence eventually replacing books and
journals.

Robotics has changed the world of manufacturing.
Automation (a combination of robotics and micro-
electronics) has made a substantial impact in
production processes, warehousing and stock control.

CASE 1

Changing face of the factory

In the automative industry, the exception today is the
car plant that does not use robots. Fiat not only use
robots for car production but have master minded a
marketing campaign for the sale of the Fiat Strada
around the theme of "hand built by robots".

Ford UK have installed thirty robots at the Halewood
plant for their new Escort line, whilst British Leyland
have gone a long way to automating their Mini Metro
line at Longbridge. In the US, General Motors are
ordering robots by the hundreds.

At present, the robot cannot see, hear or speak.
However, the crude robots we have are taking over the
human workload to the extent of three robots to sixty

human beings.

The more intelligent robot of the future is already in operation in Japan. The Yamazaki machine tool factory near Nagoya claims that they have devised a system whereby the entire operations of the factory, including accounting, the preparation of financial statements and production control, can be managed automatically. The system, already in use for the manufacture of certain machine tools is worked in three shifts - the first shift employs seven people, the second shift requires five people and the night shift runs without anybody.

A report in the Financial Times (19 May 1981), estimated that present world sales in robots is around $350 million, but the market should be worth $2 billion and upwards by 1990.

Innovation may be exciting but it also brings decline. That decline is with us.

DECLINE

Certain futurologists estimate that with the advent of micro-electronics, three to five million will be made redundant as automated machine systems substitute human labour. Current political opinion in both the US and the UK is that if both countries adopt micro-electronics more slowly than their competitors, then the effects would be more painful than three to five million unemployed.

The futurologist Keith Pavitt (1980) urges more rapid change for Britain. If the UK does not adopt sophisticated automated production systems as in Japan, then it will have to rely, in part, on human labour. Third world countries in South East Asia and Latin America will soon capture our markets as their use of cheap labour and the application of intermediate technologies in areas ranging from textiles, shoes and clothing to bulk chemical, steel and consumer durable products will mean cheaper goods for sale.

The situation has been made more difficult over the last decade. Changes in political and economic conditions have substantially shortened the forward planning time horizons of many organisations. Commodity prices and supplies have fluctuated consistently and considerably in response to political developments. There have been substantial fluctuations of price and supplies in sugar, coffee and cocoa, leaving the confectionary industry, for example, in an uncertain state.

Market swings in copper prices have created problems for management in the non-ferrous metal industries.

Raw materials price inflation leads to uncertainties

about consumer behaviour. Will people buy at a higher price?
Will wholesalers and retailers purchase bulk orders in
anticipation of price rises and horde and release
spasmodically in order to make greater profits? Will the
customer find a substitute product and thereby lessen the
real demand for the original product?

In order to cope with such pressures, the management of
decline involves cutting back, closing down, lowering
overhead costs, reducing the size of workforces through
redundancy, retirement schemes and job placement services.
The process involves breaking down old identities and coping
with anxieties, that of others and one's own.

CONTRIBUTION OF MANAGEMENT EDUCATION

What contribution can management education make to the
development of any organisation under the present conditions
of decline and new growth?

Opinions vary, but there are a number of writers who
consider traditional management education methods to be of
limited value. In this book, for example, the lecture method
is either openly or implicitly criticised by Margerison,
Nadler and Lippitt.

Case studies have been identified as being an
inappropriate vehicle for effective business education
(Cooper, Rogers and Burgoyne, 1977), as the cases tend to be
out of date and further, do not really help managers learn
about their own situation but always about somebody elses.

In a recent paper (Kakabadse and Cooper, 1980), it was
strongly argued that the MBA (Master of Business
Administration) degree, the pillar of business school
education, was not producing the business graduates capable
of attending to industry's current needs. In fact, a delphi
study conducted at Cranfield School of Management (Rushton,
1981) has indicated how outdated is MBA type education.
Certain key subjects, as world and national politics, the
politics of managerial life, women in management and the
impact of new technologies on working life, are not being
taught but are high in demand by the employers of MBA
graduates.

Equally, the multi-disciplinary management training
programmes running from one to a few weeks duration can be
similarly questioned as being of only limited value to the
manager in his work situation. The advantage of any short
course is that it offers managers a certain amount of time
away from work pressures to reflect and think about their
work situation. In addition, training in the basic
disciplines of management is provided as well as the
opportunity of mixing and sharing experiences with other
managers from other organisations. The disadvantage to
short course management training is that each manager's work

problems cannot really be examined on a multi-disciplinary programme in a business school setting. Hence, although the manager may benefit whilst he is on the course, what value to the employing organisation?

Even with the development of computer assisted learning systems, where managers are more in charge of their own training and development by sitting in front of their own computer terminal, the same question applies; just how useful is such learning to the work situation?

A number of management educationalists see management education as being only of limited value. The reason is that in virtually all schools of management, business education is seen in terms of short or long courses. The problem is that courses are not a vehicle for problem solving at work. At best, the individual course attendee may benefit from the experience, but it is unlikely that his organisation will directly benefit from the person's experience. In fact, another study recently conducted at Cranfield School of Management (Chilmeran, 1980), indicates that whatever training and development took place on management courses, individuals quickly 'slip back' to their old way of doing things once they re-enter their work organisation. It is as if they had never been away on a programme of management training and development.

In order to help managers come to terms with current changes in society in general and in work organisations specifically, additional approaches to management education are required; in this paper, that of data feedback.

TRAINING THROUGH DATA FEEDBACK

Information is the life blood of any organisation. Data that has been gathered, organised and presented in particular ways, gives people the knowledge they need to do their work, to achieve prescribed standards and to understand who has the authority to direct actions. As information and information exchange are key ingredients in the process of helping organisations operate, then the gathering of new information and its feedback to various personnel in the organisation on how effectively people and systems are functioning, is an equally powerful tool for adaption and change (Nadler 1977; 1981).

Consequently, in order to introduce changes into an organisation, it is necessary to be aware of what data should be gathered from whom and why. Equally important are process issues, namely how is data to be gathered and how should it be fed back. Managing the process of data gathering and data feedback really determines whether attempts at change will be a success or failure. Undoubtedly, the quality of the data gathered is a key area of concern but not the final determinant of successful change attempts. Knowing how to handle the various parties involved in the change programme is as vital as knowing what quantitative data analysis skills to apply.

The processes of data feedback are identified in Figure 19.1 - the 3 level data feedback process model. Six steps to introducing and successfully implementing change and three separate levels of data feedback are examined.

Data feedback process model

Step 1 : Involves someone internal or external to the organisation spotting a problem or a series of related problems. The problem(s) have to be considered sufficiently important to require some action before proceeding to step 2.

Step 2 : Formal and informal attempts are made at diagnosing the perceived problem(s) and mapping out its impact on the organisation. Informal attempts at mapping and diagnosis may simply involve talking to colleagues, superiors and subordinates. Such informal interactions may lead to more formal attempts at diagnosing and mapping by forming project teams, organising workshops or using outside consultants. If the parties involved are sufficiently satisfied that there exist good reasons to do something about the problem(s), then it is likely that the decision to go and collect data will be made.

Step 3 : Who is to collect, what data, from whom and why? At this stage, various people in the organisation will be contacted to take on different roles; to act as data gatherers; to act as participants in a data gathering exercise and offer appropriate information; to act as monitors to the whole process, debating whether the data gathered is the most appropriate data to be gathered and whether the project is or is not meeting its objectives. At this stage, consultants may be called in to advise on what data should be gathered or how a data gathering exercise could be conducted. Project teams may be created, possibly composed of line managers, technical specialists, senior executives and external consultants. The project team's brief is to identify and gather appropriate data. A steering committee may be formed with representatives from all levels in the organisation, to monitor the progress of the project team.

Step 4/first level feedback : From the decision to collect data by particular individuals to the actual collection of the data. The data could be gathered by questionnaires or other data collection instruments; by holding interviews; by holding group meetings or workshops where both the opinions of individuals and groups are taken into account; by observing the behaviour and interactions of particular individuals or groups; by examining specific documents.

As a consequence of collecting data and involving particular people in the collection process, a need arises

300

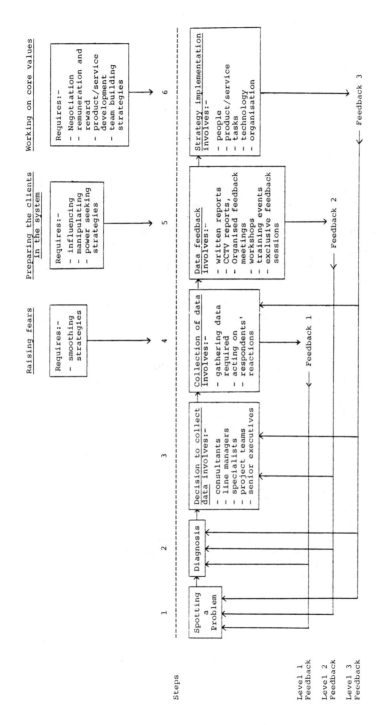

Figure 19.1 Three level data feedback process model

301

to feed data back to certain individuals and groups in the
organisation (level 1 feedback).

Numerous people in the organisation will have recognised
that new activities are taking place, such as people being
asked questions or questionnaires being distributed for
completion. As a response to the data search, people may
become fearful that unexpected or unwelcome changes may be
immenent. As a defensive measure, certain individuals or
groups may reject the data collection process by refusing
to take part in the exercise. Hence, level 1 feedback is
concerned with identifying and reducing the degree of
shared anxiety in the system to the collection of data.

In order to identify whether people's fears are being
raised, it is necessary for the data collectors to be
sensitive to the interpersonal processes involved in data
collection. For example, people may seem reluctant to be
interviewed or to offer particular documents; people may
seem defensive in interviews; it may be difficult to even
arrange for an appointment to see people. Such anxieties
have to be reduced or else people will ultimately refuse to
participate in the study.

To reduce people's fears, it is necessary to put in
practise smoothing strategies. There exist three smoothing
strategies.

1.   Prepare groups for data collection. Identify groups
     and individuals that may react adversely to a data
     collection study. Arrange for preliminary meetings
     with the groups, the individuals and their bosses,
     explaining why a data collection study is underway,
     its objectives and possible final outcomes.
     Encourage individuals at such meetings to talk
     about their fears so that all potentially
     threatening issues can be brought out into the open
     and debated.

2.   Handle each respondent's anxieties during data
     collection. It maybe necessary whilst interviewing,
     observing or gathering documentation from
     individuals to leave aside some time for openly
     discussing the data collection study. In this way,
     the respondents can begin to understand why the
     study is being conducted and hence have an
     opportunity to discuss in an informed way and in
     comfortable one to one surroundings, their reactions
     to the venture.

3.   Ensure that peoples' views are taken into account.
     As part of the smoothing process, it is neccessary
     to act on the reactions of the respondents. Their
     views and anxieties should be fed back to all the
     active members of the data feedback study. In
     addition, such process data is a good way of
     testing whether peoples' perceptions as to the

302

original problem has changed. If peoples' views of
the problem changes then approaches to diagnosis
and mapping may need to be reconsidered. That in
turn may change peoples' ideas as to what sort of
data to collect and by whom.

Level 1 feedback is aimed at reducing the level of anxiety
in the system about the survey and possible future changes
in the organisation.

CASE 2

The social services project

I recently conducted a comprehensive survey of the
social services in the UK (Kakabadse, 1982). The study
involved examining the organisation culture and
predominantly held attitudes towards work, bosses,
clients, authority and career development by all staff
in fourteen local authority social service departments.
The study required that I interviewed both on an
unstructured and on a structured interview schedule
basis, over 1,000 social service employees, ranging from
directors of social services to assistant social
workers.

Interviewing that many people was a mammoth task.
However, complications arose. People became anxious
about my presence in their organisation. They
wondered what I was doing. For this study to be
allowed to continue, it was necessary that I attempted
to reduce people's anxieties concerning the project,
how the data was to be used and what in particular
was my role.

The reason why people's anxiety level was raised was
understandable. At the time, social service
organisations were under substantial criticism from
the national press as being ineffective and not
meeting community needs. The child battering case
of Carly Taylor in Leicestershire had sparked off such
attention. Further, relations between management and
trade unions in a number of authorities had
substantially deteriorated. In fact, in some
authorities, social workers had gone on strike.
Understandably, both management and social workers
viewed me with some suspicision.

In order to be allowed access to each organisation
and in order to attract sufficient numbers of people
to interview, I adopted the following strategies:-

1. Explain to the senior management team in each
    social service department the intention of my
    project, indicating that the study was only
    an academic/information gathering exercise

303

and that all the data gathered would be treated confidentially.

2.   Once permission was granted to enter the organisation, the director of each department sent a memo to all employees, requesting that all cooperate with me on the project and stated the objectives of the project and emphasised that all information would be treated as highly confidential.

3.   From there on, I would attempt to meet supervisors, representatives of groups, trade union representatives and some middle managers to again emphasise the objectives of the project and confidentiality of information.

4.   Having obtained the support of influential groups within each organisation, I managed to attract sufficient people to interview. Before each interview began, I repeated exactly the same message that I had before so as to gain the full confidence of the interviewee in order to stimulate frank and open responses to my questions.

At the start of the project I expected the data gathering stage to last eight months. It took seventeen months to complete. Had I not attempted to reduce people's anxieties, it would never have got off the ground.

Step 5/second level feedback : At step 5, the data gathered is fed back to the interested parties. Data feedback may involve submitting written reports to certain individuals or groups; preparing video reports; offering data for discussion in small groups or large group sessions; arranging workshops to discuss the data; organising training events based on the data; providing exclusive feedback sessions to the key decision makers in the organisation, such as chairman, managing director, members of the board.

The way data is fed back depends on the impact that the data collectors wish to make on various members of the organisation. The ultimate purpose is to stimulate change in the organisation. Hence, data feedback at this stage is essentially concerned with preparing the various groups and key individuals in the system to think about change. To whom data is offered and the way it is offered are important considerations for the data collectors. The aim is to influence the opinion of particular people in the organisation in particular ways. Hence, the collectors need to have established sufficient power and influence to be able to decide:-

- who is to be fed what information?

- are all the respondents to be fed the same information?

- how is the information to be offered to various groups?

- what are the various concerns of different groups in the organisation and should the data just address each separate group's concerns?

- should further working parties be organised to analyse the value of the data?

- who should sit on the working parties?

- what is the most appropriate way to obtain a general commitment to use the data gathered in a positive way?

Peoples' views of the data and their analysis of the data should be noted by the data collectors for it may alter opinions as to what really is the problem, how should diagnosis and mapping be conducted and who should be involved in the process of data collection. In fact, a second, probably smaller data feedback survey may result from such discussions.

Level 2 feedback is aimed at influencing key individuals and groups in the organisation to think about change.

Two case examples are offered; the first (case 3) of a well conducted data feedback operation; the other (case 4) of an unsuccessful intervention.

CASE 3

Making Bankers Managers

A colleague and I were approached by a major international bank, stating that they had a problem with their domestic branch managers. Basically, the branch managers sat in their offices and did not go out searching for business in their local community. Rival banks were more proactive. This particular bank considered it was losing money in its domestic banking division due to the lack of drive and flair on the part of their branch managers. What to do?

We recommended that instead of attempting to implement a standard management programme, why not find out what the managers themselves would want. We decided to organise a series of workshops and invite all interested parties - branch managers and more senior managers - to come together and identify and analyse

305

their work situation.

Three crucial problems were identified:-

a.   the ability to manage relationships. Branch
     managers were considered insufficiently skilled
     at managing customers and staff,

b.   the ability to adapt to new job requirements.
     Branch managers had never been trained as
     managers but as technical banking specialists.
     Becoming a manager was considered a traumatic
     experience,

c.   the ability to manage superiors. Branch managers
     were considered naive in terms of organisational
     politics and too subservient towards their
     superiors. Managing your boss was considered as
     important as managing your staff.

These findings and appropriate training
recommendations were put to the main board. The board
accepted all recommendations.

Now the bank is running its own particular management
training programme just to suit its own needs. It has
also turned out to be a cheaper exercise than using
outside consultants. (Margerison and Kakabadse, 1981).

CASE 4

Training but no change: The case of British Leyland by an
OD consultant.

Ray Charlton (1982), an internal organisation
development (OD) consultant with British Leyland (BL)
recently wrote about the developments in the company that
have led to its present crisis development.

For BL, three major phases of company organisation can
be identified.

The first phase (1968-74), which followed the merger of
British Motor Holdings Limited and Leyland Motor
Corporation Limited, was one of anticipated expansion and
great hope for the future. The newly formed conglomerate
hoped to expand its production and sales to compete with
the biggest and the best. New management systems and
practises were introduced and a large number of
specialists, some outside the motor industry were
recruited, all bringing with them some ideas and techniques.

In the second phase (1974-78), the first period was
seen as a false dawn. By the end of 1974, the company
approached the government for funds. Funding was

306

granted but only after further reorganisation.
Previous car company divisions were merged into a large
centralised line and staff structure. In addition,
there was a reshuffling of management personnel and the
major functions and reporting lines were reshaped.

In the third phase (from 1978 onwards), BL was placed
under the leadership of Michael Edwardes. Further
reorganisation and rationalisation took place, whereby
inessential activities were relentlessly discarded in
an effort to keep the corporate head above water. The
new survival order was either do the job or get out.
That situation still holds.

For Ray Charlton, a number of reasons exist for BL's
demise.

Size. The company became too big too quickly.

Integration. As the company grew, there were few
attempts to bring together the various parts of the
company under some form of corporate philosophy.

Over optimism on the part of management. Simply
because the company had grown in size did not mean it
would be successful.

The lack of strategic thinking and integration on
the part of the internal OD consultants meant that
there was no coordinated effort by the very people who
were employed to provide consultancy and training to
meet the company's needs. Training in terms of short
courses and group facilitation programmes were
provided. It, however, made little impact on the
managers who in turn had to handle BL's difficulties.
The reason that inappropriate training was provided
was mostly due to the lack of data about the company
and its management. Had an effective data based
intervention been conducted, the situation may have
turned out differently.

Step 6/third level feedback : Step 6 is the final stage of a
data feedback survey and is concerned with the
implementation of particular changes. In order to
introduce changes that will be supported and recognised as
worthwhile in the organisation, the smoothing strategies of
step 4 and the manoeuvering and power seeking strategies of
step 5 must have been effectively applied.

By introducing changes in the organisation, the people who
have to implement the changes and accept the changes will
also have to adjust their attitude to the way work and
relationships are to be conducted. Step 6 is as much
concerned with the implementation of change as it is with
influencing the deeply held values with which most people
identify within the organisation. Hence, it is vital that
all the personnel involved at the implementation stage

should have been prepared to accept change.

The changes could concentrate on improving the performance of people, reorganising the range of products or services the organisation offers, re-examining task performance and productivity, reviewing the technology currently in use in the organisation and assessing whether new technologies would be required in the future, reviewing the organisational/divisional and departmental structures currently in operation. In order to achieve improvements in the area of people, products or services, tasks, technology and organisation, it is necessary to consider approaches to team building, renegotiate the remuneration and reward systems and develop new training programmes.

As part of the process of examining the practical problems of implementing change, the parties involved should again re-examine how the data feedback survey began, who collected what data and why, and whether the data collected is still of value at step 6. From these questions, an additional data feedback survey may result.

Level 3 feedback is aimed at influencing those who are involved with the implementation of change to ensure that the changes are carried out.

CASE 5

Politics of implementing change in a chemical company

The managing director of a subsidiary company of a multi-national chemical company approached a group of academic consultants stating that his company was to grow rapidly over the next few years but that he did not have the middle managers capable of managing and maintaining that growth. What should be done?

The consultants recommended that they hold exploratory discussions with a select number of senior and middle managers in the company. The MD approved. After the discussions, the consultant recommended a complete management audit including an organisation climate study, to which again the MD approved. The results of the audit were interesting.

Middle managers were identified as well qualified, technically competent, holding a wide experience of work in other functions, and companies, but extremely dissatisfied with senior management.

Senior management were identified as moderately well qualified, authoritarian; suspicious of middle managers' motives and having little faith in their abilities, with many years experience in their present position.

The deputy MD was identified as overworked, largely because all communications from senior management to the MD had to go through him and further, all decisions made by senior management had to have the deputy MD's approval.

The MD was identified as knowing only what his deputy wished him to see.

It was quickly realised by the MD and the more progressive senior managers, that the company employed all the talent it required. The immediate problem was to motivate and train the more able middle managers so as to promote them to senior management positions. Together with the consultants, the MD adopted the following strategy:-

-   establish a selection centre in order to identify the more able middle managers,

-   create the appropriate training programmes such as understanding motivation, leadership and supervisory skills, decision making skills, etc,

-   place the more able middle managers into a temporary senior management position to develop their experience,

-   identify the more vulnerable and less powerful senior managers and remove them from their position through early retirement, voluntary redundancy and transfer to another subsidiary company,

-   push the deputy MD out of the organisation and into another subsidiary company,

-   appoint able middle managers to new or vacant senior management positions.

A year later, the MD himself was promoted as group chairman. He was asked what he learnt from his recent experience of managing planned change. He replied that the secret is to have the necessary information upon which to make balanced decisions. On this basis, most people in the organisation will eventually respect the decision maker(s) and the decisions made, as the most equitable under the circumstances. In this way, any opposition will slowly turn to approval for the changes made. To try and manage major changes without a sound data base is to commit professional suicide.

SUMMARY

Data feedback is a highly effective means of influencing
peoples' values, attitudes and norms of behaviour in order
to introduce or even prevent change. In applying data
feedback approaches, it is important to realise that the
data and the process of data collection are equally
important in the change intervention. The data gathered
provides the fuel for the debate on what should be done,
how and by when. The process of data collection provides
the data collectors with information about peoples'
feelings concerning their work, their superiors,
subordinates and colleagues, their strength of identity
with the status quo and their reactions to change. Both
quantitative and qualitative data have to be taken into
account in any data feedback survey.

Final thought. Data feedback approaches to management
development are unlikely to substitute the more traditional
approaches to management development. There will still be
a place in the market for more basic management education.
However, because of the current recession, and managers, in
general, gaining a greater understanding as to the true
value of the various forms of management training, people
will be more selective. Managers will still want training
but in addition, assistance in solving their problems. The
plea is that data based feedback approaches become an
additional element of every business school's portfolio of
services.

BIBLIOGRAPHY

Charlton, R and Herlihy, F, (1982), 'Organisation Development
    in BL Cars: Practitioners Observations and Prognosis' in
    Kakabadse, A, (ed.), People and Organisations: The
    Practitioners View, Gower Press.

Chilmeran, A N A, (1980), The Influences of the Master of
    Business Administration Programme on Participants,
    unpublished PhD dissertation, Cranfield School of
    Management, Cranfield Institute of Technology, Bedford.

Cooper, C C, Rogers, A and Burgoyne, J, (1977), 'Evaluation
    of Management Education - The State of the Art' in
    Ashton, D, (ed.), Management Bibliography and Review,
    Yorkshire UK, MCB Publications.

Kakabadse, A P, (1982), Culture of the Social Services, Gower
    Press.

Kakabadse, A P and Cooper, C, (1980), 'Reflections on
    teaching organisation behaviour in the United States and
    the United Kingdom', Management Education and Development,
    Vol.11, Part 1, pp.51-54.

Margerison, C J and Kakabadse, A P, (1981), 'Making bankers managers', Management Forum, Vol.7, No.3, pp.207-211.

Nadler, D A, (1977), Feedback and Organisation Development: Using Data Based Methods, Addison Wesley.

Nadler, D A, (1981), 'Managing organisational change: An Integrating perspective', Journal of Applied Behavioural Science, Vol.17, pp.191-211.

Pavitt, K, (1980), 'Technical innovation and industrial development: The danger of divergence', Futures, February, pp.35-44.

Piatier, A, (1981), 'Innovation, information and long term growth', Futures, October, pp.371-382.

Rushton, A M, (1981), 'The future of management development: A delphi study', Working Report, Cranfield School of Management.

20 Management development for metaindustrial organisations

PHIL HARRIS

The profound transition underway in post-industrial society
has lead to many designations being utilised to try and
indicate future social systems, be they corporations,
government agencies, associations, or even institutions of
higher education. The one that seems most appropriate to
this writer is 'metaindustrial', that is an organisation
that is above and beyond the industrial stage of human
development. Today the high technology company is a
harbinger of this emerging entity, and it is spawning a new
kind of manager - a person of more vision, an
entrepreneurial type given to creative risk taking, a
technically oriented individual who values flexibility,
competency, informality, and meaning in work.

As a result, management education will experience
significant change between now and the end of this century.
In seeking to prepare managers for metaindustrial
organisations, lines of distinction will begin to erode -
between formal and informal education, between training and
education, between the role of the university in this
process and the role of the organisation in inservice
education. For example, increasingly those seeking graduate
degrees in business administration may find themselves both
studying/working in the university and the corporation
simultaneously - the future will bring a greater interchange
between these two social institutions, and probably expand
the relationship to include government. University
faculties will find themselves doing more than research and
consulting in global corporations - by the 21st century, it
will be quite common for such business professors to be
managers themselves in corporations for temporary periods,
after longer service in academia, or in university owned
businesses. Corporate management trainers, on the other
hand, may find themselves teaching in company sponsored
degree programmes, or on loan to university MBA programmes.
Management media instruction will stimulate exchanges
between both groups.

Education and training are primary means for perpetuating
a culture. One aspect for cultural analysis is how people
learn - how they transmit knowledge, information and folk
wisdom to succeeding generations. The educational practices
of a group, whether formal or informal, are culture specific.

They reflect the customs, traditions, beliefs and attitudes of both macroculture and microcultures. Thus, for management educators to better understand an organisation's culture, examine the human resource development (HRD) system of a corporation, agency or association, they must be sensitive to the organisations traditions and values. That enterprise reflects the cutlure of the society in which it is located. The philosophy, scope and manner of employee or member career development is somewhat indicative of the indigeneous macroculture. Therefore, oriental HRD programmes would have different content, emphasis, and techniques than that which might be current in accidental firms. Yet, synergy in education and training today might lead to the teaching of Zen meditation to Western executives to improve their stress management.

Corporate culture affects the entity's commitment to the development of its human resources. The quality and appearance of new recruits, the care and methods used in their placement and promotion, the ways that performance is assessed and rewarded, the procedures for terminating association - all such organisational activities reflects the institution's culture. The organisational HRD system does more than transfer attitudes, information, and skills to employees, customers and suppliers. It is more than a means to enabling personnel to earn livelihoods, to supplement previous formal schooling, to socialise and even to exercise power. This career development system is the mechanism for inculcating the organisation's wisdom, history and culture. Corporate ideas and ideals, values and priorities, norms and expectations are all passed on through orientation and training courses, management and executive development, as well as numerous conferences and conventions. Organisational behaviour is thus conditioned, consciously and unconsciously.

Some organisational cultures promote the raising of member consciousness and self actualisation. The American Red Cross, for instance, has this personnel objective - "to improve the quality of life and enhance self reliance". According to their training department, this translates into training people to help themselves. Therefore, the organisation is supportive of training. Education in many organisations is a major activity and involves considerable financial investment. The magnitude can be appreciated by examining one industry - the telephone utilities. In 1980, it was reported that the Bell System offered 12,000 courses in 1,300 training locations for 20-30,000 employees per day; such educational services involved 13-15,000 training support staff at a cost of $1.7 billion. (ASTD Report, 1980). However, the effectiveness or outcomes of this training can be aided or undermined by corporate culture as Donald Caplin reminded us in the Northeast Training News:

"In 1961, AT and T set up a training programme to teach managers how to coordinate customised sales. But when

managers returned to the job, they proved unable - or
unwilling - to implement what they had learned. In
fact, eighty-five per cent quit the company and the
programme was disbanded.

Poor training - or something else? An analysis of the
experience showed that the AT and T programme was the
victim of 'corporate culture'. Organisational culture
is a mysterious entity that has claimed a number of
training efforts - but it also can help a human resource
programme.....

In the AT and T case, for example, the problem was
that the culture valued volume and making as many sales
as possible meant mass production. Although they
learned a new set of behaviours, managers, in effect,
were not rewarded for serving individual requests.
(Caplin, 1981).

Yet corporate cultures can change for it was this very
industrial giant, AT and T, that pioneered a complete
redesigning of roles by a systemwide job enrichment
programme and another project to reward high performers!

When transnational enterprises offer training and
development on a global scale, their educational endeavours
become powerful mechinisms for local change. But their
efforts are culture bound, and need to be adapted to the
host culture if they are to be effective. Technology
transfer, when it is sensitive and appropriate, can make a
significant contribution to the development of indigeneous
peoples. Whether the corporation abroad is engaged in
literacy or skill training, management or community
development, its representatives should be aware of the
influences of their own national and organisational cultures
upon themselves. Then, they will not use the learning
processes as the means for cultural imposition, or
inappropriate and unrealistic teaching or instruction. Thus,
one does not suddenly expect management trainees to abstract
and conceptualise in a culture dominated by rote learning or
where the language itself is a limitation to such
intellectual thinking. In his book, The Cultural
Environment of International Business, Vern Terpstra (1978)
provides some guidelines for multinational corporations
engaged in worldwide worker training.

-   The general level of education locally affects the
    quality of people available for employment and
    training. Learning must be adapted to such
    realities.

-   Managers should be rewarded in proportion to their
    success overseas in training of the locals. Their
    management control systems should take into account
    the local culture and its values.

-   Every country, regardless of its stages of

development has its educational elites who are at
the top of the local educational superstructure.
The foreign manager should establish contact with
this network of individuals and the institutions
from whence they came.

The whole personnel process from entry to exit has been
popularly designated the 'human resource development
system'. Dr Leonard Nadler in his classic, Developing Human
Resources, has defined HRD as "a series of organised
activities, conducted within a specified time and designed
to produce behavioural change". (Nadler, 1979). This
George Washington University Professor maintains that:-

-   training equals job related learning experiences,

-   education equals individual related learning
    experiences,

-   development equals organisation related learning
    experiences.

He believes that HRD within organisations is moving
increasingly toward greater utilisation of media for
instructional purposes, and the presentation of instruction
through learning modules, or blocks of learning which
feature a variety of methods and techniques.

Devanna, Fombrun and Tichy (1981) propose that
organisations should have human resource management
strategies which deal with policy formulations, goal
setting, and longterm positioning of the corporation in its
environment. In Figure 20.1 there is a reproduction of
human resource functions on the strategic or longterm
level in contrast to the managerial or mediumterm level,
and the operational or shortterm level. It provides an
interesting overview of what HRD involves within
organisational culture.

Organisational human resource development leads to the
capitalisation of human assets, the enlargement of human
potential. In a knowledge or information society, the
corporation plays not only an increased role in the
education of its own personnel, but of the citizenry at
large. FORTUNE 500 companies have founded learning
corporations, while an expanding number of firms are
getting into the business of education. They provide
educational hardware, software and instruction.
Westinghouse Learning Corporation, for instance, was
involved in Peace Corps, VISTA and police training. In the
United States, the education business within the private
sector is a billion dollar plus enterprise!

And what of the future for organisational career
development? Let's use our imagination based on
contemporary trends and project ahead less than two decades
to the turn of the century.

Level	Employee Selection/Placement	Rewards (Pay and Benefits)	Appraisal	Development	Career Planning
Strategic (longterm)	1. Specify the characteristics of people needed to run business over longterm. 2. Alter internal and external systems to reflect future.	1. Determine how workforce will be rewarded over the longterm based on potential world conditions. 2. Link to longterm business strategy.	1. Determine what should be valued in longterm. 2. Develop means to appraise future dimensions. 3. Make early identification of potential.	1. Plan developmental experiences for people running future business. 2. Set up systems with flexibility and necessary to adjust to change.	1. Develop longterm system to manage individual and organisational needs for both flexibility and stability. 2. Link to business strategy.
Managerial (mediumterm)	1. Make longitudinal validation of selection criteria. 2. Develop recruitment marketing plan. 3. Develop new markets.	1. Set up five year compensation plans for individuals. 2. Set up cafeteria benefits packages.	1. Set up validated systems that relate current conditions and future potential. 2. Set up assessment centres for development.	1. Establish general management development programme. 2. Provide for organisational development. 3. Foster selfdevelopment.	1. Identify career paths. 2. Provide career development services. 3. Match individual with organisation.
Operational (shortterm)	1. Make staffing plans. 2. Make recruitment plans. 3. Set up day-to-day monitoring systems.	1. Administer wage and salary programme. 2. Administer benefits packages.	1. Set up annual or less frequent appraisal system. 2. Set up day-to-day control systems.	1. Provide for specific job skill training. 2. Provide on-the-job training.	1. Fit individuals to specific jobs. 2. Plan next career move.

Figure 20.1 Human Resources Functions*

*See Devanna, Fombrun and Tichy, (1981), pp.51-67.

YEAR 2000: MANAGEMENT DEVELOPMENT SCENARIO

Jack Armstrong is a satellite technician with Tel Com Tech, WC. Originally, this company was incorporated in the United States, until regional supranational economic authorities were established to charter 'world corporations' and supervise their planetary business activities. Back in 1995 Tel Com received its WC designation from the Pacific Basin Regional Authority, a quasi-governmental entity, because the bulk of its enterprises were centred in the Pacific Rim area. Although Jack works out of corporate headquarters in San Diego, he reports in this matrix organisation to Paula Dittmar, an attractive European executive also located at HDQ, as well as to Milton Robertson in Vancouver, Canada, and Harry Wu in Singapore. Tel Com's main operational subsidiaries are in those cities.

On the morning of 4 January 2000, Jack had scheduled an interview in the career development centre to review his semi annual career growth plan. There he will meet first with Monroe Brown, the company's HRD executive consultant, who not only heads up the centre, but is responsible for career development throughout Tel Com's global network of knowledge workers. Corporate philosophy is committed to actualising the potential of all its human assets. Since all personnel own shares in the corporation, they share in both its profits and losses (which rarely occur), so their development is a high priority in the enterprise's culture. Brown, a black former football star and scholar from USC, carries the letters CHRS after his name on the centre door. (That is a Certified Human Resource Specialist, a designation earned through the International Society for Human Resource Development. The organisation resulted from a merger of the American Society of Training and Development and like national societies with the then International Federation of Training and Development Organisations. In 1990, the formation of this HRD conglomerate dropped the words 'training' and 'trainers' from professional vocabularies).

Prior to the Armstrong meeting, Monroe had reviewed the man's career history and forecasts on the computerised video display. The office microprocessor can instantly recall personal, educational, vocational and social documentation on every Tel Com affiliate (the word 'employee' had long ago been dropped). The coded information provided not only Armstrong's performance record since joining Tel Com five years ago, but results from sophisticated career testings and simulation at the centre, along with prognostications. This was all part of Tel Com's Talent Bank, a worldwide registry called HAR (for Human Assets Registry). Through Brown every manager in their far flung enterprise can get a printout of personnel who might fit his or her unit's annual needs assessment. Each fiscal year ending, Tel Com expected managers to forecast resource needs for their operations.

With regard to workers, this was understood to include two
competency components - humans and robots. Monroe Brown's
staff was to assist management in developing a synthesis
between organisation and human career needs and
development. Their counterparts at the Robotic Research
Centre were engineering specialists who coordinated all
the mechanical 'workers' and conducted experiments on
their performance improvement.

On this particular sunny Monday morning in their Torrey
Pines Industrial Park facilities, Brown had arranged for a
tele-conference involving Jack Armstrong and Paula Dittmar
in California, Milton Robertson in Canada, and Harry Wu in
Singapore. Together they would all discuss Armstrong's
career plan for the year 2000 in terms of both his
professional needs, as well as corporate needs. Within the
context of an information processing firm's culture, the
conversation went like this:-

> Brown - "Greetings all! By now you have reviewed our
> HRD records and forecast on your bright, young
> technician, Jack Armstrong. We hope to arrive through
> this conference at some mutual consensus on a career
> development focus for him over the next six to twelve
> months. Let's begin with Jack himself. If wishes
> were to come true, and you had no constraints upon
> you Jack, what would you wish to do?"

> Armstrong - "Well, I've had five years of documented
> achievement with Tel Com, and I think that I am due for
> an educational sabbatical. I'd like to take a year off
> to go East to MIT for some technical communication
> studies. It's about time that I got exposed to some of
> that Eastern culture after being brought up in the
> West'."

> Wu - "While I'd miss you on our project team Jack, I
> can appreciate the wisdom and humour of your last
> remark about exposure to Eastern culture. I think I
> could live with your temporary absence from our
> activities if you could include some Vietnamese language
> and culture studies on your agenda for the next year.
> As you know, Tel Com has a major expansion underway in
> IndoChina, and I was anticipating that you might join
> our Hanoi operations in 2001."

> Brown - "Thanks for that input Harry. If we agree that
> Vietnam's in Jack's near future, there would be no
> problem in arranging some videotapes and holographics
> to upgrade Jack's proficiencies in Vietnamese language
> and business protocol, while he is proceeding with
> advanced information sciences."

> Robertson - "OK all. But don't forget our downrange
> plan to set up a Tel Com industrial station on the moon
> in 2005 and beyond. Jack is a prime candidate for that
> mission. If we concur that this is the right time for

extended studies, it certainly should include some long
range career preparation for that potential assignment.
A Far Eastern stint for three years is feasible for
Jack, but by 2004, he would have to devote himself
primarily to specialised orientation for that moon
launch. Since I have principal space project
responsibility, I naturally want to ensure that our
best personnel for that interplanetary team will be
ready. My staff and I envision Armstrong as a unit
leader for a mission team of five human specialists and
fifteen robots!"

Dittmar - "Well fellows, since I have everyday
interface and supervisory relations with our colleague
Armstrong, may I propose some compromises? Here in San
Diego, we cannot spare Jack to be away for twelve
months. We could release him parttime for some local
studies over the next six months, and then fulltime off
for the following six months. Further, if he enrolled
in our nearby UCSD, he could take advantage of their
unique programme in lunar studies. To meet Milt
Robertson's concerns, Jack might do two things:

1.   Finish his doctorate in telecommunications
      with dissertation research focused on problems
      related to establishing our 'moon factory'.

2.   Set up an on-line computer interaction with
      the folks up north at Edwards Air Force Base.

By staying on the West Coast, he also can pop up
regularly to the nearby NASA facilities. After that I
have no objections to a shortterm Vietnam task force
assignment. That intercultural experience might even
sharpen his coping skills for dealing with an alien
culture in outer space."

Brown - "Should Jack stay in this locale, we could take
care of Harry's concerns through the nearby Indochinese
Studies Centre, and also expose him to the large
Vietnamese community in Vista, California. Paula, your
proposals are sound, but I think I can get you a
substitute for Jack, so that he could be released for a
full year of concentrated studies and research. We
have an exchange programme with the faculty at UCSD. I
think I can arrange for one of their staff to join Tel
Com for a year to cover Jack's professional
responsibilities with us. On the other hand, Jack
might have to agree to give some lectures or teach a
course while also at the university studying .....
Well, sharpen the images on your video pictures and
tell me what you think of these alternatives? Jack, why
don't you start off replying."

SCENARIO IMPLICATIONS

Back in the present, what do we learn about future prospects for organisational culture and its HRD system? The scenario contains more facts and probabilities than fantasy. Consider then, these possibilities for the immediate decades ahead as revealed in the above case:

1. The corporate focus is upon information/communication technology.

2. There is a regional economic emphasis, and emergence of a supranational authority that charters world corporations.

3. In this matrix organisation, one operates globally and reports to people in others parts of the world.

4. A multinational workforce operates upon the authority of competence, not on your nationality race, sex or other such obsolete employment criteria.

5. A central corporate theme is meaningful career development and review in terms of larger organisational strategies.

6. The acceptance of women and minorities in executive positions is an organisational norm, along with the premise of personnel involvement and ownership.

7. The inclusion of HRD data in the total management information system for international application.

8. The utilisation of technological and personnel forecasting in comprehensive planning by HRD professionals who are more facilitators than personnel mechanics.

9. The expansion of American professional societies beyond national borders, and their certification of professional competency. The internationalisation of professional associations, both formally and informally, will be evident, especially by networking.

10. The computerisation of all worldwide personnel records and the use of a talent bank for fulltime, parttime and contract knowledge workers.

11. The establishment of a new 'personnel' entity for robotics management to counterbalance the Career Development Centre for humans (fewer in number and of high quality abilities).

12. The common use of teleconferencing and other means of telecommunications, as well as educational technology.

13. The collaborative nature and approach of the management team, though separated by distance and macrocultures.

14. The acceptance of sabbatical leaves for continuing professional growth.

15. The cooperative relations and personnel exchanges between the corporation and the university.

16. The use of other educational resources in the community for language and culture learning, especially by use of one's home communication centre.

17. The market focus on the Pacific Rim, and the international corporate headquarters in Western North America.

18. The planning for expansion into outer space commercial operations.

19. The sophisticated, cosmopolitan managerial approach with its mutual concern for the individual and institutional well being.

Since technology and its growth will dominate organisational life now and more so in the future, it is important that technical and engineering personnel not only be continuously updated, but that their educational experiences be broadening. Only then will we ensure not only their personal and professional development, and counteract overly narrow specialisation. Only then can we ensure that such persons are prepared to make more significant contributions to both society and their organisations. A recent study by HRD researchers, Rymell and Newsom (1981), recommends more selfdirected learning projects in highly technical industries, so that a wider variety of learning topics and educational resources will be utilised.

EDUCATING FOR ROLE TRANSITIONS

General Electric Corporation had a slogan, "people are our most important product." Any firm that believed in such an ideal would devote a major portion of its budget to investment in its human assets. With the spread of robotics and computerisation, there will obviously be less people at work in organisations, but these individuals will have higher qualifications and competencies. Such knowledgeable workers will not only be responsible for a wider scope of mechanised operations, they will require extensive support services. The high cost in obtaining and maintaining such personnel already demands that corporations provide creative environments to retain these valued employees. More important, company budgets will be extended to offer continuous re-education of them to ensure high performance.

Even traditional industrial age giants spend heavily today on personnel development. Westinghouse Electric Corporation, for example, has not only worldwide inservice training for hourly workers, but spends millions on management development inhouse. Most companies also send key persons off site for workshops, seminars and courses to keep them abreast of innovations in their fields, or to acquire the latest technical or managerial techniques. A few statistics may underscore the scope of this current HRD investment in people. The American Management Association, one of the largest adult education systems in the US and abroad, reports that in 1980, 81,092 managers and executives took their short courses, some 3,407 in number. Through subsidiary organisations, such management education is offered by AMA from the CEO to the supervisory level either in plush resorts or inplant. Furthermore, their management philosophy and services are offered overseas through affiliated management centres and their International Management Association. Another piece of data may make the point - in 1981, one million influential North American executives attended some type of seminar, workshop or conference at a combined fee cost of $500 million (Schrello, 1981). The billion plus business of education in industry and government has been experiencing a fifteen per cent growth rate for the past decade of the 70s. Why?

There are numerous reasons that could be cited as to why so many adults are going 'back to school', or in fact never really leave the 'classroom'. The last half of the 20th Century has been marked by an acceleration of change, an explosion of knowledge in all fields of human endeavour, and a major shift from an industrial to a postindustrial way of life. The ongoing 'metaindustrial revolution' is not only forcing the demise of many jobs and occupations, but eliminating whole functional areas within traditional industries. It has been referred to as conventional technological obsolescence. As this is being written, two newspaper reports come forth which underscore the problem and the challenge. Sony has announced a discovery of a wholly new approach to photography that will 'revolutionise' the industry and make present processes archaic. What will this do to the photographic industry and positions as now constituted? Again TRW in Hawthorne, California, reveals that it has a team of scientists and technicians working for four years under NASA contract on the establishment of outer space factories. Within the decade, materials processing platforms may be launched with a view to developing stronger alloys, more uniform crystals, and purer chemicals and serums. The vertical expansion of research and manufacturing facilities into space will not only be likely before the

322

turn of this century, it is but another catalyst for change
in the way in which we work and formulate organisations.
We are already well aware of the implications of the spread
of office automation and its impact on managers and
secretarial staff. But what will happen to traditional
careers and vocational activities brought on by the
expanded linkage of telecommunications and computer
technologies? The French have a new word for it -
'telematics' which refers to the transmission of information
(i.e. power), a different kind of network for transferring
a blend of pictures, sounds and memories that will transform
our culture (Colemen, 1981). Not just society, but
organisational culture!

New technologies are not only transforming international
trade and manufacturing, they are changing the very way in
which we do business and design people's roles in
organisations. Not only is human society globally in
transition, but our traditional roles within it are
disappearing. Consider how many jobs have disappeared
since computer programmers came into being less that forty
years ago. How many corporations today provide for the
function of 'information resource manager'? Yet with the
emergence of a watershed technology like microcomputers,
that role is already becoming a key management position.
Somebody has to coordinate the input and output of these
smart machines within organisations. If the impact of the
microprocessor may be greater upon society than the
automobile or the electric light, what will be its influence
on organisations and their cultures? Contemporary
organisational training is one arena where the impact is
most visible. The introduction of 'micros' into businesses,
for instance, has meant a proliferation of courses in
'authoring systems for managers' or 'word processing for
executives'. Furthermore, it is altering the way we learn
- like programmed instruction, computer based learning
forces one to master one part of a lesson before going on to
the next knowledge component. Still another illustration
of drastic change in the way we learn, is teleconferencing,
another spinoff of the space age. It is being now used for
medical education programming of innovative healing
techniques, for less expensive sales training in new
product lines, for updating rapidly, financial officers on
the effects of newly passed bankruptcy laws (Schaaf, 1981).
There is emphasis on moving 'brains' rather than bodies for
continuing education purposes.

So in such 'turbulent times' what are some approaches that
far-sighted managers and management educators can adopt in
their human resource development efforts? Consideration of
these four proposals may stimulate readers to undertake
many more similar endeavours for the capitalisation of
human assets:

   1.   Re-education of the masses of industrial age
       workers for the realities of postindustrial
       society. To delimit future shock and counteract

the dislocations in the workforce caused by
increased automation, business will have to
cooperate with unions, government, universities and
other social institutions in massive
'enlightenment' programmes about the profound
transitions underway in both macro and micro
cultures. For example, instead of major, sudden
layoffs of blue collar workers, a socially
responsible company might conduct orientation
sessions as to why it is necessary to discharge
them, how they can prepare for alternative careers,
and how to seek re-training in the new technologies.
Personnel departments might introduce increased
organisational communication and training on how to
make the most of increased leisure for greater
development of one's human potential. Advertising
departments might devote part of the budgets to
public service messages about social change.
Champion International Corporation (see
bibliography) has demonstrated in its advertisement
series, 'seeds for the future', that a forest
product company can successfully use advertising
for disseminating futuristic information. Few
major corporations, however, have sponsored mass
media programming to raise public awareness about
the future, and how we can influence it. What
organisations like the World Future Society and
its publication, The Futurist (see bibliography),
do for intellectual elites, corporations have the
means of doing for their publics, from employees to
customers. One healthy trend has been the emerging
issues group or task forces that are arising within
company planning departments. What is really
helpful is when they do not limit their reports to
internal distribution and make them available out
outside of the corporation as AT and T does.
(Coleman, 1981). Increasingly, companies are
establishing future studies or technological
forecasting units and departments. When their
findings are offered to personnel, customers and
interested public, it becomes a medium of
education, as well as public relations. This is
the case, for instance, with the useful newsletter,
FutureScan (see bibliography), distributed by
Security Pacific National Bank in Los Angeles.
Each of these reports deals with a different issue,
from feed to office automation. Finally, some
industries are sponsoring joint forecasting
studies of their fields in conjunction with
university futurists. When their results get
beyond privileged information reports and into
monographs and books for general use, then a public
service is performed. This happened when nine big
corporations joined the State of California in
investing in a futures research project with
scholars at the University of Southern California.
The outcomes included a remarkable volume, The

324

Emerging Network Marketplace, which we will cite
here later. (Dordick, Bradley and Nanus, 1981).

2.   Coping skill training is a valuable endeavour by
      organisations to enable their personnel and
      members to deal more effectively with dramatic
      shifts in work or life style. There are a
      variety of programmes currently underway from
      management of change workshops to stress
      management seminars. The author has been involved
      in conducting programmes and developing learning
      systems on the change management theme for over
      fifteen years with a wide variety of human
      systems. He has long maintained that when a
      company relocates an employee at home or abroad,
      productivity and profitability can be increased by
      training in the management of cultural differences,
      and especially by introduction of a foreign
      deployment system. Many corporations, like Hughes
      Tool Company in Houston, Texas, are discovering
      that human resource development in stress
      management can pay big dividends in cutting down
      sick leaves and mental breakdowns. Using the
      change inventory in Figure 20.2 reproduction,
      Hughes's Jim Pfeffer reports the results from pre/
      post administration of this instrument during
      stress management workshops. He finds that after
      the stress learning experience, individuals exhibit
      seven to nine point change per individual. He
      attributes this either to more realistic
      selfevaluation after the managers participate in
      his workshop, or more positive attitudes toward
      change as a result of this management development
      session.

      The health care industry can do much toward
preventative health programmes, both physical and
mental. These become even more meaningful when
they are undertaken in conjunction with business
and industry. Scripps Memorial Hospital in La
Jolla, California, for example,has a successful
project for coping with the transition toward
leadership. Entitled "Easing the Trauma of
Transition: Managing Your Upward Move", this
innovative two day workshop deals with the
challenge of promotion, especially when you may not
feel quite ready for it. Consultant Lorrie McGrath
reports they focus upon the problems of personnel
new to supervisory roles, selfassessment and
managerial people skill acquisition. The human
side of enterprise requires personnel assistance in
life crises management. People can be taught to be
less rigid, closed and fearful in dealing with
rapid change. They can be helped to learn how to
meet the challenge of the transitional experience.
That is those 'turning points' each person must
face from time to time in life and career. It may

325

───────Figure 20.2   Change inventory for leaders───────
(See Harris and Moran, 1981)

NOTE: On the accompanying five point scale to the right of each of the fifteen items below, please circle the number that best expresses your attitude or approach at this moment. The smaller numbers indicate that you never or rarely use this behaviour, while the higher numbers reflect that you usually or always behave in this manner.

	NEVER	RARELY	SOMETIMES	USUALLY	ALWAYS
1. Openness – willing to consider new ideas and people of differing opinions; tentative in communications, rather than dogmatic or closed minded in one's approach.	1	2	3	4	5
2. Flexibility – adaptable to new people, situations, information and developments; able to handle the unexpected and to shift position; spontaneous in responding to the 'here and now' data and experiences.	1	2	3	4	5
3. Sensitiveness – conscious of what is happening to oneself and others in the communications about the change and its effects; aware of the needs and feelings of others because of the proposed change; able to respond empathetically.	1	2	3	4	5
4. Creativeness – respond with resourcefulness to new people and situations; avoid stereotype answers and solutions; exercise initiative, imagination and innovativeness.	1	2	3	4	5
5. Person centred – concerned more about people than task or mere progress; care what happens to people involved in the change; support, encourage, inform and involve people in decisions for change they will be expected to implement; respect right of dissent.	1	2	3	4	5
6. Goal oriented planning – develop a case for change with others which takes into account long range objectives, while developing a plan with different stages or targets and shorterm steps to accomplish planning change; communicate these purposes and plans to all involved; state goals in terms that have positive value to those affected.	1	2	3	4	5
7. Group understanding – possess knowledge of the group process and skills in group dynamics; analyse the driving and resisting forces within the group relative to the proposed change; understand the character, structure, needs and wants of the group or organisation to be affected by the change; involve entire group in change process.	1	2	3	4	5
8. Communicativeness – promote open, circular interaction; able to analyse and clarify the problem and reasons for change; motivate members to desire to change and to use the available resources; develop a helping relationship with others so they can accept and live with the change.	1	2	3	4	5

Continued

326

PART II

Relative to your capacity to cope more effectively with rapid change in your personal and organisation life, indicate your present typical response by checking the category in the righthand columns which is most appropriate for each descriptive item in the paragraphs on the left. Be selfcritical.

9. Changing image - possess the capacity to re-evaluate concept of self based on new feedback, so as to expand my selfimage; fluid in my selfconception, amplifying my sense of identity as a result of new encounters and experiences.   1   2   3   4   5

10. Changing construct - willing to review periodically the way I read meaning in my life; flexible in my attitudes and perceptions, so as to make 'new sense' out of added inputs and insights; able to break out of 'old mindsets' and to develop new rationale; able to accept, at times, inconsistencies and discontinuity in my life.   1   2   3   4   5

11. Changing values - able to sense new needs in myself and others, to develop new and changing life values, to abandon past, ready made values and ideals, to revise expectations of self and others; and as a result, willing to re-examine norms or standards which I have set for myself and others and to develop new ones as appropriate.   1   2   3   4   5

12. Changing role - willing to have an unclear, hazy role in life or an organisation - one that is dynamic and responds to current relevant needs; able to live with a role definition which is open ended and subject to continuous clarification; accept new role definitions for women, parents and spouses, colleagues, professionals and other career people.   1   2   3   4   5

13. Changing society - able to be comfortable with impermanence or a lack of structure; capable of coping with constant alteration and perpetual transition; willing to live in changing times, without the traditional stability and reference groups; able to make the most of the present moment - the 'here and now' - to be 'existential' or to 'hang loose' ready to combat unwarranted resistance to change in myself and the communities in which I participate.   1   2   3   4   5

14. Changing goals - concerned about actualising my own and others' potential, as well as increasing the levels of awareness and consciousness in both; seek improvement in my capacity for feeling, and intuitiveness, for creating and risk taking; desire more knowledge and education for personal and professional development; willing to provide cultural leadership by experimenting with new life styles of adaptation to the demands of rapid change.   1   2   3   4   5

15. Changing life style - willing to be more transient and mobile within and among organisations; able to change jobs and locations when appropriate; capable of abandoning old relationships when necessary, and to search for new, more meaningful ones; willing to reject past stereotypes of other people, especially various minorities or foreigners; able to participate in team efforts to solve increasingly complex problems; able to cope with stress and urban crowding, lack of privacy, noise, pollution and other modern discomforts, while seeking to improve these situations; capable of enduring discontinuities and disconnections in my life.   1   2   3   4   5

be caused by death or loss of a beloved, by serious
illness or surgery, by career promotion or
demotion, by job relocation or layoff, by corporate
acquisition or merger, by divorce or addiction.
Such crises become an opportunity for growth or
regression, depending how the person copes with the
happening. People can learn attitude and life/work
style change; they can acquire more effective
coping skills to manage the trauma of transition.
In this period of increasing changes, individuals
and institutions must develop mechanisms and
strategies to promote ultrastability. Simply put,
"when everything nailed down is coming loose, we
have the capacity to keep our cool!"

3. Synergistic skill development is vital in a world
that is becoming ever more complex and
interdependent. Organisations can do much to
replace the obsolete industrial norm of rugged
individualism and unlimited competition. Now is
the time for corporations and agencies to teach
collaborative skills among personnel, divisions and
subsidiaries. Now is the time to foster
cooperation between companies within an industry,
between public and private sector and between
labour and management. Synergy brings about a
synthesis between divergent cultures, groups and
views so that the whole which results is greater
than the sum of the parts. It is a metaindustrial
concept that can ensure human survival and
development. Synergy can become the bridge
between the industrial and superindustrial way of
life. It can facilitate human systems renewal,
and help in the re-integration of traditional and
new forms of technologies. It can become the
means to increased national, regional and
international cooperation in both economics and
ecology, food production and distribution,
scientific and technological development. It is
already happening on an ever increasing scale, and
management and executive development can become a
forum for teaching these new team skills. (Moran
and Harris, 1981).

4. Learning to be strategists is critical for
contemporary organisational leaders. The strategist
is a professional expert who is holistic in planning
and directing large scale movements or operations.
A strategist is a person of vision who can project
beyond the moment and horizon for later effective
utilisation of combined resources. In other words,
a strategist is a futurist who can grasp the big
picture and synthesise the means for realistic
solutions with the greatest impact. A strategist
is a generalist capable of systems thinking and
integration of parts into an overall plan. The
strategist is able to plan moves that capitalise

upon weakness in other situations. The strategist creates an environment that maximises human performance. In contrast, a tactician specialises in the use and deployment of elements in an overall strategy. Within the metaindustrial organisation, the strategist is the conceptualiser who provides the models and paradigms that bring together diverse disciplines and innovations so that they fit together. Such a person can move beyond the conventional in problem solving by designing new roles, rules and rennovations.

The Western Behavioural Science Institute in La Jolla, California, recently inaugurated a School of Management and Strategic Studies. They define a strategy in their announcement as:-

> "The ability to anticipate future developments for more effective planning; to realise the limitations and possibilities of future forecasting".

WBSI maintains that today's senior executives not only face situations of enormous complexity involving unprecedented constraints, but must operate with a sense of the larger social and business context and understanding of highly interdependent social, economic and environmental systems.

It would seem, therefore, that foresighted HRD programmes would seek to prepare future top leaders who are strategic thinkers and planners. In a case book for their Organisational Strategy and Policy text, Naumes and Paine (1978) provide eight objectives which might serve any management education programme of this type. These are indicative of the strategist's competencies:-

   a.   Conceptualising the policy formation
        process .....

   b.   Developing comprehension, skill and
        knowledge for diagnosing and dealing with
        specific and unique policy and strategy
        situation.

   c.   Gaining understanding of the complex
        realities, challenging questions and
        conflicting policy making.

   d.   Analysing the organisation's environment
        and its policy generating structure.

   e.   Designing and proposing approaches that
        will help to prevent organisational
        stagnation.

f.   Developing administrative and communication
     skills in presenting and developing
     solutions to policy problems .....

g.   Integrating or tying together concepts,
     principles and skills learned separately
     in other more specialised situations.

h.   Being cautious in accepting the many
     prescriptions that exist in the
     literature .....

To put it simply, career development efforts should
aim at producing creative strategists who will
positively influence and change the organisational
culture for the purpose of more meaningful,
productive behaviour on the part of personnel or
members.

MANAGEMENT/CAREER DEVELOPMENT INNOVATIONS

Today, both the community and government look to managers to
be vehicles for both economic and social change. These
expectations are even more intense relative to the management
of multinational corporations. Great hopes are expressed on
the contribution these transnational enterprises are capable
of making within less developed countries, and with the less
developed segments of so called advanced technological
societies. Some insight into the management education
response to this broadened role for corporate leaders can be
ascertained from the McNulty Report (1981) on management
development. It contained a summary of a joint conference
between the American Assembly of Collegiate Schools of
Business and the European Foundation for Management
Development (Paris, 1981). The 600 management educators
examined the issue of "managers for the 21st century". They
agreed that management's field of vision is too narrow, and
today's career planning is obsolete. (Consultants like this
writer might dare to add that management professors' vision
is too narrow and their business teaching often unrealistic
relative to the world outside academia). In any event,
these European and American scholars did arrive at this
consensus of significance to readers:-

1.   Management curriculi will shift in orientation
     from functional to behavioural, and will include
     new teaching methods like 'hands on' project work.

2.   Management schools, now mostly structured for big
     business, will have to include the teaching of
     entrepreneurship for managers of small, capital
     venture businesses. (And this writer would again
     add, that this instruction should not be directed
     to operating within developed societies with all
     types of sophisticated support services, but also
     for business operations in less economically

330

developed societies without the infrastructure to
support multinational business).

3. Noncognitive skills will become more important for
    business students than cognitive ones, and
    negotiating skills will have to be enhanced.

4. There will be more emphasis upon ethics, morals
    and the process of learning, as well as upon the
    quality of the output.

5. There will be greater allowance in management
    education for the exercise of creativity,
    flexibility and democracy.

Since the focus of the concluding section will be on
innovation in leadership preparation within higher
education, let us concentrate here upon creative
possibilities within the traditional career development
framework. The perspective will be recruiting, selecting,
training, monitoring, counselling and evaluating, especially
with reference to management personnel within organisational
culture.

Recruiting

Among the varied prospects in this electronic age for
identifying, interesting and enticing qualified new
applicants, these are a sample of what lies ahead:-

-   the transmission of computerised personnel records
    from universities or former employees for
    evaluation purposes;

-   the exchange of data in organisational talent banks,
    facilitated by new types of employment service to
    match candidates with employers;

-   the submission of videotapes or discs by employers
    to individuals or groups of candidates about the
    advantages of working in a particular company or
    agency, and vice versa, the submission of similar
    video data about the capabilities of the
    candidate;

-   the early identification programme on an industry
    wide and international basis of future talent, the
    kind of people who fit the organisational profile
    as right for advancement within this corporate
    culture; furthermore a tracking system would be
    established to follow these future employees'
    accomplishments prior to hiring availability -
    current personnel would be rewarded for submitting
    to the organisation's computer bank these potential
    high performers and for assisting in their
    recruitment;

331

- the use of returning expatriate managers from abroad,
  or recently retired executives in a talent scout and
  counselling strategy, especially with local
  nationals overseas and incountry foreign students;

- managerial and executive search programmes seeking
  experienced management will be part of an overall
  humanpower plan that is global in scope and based on
  a performance competence criteria without
  discriminations due to gender, nationality or ethnic
  origins; it will include the physically handicapped
  person.

Selecting

The selection process would emphasise choosing persons who
are compatible with the organisation's culture and the people
now in it, as well as being concerned for their present and
future professional accomplishments and skills. However,
greater diversity and latitude for people's uniqueness would
be presented in the selection criteria of metaindustrial
organisations which might employ:-

- video documents for preliminary interviews of
  candidates and live satellite television interviews
  of prospects from all over the world; in the analysis
  of these recorded interviews, attention would be paid
  to nonverbal communication and behaviour;

- increased use of simulation techniques, both
  computer and gaming procedures, through more
  sophisticated assessment centres for both new hires
  and promotion of existing personnel; these plus other
  experiential observation methods will focus upon
  intercultural communication abilities, abstract
  thinking capability, synthesis and synergy
  competencies and technological abilities;

- utilisation of sophisticated, computerised
  instrumentation as part of a human resource inventory
  of the person's intelligence, aptitudes, interests,
  assets, personality and needs for development;

- employment of situational, group oriented problem
  solving methods in the form of videotape case
  studies, dramatised critical incidents,
  technological forecasts - all administered in
  customised scenarios to fit the corporation,
  association or agency and with a purpose of
  evaluation;

- concentration throughout the whole career development
  process upon people who excell at their present
  undertakings.

Training

This traditional management term will be broadened in the
context of human development, and the opportunities for this
will be manifold both within and without the organisation.
Some of the previous electronic and experiential methods
utilised in recruiting and selection will be employed as
part of the actualisation of human potential. Others might
include:-

-   organisational learning centres that are
    electronically connected with the employee's home
    communication system or university educational
    services;

-   special simulated preparations for unusual
    relocations or untraditional careers, similar to the
    type of orientation and training provided to the
    astronauts for their space activities and moon work;

-   content that is based upon future studies and
    technological forecasting, as well as global and
    interplanetary data collection;

-   executive development that begins as a young
    management intern and provides a senior or retired
    executive as counsellor to that individual; that
    provides a combination of line/staff experiences in
    the international marketplace; that is team
    management oriented and provides major people
    reporting responsibilities early in one's career;
    that offers skill development in coordination,
    consulting, negotiating and intercultural
    representation; that gives priority to human
    relations or people skill development, as well as
    technical and financial competencies; that
    cultivates strategic skills and systems proficiency;
    and that teaches about stress and life crises
    management for oneself; one's subordinates and one's
    family; that encourages creativity, calculated risk
    taking and diversified life and business experiences.

Monitoring

Although individuals will be encouraged in the
metaindustrial organisational culture to be more
selfregulating, the company or agency will still need some
type of tracking system to keep abreast of personnel
development. The whole personnel department function will be
mechanised and revolutionised as it converges into a broader
human resource management system:-

-   comprehensive, meaningful, current and computerised
    personnel records will be the central feature;

-   standardised human resource accounting which becomes
    part of the balance sheet and annual report relative

333

to the capitalisation of human assets;

- search and support strategies for top performing, nonconforming and exceptional workers who are then used as problem solvers, behaviour models and trainers with other employees;

- integration of total HRD systems of subsidiaries and overseas operations with emphasis upon international HRD specialist teams;

- system wide human factor data gathering and analysis for improving organisational culture, as well as employee/customer relations and performance (i.e. more HRD research);

- integration and utilisation of people differences, whether in terms of their capabilities or handicaps, culture or education, experience or aspirations, so that this is reflected in the design of facilities, provisions for career development, or accommodations of job requirements;

- variety of provisions for personal and professional growth from career exchanges and educational sabbaticals to new compensation benefits and personnel services (e.g. personality enhancement, positive drug use, dependent assistance, creative volunteerism and constructive leisure guidance).

Counselling

Since there will be fewer employees or workers in the metaindustrial organisation, time can be spent with them in a variety of HRD activities, including coaching and counselling. The latter might include dimensions that were typical in the disappearing industrial company or bureaucratic agency:-

- such corporate sponsored guidance might be for an alternative career to the one now pursued, or a second career, or retirement vocational activity;

- for returning expatriates from long service outside the home culture, it might involve re-entry counselling or even outplacement services which would not be available to all personnel;

- when reduction in force is necessary due to the nature of the high technology business, this counselling might be toward placement in another corporation or industry, or for temporary educational leave, or to assist in the establishment of some entrepreneurial enterprise by the laidoff employee;

-   relocation assignments for the organisation might
    involve a comprehensive counselling service for the
    employee's whole family, not just relative to
    housing and other resources in the new community,
    but how all members of the family could grow as a
    result in this change in their space;

-   provision for executive counselling to cope with
    inevitable uncertainties and the ambiguities of the
    unforeseen both in personal and professional life
    (this might take the form of group sessions with
    other executives and behavioural scientists within
    the total organisation, and more probably with peers
    outside in other companies or industries).

Evaluating

The assessment process begins before entry into the
organisation and after exit from it. In the metaindustrial
organisation, it will be a continuing process which is both
computerised and humanised. It might include such facets
as:-

-   review of man-machine relations or how the human and
    robot interface;

-   changes needed in personal, role and organisational
    images;

-   quality of performance in external community service
    and professional societies as a factor in career
    development;

-   degree of innovation demonstrated and contributed to
    the maintaining of a high performing company or
    association;

-   individual contribution to policy formation and
    setting of new strategic objectives;

-   performance review of past job behaviour with a view
    to increased future productive behaviour in the
    organisation;

-   examination of what changes are needed in the
    organisation's culture or system to improve
    performance.

The whole game of HRD efforts will be impacted by
electronic information technology, especially microprocessors
and video equipment. The whole process of interviewing, for
instance, is already being improved by video training tapes
and learning materials that go from selection to termination.
Figure 20.3 attempts to visually project what the human
resource management system will look like in the
metaindustrial organisation. It reminds us that the
knowledge worker may not be just fulltime employed, but also

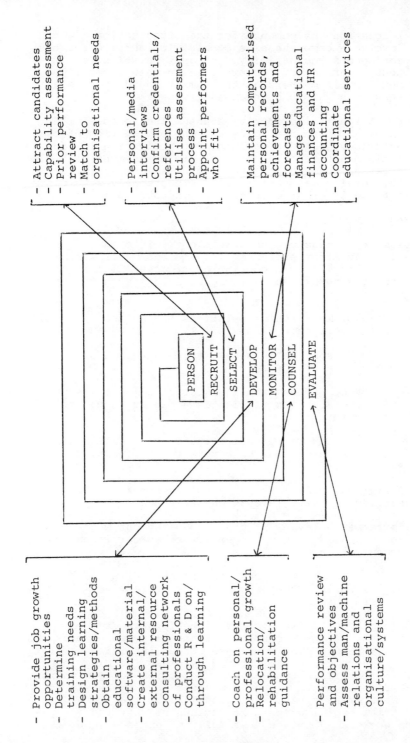

- Attract candidates
- Capability assessment
- Prior performance review
- Match to organisational needs

- Personal/media interviews
- Confirm credentials/ references
- Utilise assessment process
- Appoint performers who fit

- Maintain computerised personal records, achievements and forecasts
- Manage educational finances and HR accounting
- Coordinate educational services

PERSON
RECRUIT
SELECT
DEVELOP
MONITOR
COUNSEL
EVALUATE

- Provide job growth opportunities
- Determine training needs
- Design learning strategies/methods
- Obtain educational software/material
- Create internal/ external resource consulting network of professionals
- Conduct R & D on/ through learning

- Coach on personal/ professional growth
- Relocation/ rehabilitation guidance

- Performance review and objectives
- Assess man/machine relations and organisational culture/systems

Figure 20.3 Human resource management system

at home, in and out of the organisation for varying periods, sharing a job with a fellow employee or one's spouse, and often a contract person. Certainly the knowledge worker will be different in his or her aspirations and expectations of the organisation.

Perhaps the type of executive development programmes which global corporations like IBM now offer below should be extended downwards!

Internal	External
- Three week Advanced Management School for high potential managers focused on business process and environment. - One week Executive Seminar covering strategic issues plus external economic, social and political developments. - Two week International Executive Programme for senior executives world wide concentrating on strategic international issues.	- Participation in management programmes of major university graduate schools. - Participation in executive level leadership programmes which emphasise interpersonal effectiveness. - Participation in public affairs programmes, dealing with federal operations or national policy issues. - Participation in humanities programmes which provide courses of study on man, society and values.

PRIVATE/PUBLIC SECTOR SYNERGY IN LEADERSHIP DEVELOPMENT

Fifteen years ago Dr John Platt, distinguished physics professor and author, observed that society is going through a series of concurrent revolutions and crises. One of these, he concluded, is in the area of administration or management. Platt maintained this administrative crisis exists in all spheres of human activity, be it university, corporation or government. Essentially, this astute commentator on the contemporary scene was getting at the leadership crisis, even vacuum sometimes, which is evident in too many human systems. Many current top administrators and executives are unable to understand or cope with the accelerating changes and the profound transitions presently underway. They are literally, to use a game analogy, playing in the old ballpark, by the traditional rules, and they think they have the same players. Business as usual is their motto, as deterioration and decline set into their enterprises and organisation shock is prevalent. The crisis can be resolved, the new leaders can be developed if the principles in the drama would share and cooperate - they are universities or colleges, government agencies and multinational corporations.

In the middle ages, universities and monasteries were the great centres of learning. The latter institution was gradually replaced in this role by government agencies and trading companies. Today, more of the action in education and training seems to be shifting to industries and associations. Consider the postindustrial situation in high technology. University research which pionerred nuclear and space science, bio-engineering and other technological breakthroughs is now falling behind in the information society. Adam Osborne (1979) put his finger on one aspect of the problem when he commented in Running Wild: The Next Industrial Revolution on just the field of microelectronics:

"Frequently the advances that occur in two or three years can be so stunning that users no longer have sufficient education to understand the new product. An electronics engineer who got his degree ten years ago would understand little or nothing of what is being taught in the classroom. Moreover, the faculties in university electric engineering departments are years behind the industry. No significant developments, either in semiconductor technology or the use of microelectronic products have come out of universities, and this bleak situation does not look as though it will change in the foreseeable future.....

Universities will have to reorganise their curricula to increase the output of engineers, while simultaneously preparing to cope with lifelong learning."

Now if this can be substantiated in a facet of engineering, what about the other academic disciplines and departments? There is common realisation that many colleges and universities are offering majors and courses that are totally out of line with the world job market. Computer and space scientists are in short supply, while higher education produces an abundance of lawyers and historians. Even for the academic programmes in business and the professions, the course content is often out of touch with external needs of practioneers. The very administration of high education, from a business management perspective, is frequently archaic. The continuing education programmes, especially in management and executive development, are either too theoretical or fanciful, so that the leadership in this area has been lost to private corporations and educations. The university and colleges, like so many other social institutions, has its own crises of survival, relevancy and development in the metaindustrial age!

Some of the problems in leadership development for both university and government might be resolved if they entered into realistic collaboration in this regard with major corporations. Such synergy among the three entities already exists in Japan. Big business could enter into profitable partnership with higher education. Government could not only encourage and subsidise such endeavours, but participate in it. Here are some examples of synergistic possibilities:-

1.   Personnel exchanges - business leaders and researchers spend a year on university staffs or in government service, while faculty and public officials take comparable sabatticals in industry.

2.   Joint ventures of mutual benefit to all parties involved, such as:-

    a.   corporate executives consulting on the design of university or government administrative systems;

    b.   professors consult on corporate renewal, educational systems in business and government, while government officials consult on improved regulatory procedures and grant programmes;

    c.   all three institutional systems share their innovations in management development, the market personnel needs, the research discoveries and inventions that will impact the economy;

    d.   designing public service volunteer opportunities in which all three systems participate for the benefit of the citizenery.

3.   Sharing information on innovative educational technology which may range from the use of electronic study carrels and holography in training to advances in computer assisted instruction, voice activated computers and interactive television.

4.   Collaborative research on human problems of management that affect both public and private sectors - such as, the burnout syndrome, stress regulation, robot human interface, job displacement through automation, designing new cybernated systems to reduce costs and increase productivity, creative use of increased leisure for personnel development, expansion of high achievement, counteracting underemployment, providing meaningful living situation for the retarted and handicapped (especially economic, mental and social disadvantage), two career couples and job sharing, team management skill acquisition and production of necessary educational software.

In the superindustrial stage of human development, the

cities of the future will be built around knowledge centres, just as urbanisation in the industrial age centred around factories. These centres will be research facilities, knowledge industries and educational institutions. The latter have begun to change to meet the challenge of cyberculture. A Carnegie endowment report on alternative forms of higher education produced many innovations in existing colleges and universities, as well as the establishment of nontraditional university programmes. As a conclusion to this analysis of changing career development patterns more suitable to the needs of metaindustrial organisations, let us examine a few models that seemingly show promise and could have positive impact of leadership development:

- The USC/NIS model - The information industry may become the largest in the world. In the US, already thirty to fifty per cent of the workforce is employed in the information sector. Recognising this, the University of Southern California (School of Communication and Centre for Future Research in the Graduate School of Business) engaged in joint research with one state government and nine major corporations to study the emerging industry called network information services (NIS). Among its many applications and prospects, they also focused upon its implications for interactive training and education. The findings were shared among all participants and the public at large.

- Control Data/PLATO model is an educational data base system pioneered by Control Data Corporation. It has the capability of counteracting teacher obsolescence and permitting professional educators to interact with students or trainees in distant places, no matter how remote. It is a forerunner of the computer aided education systems that can be distributed around the world by television or video cartridges to raise the educational levels of underdeveloped peasants or managers.

- The SRI model resulted from Stanford University establishing a research institute which is now an autonomous corporation called SRI International. It acts as a conduit of university sponsored research to business and industry, or utilises its staff and university associates to undertake research investigations for clients in the private and public sector. It is one of many university stimulated owned, nonprofit or profit making corporations that are engaged into the production of everything from genetic products to cancer cures.

- The Inplant College model originally pioneered by National University in San Diego, California, and General Dynamics Corporation. Essentially, it featured:-

a.   a group of managers going through a programme
     of business or professional studies together
     until graduation;

b.   a single registration that provided a
     computerised projection of required courses
     until the degree was granted;

c.   the use of plant conference and training
     facilities for the university studies in the
     evening from 5-10 p.m.

-   The Teletuition model from the University of South
    Africa is designed for executives who operate in
    widely dispersed geographical areas. It is
    essentially correspondence tuition which includes
    in addition to written materials, TV, computers,
    radio, telephone and tapes. Regional groups of
    managers meet to discuss course materials once a
    week for four to six hours, over twelve months, and
    one day a month at the university with faculty.

-   The WBSI model, previously referred to from the
    Western Behavioural Science Institute, proposes
    postgraduate studies for executives by means of two
    eight day intensive seminars every six months in La
    Jolla, California, that continues electronically by
    means of advanced computer technology supplied to
    the participant's office or home. Computer
    keyboards, video display, recording equipment and
    printout units will provide the communication links
    to the faculty, administration and electronic
    library.

-   The INSEAD/CEDEP model is a twenty week 'sandwich'
    programme for managers to create change throughout
    a group of organisations, while engaged in
    multidisciplinary study, including the working of
    member companies. Through this Centre European
    d'Education Permanente in Fountainbleu, France,
    representatives from four European countries,
    nineteen companies, participate as members through
    study teams of ten to twelve managers, mixed as to
    age and gender.

-   The Oxford Centre model in the UK utilises top
    professors in the Oxford Strategy Unit to advise
    key management in Britain and Western Europe. These
    consultants concentrate on management and trade
    unions with emphasis on banking, insurance and public
    administration.

-   The Teknowledge model is representative of the new
    consultancies and management seminars in tune with
    metaindustrial realities. Founded in Palo Alto,
    California, by two distinguished Stanford University
    and Rand Corporation scientists, Dr Edward

Feigenbaum and Dr Frederick Hayes-Roth, it provides
expert systems executive briefings and conducts
knowledge engineering projects for major
corporations. They develop computer software
related to artificial intelligence applications and
knowledge databases.

   The above are but a sample of the innovative paradigms for
cooperation between university, corporations and government
that exist and need to be expanded in the process of
leadership development. The walls of separation between and
among these three key human systems need to be replaced by
synergistic interface if scholars, executives and
administrators are to stay on the cutting edge of
metaindustrial advances.

BIBLIOGRAPHY

ASTD National Report, (26 June, 1980), American Society for
   Training and Development, USA.

Caplin, D, (1981), 'Corporate culture: training problems and
   prospects', Northeast Training News, pp.9-11, Warren/
   Weingarten Inc, USA.

Champion ad reprints and brochure and bibliography on the
   future is available from the Champion International
   Corporation, USA.

Coleman, E R, (1981), Information and Society, AT&T/
   Corporate Planning Emerging Issues Group.

Devanna, M A, Fombrun, C and Tichy, N, (1981), 'Human
   resource management: a strategic perspective',
   Organisational Dynamics, Vol.9, No.3.

Dorick, H S, Bradley, H G and Nanus, B, (1981), The
   Emerging Network Marketplace, Ablex Publishing Company.

FutureScan, available from Hank Koehn, editor, Futures
   Research Division, Security Pacific National Bank, Los
   Angeles, USA.

The Futurist, published by the World Future Society, USA.

Harris, P R and Moran, R T, (1980), Managing Cultural
   Differences, Gulf Publishing Company. Also available from
   same source are six videotapes, workbook and manual on
   this book entitled "International Management Productivity
   Series".

Moran, R T and Harris, P R, (1981), Managing Cultural
   Synergy, Gulf Publishing Company.

Nadler, L, (1979), Developing Human Resources, Learning
   Concepts/University Associates, p. 254 and 298.

Rymell, R G and Newsom, R, (1981), 'Selfdirected learning in HRD', Training and Development Journal, Vol.35, No.8, American Society for Training and Development.

Schaaf, D, (1981), 'Teleconferencing: will it change the way you train?', Training/HRD, Vol.18, No.7, pp.49-50 and 60, Lakewood Publications Inc, USA.

Schrello, D M, (1981), The Seminar Market, Schrello Enterprises.

Terpstra, V, (1978), The Cultural Environment of International Business, pp.167-173, South Western Publishing Company.

21 Management education in an interdependent world

LEN NADLER

It has been said that "the future isn't what it used to be" and in no place is this more apparent than in the work of managers. There was a time, and not too far in the past, when it was possible for a person to achieve the rank of manager and to function adequately, having learned how from two sources. One was the academic, where the individual attended a college or university. Courses and degrees were available in management or management science. This is still true today.

The second source was the use of role models. That is, the rising manager was able to work under people who were successful managers. By emulating what they saw being done, the new managers had some reasonable expectation of being successful.

These sources still exist today and will tomorrow, but must be used with caution. The university curricula tend to be increasingly less reflective of the real world. This should not be taken as a criticism of universities, but as recognition that curricula change slowly. At one time, this was not only necessary but desirable. Continuity was provided and change was not introduced until the benefits had been proven. This is no longer possible. We live in a rapidly changing world, one which requires that what is being taught at the university level also change, perhaps not as rapidly, but sufficiently to prepare managers for that rapidly changing world.

We will continue to need the contribution that the university makes towards preparing managers. It requires, however, that we recognise the gap that will probably always exist between university degree granting programmes and the rapidly changing world. Universities have tried to accommodate to this by supplementing their regular degree programmes with workshops, seminars, and certificate programmes. To the extent that a university does this, attempts to provide flexibility and a rapid response to timely issues, they are to be commended, and should be utilised as a source for training and educating managers.

The use of role models, for educating managers, is more

difficult. This is not a criticism of practicing managers, but rather a reflection of changing values and problems. Those behaviours that make a manager successful today could be completely counter-productive when used by a new manager tomorrow.

THE INTER-DEPENDENT WORLD

It may be almost too obvious to discuss inter-dependency, but there are still many managers who prefer to see the world as insular. It is easier, of course, to try to ignore rest of the world over which the manager may have little or no influence. This does not make the rest of the world any less important for the manager.

Not every manager is impacted upon by other parts of the world, but the number who are not, is exceedingly small. Goods, in increasing quantities are being sold by one country to another. Raw materials are being shipped, and trans-shipped. High level technology is no longer the property of only two or three major powers, but is readily available throughout most of the world. Finished goods cross borders in an endless and increasing flow. Even partly manufactured goods are a major trade item. There are companies that have sub-contractors in many countries, though the final assembly may be in one country. Thus, the final product bears the label of one country, even though parts have been manufactured by many.

People are likewise moving across borders in unprecedented numbers. This, despite the limitations on international travel imposed by some countries. The movement is not like that of the last century or the early part of this century. It is not immigration, but rather, people going to other countries to work. There are the 'guest workers' who have been so important to the economy of Europe for the past two decades. They are supplemented by the 'undocumented aliens' (i.e. illegal) who can be found in many countries of the world and provide a source of cheap labour within the host country.

At the managerial level, we find the 'expatriates', or those who have gone to another country to work at high level jobs. These expatriates do not intend to stay in the host country, though some do remain for long periods of time. Expatriates may be sent by a multi-national company, or may have moved on on their own initiative and function as self employed. We find, generally, that expatriate managers are sent by multi-national companies.

It is possible for a manager to meet the interdependent world without crossing an international border. Within one's own country there are also the guest workers, referred to above. A person who expects to manage a work force made up of people from that country, may find that there is responsibility for an international work force! In too few

instances has a manager been prepared to cope with
internationalism within the confines of the organisation.
International was always something 'out there - having to do
with foreigners.' Out there has now become 'in-here' and the
foreigners are now subordinates.

Up to the late 1970s, it was customary for developed
countries to send managers to lesser developed countries.
For a variety of reasons this began to change in the late
1970s. Industrialised countries began to receive investment
and managers from the so-called 'Third World', which includes
many of the lesser-developed countries. Those countries began
to export first capital, and then managers to oversee the use
of that capital. Developed countries began increasingly to
buy into other developed countries. The USA, for example,
began to experience unprecedented numbers of foreign managers
supervising people in the USA.

A manager in the USA or in other developed countries, could
no longer count on the fact that those at higher levels would
be from the same national background. Indeed, it also meant
that some managers could not expect to be promoted, because
those upper level spots were reserved for those from another
country.

What does all this mean to managers? The world has been
changing, more rapidly now than before, and therefore the
education of managers must reflect the changing conditions.

UNDERSTANDING OTHERS

The interdependency, particularly of people, has introduced
a new dimension into management education. It is no longer
optional but has become essential that managers have
competencies in cross cultural and international areas. This
need is not limited, as noted above, to those who are working
in the international field. It is a need of all managers,
in all countries.

Culture

Perhaps the most important addition to existing management
education programmes is the area of culture. For those who
want to deal in exact definitions, this term 'culture'
presents some problems. There is really no one generally
agreed upon definition of this term. Therefore, for purposes
of this chapter, the term needs to be defined so that we can
communicate.

When we speak of culture, we mean the habits and customs
that people develop to cope with change. It is not legal
behaviour (that which is set down in writing as laws, company
manuals, and other written documents). There are times
when cultural behaviour becomes codified, but then it is no
longer cultural behaviour.

346

For example, there is the use of 'bribes'. That is not, perhaps, the correct word, but hopefully, it communicates. It is the use of money to facilitate making or implementing a decision. It takes many forms, and in some countries it is not considered either illegal or immoral. It is a fact of life. Historically, we know that in the late 1970's the U.S. government imposed restrictions on U.S. companies and penalized those who engaged in that practice in the international market place. All of this was despite the protests of U.S. companies that pointed out that if they could not use alternative monetary incentives (i.e. bribes) they would be hurt in that market place. It was a conflict of cultures between that generally agreed upon in the U.S.A. and the cultural practices in some other parts of the world.

A manager cannot deal with this cultural conflict from the context of only one country. Of course, a manager must obey the laws of the country where the company is operating, as well as the laws of the manager's country. This is difficult enough, but the manager finds that, in addition, there are cultural conflicts.

A more subtle area than money, is the question of loyalty. This too is a cultural factor. What loyalty does a subordinate owe to a manager? In some countries, culturally, the manager actually stands in 'locus parentis' or in the place of a parent of the subordinate. This is not a choice a manager makes, but one that is imposed by the culture. The manager has, in fact, become a member of the family! This imposes responsibilities and behaviours on the manager that had not previously been contemplated.

There are other countries where the manager will always be considered an outsider because the culture imposes that behaviour. If the manager is not a 'member of the tribe', (and there is no way for an outsider to become a member) the loyalty of the subordinates will be to the tribe and not to the manager or the employer.

A manager should recognise and understand this. It is not rejection of the manager by the subordinates, but their acceptance of the cultural norms.

Another cultural norm has to do with leadership. In some cultures, it is expected that the manager will be the leader, make the decisions, and give the orders. It would be culturally inappropriate for the manager to consult with the subordinates, to share leadership, or in any other way relinquish a command position. There must always be a gap between the manager and subordinates. That is the expected cultural behaviour.

It is equally possible that in another place (another culture) the manager is expected to be part of the group, to discuss decisions with subordinates, and generally expect a small gap between the manager and those of lesser ranks. It is recognised by all involved that the manager is the leader, but not the 'boss' in a traditional sense.

Note that these two kinds of leadership are not a function of whether a country is developed or less developed. They do not even depend upon which countries are industrialised as contrasted with those that are predominantly agricultural. It is cultural behaviour that varies greatly from country to country and will have its own reasons for being culturally acceptable in a particular country.

Communications

There are many forms of communication, and almost all have cultural implications. In some countries of South East Asia, for example, one can use a puppet to say things that would otherwise put the speaker in jail. The ubiquitous television has altered some forms of communication, but even with television, there are cultural norms as to what is appropriate. Therefore, films are usually edited for television, to eliminate scenes of physical intimacy, to reduce violence, and to cut out improper language.

For a manager, a major form of communication is language. Actually, language relates very directly to culture and is part of culture. We have been told that 'language is a manifestation of culture'. In this chapter, it is being discussed separately from the previous section, since language and communication are so essential to the success of a manager.

In an interdependent world, what is the language requirement for a manager? At one time, English and French were presumed to be all that was needed. Even then, many managers from countries other than France, did not speak French!

In the interdependent world of today, knowing more than one's own native language has assumed a different role. It is not only necessary to be able to communicate, but it is a way of showing respect and concern for the country where one is working. When I worked in Japan, I studied Japanese. I tried to use it in my work, but it proved extremely difficult. In despair, I began to use less Japanese in my work conversations until one of my Japanese colleagues commented, "You will never be able to speak good Japanese for you have to be born here in Japan to be able to do that. But, we do appreciate that you are trying". That is the value of a manager at least trying to learn the language of the country of assignment.

The manager should not attempt to become a scholar, but should learn at least some of the basic language, common phrases, and generally those things that can help socially. It will also give the manager insight into some of the cultural practices that appear to be inscrutable. (The cultural practices of others which we cannot understand are generally labelled 'inscrutable'). Of course, a manager who can develop fluency may find that highly desirable, but on the other hand, it might also mean that that manager could be locked into that country. There is always the possibility that the home office will find that manager so proficient in the language, that they will hesitate to give him another assignment, one which might have led to promotion.

348

Management education should at least include some work on the more common languages, if only to contrast greetings, salutations and the more prevalent phrases. At the very least a manager will be sensitised to the fact that all people do not say 'hello' (whatever that means) and 'goodbye' (a religious contraction of God be with you) in the same way.

Where language is a factor, a manager may have to rely on interpreters. Therefore, management education should include some competency in working through interpreters.

There are two major ways in which interpreters are used. One is for consecutive translation, while the other is for simultaneous translation. The difference is important and if the manager does not understand and have competency in both patterns, communication will either be distorted or impossible.

In consecutive translation, the manager will speak first and then the interpreter will translate. In simultaneous translation the interpreter will translate at the same time the manager is speaking. This latter approach requires equipment which at one time, was cumbersome but technology has reduced the size and complexity to the point where it is readily available and usable.

Competency in both forms is essential for any manager who will be working with people who speak a different language, no matter which country. It is a competency that takes time to develop, particularly if the manager does not have a regular interpreter but must use different interpreters in different situations. An interesting example was provided in the film 'Reds' which was a success in the U.S.A. in 1982. It was the story of John Reed and there was one incident where a speech he had written, in English, was translated into many languages. To his dismay, he found that where he wrote of a 'just war', it had been translated into a 'holy war'! For Moslems, the change of that one word made a tremendous difference in what he had proposed.

Context

Recent work by some researchers has identified another cultural difference which has long been overlooked. 'Context' refers to relating to something in the general field in which it is taking place. It is much like 'gestalt' in that one must see the whole picture to understand any of the pieces.

A high context society is one in which the habits and customs of people must be seen in light of general relationships and trends. There is a high level of implied trust among those who know and accept that context. A particular event or decision can only be understood as part of a general pattern. It assumes that taking a thread of a rug, and examining it, tells you little about the rug. Indeed, once the thread is out, it is no longer part of the rug, but is something else. In a high context society, one seldom examines the threads but is content to share the rug.

In a low context culture, things must be spelt out. It is
not the context which communicates but the written document
or the explicit order. Written communications are extremely
important and can be taken by themselves without any
relationship to a context. Indeed, it is assumed that the
correct language will take care of all possibilities and
avoid the misunderstandings that can result when one relies
on the context to communicate.

The research on contexts is still in its early stages.
As the work progresses, other implications may be forthcoming.
For the manager of today and tomorrow, understanding contexts
is extremely important. It can help explain how decisions
are made and carried out, in some cultures, as well as the
appropriate form of communication with a particular group.

OPERATIONAL FACTORS

A manager functions in a wide variety of operational areas.
In this section, we will explore just a few of these as they
relate to management education and the interdependent world.

Staff Meetings

Despite all the criticisms and snide remarks about staff
meetings, most managers find it advantageous to have such
meetings. Many managers have not been prepared (e.g.
educated) to handle staff meetings and fall into predictable
traps. Too many managers have learned how to conduct staff
meetings by being participants in somebody else's meeting,
experiencing dissatisfaction, but not really knowing why the
meeting was unsuccessful or what they could have done to
improve it. More attention must be given to helping managers
conduct productive and satisfying meetings.

To start with, managers should know why they have staff
meetings. There are many reasons and these should be clear
to the manager and to those who will be attending the meeting.
Of course, there are meetings where the only purpose is - to
meet. These generally become ritual affairs, such as, we
meet every Monday morning - whether we need to or not.

There is nothing wrong with such meetings, if the purpose
has been made clear. Ritual meetings can serve a very valid
purpose. They can keep open a continual line of communication.
The meeting can also serve as a way for the manager to let
everybody know he is concerned with them as people, as well as
subordinates. The ambiance can be set with appropriate drinks
(coffee, tea, etc.) or edibles (pastry, cheese, fruit, etc.).
Particularly where the staff consists of individuals from
different cultures, the morning sharing of food can be
perceived as a very positive indication of the concern of the
manager. Most cultures have such shared morning repasts.

Where the staff is multi-cultural, the manager may find that
a small United Nations meeting is in progress. There may even

350

be a need for interpreters! The UN endeavours to minimise confusion at meetings by having papers prepared before the meeting and distributed at an appropriate time. The manager conducting a staff meeting, may require such reports but they are not absolutely necessary. What can be more helpful is some kind of visual reinforcement through prepared flip chart paper (also known as rotofolio, butcher paper, artist paper, newsprint, etc.) so that some of the major points are visible to all. The overhead projector is a very flexible device and highly desirable as a way of focusing attention on particular agenda items.

The purpose of written statements, for all to see, is to make sure that as little as possible is lost through translation or by the pattern of speech of the manager or others who are going to make presentations. Such pre-meeting preparation can reduce the need for post-meeting corrections and apologies.

If the purpose of a meeting is to make or convey decisions, these should be in writing as far as possible. All to often, at a meeting attended by participants from several cultures, there is a confusion as to just what the decision is, and even when it is made. People who are attuned to a democratic pattern will look to the final vote for the decision. Others may seek different clues for the decision-making and pay little attention to the voting.

The period that follows a staff meeting is almost as significant as the meeting. During the meeting, assignments may have been made. For some managers, this is done by a nodding of the head, and for some participants this may be all that is necessary. In other situations, a direct order may be given, though in some cultural situations a direct order in a group situation is considered impolite and should be avoided.

Difficulty in identifying decision points, and the intent of the leader (manager) is nothing new. History has given us many examples of subordinates carrying out what they thought were the implied orders of their leaders, only to cause disaster for all concerned. The aftermath of a staff meeting may be almost as traumatic, even if not recorded for posterity.

Job Rotation

In some parts of the world, job rotation is a common practice. An individual is moved from one job to another. The question that is significant is: why the movement? There are several possibilities.

One of the most common reasons is to provide the individual with a broad background, to facilitate future movement through the organisation. The intent is learning, though the individual may be expected to be productive while on each

351

assignment. Indeed, the performance on each assignment can be the significant factor that determines the future career patterns of that individual within the organisation.

This type of job rotation, for management education, is frequently referred to as a management internship. For the most part, management interns (MI) will be recruited directly from a college or university for internships of about two years. At the termination of that period, the MI will either be offered a position as a manager or encouraged to seek employment elsewhere.

In some countries, where life-long employment of managers is the cultural practice, the MI is seen as going through an 'apprenticeship' to the company. The MI position is considered a long term orientation and acculturation for this new employee. Failure is reduced to a minimum through the use of extensive testing and investigation before employment as an MI.

There is also a lateral type of job rotation. This rests on the concept that an individual manager working for the organisation should be capable of moving readily from one part of the organisation to another. This creates a generalist who is never allied with a particular part of the organisation, or a career speciality. When this type of job rotation is used, the movement will take place about every three - five years.

A third type of job rotation is focused strictly on learning. The manager has a regular job, but is rotated to a different position in order to learn more about that part of the company operations. The intent is that, upon completion of the rotational assignment, the manager will return to the original position.

A fourth type of job rotation could also be considered a temporary job assignment. A manager may be sent to another job because of immediate, but short term need. It may be a result of an unusual flow of work, an industrial dispute, a political crisis, or the unavailability of the regular manager. In each case, the organisation seeks a manager who can respond rapidly to the new job situation, but who will, at some indefinite time, return to the original position.

The normal confusion surrounding job rotation is compounded when we include the interdependent world. In some parts of the world, job rotation is not only accepted, but expected. If a manager is not rotated within the culturally approved periods of time, that can be a signal to others that this particular manager has not been successful and will not be moving into higher levels of the organisation.

A manager, going from one culture into another, must be very careful about carrying along the presumed use of job rotations from the original culture. The purpose for using job rotation in the new setting must be identified, and how it is being used must be understood. To do less will certainly lead to failure.

Delegation

In some ways, delegation is related to job rotation. The major difference is that job rotation is a specific work assignment for which the individual being rotated has responsibility. In delegation, the delegator is giving work to a delegatee that is usually done by the delegator. Delegation is always temporary. When it becomes a regular part of the delegatee's job it is no longer delegation but a work assignment.

Delegation is impacted upon very heavily by culture. In some cultures, it is almost impossible to delegate. Only the manager who has the authority can exercise that authority. It cannot be given (delegated) to another. Particularly where authority is based on seniority, delegation becomes almost impossible. Where the authority of the manager is based upon another source (the home office), it may also be difficult to utilise delegation.

There are cultures, however, where delegation is frequently used as the manager has the responsibility but is considered too high level an official to be bothered with 'small details'. In a protective mode, delegation may occur even without a specific act by the manager. That is, what may be assumed to be managerial functions are done by others in the name of the manager. In some cultures, this is also done to avoid possible embarrassment to the manager.

Managers will have to learn much more about delegation as a regular process, and how delegation varies, depending upon differences in our interdependent world.

MINORITIES AND QUOTAS

Every country in the world has minorities! Indeed, some countries have numerous minorities that are officially recognised. In the People's Republic of China, for example, there is a Ministry of Minorities which has responsibility for the sixty specified minorities. In India, the castes represent minorities. In some countries, the minorities exist by virtue of religion, kind of citizenship, country of origin, race, etc. The list is virtually endless.

Within one's own country, a manager can also expect to have to work with minorities. Indeed, some of the managers will be minorities! Managers are expected to know the legal requirements related to minorities and to be sensitive to the cultural expectations that are likewise related to minorities.

Despite this obvious need, colleges and universities offer very little for managers in relation to minorities! In part, this reflects a lack of sensitivity to the unique situations that confront a manager in relation to minorities. It is understandable that some of our institutions of higher education may prefer not to become embroiled in this delicate issue. The manager, however, cannot avoid becoming involved and therefore learning about minorities should be a required part of management education.

A foreign manager going to the U.S.A., for example, should have learned about the various minorities there. This would include the national laws relating to equal opportunity, the applicable state laws, as well as the cultural behaviour related to minorities in the particular part of the country where the manager will be working.

In a similar vein, a manager from any country might go to work in South Africa, where there are numerous laws relating to minorities that are strictly enforced. The manager must know those laws, how they are enforced, and what is required of a manager working in that situation. As with any other country, there are also cultural behavioural expectations which may not have been spelt out but which the manager is expected to know, or to learn about rapidly.

It is not a question of whether or not the manager likes those laws. A manager who has any hesitation about the laws of the country of assignment, should make this known before taking the assignment. Of course, this involves risks related to a managerial career. That is the choice a manager must make.

In some countries, there are quota systems related to minorities. These can work both ways. That is, an employer may be required to have a certain percentage of the work force from a particular minority (e.g. the Bumiputra plan in Malaysia). In other countries, there may be quotas that indicate how many of each minority can be employed by a company. A manager must know this to avoid putting the company into disfavour with the host.

In the U.S.A., as of this writing, there are court cases related to the employment of foreign managers by companies operating in the U.S.A. Specifically, legal action has been brought by some employees against a Japanese company that brought Japanese managers to work in the U.S.A. The U.S.A. citizens who are suing have complained that such action deprived them of the right to rise to managerial positions. No matter which way this is finally adjudicated, the Japanese company has already lost in public relations and is seen as being insensitive to the laws of the U.S.A.

Multi-national companies operating in various parts of the world have found themselves under increasing pressure to employ local managers. The rising expectations of some of the developing countries of the world has increased the significance of that issue. Therefore in some countries, foreign managers are expected to show positive actions to prepare their replacements from the local population.

FOREIGN MANAGERS AS CONSULTANTS/ADVISORS

One effect of the situation just discussed is that some
managers are expected to exhibit competencies that are not
usually associated with that position. Generally, managers
are expected to be problem solvers and decision makers. This
can change under the impact of working in a foreign country.

Multi-nationals may still send managers to foreign countries,
but the trend is towards using local managers. To facilitate
communication and relationships with the home office, the
local managers may be brought to corporate headquarters. This
is a good practice but it has been found that this may not be
sufficient to assure that corporate policy is continuously and
adequately communicated.

As a result, a new type of manager is emerging. Indeed, the
title 'manager' may no longer be appropriate and at some
future point a new title will be coined. This new manager is
more of a consultant/advisor and as such is less involved in
problem solving and decision making.

Rather, as a consultant/advisor, this individual will be
expected to assist others in solving problems. This is much
different than having direct responsibility for solving
problems and being directly involved in the solutions.

In a sense, it is much like what happened in the foreign
aid field during the 1950 - 1970 period. Developed countries
sent vast numbers of technicians to assist the developing
countries. The job of those technicians was to train and
educate local people who would then replace the technicians.
In too many cases this did not happen. It was not that the
local people were inadequate. Rather, the technician had
been selected based on technical proficiency, not on the
skills of training and educating. The technician was an
operational person who was good at getting the work done,
even through the efforts of others. But those efforts were
by giving orders, not by helping the others to learn so they
could do it themselves.

The problem which faced the technicians in those days is an
important factor in the life of managers as we race to the
end of the twentieth century. Too few managers have received
any preparation for being consultant/advisors, rather than
practitioners.

POLITICS AND ECONOMICS

The manager of the future will have to study much more about
politics and economics than is generally the case at present.
There has been an increasing tendency for managers to study
about management, and those areas directly related to
management such as finance and marketing. Less common, in
management programmes, have been courses on political history
and structure. Sometimes, some work is included in economics,

particularly when the manager expected to go into international work. Even in those cases, however, the study of economics was limited and tended to be almost superficial.

The areas of politics and economics can no longer be considered as electives or optional courses. At the university level, those courses are as essential as those that have emerged dealing with human systems or organisational behaviour.

POLITICAL SENSITIVITIES

Existing managers, as well as new ones, must learn to be sensitive to the political structure of other countries. Too many managers are prone to ethnocentricism - or seeing the rest of the world as less desirable than their own ethnic background. A major example of this relates to democratic governments.

To begin with, it is extremely difficult to get agreement on just what is a 'democratic government'. Some say it is sufficient if people can vote. The same people have difficulty, however, when they learn that the candidates being voted for have been previously selected, and that the outcome is fully predictable. This discussion of various forms of democracy could continue for many pages, but that is not the point, for managers. Rather, managers (as do others) have to recognise that they are assuming that all people prefer some form of democractic system. This assumption is at the root of much of the difficulty that managers from 'democratic' countries experience when they work in a country with a different political system.

An example comes from India, specifically from the city of Lucknow. That was the site, in 1857, of what has been referred to as the Sepoy Rebellion. One of the historical points, shown to visitors, is the remains of the building which was the last bastion of the British defenders, who were subsequently relieved. Nearby stands an obelisk which also commemorates that struggle. One group looking at the site may comment with awe on the valiant struggle of the British at that site against the rebels. An Indian, at the same site, will point to the same obelisk monument, as commemorating the struggle of the freedom fighters of that period!

When working in a foreign country, a manager must become almost apolitical. Every country has continuing struggles with control. These can be acted out in the political arena or on a battlefield in a national struggle. The manager cannot ignore those activities, but as an expatriate must steer clear of them. If the manager cannot do that, it is best that the manager return to the home country. Not taking part does not mean being insensitive. The manager must know enough about the politics of the situation to know what to avoid. For those managers who have come from an interactive society where most people take part in government such a withdrawn stance can be a problem. It requires a significant change in thinking and behaviour for the manager.

Economics

Coupled with the above, a manager can have difficulty when
it comes to understanding the distribution of wealth within
a country. A manager for the U.S.A. in 1981, might have been
proud that the U.S.A. had an average national income of about
U.S.$9,000 per person. It can be a severe blow to the ego of
that manager to learn that in the same year, the United Arab
Emirates had an average national income of U.S.$72,000!

It would be of no avail for the U.S. manager to try to
rationalise statistics, or attack the form of government of
the U.A.E. which does not distribute the income in a form that
the U.S.A. might find more acceptable. Rather, the U.S.
manager must learn about 'average national income' - what it
means, and what it can tell us about a country, while still
withholding any value judgements.

Sometimes it is easier to compare similar countries, two
industrial countries like Japan and the U.S.A. Yet, when it
comes to international trade, Japan has created a significant
surplus during the decade of the 1970's. In the 1980's, one
reaction in the U.S.A. has been to try to change the hidden
import restrictions which, the U.S.A. contends, have been a
significant factor in creating that surplus.

A U.S. manager, whether in the U.S.A. or Japan, should have
learned enough about economics to understand the nature of the
surplus - and the same applies to the Japanese manager. By
having studied economics, these managers can be more effective
for their organisations - particularly if they are functioning
in the international market in this interdependent world.

Earlier, reference was made to guest workers, from a
cultural viewpoint. The underlying reason for guest workers
is in the economic sphere, although sometimes also in the
political one. Managers need to know and to understand the
reasons for the use of guest workers, and their impact on the
economy, and to be prepared to influence their own government
policies related to guest workers, as well as undocumented
aliens.

THE FUTURE

It is always risky to write of the future, yet it must be
done. Let us look at some of the factors, over the horizon,
that can be expected to have an impact on management
education - both for those who are managers and for those
preparing to be managers.

There was a time when managers did not have to be concerned
about the future. The 'future' was something that would
happen after the manager had retired! This is no longer
possible. The rapidity of change requires that all managers

be futurists! For those functioning in an interdependent
world this is even more crucial for we still know too little
about living in an interdependent world.

MORE INTERDEPENDENCY

There is little question but that the world will become even
more interdependent. Advances in technology have consistently
narrowed the gap between countries. Geographical borders
become less meaningful, particularly with the technology which
does not stop at the borders. A war, economic decline,
population explosion, etc. in any part of the world has its
effects on all parts of the world.

A manager cannot ignore this increasing interdependency.
It means that managers will have to constantly be learning
about areas which traditionally have not been in the
management curriculum.

POPULATION

It appears that the population explosion will begin to slow
down in the early twenty-first century. By no means will we
approach the elusive goal of ZPG (zero population growth),
for we will continue to have increased population, but at a
slower rate.

The problem with this statistic is that it is averaged out
internationally! As with any average, there will be some
countries with a three percent growth rate which means
doubling their population in about twenty five years. There
will be other countries in which the slow increase in the
population will produce a much higher average age population
than in the three percent growth rate countries. The
discrepancy in the work forces of these two groups of
countries can be expected to have an impact on the manager in
both countries. One obvious effect will be the increased
movement of work forces between the countries. Those with
expanding birth rates may find that their own economy cannot
expand rapidly enough to absorb all those who are entering
the work force. The numbers of guest workers will increase,
immigration may increase, and some countries may be exporting
labour!

ENERGY

As we approach the end of the twentieth century, too few
managers are aware of the fantastic changes that have taken
place during this century, and particular in the last quarter
of this century.

We can pinpoint the energy situation by noting that prior
to 1973, the control of a major source of energy (i.e. oil)
was in the hands of the energy consuming nations. In the

space of about one year, control shifted to the energy producing nations! Rarely, if ever in history, has such a major shift in control taken place in such a short period of time. Indeed, many managers are still thinking in pre-1973 terms.

Alternative forms of energy may bring about changes that one cannot possibly foresee at this time. Suffice it to say that all managers must be familiar with energy and energy sources, since this is the mainstay of industrialised societies, but one that also impacts on agricultural economies.

CONCLUSION

The manager of the future will be concerned with much more than is currently included in the study of management. A manager will have to be a broader person and have an understanding that far surpasses what is currently expected.

The job of the manager is becoming more exciting, particularly for those who are prepared to cope with interdependency and turn it from a problem into a resource.

Management is important now, but the importance of management can be expected to accelerate in the future, requiring new ways to educate managers about topics which are not now generally a part of management education.

22 The preparation and nurturance of managers: For today and tomorrow

RONALD LIPPITT

As we approach the task of developing the new managers of the 80s and 90s, one of our challenges is tounderstand the emerging contexts in which managers must be able to function effectively, i.e. to be proactive leaders. Let me first address this challenge, then derive some implications for managerial skill, and conclude with an examination of some of the procedures and strategies of preparing and supporting managers to learn and utilise these competencies.

SIX 'CUTTING EDGE' CONTEXTS FOR MANAGEMENT

I believe the six 'cutting edges' or contexts of change identified below have major implications for significant changes in leadership roles and represent very important challenges for managers in all types of social contexts - communities, human service organisations, business enterprises, government departments, and social action groups.

Context 1 - The double bind of maintaining quality in a downsizing environment

Most committed leaders today are experiencing a difficult double bind. There are pushes to respond to the needs and expectations of customers for better products, or clients for better services, or of subordinates for more adequate response to their needs. The more sophisticated and sensitive leaders are, the more they feel a gap between 'what ought to be' and 'what is', between 'meeting needs' and 'getting by'. The threat of strikes, the loss of competitive advantage, the feedback from alienated employees, are all symptoms of a push towards putting energy into improving the effectiveness and quality of leadership.

But, in the light of these upgrading thrusts, the message that 'smaller can be beautiful' is not a very compatible or congenial message. The message of budget cuts clearly seems to mean reductions in quantity and quality of personnel and of programme and production resources. The messages that attempt to justify the cuts seem to downgrade the value and quality of our leadership efforts. Priorities do not seem to be understood or listened to. Standards of leadership achievement and competence feel threatened. Leaders hear puzzling messages about critical functions being entrusted to untrained types of personnel. Subordinates feel threatened and unappreciated.

Managers are in a double bind of pressure for improvement of quality in the face of downsizing demands. Subordinates are in a double bind of pressures for accountability and loyalty in the face of insecurity and reduction of resources to get their tasks done.

Context 2 - Shared power and responsibility expectations

A major trend of the postindustrial society is what has been referred to as the 'flattening of the organisational chart'. This means shifts toward a wider delegation of responsibility and power, and expectations for more initiative and risk taking on the part of those who have previously been dependent followers. Along with decentralisation of decision making responsibility and authority goes a complementary trend of centralisation of accountability for the quality of output and organisational functioning. Many new centralised managerial functions emerge, those of coordination, communication linkage, and quality control. These shifts in leadership functions add up to great stress for both top leadership and the subordinates who find themselves in the new roles of risk taking responsibility. Leaders feel uncertainty and fear of loss of control and the subordinates feel the challenge but avoid the risks of new task requirements for which they lack skill and support.

Context 3 - Interdependence, collaboration and communication

One of the consequences of decentralised organisational functioning is the increase in interdependence and the need for collaboration between the managers and supervisors in the different units of the system. But the traditions of sibling rivalry and protected turfdom are so great that shifts toward collaboration and toward new norms that 'asking for help' is a sign of strength are very difficult to develop. And the needs for a great increase in openness of communication and feedback between centralised coordination and decentralised initiative are hard to achieve.

One of the most important issues is that with decentralised initiative there is a great increase in the amount of innovational practice which does not get shared by adequate dissemination through the organisation or community or company. The new manager subordinate pattern of the 80s requires a tremendous new awareness of interdependence, new values and skills of collaboration, and new openness of two way communication.

Context 4 - More different heads for problem solving

The futurist, Esfandiary, has pointed out that with each succeeding decade, the problems to be solved in the world have become more complex, requiring an understanding of more different variables and factors in order to do creative problem solving. Analysis by decades beginning in 1900 of the number of different persons involved in the creating of significant inventions and innovations reveals that in the decade of 1900-1910, the average number of heads involved in significant innovations was two, while in the 70s, the average number of heads was twelve. Many leaders, aware of this fact, are developing resource banks and skill banks to record and store the variety of skills and expertise of each member of the organisation so that for any new problem or task the right heads can be put together to tackle the job. This growing trend of problem solving through temporary task forces is requiring flexible leadership and followership, new abilities and readiness to relate to different persons in different combinations with a much greater tolerance and acceptance of differences in background and orientation than has been traditional.

Context 5 - Integrating technological and human resources

Becoming comfortable with the computer has become a new managerial challenge. 'Computer persons' are a more and more frequent part of problem solving teams. Sometimes it seems hard to diagnose whether computers are leaders or followers. Clearly it is a current struggle to discover how the computers, and their programmers, can be collaborators rather than controllers or underutilised servants. Many older managers are feeling very threatened today by the computer oriented competences of their younger subordinates, and frequently subordinates are using their relationship with the computer as a support system for confronting leadership with demands for change.

Context 6 - Reorientation, renewal and new competency development

Achieving changeability is a requirement for the managers and subordinates of the 80s and for the systems they are part of. This requires a proactive, rather than a defensive, reactive posture toward the pressures and opportunities for change. It requires an acceptance and understanding of the fact of universal ambivalence, in all of us, about putting energy and risk into change effort. It requires the acceptance of the continuing role of learner, of commitment to a renewal process for self, the investment in and support of continuing training programmes for employees, and research and development as a major organisational priority.

I believe that with each succeeding year of the 80s, these six trends will become more obvious and more crucial as challenges for managers in all sectors of the society.

THREE BASIC CHANGE CHALLENGES FOR THE MANAGER

For many managers the most confronting challenge in moving

into the 80s is the necessity to root out years of
socialisation in three traditional orientations of our
culture.

One of these is the model of the vertical dimension of
authority and dependency, of superordinate and subordinate,
of decision maker and implementer, of master and servant.

A second ingrained orientation is that 'doing it by
yourself' is a sign of strength. Movement from pride in
independence and autonomy to pride in interdependence and
mutual help is one of the toughest and one of the most
necessary.

The third difficult confrontation is moving from the
assumption that competition is a necessary and needed
support for motivation to achieve. This orientation is one
of the greatest blocks to the competent asking for help and
sharing of resources and pooling of complementary
differences which is required for survival, growth, and
development in the decades ahead.

SEVEN AREAS OF NEEDED COMPETENCY DEVELOPMENT

Let me briefly define what I see as some of the challenges
and competency requirements for leaders on the cutting edge
of the 80s and 90s.

1.   Attitudes and skills of proactive responses to change

The natural, first reactions to downsizing and cutback
demands are to defend, to be equitable by cutting everybody
by the same amount, to eliminate research and development and
the other mechanisms for development and growth, to
sacrifice the most vulnerable personnel (e.g. internal
trainers and external consultants), and to permit the
obsolescence of technical and material resources. The
reactive temptation is to become more authoritative at a time
when democratic participation is more crucial than ever.

Competent managers in similar situations manifest what I
would describe as proactive responses such as, restudying
priorities, reassessing payoffs of different activities,
exploring the exchanging of and sharing of resources with
others, searching for alternative sources of support,
scanning for innovative, new models of service and production
that require less resources, restructuring roles and
reorganising operations to maximise use of human and
technical resources, mobilising volunteer time and energy.

Avoiding the reactive, defensive, depressive posture of
response to confrontation and downsizing is one of the
critical competency challenges for all managers in this and
future decades.

2. Mobilising resources for the self

Giving up authority and taking on more responsibility are
both sources of stress for the manager and subordinates. The
skillful mobilising of resources for the self, and from the
self, are the key ways to reduce these stresses. These
skills involve learning how to ask peers for consultation, to
use them for support, and to form coalitions for action, the
utilisation of subordinates to brainstorm creative ideas for
problem solutions, to provide guiding data about their own
needs and corrective ideas for one's own role. A second
challenge is to mobilise the resources from within oneself.
This requires developing the special skills of listening to
one's own internal dialog between the various voices within
the self which are expressing pro and con feelings, supports
for risk taking and supports for caution, and reflecting on
different alternatives for action. Listening to and
utilising these resources requires achieving a reflective
attitude and reflective time, a crucial necessity for every
successful manager.

3. Achieving a balance of decentralisation and
   centralisation

Moving decision making and responsibility closer to the
action is a basic gain in leadership potential, if there is
also a centralisation of the function of planning for and
providing the learning experiences required to support the
skill development needs of decentralised leadership
personnel.

   Getting more persons and competencies involved in
managerial functions is great, if there is centralised,
systematic coordination and integration of their initiatives
and decisions.

   Getting localised mechanisms for using the experience and
ideas of these down the line is a great gain, if there is
centralised initiative to retrieve other perspectives from
outside and to introduce quality assurance procedures into
the ongoing system.

   These are illustrations of some of the challenges of
achieving balance between centralised management functions
and decentralised subordinate responsibilities. In the
current enthusiasm for shared power and decentralisation,
there is a serious trap in neglecting the complementary,
supportive central functions which require very different
types of leadership competencies.

4. Achieving a balance of task work focus and process work
   focus

Probably the most significant contribution of the NTL
laboratory movement has been the discovery that if groups
that are engaged in production and problem solving tasks of
various kinds will also focus on their process of interacting

with each other, they will achieve significant improvements
in productivity. In many committees, staffs, and task
forces, it has become a regular part of their work to have
brief 'stop sessions' where they share data about 'how
things are going' and what could be done to improve the
utilisation of each member and increase productivity or
problem solving effectiveness. Managers must be ready to
take the risk of this type of intervention, and to model
openness in seeking and responding positively to feedback in
such process reviews.

5.   Diverse person team building

Getting persons with very different types of backgrounds,
specialities, and discipline to work together effectively is
one of the toughest leadership challenges of the 80s. The
first question is who to put together, for what, and for how
long. The technology of the resource inventory is developing
rapidly. Leaders of any size group or system need to have
some type of procedure for identifying, recording, and storing
of the skills, competencies, and training of the personnel
they manage.

    But the more difficult challenge is how to get them to work
together. Rather typically, the assumption is that
differences are a source of problems and conflicts. The
effective manager must convert this posture into an attitude
that differences are one of the greatest resources we have if
we can accept the challenge of utilising them effectively.
This means developing such procedures as using techniques of
process review to assess the effectiveness of the task work
and of the problems of cooperation between the team members,
developing the concept of 'creative compromise' or finding
win-win approaches to problem solving, and the extensive use
of nonevaluative brainstorming by the different heads in the
group before turning to critical evaluation. Many skills of
this type must become part of the repertoire of the manager
who is building for the future.

6.   The teaming of technology and humans

One of the challenges of the manager must be to help the
machine oriented and the person oriented task members
understand and appreciate each other. This involves setting
up procedures for teaching each other, for cooperative dry
runs on simulation projects where they are not playing for
keeps, and understanding and accepting some of the typical
cross generational differences in orientation. This will
often involve a development of co-leadership of teams and
projects by a younger, technically sophisticated person and
an older worker more experienced and skilled in the human side
of the enterprise.

7.   Leaders have neighbors and outsiders as potential
      resources

There is a temptation in a downsizing world to define

boundaries and emphasise turfdom. But a creative managerial
role requires the opposite posture. There must be readiness
to actively explore the sharing and exchanging of resources,
including the sharing of successful practices which are
helping the group or organisation to survive, grow, and
profit in the changing environment of the 80s. Such an
orientation to securing resources and being a resource to
other managers and systems requires a special orientation
toward documentation and evaluation. To be able to share
requires a much more systematic orientation toward what we do
and how we do it and how well it works. Another temptation
in the downsizing world is to withdraw connections with and
use of outside sources of consultation, critique, and review.
Usually the need for resources is even greater and the
competent manager is always improving his/her techniques of
utilising external resources.

DESIGNS AND STRATEGIES FOR DEVELOPMENT OF MANAGERIAL
COMPETENCE AND MAINTENANCE OF HIGH PERFORMANCE

We now turn to the third question of the analysis. What
conditions for learning can we create, and what strategies of
training and development can we mobilise that will help
develop the kinds of competencies we have identified above?
Here are our suggestions and observations regarding this
question.

1.   The learning programme must be 'linkage oriented'

Most learning programmes fail to connect information input
(knowledge) with relevance to the self and one's own
situation. There is a lack of emphasis on 'application
thinking' about the concepts and theory that are presented.

   A related typical weakness is that ideas for action do not
become connected to actual behaviour, to the skills of
carrying through from intentions or goals to competent
performance. This linkage requires that every learning
design include behavioural reality practice in safe
situations where one can risk new behaviours without danger
and with the benefit of constructive feedback and a chance to
re-practice. The neglect of reality practice opportunities in
managerial training programmes is one of the most serious
weaknesses.

2.   An opportunity to set growth objectives

The learning programme must provide opportunity and guidance
for each learner to clarify their development needs and to
set growth objectives as a contract with the teachers and
with themselves.

3.   The use of co-learner teams

We have discovered that more efficient participative learning
happens when learners do learning work in small subgroups,

366

such as trios. Their sharing of ideas, support of risk taking, and debriefing and conceptualising learning result in more productive and complete learning of managerial concepts and skills.

4. Supervised observation and analysis

An adequate search by the teacher will uncover examples of good practice in the surrounding environment to be observed and to be interviewed. This type of guided fieldwork with reporting and interview analysis by the learners is a very significant part of a good management development programme. Our studies indicate that high quality practice, 'windows on the future', are identifiable in almost any organisation or cluster of neighbouring organisations if we do a bit of searching.

5. Tutorial modeling and apprenticeship

One of the exciting uses of retirees and senior managers in some companies is the assigning of new, young management learners to them for consultative tutorial teaching and demonstrating. Through the centuries this has been one of the most used techniques of training the next generation.

6. Laboratory situation practice and repractice opportunities

The case study analysis was one of the early models of learning from reality practice in situations of intensive analysis and revision of judgements. But the actual behavioural skill practice of simulations and role playing rehearsal have added a new dimension of behavioural skill development. We would never conceive of a design for learning to play a musical instrument, or to paint, or to perform athletically that did not have a programme of practice, feedback, repractice as a major core of the learning design. This model is even more council in learning the human interaction skills and decision making that are a core part of managerial competence.

7. At the elbow support of risk taking

The greatest loss of payoff from management training programmes comes in neglecting the critical linkage between learning in the protected, safe learning environment and the playing for keeps risks of performing in the job situation. There are several things trainers have done to design such support. One procedure is to help the supervisor be aware of the risk taking and to be ready to be supportive. Another is to provide for debriefing discussions, even on the phone, after a risk taking effort. Another is to have training designs where peer pairs are taking the risk together. Another help from the trainer is to be sure there has been realistic anticipatory rehearsal in direct preparation for the on the job risks.

367

8.   Membership in a peer support group or network

If the training activity has involved peer teams from the
same setting, the trainer can help the peer managers
practice asking for and giving help to each other during
the training. But if this has not been feasible the
trainer needs to help the trainees with the strategies and
skills of creating support groups. Even though they may
work at a distance from each other, very often it is
feasible to help trainees develop a design and time
commitments for telephone and correspondence networking.

9.   A recognition, reward for merit environment

In a good training programme, the trainees develop goals for
their own action initiatives and performance improvements.
Then it is important to define criteria of progress toward
these goals and to help develop plans for celebrating
progress and for getting recognition for successful effort.
If the trainer is concerned about the payoff of training,
he/she will include this aspect of management development
design as a part of their effort.

SEVERAL SOURCES FOR FURTHER INFORMATION

These are several of the most important types of learning
designs and models to ensure the development of the
orientations and skills we have identified as critical to
the growth and expression of the high quality management
skills needed to day - and in the decade ahead.

   Below, we are listing some of the resources we have found
helpful to management developers:-

Benne, Bradford, Gibb and Lippitt, (Eds.), (1975), The
   Laboratory Method of Changing and Learning, Learning
   Resources Corporation, California, USA.

Bennis, Benne and Chin, (Eds.), (1969), The Planning of
   Change, Rinehart and Winston, New York

Burke and Beckhard, (1970), Conference Planning, Edition 2,
   University Associates, California, USA.

Capelle, R, (1979), Changing Human Systems, International
   Human Systems

Chesler and Fox, (1966), Role Playing Methods in the
   Classroom, Science Research Association, Illinois, USA.

Davis and McCallon, (1974), Planning, Conducting and
   Evaluating Workshops, Learning Resources Corporation,
   California, USA.

Fox, Luzki and Schmuck, (1966), Diagnosing Classroom Learning Environments, Science Research Associates Inc., Illinois, USA.

Lindaman and Lippitt, (1979), Choosing the Future You Prefer, Development Publications, Washington DC, USA.

Lippitt, G, (1982), Organizational Renewal, Prentice Hall, London.

Lippitt, G, and Lippitt, R, (1978), The Consulting Process in Action, University Associates, California, USA.

Lippitt, P, Lippitt, R, and Sproule, G, (1981), Reality Practice: Methods and Theory of Role Playing, Development Publications, Washington DC, USA.

Lippitt, R, (1958), The Dynamics of Planning Change, Development Publications, Washington DC, USA

Pfeiffer and Jones, (1973-1979), The Annual Handbook of Structured Experiences for Human Relations Training, Vols.1-7, University Associates, California, USA.

Schindler-Rainman, E, and Lippitt, R, (1975), The Volunteer Community, Ed.2, University Associates, California, USA.